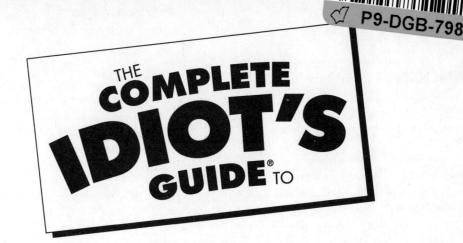

THE COMPLETE IDIOT'S GUIDE® TO

American History

Fourth Edition

by Alan Axelrod, Ph.D.

ALPHA

A member of Penguin Group (USA) Inc.

P9-DGB-798

As ever, for Anita

ALPHA BOOKS

Published by the Penguin Group

Penguin Group (USA) Inc., 375 Hudson Street, New York, New York 10014, U.S.A.

Penguin Group (Canada), 10 Alcorn Avenue, Toronto, Ontario, Canada M4V 3B2 (a division of Pearson Penguin Canada Inc.)

Penguin Books Ltd, 80 Strand, London WC2R 0RL, England

Penguin Ireland, 25 St Stephen's Green, Dublin 2, Ireland (a division of Penguin Books Ltd)

Penguin Group (Australia), 250 Camberwell Road, Camberwell, Victoria 3124, Australia (a division of Pearson Australia Group Pty Ltd)

Penguin Books India Pvt Ltd, 11 Community Centre, Panchsheel Park, New Delhi—110 017, India

Penguin Group (NZ), cnr Airborne and Rosedale Roads, Albany, Auckland 1310, New Zealand (a division of Pearson New Zealand Ltd)

Penguin Books (South Africa) (Pty) Ltd, 24 Sturdee Avenue, Rosebank, Johannesburg 2196, South Africa

Penguin Books Ltd, Registered Offices: 80 Strand, London WC2R 0RL, England

Copyright © 2006 by Alan Axelrod

THE COMPLETE IDIOT'S GUIDE TO and Design are registered trademarks of Penguin Group (USA) Inc.

International Standard Book Number: 1-59257-476-9
Library of Congress Catalog Card Number: 2005935929

08   07   06   8   7   6   5   4   3   2   1

Interpretation of the printing code: The rightmost number of the first series of numbers is the year of the book's printing; the rightmost number of the second series of numbers is the number of the book's printing. For example, a printing code of 06-1 shows that the first printing occurred in 2006.

Printed in the United States of America

Note: This publication contains the opinions and ideas of its author. It is intended to provide helpful and informative material on the subject matter covered. It is sold with the understanding that the author and publisher are not engaged in rendering professional services in the book. If the reader requires personal assistance or advice, a competent professional should be consulted.

The author and publisher specifically disclaim any responsibility for any liability, loss, or risk, personal or otherwise, which is incurred as a consequence, directly or indirectly, of the use and application of any of the contents of this book.

Most Alpha books are available at special quantity discounts for bulk purchases for sales promotions, premiums, fund-raising, or educational use. Special books, or book excerpts, can also be created to fit specific needs.

For details, write: Special Markets, Alpha Books, 375 Hudson Street, New York, NY 10014.

Publisher: *Marie Butler-Knight*
Editorial Director: *Mike Sanders*
Senior Managing Editor: *Jennifer Bowles*
Acquisitions Editor: *Tom Stevens*
Development Editor: *Lynn Northrup*
Production Editor: *Janette Lynn*
Copy Editor: *Kelly D. Henthorne*

Cartoonist: *Shannon Wheeler*
Book Designer: *Trina Wurst*
Cover Designer: *Bill Thomas*
Indexer: *Brad Herriman*
Layout: *Becky Harmon*
Proofreading: *Mary Hunt*

Contents at a Glance

Contents

Foreword

As a professor of history at a major university and director of research for a public history center, it's my job to take the past seriously. And I do. I research, write, and teach about the past, because I believe that understanding history is fundamental to understanding how our world got to be the way it is. Through the study of American history, we gain crucial perspectives on how we as a people and as a nation came to be who and what we are today. Armed with historical information, we're equipped to draw distinctions and connections between past and present. With this knowledge, we're far better prepared to face the challenges of the future.

Reading Alan Axelrod's *The Complete Idiot's Guide to American History, Fourth Edition*, reinforced for me the importance of knowing history. As a guidebook should, Axelrod's text provides a brief yet remarkably thorough and well-balanced tour of American history. It begins by sorting out the mysteries of North America's pre-Columbian societies, and it continues through to the tumultuous political controversies and international conflicts that have unsettled the early twenty-first century. In between, it explains the key events, individuals, technological innovations, and social developments that shaped the course of American history. Here and there, I found myself arguing with Axelrod's interpretation, but, at the end of the book, I marveled at the text's breadth and evenhandedness. Attentive to the triumphs that have marked the history of the United States, Axelrod's text is also attuned to the tragedies that have marred it.

Reading *The Complete Idiot's Guide to American History, Fourth Edition*, also reminded me that what drew me to study the past was not only that I believe it mattered, but also that I thought it exciting. The history that unfolds in the pages that follow is undeniably important; as significant, the narrative is refreshingly entertaining. The analysis is always accessible, the prose ever engaging, and the chapters easily digested. Especially illuminating—and fun—are the delicious cocktail of vital statistics, insightful vignettes, memorable biographies, interesting definitions, stirring quotations, and just plain wonderful trivia that accompany each chapter. These inserted features alone make this guide a tour worth taking.

As far as I'm concerned, this is a book for readers wise enough to know that while history matters, it need not be painful.

Stephen Aron is professor of history at UCLA and executive director of the Institute for the Study of the American West at the Autry National Center.

Introduction

Most of the world's nations are *places*—places with a past, certainly, and with traditions and a heritage, but places nevertheless. The United States is different. It's a place, but it's also an *idea*. Sure, democracy was not exactly a new idea in 1776—the word *democracy*, meaning "government by the people," was coined in ancient Greece—but no one had really tried it before. Few people thought it would actually work.

The story of gambling on an untried notion is bound to be fascinating. When you have a stake in that gamble, the story can be downright riveting. And make no mistake, living in a world where most people are hungry, terrified, tortured, and not free, you do have a big stake in the story.

My purpose is to give you a quick and comprehensive overview of American history. Although I've tried not to grind any axes, I'd be less than a living, breathing human being if I told you what I've written is totally impartial and neutral. Obviously, a book of this length is also grossly incomplete. Walk through a bookstore or library, and thousands of books on American history will leap at you from the shelves. The great thing is that many of them are well worth reading. However, you now hold in your hands a good place to start, a road map of the American story.

Part 1, "The New World," takes us back some 45,000 years to the epoch of the first immigrants, the people who crossed the long-vanished Bering "land bridge" from Asia to North America. The discussion then shifts to the collision of Old World and New as Europe invaded the realm of the Native American beginning in the fifteenth century, transforming the continent into a battlefield on which a nation was forged.

Part 2, "The World Turned Upside Down," covers the period of the American Revolution, from origins to outcome, including issues of economic, political, and spiritual independence.

Part 3, "Building the House," discusses the creation of the Constitution, the War of 1812, the rise of Andrew Jackson, and the era of the common man, as well as the forced removal of the Indians from the East to the West.

Part 4, "The House Divided," analyzes the causes of the Civil War, the early steps toward western expansion—including the Mexican War, by which much of the Southwest was acquired—the Civil War itself, and the Reconstruction era following the Civil War.

Part 5, "Rebuilding the House," covers the major period of western expansion, including the homestead movement, the building of the transcontinental railroad, the

Indian Wars, the growth of the western cattle empire, and the economic and techno-logical boom of the later nineteenth century. This part also discusses the immigrant experience, the labor movement, and the rise of urban political machines.

Part 6, "World Power," charts the nation's evolution as a world power (beginning with the Spanish–American War and World War I), the isolationist reaction against that evolution, the culture of the Roaring Twenties (including the heyday of Prohibition Era gangsters), the stock market crash, and the Great Depression. This part also outlines the origins of World War II and the nation's fight to victory in that war, from which it emerged as a nuclear superpower.

Part 7, "Superpower," covers the Cold War years, the Korean War, the Civil Rights movement, and the social revolution wrought during the administrations of John F. Kennedy and Lyndon Johnson. The part concludes with the Vietnam War.

Part 8, "Identity Crisis," surveys the turbulent home front during the Vietnam era, including such high points as the *Apollo 11* moon landing and such low points as the Watergate scandal. The women's liberation movement is also discussed in this part, as are the energy crisis and the economic crises of American cities and industry, which created fertile ground for the growth of Reaganomics.

Part 9, "A New World Order?" begins with the Reagan years and covers the end of the Cold War, including the experience of the Persian Gulf War. The final two chap-ters in this part look at recent events, including the terrorist attacks on the United States, the financial and ethical collapse of some major corporations, and the division of the nation into "red states" and "blue states," all of which indicate the challenges American democracy faces during these first years of the new century and the new millennium.

Extras

In addition to the main narrative of *The Complete Idiot's Guide to American History, Fourth Edition*, you'll find other types of useful information, including capsule histories of major events, brief biographies of key people in American history, digests of impor-tant statistics, and quick definitions of historical buzzwords. Look for these features:

American Echo

These are memorable statements from historically significant figures and documents.

What's the Word?

This feature defines the buzzwords that defined a time and place.

Remember This

Here you'll read about the most significant or representative single event of an era, ranging from historical milestones to pop culture landmarks.

Vital Statistics

Here you'll find key numbers relating to an era or event, including such items as population statistics, war casualties, costs, and so on.

American Life

This feature provides biographical sketches of an era's most significant and representative figures.

Trademarks

All terms mentioned in this book that are known to be or are suspected of being trademarks or service marks have been appropriately capitalized. Alpha Books and Penguin Group (USA) Inc. cannot attest to the accuracy of this information. Use of a term in this book should not be regarded as affecting the validity of any trademark or service mark.

Part 1

The New World

The "New World" was new only to Old World eyes. North America has been populated for perhaps nearly 50,000 years, and the people Christopher Columbus misnamed "Indians" might well be members of the oldest identifiable human race on the planet. Except for a brief visit from Vikings about 1000 C.E., the "New" World and the Old remained unknown to one another until October 12, 1492, when Columbus, the prodigal son of a Genoese weaver, claimed a Caribbean island for Spain. For the next 150 years, the people of Europe carved up the land of the Indians, and for the next 400 years the colonists, settlers, and citizens of Euro-America fought the Indians, fought one another, and managed eventually to forge a nation. This part of the book tells the story of that long, exciting, and often tragic process.

Chapter 1

The First People (43000 B.C.E.–1500s C.E.)

In This Chapter

- Where the first Americans came from
- The Mayas, Incas, and Aztecs
- The Anasazi, Mound Builders, and Pueblos
- Leif Eriksson, first European in America

Look at a map that shows the north Pacific Ocean. You'll find the Bering Sea, an arm of the Pacific bounded on the east by Alaska, on the south by the Aleutian Islands, and on the west by Siberia and the Kamchatka Peninsula. Near the north end of the Bering Sea is the Bering Strait, which, lying between Alaska and Siberia, connects the Bering Sea with the Chukchi Sea of the Arctic Ocean. At its narrowest, the strait is only 55 miles across, the shortest distance between the continents of North America and Asia. Fifty-five miles in icy cold water is a long swim, but not much of an ocean voyage. Historians believe that once upon a time, there wasn't even that 55 miles of water between the continents.

People of the Land Bridge

Several times during what paleontologists call the Quaternary Period—that's their name for the last two million years—a "land bridge" emerged in the Bering and Chukchi Seas as the sea level dropped due to the expansion of the ice cap surrounding the North Pole. The theory is that anywhere from 10,000 to 45,000 years ago, human beings used the Bering land bridge to enter the New World, migrating from what is now northeast Asia to northwestern North America. Beringia, as the land bridge is sometimes called, disappeared when the major continental ice sheets and other glaciers melted, causing the sea level to rise again.

45,000 Years of American History (Abridged Version)

The trek across Beringia was no evening stroll. In fact, it must have consumed thousands of years. By 9000 B.C.E., it's likely that the former Asians reached Patagonia, at the southern tip of South America. In between, in the area that is the present-day United States, the population of what we now call *Native Americans* may have reached 11 million or more.

Vital Statistics

Eleven million is the current consensus. However, estimates of the prehistoric population of the area encompassed by the United States range wildly—from 8.4 million to 112 million. By comparison, in 2000, 2,475,456 Native Americans, including Eskimos and Aleuts, lived in the United States.

These Native Americans, thinly distributed over a vast area in bands of 100 or even fewer individuals, lived for thousands of years on the ragged edge of subsistence. They didn't develop great cities, but, as nomads, wandered, hunted, and foraged together. Then, perhaps 9,000 years ago, some bands began to domesticate plants in order to supplement foraged and hunted food. By the beginning of the sixteenth century, when Europeans first made contact with Native Americans, they were cultivating maize, beans, and squash, as well as manioc, potatoes, and grains.

Agriculture fostered a more stable lifestyle than hunting and gathering, and the horticultural groups organized themselves into tribes.

The Anasazi

In the Southwest, archaeologists have identified a people they call the Anasazi (from a Navajo word meaning "the ancient ones"). The Anasazi appeared as early as 5500 B.C.E. and are also called "the Basket Makers," because of the many skillfully woven and often remarkably beautiful baskets that have been discovered in sites associated with their culture. During the period of 700 to 1100 C.E., the Anasazi began building what Spanish invaders would later call *pueblos* (Spanish for "town" or "village" and also "people"). These were fantastic groupings of stone and adobe "apartment buildings," cliff dwellings seemingly hewn out of lofty ledges, the most spectacular of which survive at Mesa Verde National Park in southwest Colorado.

The Mound Builders

In the meantime, to the east, in a vast area stretching from the Appalachian Mountains to the eastern edge of the prairies, and from the Great Lakes to the Gulf of Mexico, other Native Americans were building cultural monuments of a different kind. From about 1000 B.C.E. to after 1500 C.E., many different Indian societies constructed earthworks that modern archaeologists classify as burial mounds, "platform" or temple mounds (that served as the foundations for important public and private buildings), and other circular and geometric ceremonial earthworks. The largest and most elaborate of the mounds were built in southern Ohio by people of the Hopewell culture (named after mounds found near the Ohio hamlet of Hopewell).

Beyond the Aztec Horizon

If you could see a map of the Americas in the days before the European invasion, you would behold great Indian empires in South and Central America, but nothing more than a collection of thinly distributed tribal communities in North America, the vast region beyond the Aztec frontier of Mexico. In the southwestern part of this region, the Pueblo culture developed. Far to the northeast of the Pueblos were the "Temple Mound" people.

The Pueblos and the Temple Mound people diversified into many tribes, which overspread the region now encompassed by the United States. Unlike the Maya, Aztec, and Inca, these North American cultures had no written language and left no historical records, so it is impossible to present a "history" of the North American Indians

> **What's the Word?**
>
> **Native American** is the term used by most historians and anthropologists to describe the aboriginal peoples of the Western Hemisphere. In this book, I also use the more familiar term "Indian." That designation was coined by Christopher Columbus, who, on October 12, 1492, thought that he had landed in Asia—"the Indies"—and, therefore, called the people he encountered Indians. The name stuck.

before their contact with Europeans. In fact, some scholars have gone so far as to suggest that most North American Indians lived apart from linear time, harmonizing their lives with the cycles of the seasons and the biological processes of propagation, birth, and death. Europeans, forever *doing* and *getting*, were obsessed with recording *events* and measuring time. The Native Americans were focused instead on *being*. Therefore, time itself was different for them.

Leif the Lucky

Momentously—and tragically—the *time* of the Old World would collide with the *time* of the New. For 400 years, from a clash between "Indians" and Christopher Columbus's men in 1493 to the massacre of Native Americans by the U.S. 7th Cavalry at Wounded Knee on December 29, 1890, the history of America would be in large part the history of racial warfare between the white and the red.

The first European contact, some 500 years before Columbus sailed, ignited no great tragedy, however. It seems likely that Vikings reached the Faeroe Islands by 800 C.E. and that they landed in Greenland in 870 C.E. The very first Old World dweller to set eyes on the continent of North America was most likely a Norseman named Bjarni Herjulfsson in 986 C.E., but that sighting came as a result of a mistake in navigation. Herjulfsson had been blown off course, and he had no interest in actually exploring the land he sighted.

It was not until the next decade, about the year 1000 C.E., that the Norse captain Leif Eriksson led an expedition that touched a place called Helluland (probably Baffin Island) and Markland (most likely Labrador). Most historians believe that Leif— celebrated as "Leif the Lucky" in the great Icelandic sagas of the thirteenth century— and his men spent a winter in crude Viking huts hastily erected on a spot abundant with berries and grapes and, for that reason, called Vinland, which was probably located at a place now called L'Anse aux Meadows on the northernmost tip of Newfoundland. After Leif the Lucky left Vinland, his brother Thorvald paid a visit to the tenuous settlement in about 1004. Next, in 1010, Thorfinn Karlsefni, another Icelandic explorer, attempted to establish a more permanent settlement at Vinland. According to two Icelandic sagas, Thorfinn, a trader as bold as he was wealthy, brought women as well as men with him. They carried on a lively trade, but they also fought fiercely with the Native Americans, whom the sagas call Skraelings—an Old Norse word signifying "dwarfs" or "wretches" or, perhaps, "savages." The Skraelings attacked tenaciously and repeatedly.

American Life _____

The adventures of Leif Eriksson (ca. 970–1020) are known exclusively through semi-legendary, sometimes contradictory sagas. Leif the Lucky was the son of Eric Thorvaldsson, better known as Eric the Red, who established in Greenland the first enduring European settlement in the New World in about 985 C.E. Through his fearsome father (Eric the Red was banished from Iceland after having murdered a man), Leif Eriksson was descended from a line of Viking chieftains. Leif explored the lands that had been first sighted by Bjarni Herjulfsson.

After three lethal winters, Thorfinn and the other would-be settlers abandoned Vinland forever. The Viking expeditions to North America led, then, to nothing—at least not right away. Christopher Columbus, half a millennium removed from the Vikings, heard of the Vinland tradition and was excited by stories about a New World across the "Ocean Sea."

The Least You Need to Know

- ◆ Native Americans almost certainly immigrated to the Americas from Asia across an Ice Age "land bridge" where the Bering Strait is today.

- ◆ Pre-Columbian Native American cultures varied widely, with the most elaborately developed in South and Central America.

- ◆ The early Indians of North America may be thought of as the peoples of the northern Aztec frontier.

- ◆ The European discoverer of America was (most likely) Leif Eriksson in about 1000 C.E.

West to East (1451–1507)

In This Chapter

- ◆ The round Earth hypothesis
- ◆ Columbus's early life and struggle for a sponsor
- ◆ The voyages of Columbus
- ◆ Contact—and clash—with Native Americans
- ◆ The voyages of Amerigo Vespucci and the naming of America

Everyone's heard the Columbus story so many times and in so many bits and pieces that most of us just stop listening, and we fail to imagine the combination of creativity, the capacity for wonder, the courage, and the sheer madness that sent a Genoese seafarer and crew in three small ships across an unknown expanse of ocean to (it turns out) they knew not where.

The Round World Myth

Before we tell the Columbus story yet again, let's whisk away the myth many of us recall from childhood that, when he sailed, Columbus was about the only person in the world smart enough to believe that the Earth is round. In truth, the notion of a round Earth was hardly new by the end of the fifteenth century. The ancient Greeks said the Earth was a sphere, and one of them, Eratosthenes of Cyrene (ca. 276–195 B.C.E.), even performed a remarkable calculation that measured the Earth's circumference with great accuracy.

The Weaver's Boy

What we've got to give Columbus credit for was *believing* the wisdom of the ancient Greeks, which many people as indifferently educated as he was, either knew nothing of or simply couldn't accept.

Cristoforo Colombo—to use the native Italian form of his name—had been born in Genoa in 1451 to a weaver and did not learn to read and write until he reached adulthood. As a youth, he took not to books, but to the sea, and claimed to have sailed as far as Iceland. If this was so, might he have heard there the old, old stories of a place called Vinland?

Columbus returned from his early voyages to Genoa in 1479, and then went to Portugal, where he married. His wife died while giving birth to their child, Diego, the following year. But by this time, the seafarer's thoughts had sailed far from his family.

Having learned to read, he devoured shadowy accounts of westward voyages. It must have been at this time that he decided the world was indeed round. He was right about that, of course, but he was wrong to swallow whole Marco Polo's calculations concerning the location of Japan—1,500 miles east of China—and the work of the Greek astronomer Ptolemy (ca. 100–70 C.E.), who grossly underestimated the circumference of the earth and overestimated the size of the Eurasian land mass. Confirmed in these errors by reading the miscalculations of the Florentine cosmographer Paolo dal Pozzo Toscanelli, Columbus decided that Japan—he knew it as Cipangu—was a mere 5,000-mile voyage *west* of Portugal, over an ocean covering a round Earth.

Now, 5,000 miles is a long trip, but it was one that (Columbus believed) could be made by the vessels of the day. Communicating his confidence in Renaissance sea craft to others, however, was not so easy.

Vital Statistics

The actual circumference of the earth at the equator is 24,902 miles. The distance from the Spanish coast to the Bahamas, via the route Columbus took, is about 3,900 miles.

In 1484, Columbus tried to persuade King John II of Portugal to fund a voyage to Japan. There were excellent reasons for sailing to the East—all of which involved lucrative trading opportunities, chief among which was the commerce in spices. In the age of Columbus, aromatic spices were not just pleasant condiments, they were rare and costly substances *essential* to the preservation of food in a world without refrigerators. Nevertheless, King John II turned Columbus down, correctly believing that the distance between Europe and Asia was about twice as great as Columbus had guessed. Besides, John was already financing the efforts of his own seafarers to navigate a more practical route to Asia by rounding the coast of Africa.

Not one to give up, Columbus next approached Don Enrique de Guzmán, Duke of Medina Sidonia, only to be rebuffed. He appealed next to Don Luis de la Cerda, Count of Medina Celi, who was sufficiently intrigued to arrange an audience, on or about May 1, 1486, with Queen Isabella I of Castile.

She was not one to make up her mind quickly. For a half-dozen years, Columbus, with his son Diego in tow, cooled his heels in the Spanish court of Isabella and her husband, Ferdinand II of Aragon. He did not idle, but used the time to make a host of influential friends and, unfortunately, some powerful enemies. Among the most influential of his friends was a courtier named Luis de Santangel, who, after the monarchs apparently turned down Columbus once and for all early in 1492, intervened and succeeded in persuading the royal pair to sponsor the voyage after all.

Commissioned "Admiral of the Ocean Sea," as well as viceroy and governor of whatever lands he might discover, Columbus set sail from Palos on August 3, 1492. He was in command of three small ships, the *Niña* (skippered by Vincente Yáñez Pinzón), the *Pinta* (under Vincente's brother, Martin Alonso Pinzón), and his own flagship, the *Santa Maria*.

Trouble on the Horizon

During its first month and a half, the voyage went well, as the three vessels were propelled by highly favorable winds. Then, between September 20 and 30, the winds petered out into deadly doldrums. The cowering crews of all three ships began to grumble their doubts concerning the Admiral. Columbus, unfazed, began to keep two logbooks—one, for the benefit of the crew, containing fictitious computations of distances, and another, for his own records, consisting of accurate figures. The deception worked for a time, but, by the second week in October, the crews of all three ships verged on mutiny.

Columbus Day, 1492

As if cued by a hack playwright, land suddenly hove into view on October 12, 1492. What the *Santa Maria*'s lookout sighted was a place the natives called Guanahani, and Columbus christened San Salvador. Most modern historians believe that the three ships put in at present-day Watling Island, although, in 1986, a group of scholars suggested that the true landfall was another Bahamian island, Samana Cay, 65 miles south of Watling.

The seafarers were greeted by friendly Arawak tribes people. Believing that he had reached Asia—the "Indies"—Columbus logically enough called these people *Indians*. He then sailed on to Cuba in search of the court of the great Khan, the Mongol emperor of China, with whom he intended to negotiate a trade agreement for spices and gold. Finding no great capital, let alone a palace and a Khan, Columbus set off for an island he called Hispaniola (today divided between Haiti and the Dominican Republic), where, in a Christmas Day storm, the *Santa Maria* was wrecked near Cap Haitien. The Admiral ushered his crew safely onto shore and, seeing that the Indians were docile, left a garrison of 39 at the place he named La Navidad. Then, on January 16, 1493, Columbus returned to Spain on the *Niña*.

At the Canary Islands, Columbus paused on February 15 to replenish supplies and to dash off and dispatch a letter to his patron Luis de Santangel. That worthy immediately had the letter printed, and he published to all the Old World the discovery of one that was new:

> Hispaniola is a marvel. Its hills and mountains, fine plains and open country, are rich and fertile for planting and for pasturage, and for building towns and villages. There are many spices and vast mines of gold and other metals in this island. They have no iron, nor steel, nor weapons, nor are they fit for them, because although they are well-made men of commanding stature, they appear extraordinarily timid. The only arms they have are sticks of cane, cut when in seed, with a sharpened stick at the end, and they are afraid to use these.

First Blood

In addition to the observations Columbus made in his letter regarding the timid nature of the Indians, he recorded in his private journal on October 14, 1492, that no Spanish fortress would be required to secure La Navidad, "for these people are very simple as regards the use of arms."

No sooner had Columbus departed unfortified La Navidad than the 39-man garrison he left behind set about pillaging Indian goods and raping Indian women. The "timid" Indians retaliated, and when Columbus returned in November 1493, on his second voyage to America, not a single Spaniard was left alive.

Carving Up

The first voyage of Columbus triggered a dispute between Spain and Portugal, whose king had rebuffed the Great Navigator back in 1484. The failure to back him notwithstanding, the Portuguese crown pressed claims to all Columbus had discovered, which soon led Pope Alexander VI to issue a pair of papal bulls (*Inter Caetera* and *Inter Caetera II*) in 1493 that divided the newly discovered lands as well as those that might yet be discovered between Spain and Portugal. The two nations formalized this decree with the Treaty of Tordesillas (June 7, 1494), which established a line of demarcation at 370 leagues west of the Cape Verde Islands.

Thus, Spain and Portugal divided the New World between themselves. No one asked the Indians.

Three More Voyages

In the meantime, Ferdinand and Isabella sent Columbus on his second voyage (from Cadiz, on September 25, 1493), this time grandly outfitted with a fleet of 17 ships and nearly 1,500 men. After discovering the grim fate of the La Navidad garrison, Columbus set up a new colony, named Isabella, about 70 miles east of that bloody site. He explored the Caribbean for some 5 months and then tried to govern the fledgling colony he had planted, only to reveal himself as a disastrously inept administrator.

Columbus returned to Spain in 1496, leaving his brother Bartolomé in charge with instructions to move the settlement to the south coast of Hispaniola. Renamed Santo Domingo, this became the first permanent European settlement in the New World.

In June 1496, when Columbus landed at Cadiz, Spain, it was not to a hero's welcome. Although he continued to protest that he had found a shortcut to gold- and spice-rich Asia, he had clearly failed to find the mainland (where, presumably, some great hoard was stashed), and discouraged colonists trickled back to Spain with complaints about the Admiral's abusiveness and incompetence. Nevertheless, growing competition from Portugal, which sent Vasco da Gama to India in 1497, prompted Isabella and Ferdinand to fund a third voyage. With difficulty—due to his tarnished reputation—Columbus gathered a crew to man six ships, which departed Spain in May 1498, reaching Trinidad on July 31, 1498. On August 1, they landed on the mainland, and Columbus thereby became the discoverer of South America.

He also discovered pearls on islands near the coast. This must have been a great relief, for his royal sponsors were continually fuming about Columbus's failure to harvest the treasure trove he had promised and they expected.

But then came the bad news. Sailing across the Caribbean to Hispaniola, Columbus found the colonists in a full-scale revolt. In the meantime, the disgruntled Spanish sovereigns had dispatched a royal commissioner, Francisco de Bobadilla, who arrived from Spain in 1500 to straighten matters out. He summarily stripped the Columbus brothers of governing authority and sent them back to Spain—bound in chains.

The captain of the returning vessel thought Columbus had gotten a raw deal and removed the shackles, but the Admiral, with a theatrical flourish, insisted that he appear before Isabella and Ferdinand in his chains. Stricken by the pathetic sight of the Great Navigator weighed down by iron, the royal pair ordered him freed, and, in May 1502, sent him on a fourth and final voyage.

Landing briefly at Martinique, Columbus sailed on to Hispaniola, only to be refused permission to land. He explored the Central American coast and was marooned for a year in Jamaica because his wooden vessels had been thoroughly rotted by shipworm. Subsequently rescued, he reached Spain in November 1504 and died two years later (on May 20, 1506) at Valladolid, still claiming that he had reached Asia and arguing with limited success for his family's right to a share of whatever wealth and power his discoveries might yet yield.

Why We're Not Called Columbia

In the end, Columbus was cheated even of the honor of having his major discovery named for him. The Florentine explorer Amerigo Vespucci (1454–1512) claimed to have made four Atlantic voyages between 1497 and 1504, although historians have confirmed only two: one in 1499, commissioned by Spain and resulting in the discovery of Brazil and Venezuela, and another in 1501, to Brazil on behalf of Portugal. Following the 1501 voyage, Vespucci coined the phrase *Mundus Novus*—New World—to describe the region. The name stuck. Then, in 1507, the German cartographer Martin Waldseemüller published an account of Vespucci's voyages, along with a map and *Cosmographiae Introductio* (*Introduction to Cosmography*), a treatise on mapmaking. It was Waldseemüller who used a Latinized form of Vespucci's first name—America—to label the region Amerigo Vespucci had explored.

The Least You Need to Know

◆ Columbus was not unique in believing the earth to be round. However, he did set sail and persuade a crew that they would not fall off the edge of a flat world.

◆ Columbus thought he was sailing to spice-rich Asia; he had no intention of finding a "New World."

◆ Despite the Native Americans' friendly overtures, the Spanish attacked and suffered retaliation. This inaugurated 400 years of white–Indian warfare in the Americas.

◆ Columbus derived little benefit from his four voyages; even the land mass he discovered, America, was named for a later explorer, *Amerigo* Vespucci.

3

New Blood for Old Spain (1400–1600s)

In This Chapter

- Spanish voyages after Columbus
- Conquest of the Aztecs and Incas
- Coronado's search for the Seven Cities of Cibola
- The "Black Legend" and native revolts

In the wake of Columbus, the Portuguese scrambled to launch a series of expeditions, including that of Amerigo Vespucci and, in 1500, an expedition to India led by Pedro Alvares Cabral. To put it mildly, Cabral steered a bit wide in the South Atlantic and ended up in Brazil.

Yet another Portuguese, Ferdinand Magellan, sailed not under the flag of his native country, but on commission from Spain, charged with proving that the aptly named Spice Islands lay on the Spanish side of the line of demarcation established by the Treaty of Tordesillas.

Magellan sailed west in 1519, found the Strait of Magellan separating the southern tip of South America from Tierra del Fuego, and crossed the Strait into the Pacific. That big ocean had been discovered on September

25 or 27, 1513, by Vasco Nuñez de Balboa, but Magellan named it. Magellan explored the Philippine Islands and even persuaded the ruler of Cebu, one of the islands, to accept Christianity—a move that quickly triggered a local war, in which Magellan was killed on April 27, 1521. One of Magellan's captains, Juan Sebastian del Cano, brought his ship, the *Victoria*, back to Spain, thereby completing (in 1522) the first circumnavigation of the globe.

The voyages of Spain, as well as those of Portugal, were undertaken not to explore, but to conquer and colonize—while, in the bargain, also converting the "heathen" to Christianity. Accordingly, two classes of professionals were represented among the early Spanish explorers: *conquistadors* ("conquerors") and priests.

The Sword of the Conquistador

For Spain, the discovery of the New World came just in the nick of time. Like much of Europe, Spain labored under the yoke of *primogeniture*, the legally enforced tradition dictating that the first son in a family inherited all titles and property upon the death of the father. This cramped the style of younger sons, who were left with whatever scraps number-one son gave them, which might well be nothing at all. For all practical purposes, Spain was all used up—all titles were taken; all property was claimed. And if things were bad for the disinherited sons of the rich, they were downright hopeless for the Spanish poor. The New World represented a new chance, a world of opportunity.

The conquistadors followed in the footsteps of Columbus. Puerto Rico was subjugated during 1508 to 1509 by Juan Ponce de León (ca. 1460–1521), who, according to partially credible legend, had come to the New World in search of the fabled Fountain of Youth. (What he found was death: Ponce de León was mortally wounded by an Indian arrow in Florida.) Next, Jamaica and Cuba fell easily to the Spaniards in 1510 and 1511.

Far more spectacular was the brief, bloody war by which Hernán Cortéz conquered the Aztec empire of Mexico by August 13, 1521.

What's the Word?

The word **primogeniture** is Latin, meaning "first" (*primo*) "birth" (*geniture*). It signifies the right of the firstborn child—almost exclusively the male child—to inherit the whole of his family's wealth, titles, and privileges.

Borderlands

Cortés achieved what every conquistador sought: wealth beyond imagining. The example of his success would be the golden carrot that led a legion of conquistadors in his trail. The only one of these whose success even began to approach that of Cortés was Francisco Pizarro, who twice attempted to conquer the Incas of Peru during the 1520s and finally achieved his objective on a third try in 1531.

Like Cortés, Pizarro was esteemed a great conqueror, and his exploits inspired Spanish expeditions into the borderlands—the area of the present United States. After all, back in 1492, Indians had told Columbus tales of distant inland villages containing vast treasuries of gold. Eager to believe, and seizing on the examples of Cortés and Pizarro, one Spaniard after another traipsed across America, looking for the Seven Cities of Cibola, the Seven Cities of Gold.

Estevan, a black slave who had survived the typically calamitous 1520 expedition of Panfilo Narváez, joined an expedition led by Marcos de Niza in 1539, in search, naturally, of the Seven Cities. Zuni Indians killed the unfortunate Estevan in a battle outside the Hawikuh pueblo in New Mexico, but de Niza returned to the Spanish colonial capital of Mexico City, and there delivered a sparkling account of the pueblo and its treasures. Never mind that he had failed to gain entry into Hawikuh.

The tale was enough for Francisco Vázquez de Coronado. As with so many others who would journey to the American West in the centuries to come, all that was necessary to propel Coronado was a *dream* of riches. Proof was superfluous. During 1540 to 1542, he traveled throughout the Southwest, as far as present-day Kansas. Early in the expedition, during July 1540, he and his troops rode into Hawikuh and imperiously demanded the surrender of the pueblo. In response, the Zuni showered stones upon the conquistadors, knocking Coronado himself unconscious. Within an hour, however, Hawikuh fell, Coronado and his men entered it, and they found—drum roll, please—very little and, among that very little, absolutely no gold.

Coronado pressed on, in fruitless search of the elusive Seven Cities. Traveling through the pueblo region along the Rio Grande, he captured one Zuni or Hopi town after another, forcing the inhabitants into slavery and taking from them whatever food and shelter he required. In the wake of Coronado's visit, during the summer of 1541, the pueblos, led by an Indian named Texamatli, rebelled, but they were quickly defeated by the forces of Niño de Guzmán, governor of New Spain.

Oñate the Terrible

With Coronado's disappointment, the legend of the Seven Cities of Cibola dimmed, as did Spain's interest in the American Southwest. Then, in 1579, the English *sea dog* Sir Francis Drake landed on the central California coast and laid claim to territory he

What's the Word?

Whereas Spanish seafarers favored such grandiose titles as "Admiral of the Ocean Sea" and "Marquis of this or that," the great British navigators who sailed for Queen Elizabeth I gloried in the title of **sea dog,** coined during the sixteenth century and used to describe only the most daring and seasoned salts.

christened "New Albion," using the old poetic name for England. Alarmed, the Spanish viceroy in Mexico City alerted the royal court in Madrid that Spain's New World monopoly was imperiled. Busy with the usual European wars, the Spanish crown did nothing to reinforce the northern frontier of its colonies for another 20 years. At last, in 1598, the ambitious Don Juan de Oñate led an expedition northward from Mexico. At the site of present-day El Paso, Texas, Oñate claimed for Spain—and his own governance—all of "New Mexico," by which he meant a region extending from Texas to California.

With 400 men, women, and children—plus 7,000 head of cattle—Oñate colonized deep into pueblo country, depositing clutches of settlers at various sites. In no place, except at the Acoma pueblo, in western New Mexico, did he meet resistance. There Indians killed 13 members of Oñate's advance guard. Perched atop a high-walled mesa, the defenders of the pueblo believed their position impregnable. But in January 1599, the main body of Oñate's troops fought their way to the top of the mesa, killed most of the pueblo warriors, and took captive 500 women, children, and noncombatant men. Of the latter, 80 over the age of 25 were condemned to the amputation of one foot and a period of 20 years of enslavement. (Whether or not Oñate considered the limited utility of 80 one-footed slaves is not recorded.) The women—as well as children over age 12—were permitted to retain their extremities, but were likewise enslaved. Children under 12 were considered ripe for conversion to Christianity and were delivered into the care of priests. A pair of Hopis who had the ill fortune to be visiting Acoma at this time were seized. The governor ordered their right hands to be severed, and he sent the maimed visitors back to their own pueblo as a bloody warning of the consequences of rebellion.

The "Black Legend"

In 1514, the Spanish Dominican friar Bartolomé de Las Casas (1474–1566), known as the "Apostle of the Indies," catalogued with outrage a litany of his countrymen's atrocities in his *Historia de las Indias* (*History of the Indies*) and in the briefer *A Short Account of the Destruction of the Indies.* Published in 1552, the latter book was addressed directly to Prince Philip of Spain in the hope that he would take measures to put a stop to the cruelties of the conquistadors and others responsible for the Spanish New World colonies. Las Casas may be seen as the very first in a long line of American voices of reform and humanity.

The writings of Las Casas paint a picture of what might be called the genocidal colonization of the Americas. Because of his works and the records left by other witnesses, the history of Spanish brutality in the New World became what historians called the "Black Legend." Tragically, this legend contained a great deal of truth; for the conquistadors had come to the Americas already steeped in a bloody eight-century tradition of racial warfare against the Moors. Moreover, colonizers such as Oñate had a great deal at stake. They financed operations not with royal funds, but their own fortunes, and when Oñate failed to find the gold he had hoped for, he worked the Indians ruthlessly in an effort to wring a profit from agricultural enterprise. As it turned out, the people he had subjugated failed to produce enough food even to sustain the colonists, let alone to sell for profit, and, after Oñate's cruelty became obnoxious even to royal officials, he was fined and stripped of all honors.

The Black Legend was also fostered by the *encomienda system*, which dominated Spanish colonial government from the sixteenth through the eighteenth centuries. By 1503, the crown began granting loyal colonists a type of deed (called an *encomendar*) to specific tracts of land with the additional provision that the Indians living on the land could be used as laborers for a specific number of days per year. They weren't called slaves, but they might as well have been. They were worked and overworked, even unto death.

 What's the Word?

The **encomienda system** was the Spanish method of colonization, whereby certain settlers were granted a type of deed (called an **encomendar**) to specific tracts of land, which also entitled them to the labor of the Indians living on the land.

To some extent, the cruelty of the encomienda system was balanced by the ministry of the Spanish missionaries, at least some of whom behaved with benevolence. It is true that the Indians were given no choice in deciding whether or not they *wanted* to be "saved" by conversion to Christianity, but the best of the missionaries, beginning with Las Casas, did have an abiding concern for the spiritual, as well as physical, welfare of their charges. Tragically, such concern might have served to perpetuate the horrors that Oñate and others visited upon the Indians. On economic grounds alone, it is not likely that Spain would have continued to support its colonial outposts north of the Rio Grande. Gold was not forthcoming, and agricultural enterprises produced marginal profits at best and, in most cases, ruinous losses. But throughout the Spanish experiment in the Southwest, the friars had been creating a population of new Christians, whose now-sanctified souls, the priests argued, could not simply be abandoned.

The First American Revolutions

By the middle of the seventeenth century, after 50 years of tyranny, some of the Pueblo Indian groups were moved to take desperate action. They forged an alliance with their hereditary foes, the Apaches, universally feared for their skill as warriors (the very word "apache" comes from a Zuni term meaning "enemy"). After several abortive attempts at rebellion, the Apaches finally seized the initiative and, during the 1670s, terrorized the Spanish Southwest. In this, they were soon joined by the Pueblos, and the unlikely alliance waged a long and disruptive guerrilla war against the Spanish. At last, Governor Antonio de Oterrmín moved against 47 "medicine men" whom he identified as instigators of the rebellion. He hanged three and imprisoned the remainder in Santa Fe, the territorial capital. Among the prisoners was an Indian leader from the Tewa pueblo named Popé. Released after several years of cruel confinement, Popé went into hiding in Taos, where he began covertly organizing what he planned to be the decisive rebellion.

Through charisma and a genius for organization, Popé managed to persuade all but the most remote pueblos, which were the least oppressed by the Spanish, to join him. Next, to coordinate the uprising, he sent runners to the various towns, each bearing a knotted cord designed so that the last knot would be untied in each pueblo on the day set for the revolt: August 13, 1680. So determined was Popé to maintain secrecy that he had his brother-in-law murdered when he suspected him of treachery. Despite such precautions, word of the rebellion leaked to colonial authorities, and Popé was forced to launch his revolution early, on August 10.

Despite the last-minute change in schedule, the rebellion was devastating. The major missions at Taos, Pecos, and Acoma were burned, and the priests murdered; their bodies were heaped upon the altars of their despised religion. The lesser missions were crushed as well, and outlying ranches destroyed. Those who did not flee were killed.

On August 15, Popé led a 500-man army into Santa Fe, having so far killed 400 settlers and 21 of 33 missionaries. Although the armed garrison at Santa Fe consisted of only 50 men, they were equipped with a brass cannon, which they used to resist the invasion for four days before evacuating—Governor Oterrmín included—on August 21. Some 2,500 survivors of the onslaught fled as far as present-day El Paso, Texas, abandoning all their possessions to Indian looters.

Sadly for the native people of the pueblos, Popé capped his triumph by installing himself as absolute dictator and proceeded to become as oppressive as any Spanish overlord. For the next 8 years, he extorted a ruinous tax from his people, executing anyone who resisted. By the time of Popé's death (from natural causes) in 1688, the pueblo region was in a state of chronic civil war. The Indians were vulnerable, and, a year after Popé's death, the Zia pueblo was retaken by the Spanish. In 1692, Governor Don Diego de Vargas laid siege to Santa Fe, entirely cutting off its water and food until it collapsed in surrender. Within another 4 years, all of the pueblos had submitted once again to Spanish rule—except for the Hopis, a quiet people who were somehow overlooked by colonial authorities.

But the Spanish frontier did not long remain at peace. In 1695, the Pima Indians of lower Pimeria Alta—the region of present-day Sonora, Mexico, and southern Arizona—looted and burned Spanish settlements. The uprising was quickly suppressed, however, and more than 50 years would pass before the Pimas—these of upper Pimeria Alta, many descended from earlier rebels who had fled north—staged another uprising, which guttered out then smoldered as a century and a half of guerrilla wars—first against the Spanish, then the Mexicans, and finally the Americans.

From Black Legend to Black Robes

Enslavement and warfare were not the sole legacies of the Spanish in the American Southwest. The priests—the Indians called them "black robes"—who accompanied the conquistadors not only brought their religion to the Americas, but also created a Euro-Indian culture centered on the many missions they established. The first of these, in New Mexico, was founded during the administration of Oñate in 1598. Over the course of the next century, Franciscan friars founded more than 40 more, mainly along the Rio Grande. By 1680, missions had been built among most of the Indians in New Mexico as well. As the presence in California of the Englishman Sir Francis Drake had stirred Spanish concerns in 1579, a French landing on the Texas coast led by Robert Cavelier, Sieur de La Salle, in 1684 prompted the Spanish to build missions in that area.

Between 1687 and 1711, Father Eusebio Kino established many missions in northern Mexico and Baja, California, as well as some in southern Arizona, the most famous of which was Mission San Xavier del Bac. But it is for the chain of 21 Franciscan missions, linked together by El Camino Real ("The Royal Road"), extending along the California coast from San Diego in the south to Sonoma in the north, that the Spanish missionaries are best known. The first, Mission San Diego de Alcala (at San Diego) was founded by Father Junipero Serra in 1769. Serra would go on to found nine more.

The missions were communities, and, like other communities, they varied widely in their success. Some faltered and collapsed, while others spawned fertile fields, vineyards, and vast herds of cattle. By bringing large numbers of Indians into a small space, the missions also tended to spread epidemic disease, which greatly reduced some native populations. Beyond this, depending on one's point of view, the missions either enriched or disrupted native culture and traditions.

The way of the conquistador and the way of the Black Robe represent two distinctive aspects of the Hispanic Southwest. But whereas the conquistadors treated the Indians as bestial enemies, to be subdued and enslaved, the Catholic padres regarded them as miscreant children to be supervised and regulated. Neither extreme admitted a full appreciation of their humanity, but both traditions shaped the character of the Southwest in an enduring fashion. Both, too, created implacable enmities between white and red, leaving scars on the history of the region so deep that they would not begin to fade until the end of the nineteenth century.

The Least You Need to Know

- The sensational exploits of Cortés in Mexico and Pizarro in Peru inspired exploration of the "borderlands" (the area of the present American Southwest).

- Don Juan de Oñate was typical of the oppressive colonial authorities who ruled the borderlands.

- In addition to a hunger for wealth and power, the Spanish colonizers were driven by a desire to convert the Indians of the New World to Christianity.

- The encomienda system, at the heart of Spanish colonial policy, made virtual slaves of many Indians in Spanish-controlled territory.

4

England's Errand in the Wilderness (1497–1608)

In This Chapter

♦ The search for a Northwest Passage

♦ The "Lost Colony" of Roanoke

♦ Jamestown: first permanent English settlement in America

♦ Captain John Smith and Pocahontas

Sometime in the twenty-first century, people of Hispanic heritage will become the single largest ethnic group in the United States. History is always being rewritten, and, doubtless, it will get rewritten then as well. However, up to the present, most American history has been told from a distinctly Anglo point of view. Spain often acted cruelly in the New World, but it is also true that the history of Spain in the New World has been written, mostly, by Anglo historians who, over the years, have narrated that record of cruelty with relish and even an attitude of superiority. Often, they have contrasted the Spanish colonial experience—driven by greed for gold and absolute power—with the English experience, motivated by a quest for religious freedom.

Well, things weren't quite that simple.

England Joins the Age of Discovery

Henry VII (1457–1509) instituted a strong central government for England, replenished a treasury drained by the costly Wars of the Roses, and, in 1497, sponsored the first English voyage of exploration to the New World.

Henry's Hired Sailor

Giovanni Caboto, born in Genoa about 1451, but a citizen of the seafaring city-state of Venice, finally settled in England with his family. A cartel of merchants in the seaport town of Bristol hired Caboto, whom they called John Cabot, to pioneer a direct route to the spice-rich Indies. The plan was logical and potentially lucrative. England, on the westernmost end of the traditional overland caravan routes from the East, paid premium prices for spice. If the East could be reached more directly by sailing *west*, English merchants would get a jump on the worldwide spice market and enjoy unheard of levels of prosperity. King Henry VII made it official by granting Cabot letters of patent, empowering him to claim hitherto unspoken-for territories.

Cabot sailed from Dursey Head, Ireland, in May 1497 with no more than 20 men on the ship *Matthew* and landed in Newfoundland on June 24. It is likely that he probed as far south as Maine. After looking around for no more than three weeks—long enough to come to the confident and erroneous conclusion that he had reached the northeast corner of Asia—Cabot returned to England with the exciting news. Eager to believe that Cabot had indeed opened a door to the wide world, a grateful Henry VII granted him an annual pension of £20.

Cabot rushed to outfit a second voyage, bound for what he thought was Japan. Setting out in May 1498, this time with 200 men in 5 ships, he and his crews were lost at sea. (Some authorities claim that one ship did return to Ireland, but no official record exists of the expedition's fate.)

Passage to India? No Way

The loss of John Cabot was hardly the end of English exploration. His son Sebastian (ca. 1482–1557) was commissioned by Henry VII to make a voyage in 1508 and probably reached what would later be called Hudson Bay. Appointed Henry's official cartographer, Sebastian Cabot nevertheless later transferred his allegiance to England's great rival, Spain, in 1518. After failing, in 1526, to complete a voyage intended to follow the route of Ferdinand Magellan, he was prosecuted by his Spanish paymasters in 1530 and found his way back to England in 1548. There King Edward VI granted him a pension, and he became governor for life of the English Muscovy Company, which traded with Russia. In that capacity, he sent Sir Hugh Willoughby and Richard Chancellor in search of a "Northeast Passage" connecting the Atlantic and Pacific oceans along the northern shores of Eurasia. Willoughby and his crew were lost, but Chancellor, although he failed to find the passage, did reach Moscow, and trade was opened up between English merchants and those of Russia.

Remember This

It was Russian sailors who finally found the Northeast Passage in 1648. Semen (or Semyon) Ivanov Dezhnev sailed from the Kolyma River through the Bering Strait to the mouth of the Anadyr River on the Pacific Ocean. Vitus Bering, the Danish seafarer for whom the strait is named, sailed from the Pacific to the Arctic Ocean between 1725 and 1730, and Baron Nils A. E. Nordenskjold, a Swede, made the first through passage from west to east in 1878 to 1879, wintering off the Chukchi peninsula.

In the meantime, even greater interest developed in the prospect of a north*west* passage. Despite the claims of Columbus and John Cabot that they had reached Asia, it began to dawn on explorers and cartographers alike that the New World really was a *new* world—a continental land mass separating the Atlantic and Pacific oceans and, therefore, separating Europe from Asia, at least as far as any western shortcut was concerned. However, the early explorations had also revealed the presence of many bays and rivers along the northern coast of the new continent, and this suggested the possibility of a water passage clear through the land mass, maybe all the way to the Pacific Ocean and spice-rich Asia. As it became increasingly clear that the Americas would yield no great treasures of gold, the New World was perceived by some as less of an objective than an obstacle.

The search for the Northwest Passage may be traced to the 1534 voyage of the French navigator Jacques Cartier, who explored the St. Lawrence River with the express purpose of finding a passage to China. The English weighed in when 29-year-old Sir Humphrey Gilbert (ca. 1539–1583) published *A Discourse to Prove a Passage by the Northwest to Cathia* ("Cathia" = Cathay = China) in 1566, which, 11 years later, indirectly led Sir Francis Drake to sail his famed vessel, the *Golden Hind*, down the Atlantic coast of South America, around Tierra del Fuego, and northward, just beyond San Francisco, California. But Martin Frobisher (ca. 1539–1594) was the first Englishman to deliberately search for the Northwest Passage. He made three attempts. The first, in 1576, yielded the discovery of an inlet in Baffin Island, now known as Frobisher

Bay, which Frobisher believed was the opening of the Northwest Passage. He also became excited by the presence of an ore that looked a lot like gold. (Hey, maybe America was not such a bad place after all!) The ore attracted a cartel of investors, who created the Company of Cathay, which backed a second voyage in 1577, and a third in 1578.

Neither subsequent expedition found gold, but in July 1578, Frobisher sailed up what was later named Hudson Strait, which was an interesting discovery in itself, but hardly the Northwest Passage. Frobisher named it "Mistaken Strait," and gave up the search. Next, another Englishman, John Davis (ca. 1550–1605), made three voyages between 1585 and 1587, exploring the western shores of Greenland, Davis Strait, and Cumberland Sound. Failing to find the Northwest Passage, he became one of the first explorers of the Arctic. Then, in the opposite hemisphere, he discovered the Falkland (Malvinas) Islands, 480 miles northeast of Cape Horn, which would become the object of a brief but violent 1982 war of possession between Argentina and Great Britain.

Davis met his end in 1605 at the hands of Japanese explorer-conquerors in Sumatra. Henry Hudson, the next seeker of the "passage to India," became the victim of his own crew. In 1610 and 1611, after fruitlessly exploring Hudson Bay—an inland body of water so vast that it seemed certain to be the fabled passage—his sailors mutinied, casting adrift and to their deaths Hudson and a few loyal men.

Still, the search continued. Between 1612 and 1615, Thomas Button, Robert Bylot, and William Baffin, Englishmen all, made additional voyages to Hudson Bay looking not only for the Northwest Passage, but for any sign of the missing Henry Hudson. Although these expeditions failed to achieve either of their objectives, they did create interest in the region and led, in 1670, to the creation of the Hudson's Bay Company, which became one of the most powerful forces for trade and settlement in North America.

A Colony Vanishes, Another Appears

A passage to the East was not the only reason for English interest in the New World. Sir Humphrey Gilbert, author of the provocative tract on the Northwest Passage, earned renown as a soldier in the service of Queen Elizabeth I. She knighted him in 1570 and, 8 years later, granted him a charter to settle any lands not already claimed by a Christian nation. The ambitious Elizabeth wanted her island realm to become the center of a new world, the locus of a great trading empire—and she wanted to do this before Spain and Portugal succeeded in grabbing all of that new world for themselves. With her blessing, then, Gilbert sailed in 1579 but was compelled to return when his fleet broke up. He set sail again in June 1583 and reached St. John's Bay, Newfoundland, in August, claiming that territory for the queen. On his way back to England, however, Gilbert's ship, badly overloaded, foundered with the loss of all hands. The charter was inherited by Gilbert's half brother, Sir Walter Raleigh, the 31-year-old favorite of Queen Elizabeth.

What Happened to Roanoke?

In 1584, Raleigh sent a small reconnaissance fleet to what would become Croatan Sound in the Outer Banks of North Carolina. They returned with glowing reports of a land inhabited by "most gentle, loving and faithful" Indians who lived "after the manner of the Golden Age." Knighted by his "Virgin Queen," Raleigh (acting on royal instructions) named the new land after her: Virginia. In 1585 and 1586, he dispatched Sir Richard Grenville with a small group of would-be settlers. Sir Francis Drake encountered them a year later, starving and wanting nothing so much as passage back to England. Undaunted, Raleigh launched three ships and 117 people (men, women, and children) to what is now called Roanoke Island, off the coast of North Carolina, in 1587. After establishing them on the swampy island, their leader, John White, decided to sail back to England to fetch the supplies that Raleigh had promised to send. (Unknown to White, the supply ships were stalled because of the attack of the Spanish Armada against England.)

When White returned to the colony in 1590, he found no settlers and only the barest trace of a settlement—a few rusted items and what was apparently the name of a neighboring island carved into a tree: CROATOAN.

Had the colonists fallen prey to disease? Starvation? Hostile Indians, who took them captive to a place called "Croatoan"?

To this day, no one knows.

Starving in Jamestown

Raleigh's disaster did not shatter English dreams of colonial expansion. At the start of the seventeenth century, England was still militarily and commercially weak in comparison with Spain and Portugal. Domestically, as the ancient feudal system decayed, the nation was burdened on one hand by a displaced peasant class it could no longer feed, and, on the other, it saw the rise of a merchant and artisan class whose markets were exceedingly limited. Like Spain, then, England *needed* a new world.

In 1605, two groups of merchants, one calling itself the Virginia Company of London (usually abbreviated the London Company) and the other the Plymouth Company, recruited a cartel of investors and joined in a petition to James I for a charter to establish a colony in the territory of Raleigh's patent, which, as far as anyone knew, was vast, encompassing whatever portion of North America had not been claimed by Spain. The Virginia Company was granted a charter to colonize southern Virginia, and the Plymouth Company was given rights to northern Virginia.

The Virginia Company moved swiftly to recruit a contingent of 144 settlers, including the families of moneyed gentlemen, as well as poor people. The latter purchased their passage to America and the right of residence in the colony by binding themselves to serve the Virginia Company for a period of 7 years, working the land and creating a settlement. In Decem-ber 1606, the hopeful band of men, women, and children boarded the *Susan Constant*, the *Discovery*, and the *Goodspeed*. Thirty-nine perished in the course of the voyage. The remaining 105 arrived at the mouth of a river—they called it the James—on May 24, 1607, and, where river joined sea, they scratched out the settlement of Jamestown.

What's the Word?

Most of the colonists obtained passage to the New World by signing a contract called an **indenture,** thereby becoming **indentured servants**— in effect, slaves for the 7-year term of the agreement. This would prove a very popular method of bringing settlers to the fledgling English colonies.

Historians blithely refer to Jamestown as "the first permanent English colony" in the New World. At the time, *permanent* would have seemed too strong a word. Jamestown was established in a malarial swamp well past the time of year favorable for planting crops. In any case, the "gentlemen" of the venture—those who were not *indentured servants*—were unaccustomed to manual labor, and hacking a colony out of the wilderness required the hard work of all hands. Within months, half the colony was dead or had fled to the mercies of the local Indians.

Things only got worse from there.

John Smith and Pocahontas

In 1609 came what the colonists called "the starving time." Desperate, the survivors resorted to acts of cannibalism and even looted the fresh graves of their own number, as well as those of local Indians.

Jamestown would certainly have joined the Roanoke colony in a common oblivion had it not been for the presence of the soldier of fortune the Virginia Company had hired to look after the military defense of the colony. The intrepid Captain John Smith (ca. 1579–1631) managed to get himself adopted by the local Indians, who were led by the powerful old chief Wahunsonacock—called Powhatan by the English—and obtained enough corn and yams from them to keep the surviving colonists from starving. He also instituted martial law in the colony, sternly declaring that only those who worked would eat. Enforcing this iron discipline, Smith saved the fledgling colony.

Relations between the colonists and the "Powhatans" (the English used the same name for the chief and the numerous Algonquin villages he controlled) were always strained. Simply by refusing to share their food, the Powhatans could have wiped out the struggling colony at will. Yet they did not do so, although they repeatedly threatened war. Doubtlessly in an effort to intimidate Chief Powhatan and his people into maintaining peaceful relations, in 1613, Captain Samuel Argall kidnapped his daughter Pocahontas and took her to Jamestown (and, later, to Henrico) as a hostage. Fascinated by the English, the "Indian princess" quickly learned their language and customs—and rapidly evolved from hostage to ambassador. In 1614, with the blessing of her father, she married John Rolfe, a tobacco planter. The union brought 8 years of peace between the Indians and the settlers, a period crucial to the survival and development of the colony. (Rolfe took his bride on a voyage back to England, where she was a favorite with London society, as well as the royal court. Sadly, this remarkable young woman succumbed to an illness and died in England, on March 21, 1617, at the age of 22.)

To what must have been the great surprise of anyone who had witnessed the first terrible year at Jamestown, the colony survived and even prospered. The indentured colonists, having fulfilled their obligations, took control of their own land, on which they planted tobacco, as the Indians had taught them. A great fondness for the weed developed in Europe, and America found its first cash crop and significant export product. The prospect of growing rich from the cultivation of tobacco attracted more settlers. The Virginia enterprise was, at long last, successfully launched, and the world—New and Old—would never be the same.

 Remember This _____

Pocahontas is probably most famous for saving Captain John Smith's life when he was captured by Powhatan. Here is the story, as related in *A History of the Settlement of Virginia,* by the early Virginia merchant Thomas Studley and Smith himself:

"At last they brought Captain Smith to Powhatan, their emperor. ... Having feasted him after the best barbarous manner they could, a long consultation was held. At last two great stones were brought before Powhatan. Then as many as could lay hands on Captain Smith dragged him to the stones, and laid his head on them, and were ready with their clubs to beat out his brains. At this instant, Pocahontas, the king's dearest daughter ... got his head in her arms, and laid her own head upon his to save him from death. Thereupon the emperor was contented to have him live."

The Least You Need to Know

◆ The earliest English interest in the New World was motivated by a desire to strengthen the tiny nation through dominance in trade.

◆ England's first foray into the New World, the Roanoke Colony, vanished virtually without a trace.

◆ In 1607, Jamestown became the first permanent—albeit precarious—English settlement in America.

◆ The Jamestown experience occasioned the emergence of the first American hero-heroine pair, John Smith and Pocahontas.

5

A Rock and a Hard Place (1608–1733)

In This Chapter

- ◆ Puritans, Separatists, Pilgrims
- ◆ The settlement of Plymouth and Massachusetts Bay colonies
- ◆ Religious tolerance in Rhode Island, Maryland, and Pennsylvania
- ◆ Oglethorpe's utopian experiment
- ◆ The introduction of slavery

The settlement of Virginia was motivated by a combination of commercial enthusiasm and the intense social and economic pressures of an England that had outgrown its ancient feudal system. Farther north in America, in the area still known today as New England, settlement was motivated more immediately by religious zeal.

As early as the reign of Elizabeth I, certain members of the Church of England (which the queen's father, Henry VIII, had severed from the Roman Catholic Church during 1534 to 1540) had become extremely critical of what they considered compromises made with Catholic practice. A group of Anglican priests, most of them graduates of Cambridge University, advocated such articles of religion as direct personal spiritual experience, rigorously upright moral conduct, and radically simple worship services. They felt that the mainstream Anglican Church had not gone far enough in reforming worship and purging it of Catholic influence. When James I ascended the throne in 1603, Puritan leaders clamored for reform, including the abolition of bishops. James refused, but Puritanism (as the new reform movement came to be called) gained a substantial popular following by the early seventeenth century.

The government and the mainstream Anglican Church, especially under Archbishop William Laud, reacted with repressive measures amounting to a campaign of persecution. Some Puritans left the country, settling in religiously tolerant Holland, but others remained in England and formed a powerful bloc within the Parliamentarian party that, under the leadership of Oliver Cromwell, ultimately defeated (and beheaded!) Charles I in the English Civil War (1642–1646).

Promised Land

The Puritans who left England were, logically enough, called Separatists. Most of them were farmers, poorly educated, and of low social status. One of the Separatist congregations was led by William Brewster and the Reverend Richard Clifton in the village of Scrooby, Nottinghamshire. This group left Scrooby for Amsterdam in 1608; then, the following year, they moved to another Dutch town, Leyden, where they lived for a dozen years. Although the Scrooby group had found religious freedom, they were plagued by economic hardship and were concerned that their children were growing up Dutch rather than English. In 1617, they decided on a radical course of action. They voted to emigrate to America.

Brewster knew Sir Edwin Sandys, treasurer of the Virginia Company of London, and, through him, the Scrooby congregation obtained a pair of patents authorizing them to settle in the northern part of the company's American territory. With supplementary financial backing from a London iron merchant named Thomas Weston, somewhat less than half of the congregation finally chose to leave Leyden. They boarded the *Speedwell*, bound for the port of Southampton, England, where they were to unite with another group of Separatists and pick up a second ship. However, both groups were dogged by delays and disputes. Ultimately, 102 souls (fewer than half of whom were Separatists) piled into a single vessel, the *Mayflower*, and embarked from Plymouth on September 16, 1620.

After a grueling 65-day voyage, the Pilgrims (as their first historian and early governor, William Bradford, would later label them) sighted land on November 19. Some believe that rough seas off Nantucket forced the *Mayflower*'s skipper, Captain Christopher Jones, to steer away from the mouth of the Hudson River, where the Pilgrims were supposed to establish their "plantation," to a landing at Cape Cod instead. This lay beyond the Virginia Company's jurisdiction, and some historians believe that the Pilgrims were not victims of rough seas, but actually bribed Captain Jones to alter course in order to ensure the group's independence from external authority. Be that as it may, the *Mayflower* dropped anchor off present-day Provincetown, Massachusetts, on November 21.

There remained two problems. First, the settlers consisted of two distinct groups: the Separatists, united by their religious beliefs, and the others (whom the Separatists called "Strangers"), united by nothing more or less than a desire for commercial success. Second, neither group had a legal right to settle in the region, which was beyond the boundary of their charter. While riding at anchor, the two groups drew up the "Mayflower Compact"—considered by historians the first constitution written in North America—in which they all agreed to create a "Civil Body Politic" and abide by laws created for the good of the colony.

The settlers searched for a good place to land and soon discovered Plymouth Harbor, on the western side of Cape Cod Bay. An advance party set foot on shore—supposedly on a rock now carved with the year 1620—on December 21, with the main body of settlers disembarking on December 26.

They could hardly have picked a less favorable time and place for their landing. A bitter New England winter was blowing, and the site boasted neither good harbors nor, given its flinty soil, extensive tracts of fertile land. As at Jamestown, people began to die: during the first winter, more than half of them. But these settlers were also very different from their Jamestown predecessors. They were neither moneyed gentlemen nor indentured servants. Most were yeoman farmers, hard workers who were by right and inclination free.

From their number emerged a succession of able leaders, including John Carver (ca. 1576–1621), the first governor of Plymouth Colony; William Bradford (1590–1657), governor for more than 30 years, the colony's most able early historian, and the author of *History of Plymouth Plantation, 1620–1647*; William Brewster (1567–1644); Edward Winslow (1595–1655), the colony's indispensable diplomat, who negotiated a treaty with local Indian chief Massasoit, established vital fur-trading enterprises, and managed relations with England; and Myles Standish (ca. 1584–1656), not a Puritan, but a brave professional soldier who served as the colony's military adviser, established its defenses, negotiated with Indians, represented the interests of Plymouth in England (1625–1626), and was a founder of Duxbury, Massachusetts, in 1632.

But even able leadership would have failed to bring the colony through the first dreadful winter without the aid and succor of the neighboring Wampanoag Indians. Two in particular, Squanto (a Pawtuxet living among the Wampanoags) and Samoset (an Abnaki), gave the Pilgrims hands-on help in planting crops and building shelters. Samoset introduced the settlers to Massasoit, principal leader of the Wampanoags, and Squanto served as interpreter between the chief and the Pilgrim leaders. Throughout his lifetime, Massasoit (that was what the English called him; his Indian name was Wawmegin, "Yellow Feather") treated the settlers as friends.

 **American Life**

> In the fall of 1621, the Pilgrims invited their Native American benefactors to a feast in celebration of the first harvest, in which Indian aid had been so instrumental. The event was the first Thanksgiving (unless you count the collective prayer of thanksgiving offered on December 4, 1619, by members of the Berkeley plantation near present-day Charles City, Virginia). Our first president, George Washington, proclaimed the first national Thanksgiving Day, on November 26, 1789, but it wasn't until 1863 that President Abraham Lincoln made Thanksgiving an annual holiday to be commemorated on the last Thursday in November. During 1939 to 1941, by proclamation of President Franklin D. Roosevelt, the day was celebrated on the third Thursday in November, but then was returned by act of Congress to the date set by Lincoln.

Massachusetts Bay

Inspired by the success of the settlement of Plymouth (but ignoring the hardships involved in it), another group of Puritans—these only somewhat less radical than the Pilgrims—landed at Massachusetts Bay in five ships in 1630. Eleven more ships arrived the next year. Under the auspices of the Massachusetts Bay Company, a joint stock trading organization chartered by the English crown in 1629, 20,000 immigrants, mostly Puritans, would arrive by 1642, authorized to colonize a vast area extending from three miles north of the Merrimack River to three miles south of the Charles River. Led by John Winthrop, the new Massachusetts Bay Colony was centered in a city called Boston, and it soon prospered.

The Puritans wanted to create in the New World a new center of right religion, to build what their sermons (with reference to the Old Testament) frequently called "the city on a hill," a place of holiness that would be a shining example for all humankind. Toward this end, the Puritans laid great emphasis on family life and, in particular, on the education of children, as well as the education of a class of clergymen sufficiently learned to interpret the Scriptures as authentically as possible. The Puritans intended to guide their actions by an intensive interpretation of the Bible, since they saw themselves as living out a kind of Biblical allegory and prophecy in which they were on an "errand into the wilderness," chosen by God to build the "New Jerusalem." The most immediate practical effects of these beliefs were the creation of Boston's High and Latin Schools as early as 1635 and Harvard College the very next year. Moreover, the Puritan character rapidly evolved into an unlikely combination of a limitless appetite for brilliant religious disputes and flinty intolerance of nonconforming beliefs.

 Remember This _____

In February 1692, two daughters of the Reverend Samuel Parris and some of their friends were diagnosed by a Salem, Massachusetts, physician as victims of witchcraft. Under questioning, the girls accused certain women of being witches. The town magistrates proceeded against the accused on February 29. By the end of the year, accusations multiplied: 140 were accused, 107 of them women. The royal governor of Massachusetts, Sir William Phips, established a special court to try more than 70 of the cases. Of 26 individuals convicted, 19 were executed and one man, Giles Corey, was pressed to death under heavy stones as punishment for defiantly refusing to stand trial.

The Salem witchcraft epidemic, although extreme, was hardly unique. Witches had been tried before 1692 in Massachusetts as well as Connecticut and, even more frequently, throughout Europe. Who stood accused in *all* these places? "Witches" were usually poor, elderly women (sometimes men) who quarreled with their neighbors and were generally disruptive, disagreeable social misfits.

Rhode Island: Haven for the Heterodox

One of the most brilliant masters of religious debate was the Reverend Roger Williams (ca. 1603–1683), who emigrated from England to Boston in 1631. He declined an offer to become minister of the first Boston congregation because it had not formally separated from the Anglican Church. Instead, Williams moved first to Salem, then to Plymouth, and back to Salem. In each place, he was criticized for his "strange opinions," which included a conviction that the lands chartered to

Massachusetts and Plymouth belonged by right to the Indians, that a civil government had no right to enforce religious laws ("Coerced religion stinks in God's nostrils," he said), and that religion itself ultimately rested on profoundly individual conscience and perception. Ordered by the Puritan hierarchy to change his views, Williams refused and was banished from the Bay Colony by the Massachusetts General Court in October 1635. He and a handful of followers found refuge in January 1636 among the Indians on Narragansett Bay. At the head of that bay, Williams purchased from his protectors a small tract and founded a town he called Providence, the first settlement in Rhode Island.

During the next four decades, Williams welcomed to Rhode Island those of all Protestant persuasions. In 1644, during the English Civil War, he secured a patent for the colony from the Puritan-controlled Parliament, and he established a genuinely representative government founded on the principle of religious freedom. Williams returned to England again, where he successfully defended his colony's grant against the onslaught of Puritan objections, and after the restoration of Charles II to the British throne, he secured a royal charter in 1663, sanctioning the liberal institutions he had created.

Maryland: Catholics Welcome

The founding and survival of heterodox Rhode Island made it clear to the Puritans that their "city on a hill" would not stand alone in America. In yet another colony, the interests of a group even more repugnant to the Puritans were taking root.

In 1632, King Charles I of England, under siege from the Puritan faction that would soon overthrow him, granted the Roman Catholic George Calvert, First Baron Baltimore, a charter to settle North American lands between the 40th parallel and the south bank of the Potomac. The First Baron Baltimore died before the papers were executed, and the charter passed to his son Cecil Calvert, Second Baron Baltimore. In November 1633, 200 Catholic colonists set sail from England in the *Ark and the Dove*, which landed on March 24, 1634, on an island at the mouth of the Potomac they named Saint Clement (now called Blakistone Island). The colonists purchased the Indian village of Yaocomico and called it St. Mary's (it is present-day St. Mary's City), which served for the next 60 years as the capital of the colony. Under Lord Baltimore's direction, in 1649, the Colonial Assembly passed the Act Concerning Religion, the first law in the American colonies that explicitly provided for freedom of worship, although it applied only to Christians.

Pennsylvania: Quaker Colony

Freedom of worship was the theme for the creation of yet another non-Puritan colony. The Society of Friends—commonly called Quakers—was founded in seventeenth-century England by a visionary leader named George Fox. His belief was in the *immediacy* of Christ's teaching; that is, divine guidance was not "mediated" by Scripture, ceremony, ritual, or clergy, but came directly to each individual from an "inward light."

By its nature, Quakerism is subversive of authority imposed from the outside, and although a prime tenet of Quakerism is nonviolence and supreme tolerance of all points of view, the religion was quickly perceived as a threat to the dominant order. Quakers were officially and unofficially persecuted. Some immigrated to America, settling in the Middle Atlantic region, as well as North Carolina. An early enclave was established in Rhode Island.

The Quakers had some powerful adherents, one of whom was William Penn, the brilliant young son of a prominent British admiral. On March 14, 1681, Penn obtained from King Charles II a charter granting him proprietorship of the area now known as *Pennsylvania*. In 1682, Delaware was added to the charter. The region was occupied by some 15,000 Delaware, Shawnee, and Susquehanna Indians, as well as tribes associated with the Iroquois League. During the seventeenth century, it was claimed by Dutch, Swedish, and English interests.

In 1682, Penn founded Philadelphia, a name he formed from two Greek words together meaning "brotherly love." The name expressed the intent of what Penn planned as a "holy experiment" in harmonious living.

Under Penn, "The Great Law of Pennsylvania" extended male suffrage to those who professed a belief in God and met modest property requirements; it all but eliminated imprisonment for debt, one of the great scourges of life in England; and it restricted the death penalty to cases of treason and murder. In a combination of the best tradition of English common law and a dramatic foreshadow of the U.S. Bill of Rights, the Great Law specified that no person could be deprived of life, liberty, or "estate" (property) except by due, fair, and impartial trial before a jury of 12.

Georgia: Utopia, Prison, and Profit Center

Founded on firm—although diverse—religious principles, Plymouth, the Massachusetts Bay Colony, Rhode Island, Maryland, and Pennsylvania were all expressions of hope, variations on a theme of desire for a better life. The origin of Georgia was even more explicitly utopian.

In 1732, James Edward Oglethorpe, whose character combined military discipline (he was a general) with a passion for philanthropy, organized a group of 19 wealthy and progressive individuals into a corporation that secured a royal charter to colonize Georgia as the southernmost of Britain's North American colonies. Oglethorpe's bold plan was to create a haven for various Protestant dissenters, but, even more important, a settlement for the vast and ever-growing class of insolvent debtors who languished in British prisons and also for persons convicted of certain relatively minor criminal offenses. Oglethorpe reasoned that the colony would give the debtors a fresh start and would reform and rehabilitate the criminals.

Selflessly, Oglethorpe and the other philanthropists agreed to act as trustees of the colony without taking profits for a period of 21 years. To promote a utopian way of life, Oglethorpe prohibited the sale of rum and outlawed slavery in the colony. He also set regulations limiting the size of individual land holdings in an effort to create equality.

The first colonists who arrived with Oglethorpe in 1733 were placed on 55-acre farms, which they were forbidden to sell or transfer. They were permitted to acquire no more than a total of 500 acres of property. But this arrangement, key to the project, was quickly abandoned. To begin with, few of the original 100 colonists were debtors, victims of religious persecution, or criminals ripe for rehabilitation. They were speculators looking for opportunity. They soon found ways of circumventing the 500-acre limit to land holding, and after large plantations were established, slavery followed. Georgia was now no different from England's other southern colonies: land on which a few grew wealthy.

The introduction of slaves into Georgia was the hardest blow to Oglethorpe's dream, and he returned to England, disgusted with the entire enterprise. Like most other even modestly enlightened individuals, Oglethorpe regarded slavery as evil. Yet it persisted, even in a would-be utopia, and would persist until it tore the nation apart.

Slave Country

Just as Georgia was a latecomer into the British colonial fold, so it had adopted slavery late in the scheme of things. In 1619, just 12 years after Jamestown got its shaky start, Dutch traders imported African slaves at the behest of the Virginia tobacco farmers. The first 20 or so landed at Jamestown and were not racially discriminated against but were classed with white indentured servants brought from England under work contracts. Indeed, many years passed before African slaves were brought to the colonies in large numbers. At first, they were purchased primarily to replace indentured servants who had either escaped or had served out the term of their indentures.

As the plantations of the southern colonies, Virginia, the Carolinas, and Georgia, expanded, demand for slavery grew, as did commerce in slaves. The so-called "triangle trade" developed: Ships leaving England with trade goods landed on the African west coast, traded the merchandise for African slaves, transported this "cargo" via the "Middle Passage" to the West Indies or the mainland English colonies, where the slaves were exchanged for the very agricultural products—sugar, tobacco, and rice—slave labor produced. The final leg of the triangle was back to England, laden with New World produce.

Nor were the northern colonies untouched by the "peculiar institution" of slavery. Although a later generation of New Englanders would pride themselves on being fierce abolitionists, fighters for the freedom of the slaves, their forefathers had profited from the trade. New England ports became a regular stop for vessels about to return to Old England. The sugar and molasses acquired at southern ports was often unloaded here in order to manufacture rum, an important New England export.

The Least You Need to Know

- The Pilgrims were Puritans who left England, settling first in Holland and then in New England (at Plymouth) in 1620. Separatists were somewhat less radical Puritans who settled in New England (at Massachusetts Bay) beginning in 1630.

- The Puritan colonies combined religious fervor with respect for intellect and learning—as exemplified by the founding of Harvard College—but were also deeply tinged by cruel superstition, as evident in the Salem witch trials.

- The other major English colonies were also established as havens for freedom of worship; Georgia was meant to be a utopia.

- Intolerance among the Puritans and slavery in the South marred the colonies' ideal of liberty.

Chapter 6

Colonial Contenders (1608–1680s)

In This Chapter

- ◆ Champlain founds Quebec
- ◆ Jolliet and Marquette discover Mississippi and claim "Louisiana"
- ◆ The Dutch West India Company creates New Netherland
- ◆ New Sweden
- ◆ The English seize New Netherland and rename it New York

Compared to the Spanish, the English got off to a slow start in the New World, but they soon became one of the three principal forces in the Americas. Besides Spain, the other was France, which directed its main efforts at settlement along the St. Lawrence River in present-day Canada and in the West Indies. Although "black robes," Catholic priests, came in the wake of French exploration and set up missions among the Indians, religion was never as strong a component of settlement as it was for the Spanish, nor so compelling a motive for settlement as it was for the English. The fact was that the ambitious Cardinal Richelieu (1585–1642), who, in effect, ruled France as prime minister under the weak-willed Louis XIII, needed money to finance his campaign to make France the dominant power in Europe. And the New World offered opportunity for profit.

Champlain Sails In

As a boy growing up in France, Samuel de Champlain (ca. 1570–1635) showed a distinct flair for drawing. He especially liked to design maps—inspired in large part by the tales of adventure his naval captain father brought home. Champlain followed in his father's footsteps and was commissioned by the French government no fewer than a dozen times between 1603 and 1633 to probe the waters of North America and also explore inland. As with so many other explorers of the time, Champlain's primary objective was to find the Northwest Passage through to Asia, but he also worked to promote trade in furs and other commodities. When Richelieu became convinced that money was to be made from North America, even if the Northwest Passage were never found, he also authorized Champlain to establish colonies and (because Richelieu was a cardinal of the Roman Catholic Church) to promote Christianity as well.

Champlain established a broad beachhead for France in North America. During the seven voyages made between 1603 and 1616, he thoroughly mapped the northern reaches of the continent (accurately charting the Atlantic coast from the Bay of Fundy to Cape Cod), he established settlements, he got the French fur trade off to a most promising start, and he struck alliances with the *Algonquin* tribes and Hurons against the tribes of the powerful Iroquois League. These alliances would strengthen the French position in the New World at the often bloody expense of their archrivals, the British, who, during the next 150 years, would make few Indian friends, but many Indian enemies. Beginning with Champlain, the lines of alliance and enmity among Frenchman, Englishman, and Indian became sharply drawn. These would, by the middle of the next century, deepen into the wounds of the long and tragic French and Indian War.

Champlain built a crude settlement at Sainte-Croix in 1604 and then moved it to Port Royal the following year. This was the nucleus around which the

> **What's the Word?**
>
> The terms **Algonquin** and **Algonquian** cause confusion. "Algonquin" describes any of various Native American peoples who live or lived in the Ottawa River valley of Quebec and Ontario. "Algonquian" is a family of Indian languages. Tribes linguistically related through dialects of this language are referred to as Algonquian— *not* Algonquin. The other major Indian linguistic family in eastern North America is the Iroquoian.

colony of Acadia formed. In July 1608, Champlain directed the digging of a ditch and the erection of a stockade. He called this *Quebec*.

In 1609, operating from his base in Quebec, Champlain sailed up the St. Lawrence, and the river he named after his patron, Richelieu, to the lake that was subsequently named after Champlain himself. Here he attacked a group of Iroquois, on behalf of his Algonquin allies, thereby cementing the French-Algonquin alliance in blood. Later, in 1615, he would venture farther west, across the eastern end of Lake Ontario, and help the Huron Indians in an attack on the Oneida and Onondaga (two tribes of the Iroquois League). In these actions, Champlain was determined to secure the St. Lawrence region for France. He saw that this served as a major avenue of trade for the Indians. Whoever commanded the region would also command trade in the upper Northeast.

Of course, securing alliance with one Indian group meant incurring the wrath of another. And the Iroquois were enemies to be feared. Highly organized, the Iroquois League—five tribes, whose territory stretched from the East Coast west to Lake Ontario—waged war mercilessly, employing tactics of torture and terror to intimidate, subdue, and utterly conquer their enemies.

Champlain was an enthusiastic booster of Canada, promoting it in the French court of Louis XIII and Richelieu, yet he initially discouraged out-and-out colonization. Little wonder, for Champlain was interested in operating Quebec as a kind of private trading post, with himself in a position to collect a healthy portion of the profits. Nevertheless, the settlement was the nucleus of a French North American fur-trading empire that would endure for the next 125 years.

What's the Word?

Canada and the northeastern United States are filled with French-Indian place names. **Quebec** is how an Algonquian Indian word meaning "abrupt narrowing of the river" sounded to Champlain's French ears. Quebec City is located at the narrow head of the St. Lawrence River estuary.

The Sun King Beams

Louis XIV was born to Louis XIII and his queen, Anne of Austria, on September 5, 1638. Four years later, Louis XIII died, and his son ascended the throne under the regency of Cardinal Mazarin. Only on the death of Mazarin in 1661 did Louis XIV begin to rule in his own right, and thoughts of New France, although not uppermost in his mind, were at least *in* his mind. Unlike his father—and Cardinal Richelieu— Louis XIV did not want New France to serve merely as a source of quick trade profit.

What's the Word?

Coureurs de bois, runners of the woods, was a name applied to a class of men who made their living by trapping furbearing animals. Their profession required them to combine the roles of explorer, woodsman, diplomat, trader, hunter, and trapper. The coureurs, although often barely civilized themselves, were the pioneers of civilization in the upper Northeast.

He understood that, in order to hold the colony, it had to be a genuine colony, populated not just by *coureurs de bois*, but by sturdy, stable yeoman farmers.

What happened in 1671, then, shouldn't have come as a surprise. Pierre-Spirit Radisson and Médart Chouart, two coureurs, proposed to the emperor a scheme to create a company that would effectively monopolize the northern fur trade. But that wasn't all. They promised also to find the Northwest Passage, which (they said) would become an exclusively French route for the transportation of fur directly to Asia. In Japan and China, a little fur would buy a lot of spice. But the king was not interested in sending his subjects on such errands. In response to the proposal, he sent women to New France, hoping to entice trappers like Radisson and Chouart to settle down; he also offered a bounty to be paid to those who sired large families in New France; and, finally, he urged the Church to excommunicate men who abandoned their farms without the government's permission. In turn, Radisson and Chouart made their own response: they went to the English and secured backing to create the Hudson's Bay Company, which would be for many years the single most powerful mercantile force on the North American continent.

Two years later, the French intendant (chief administrator) in Canada, Jean Baptiste Talon, stuck his neck out, defying royal policy by hiring a fur trader named Louis Jolliet to follow up on something he had heard from the Indians—tales concerning a "father" of all the rivers. Perhaps this would prove to be the passage to the Pacific, Talon thought. The Indians called it the "Mesippi." But Talon despaired of ever actually getting Jolliet on the move, because a new governor was due to arrive from France, and surely he would nip the expedition in the bud.

To Talon's surprise and delight, the governor, Le Comte de Frontenac, a crusty old man who nevertheless possessed a combination of shrewd practicality and vision for the future, approved the expedition. Even if Jolliet failed to find a passage to the Pacific, Frontenac reasoned, pushing the claims of France westward was of great strategic importance in and of itself.

Jolliet, accompanied by a Jesuit priest named Jacques Marquette, did not find a shortcut to the western ocean, but he did find the Mississippi River, thereby establishing France's claim to a vast portion of what one day would be the United States. In honor of their monarch, they called the territory Louisiana, and it encompassed (as the French saw it) a vast, although undefined, expanse of land between the Appalachian and Rocky Mountains.

Not that the French really knew what to do with all they had found. Louis XIV—called the "Sun King" because of the magnificence of his opulent court and his even more opulent dreams of greatness for a French empire—had visions of an immense agricultural kingdom to reflect in the New World the glories of the Old. But, by the end of Louis's long reign and life, New France consisted of nothing more than a scattering of precarious settlements in Nova Scotia, along the St. Lawrence, and one or two isolated outposts in Louisiana.

A Small Investment

In 1609, Henry Hudson, an Englishman sailing in the Dutch service, reached the site of present-day Albany. Like everybody and his brother, he was looking for the Northwest Passage, and, like everyone who looked for it, he failed. However, his search did give the Netherlands a claim to the richest fur-bearing region of North America south of the St. Lawrence.

This did not bring an immediate rush of colonization. Instead, a handful of Dutch sea captains traded for furs with the Indians—often bartering hard liquor for them—but a full-scale colonial movement did not get under way until the Dutch West India Company was founded in 1621.

Until 1581, when it declared independence, Holland was one of Spain's seven Northern Provinces. Spain refused to recognize the claim to independence, and the young Dutch Republic founded the Dutch West India Company as part of its struggle to maintain sovereignty. The company was authorized to commission privateers (state-sanctioned pirates) to disrupt Spain's trade with its American colonies and, a little later, to undertake colonization efforts in Brazil, Dutch Guyana (now Surinam), the Antilles, and in the North American region staked out by Henry Hudson, which, in 1623, was christened New Netherland. The following year, the company established a trading post at Fort Orange (present-day Albany), and in 1626 dispatched Peter Minuit (ca. 1580–1638) to serve as the colony's first director-general.

The conquistadors of Spain, when they came to the Americas, simply took the Indians' land. But most of the other European colonizers made attempts to *buy* the land. It seemed more legal that way. Minuit's first step, then, was to legitimize Dutch claims to New Netherland by purchasing Manhattan Island from the Manhattan

Indians, a band of the Delaware tribe, for trade goods valued in 1626 at 60 guilders. Now, that figure was computed by a nineteenth-century historian as being the equivalent of $24, but, with a hundred and more years' worth of inflation, that computation hardly stands as an eternal truth. Still, it is interesting to contemplate the fact that, today, all $24 will buy you is a slot in a Manhattan parking garage near Radio City Music Hall for about 10 hours, and generations of self-satisfied readers of history have chuckled over what has been called the greatest real estate bargain in history. Few have stopped to think, however, that the joke was not on the Indians. After all, *they* never claimed to own Manhattan Island. The concept of land ownership was essentially foreign to most Native American cultures. For them, land was part of the natural world, and you could no more own the land you walked on than you could own, say, the air you breathed. If Minuit wanted to part with a load of trade goods just because an island was named after them, the Manhattan Indians were not about to explain to him the error of his ways. In any case, Minuit built a fort at the tip of the island and called it New Amsterdam.

The Dutch established a profitable trade with the Indians of New Netherland during the 1620s and 1630s, a period (as you see in the next chapter) during which New England settlers were locked in bloody war with their Native American neighbors. It wasn't that the Dutch were kinder and gentler than the English, but that, at first, they were interested in trading rather than settling down on farms. When the local supply of beavers (whose pelts were the principal trade commodity) became depleted due to over-hunting, the Dutch also started to stake out farms, thereby displacing the Indians and creating a cause for war.

Kieft the Butcher

By 1638, when Willem Kieft (1597–1647) arrived in New Netherland as the colony's fifth governor, two intimately related truths were operative: violence between the Dutch and Indians had become frequent, and aggressive territorial expansion had become a prime Dutch objective. Kieft was appalled by the condition of New Amsterdam. Its defenses were practically nonexistent, and its capacious harbor boasted only a single seaworthy vessel. Assuming dictatorial powers, he made sweeping reforms in civil and military administration. Among these was a heavy tax imposed on the local Indians in return for defending them against "hostiles," mainly the Mohawks. In truth, the Mohawks had become important trading partners with the Dutch and were now allies—henchmen, really—whom Kieft deliberately used to terrorize other tribes. The "defense" tax was a shakedown, a protection money racket, and Kieft was behaving no better than a gangster.

When the Raritan Indians, living near New Amsterdam, refused to pay the protection money in 1641 and attacked an outlying Dutch colony, Kieft declared brutal war on them. Two years later, he put the squeeze on the Wappinger Indians, who lived along the Hudson River above Manhattan. To persuade them of the wisdom of paying tribute, he unleashed the Mohawks on them. The Wappingers fled down to Pavonia (present-day Jersey City, New Jersey), just across the Hudson from Manhattan. Failing to understand the situation, they appealed to Kieft for aid. In response, he dispatched the Mohawks to wreak havoc on Pavonia, and then he sent Dutch troops in to finish off what refugees the Mohawks had spared. During the night of February 25–26, 1643, Dutch soldiers killed men, women, and children in what was later called the "Slaughter of the Innocents." The heads of 80 Indians were brought back to the dusty streets of New Amsterdam, where soldiers and citizens used them as footballs. Thirty live prisoners were publicly tortured to death.

Following the atrocity, 11 local tribes united in waging war against the settlers of New Netherland. Kieft frantically parleyed with the Indians, trying to undo the catastrophe he had created and fruitlessly seeking peace. His own colony, panic-stricken, threatened rebellion. At last, in 1645, the Dutch West India Company recalled Kieft to Holland and replaced him with a crotchety one-legged son of a Calvinist minister, Peter Stuyvesant.

Stuyvesant Takes Command

The autocratic Stuyvesant immediately set about whipping the colony into shape, restricting the sale of alcohol and persecuting Quakers and Lutherans, whom he feared would lead the impending revolt. On the positive side, he tried earnestly to provide an honest and efficient administration, including a limited public works campaign of improving roads, repairing fences, constructing a wharf on the East River, and building a defensive wall on the northern edge of New Amsterdam along a "cross-town" pathway that would be named for it: Wall Street.

As to the Indians, Stuyvesant strove to re-establish trading relationships, but he continued Kieft's policy of ruthlessness, especially against the Esopus, whose children he took and held as hostages in 1659 to ensure the tribe's "good behavior." And when the Esopus refused to yield *all* their children as directed, Stuyvesant sold those he held into the West Indian slave trade. Their parents never saw them again.

It was, however, Stuyvesant's despotism in governing the colony itself that led to the decay of his power, as the burghers of New Amsterdam clamored for increased self-government, which the West India Company finally granted them. Beyond the confines of New Netherland, Stuyvesant had mixed success in dealing with the colonies of other European powers, beginning with New Sweden.

Sweden in the Delaware Valley

In 1655, Stuyvesant expanded his colony into the Delaware Valley. The fact that the region was already held by Sweden did not deter him. He simply invaded, and New Sweden just as simply yielded. The colony had been founded by Manhattan's own Peter Minuit, who, having been recalled from New Netherland to Holland in 1631, subsequently entered into the service of Sweden (Minuit was neither Dutch nor Swedish by nationality, but had been born in the Duchy of Cleves, a Germanic state). In any case, the New Sweden Company, formed in 1633, was a joint Swedish and Dutch enterprise. Minuit led the company's first expedition in 1638 and established a settlement on the site of present-day Wilmington, Delaware, which he named Fort Christina in honor of the Swedish queen. Within a short time, the Dutch dropped out of the colony, and New Sweden, lying along the Delaware River in what is now Delaware, New Jersey, and Pennsylvania, became exclusively Swedish. Under the administration of governors Johan Bjornsson Printz (1643–1653) and Johan Claesson Rising (1654–1655), friction developed with New Netherland, and Stuyvesant invaded, annexing the territory. Thus concluded the cameo appearance of Sweden as an actor on the New World stage.

New Netherland Becomes New York

For Stuyvesant, it was win a little, lose a little, and then lose it all. Relations between New Netherland and New England became increasingly strained as the colonies competed for Indian loyalty and trade. The Dutch were at a disadvantage not just militarily, but also as victims of the settlement scheme established by the Dutch West India Company. Whereas the English settled New England and the southern colonies with relative speed, putting in place a combination of wealthy planters and yeoman farmers, the Dutch settlement was hampered by the patroon system, whereby land grants approximately 16 miles along one side of the Hudson (and other navigable rivers) or about 8 miles on both banks (and extending for unspecified distances away from the river) were made to absentee landlords who installed tenant farmers. Thus, New Netherland was largely a colony of tenants rather than property holders, and this state of affairs retarded settlement and made patriotism among the New Netherlanders pretty much a lost cause. Who wanted to fight and possibly die for a rented country?

By the 1660s, New Netherland was weak and torn by dissension. Peter Stuyvesant stumped about on his peg leg and rattled his saber, but he could not rally his country-men. On September 8, 1664, a fleet of British warships sailed up the Hudson. The Dutch colonists simply declined to offer resistance, leaving a supremely frustrated Stuyvesant no choice but to surrender, albeit on the important condition that the West India Company continue to enjoy substantial trading rights. The British promptly renamed both the colony and its chief town after the Duke of York (the future King James II), and Stuyvesant retired peacefully to his farm, which he called the Bouwerie. Through the years, the tranquil country path passing through his farm became first a racy street of cheap theaters, and, by the early twentieth century, a gray and dilapi-dated avenue of dead-end bars known as the Bowery and symbolic of other American dreams that had somehow gone awry.

The Least You Need to Know

- ◆ The French claimed vast tracts of land but failed to adequately colonize them.

- ◆ Although they set up a lively trade with the Indians, the Dutch likewise failed to create an enduring colony.

- ◆ The cruelty of New Amsterdam's Willem Kieft brought on years of destructive Indian warfare between the Dutch and Indians.

- ◆ The British easily displaced the Dutch in New York, creating the most powerful colonial presence on the East Coast of North America.

Fires in the Wilderness (1636–1748)

In This Chapter

America has long been a place of hopes and dreams. America has brought out the best of which humanity is capable—a dream of justice, a hope for liberty—and it has brought out the worst. First, it became a battleground on which Native Americans fought against an invasion from Europe. Then it became a battlefield on which the invaders fought one another, embroiling the Native Americans in their conflicts. At times, the invaders retreated into the distance and let the Native Americans fight their wars for them. It was, all in all, a place of most bloody beginnings.

New England Bleeds

The only thing certain is that the murder of Captain John Stone in 1634 was *not* the work of Pequots. As to the rest, the accounts of the Indians and the Englishmen differ sharply.

The Pequots were a powerful Algonquian tribe settled along the Connecticut River. Resenting the intrusion of Dutch traders in the Connecticut valley, they waged a small, bitter war against the Dutch. Then, in 1634, Stone, an Englishman, was killed as his ship lay at anchor at the mouth of the Connecticut River. Never mind that Stone was a pirate, who had tried and failed to hijack a vessel in New Amsterdam, had brandished a knife in the face of the governor of Plymouth Colony, and had been deported from the Massachusetts Bay Colony for drunkenness and adultery, and never mind that the Indians claimed Stone had kidnapped some of their people. Tensions ran so high between colonists and Indians that the New Englanders demanded action against the Pequots for the murder of John Stone.

The Pequot War

For their part, the Pequots wanted no trouble. Although no one accused any Pequot of having laid a finger on Stone, the murder was clearly the work of western Niantics, a tribe nominally under Pequot control. Seeking to avert a war, the Pequots accepted responsibility and signed a treaty with the Massachusetts Bay Colony in which they promised to surrender those guilty of the murder. They also agreed to pay an exorbitant indemnity, relinquish rights to a vast tract of Connecticut land, and trade only with the English, to the exclusion of the Dutch. By and by, a portion of the indemnity was paid, but the Pequots claimed that, of the murderers, all were dead (one at the hands of the Dutch, the others of smallpox), except for two, who had escaped.

For two years, the Massachusetts Bay colonists did nothing about what they saw as a breach of treaty. Then, on June 16, 1636, Mohegan Indians warned the English that the Pequots, fearful the colonists were about to take action against them, had decided on a pre-emptive strike. A new conference between the Pequots and the colonists was called at Fort Saybrook, Connecticut, and agreements were reached, but word soon arrived of the death of another English captain, John Oldham, off Block Island. This time, the perpetrators were Narragansetts (or a tribe subject to them), and although the Narragansett sachems immediately dispatched 200 warriors to avenge the deaths on behalf of the colony, the English sent Captain John Endecott to Block Island with orders to seize the Indians' stores of wampum, slaughter all the men they could find, and take captive the women and children to sell as slaves in the West Indies.

The Indians, anticipating just such action, had fled. A frustrated Endecott paid a visit to the Pequots outside of Fort Saybrook and set about burning their villages.

Soon, the Connecticut valley burned, as Indians put the torch to one English settlement after another, and the colonists responded against the Pequots in kind.

The Pequots were now defeated at every turn. On September 21, 1638, the Treaty of Hartford divided the Pequot prisoners of war as slaves among the allied tribes—Mohegans, Narragansetts, and Niantics—and further stipulated that no Pequot could inhabit his former country again. Indeed, the treaty proclaimed the very name "Pequot" would be forever expunged.

King Philip's War

An even more destructive war broke out in New England less than 40 years later, again over a murder. On June 11, 1675, a farmer saw an Indian stealing his cattle. He killed the Indian. The local Wampanoag chief, called Metacomet by the Indians and (with contempt) King Philip by the English, sought justice from the local garrison. Rebuffed, the Indians took justice into their own hands, killed the hot-tempered farmer, and then killed his father and five other settlers.

This blew the lid off a war that had actually been brewing for some time.

King Philip was the son of Massasoit, the chief who had been so friendly to the New Englanders. Faced with the colonists' insatiable land hunger, their rising population, and their highhanded, contemptuous treatment of himself, King Philip was not inclined toward perpetuating the friendship. Beginning about 1662, he stirred rebellion among the Narragansetts and the Nipmucks, as well as his own Wampanoags.

At first, the colonists were hobbled by the same problem they had during the Pequot War. Disorganized and apparently incapable of unified action, the New Englanders suffered very heavy losses during the first months of the war. It was only after they managed to join forces as the "United Colonies" that Massachusetts, Plymouth, Rhode Island, Connecticut, and the more remote "Eastern Colonies"—Maine and New Hampshire—began to seize the initiative.

King Philip's War was an unmitigated catastrophe for colonists and Indians alike. Between

 Vital Statistics

Among the colonists, 1 in 16 men of military age was killed in King Philip's War. At least 3,000 Indians died; many more were deported and sold into slavery in the West Indies.

1675 and 1676, half the region's towns were badly damaged and at least 12 utterly wiped out. The colonial economy was left in tatters because of the disruption of the fur trade, coastal fishing, and the West Indian trade. The Wampanoags, Narragansetts, and Nipmucks lost a great many of their number. As for the colonists, proportional to the population at the time, King Philip's War stands to this day as the costliest conflict in American history.

The French and Indian Wars

The Pequot War and King Philip's War were strictly colonial tragedies. The series of wars that followed, however, were reflections of conflicts also engulfing Europe. Collectively, historians refer to them either as the colonial wars or as the French and Indian *wars*—in the plural; the French and Indian *War*, singular, would come a little later, in the mid-eighteenth century, and would make the earlier conflicts seem all but inconsequential by comparison.

King William's War

King William III ascended to the English throne in 1689, after James II had been ousted in a Protestant revolt. William almost immediately (May 12, 1689) committed his nation to the Grand Alliance, joining the League of Augsburg and the Netherlands to oppose French King Louis XIV's invasion of the Rhenish Palatinate. In Europe, this resulted in an 8-year conflict known as the War of the League of Augsburg. In America, the struggle was called King William's War and pitted the French and the Abnaki Indians (of Maine) against the English and their allies among the Iroquois.

The New World theater of this war gave rise to a new kind of fighting. In 1689, Louis XIV dispatched Louis de Buade, comte de Frontenac, to America as governor of New France. He had served in that capacity before—from 1672 to 1682—but, proving himself a strong-willed tyrant, was recalled to France at the request of those he governed. Louis understood that what his colonies needed now was precisely what this tough 70-year-old had to offer: a stomach for relentless aggression.

Frontenac proposed not merely a defensive strategy against the British, but an invasion of New York. His only problem, he soon realized, was that he did not have the manpower to invade anybody. The solution, Frontenac decided, was to fight a *petite guerre*, or "little war," a war consisting not of grand strategies and the mass movement of great armies fighting European-style battles, but a war of ambushes, murders, and terror—mostly carried out by Indian allies.

Frontenac's "little war" was a dreary pattern of raid and counter-raid, without much decisive action but with plenty of misery to go around. In September 1697, the Treaty of Ryswyck ended the War of the League of Augsburg in Europe and, therefore, officially ended King William's War in America, but raids and counter-raids continued through the end of the seventeenth century.

What's the Word?

In French, "little war" is *la petite guerre*. This phrase soon evolved into the single word **guerrilla** to describe a limited, covert style of warfare as well as the combatants who fight such wars.

Queen Anne's War

Now it's time to return to the cheerful precincts of "civilized" Europe. England, Holland, and Austria had the jitters over an alliance struck between France and Spain when King Charles II of Spain, a Hapsburg (that is, originally an Austrian), died in 1700, having named a Bourbon (that is, originally a Frenchman) as his successor. The French, naturally, backed Charles's nominee, Philip of Anjou, the grandson of Louis XIV. England, Holland, and Austria threw their support behind the Bavarian archduke Charles, second son of the Hapsburg emperor Leopold I. These three nations then formed a new Grand Alliance in 1701, and the War of the Spanish Succession was declared between the Grand Alliance and France and Spain on May 4, 1702.

In America, the conflict was called Queen Anne's War. It began on September 10, 1702, when the South Carolina legislature authorized an expedition to seize the Spanish-held fort and town of Saint Augustine, Florida. When a combined force of 500 colonists and Chickasaw Indians failed to breach the fort, they settled for burning the town instead.

Not unexpectedly, this act brought a series of counter-raids from Spanish-allied Appalachee Indians, which prompted South Carolina governor James Moore to lead a force of militiamen and Chickasaws in a devastating sweep of western Florida during July 1704. The result: seven villages and 13 Spanish missions (out of 14 in the area) were razed, and the Appalachee were effectively annihilated as a tribe. Strategically, Moore's campaign opened a path into the heart of French Louisiana. Anticipating this, French colonial authorities heavily bribed the Choctaws into an alliance, which blocked Moore's advance into Louisiana.

The war raged—from Saint Augustine, Florida, to St. Johns, Newfoundland (captured by the French just before Christmas of 1708)—not in a series of great battles, but in a string of murders, raids, and counter-raids.

In 1713, Louis XIV, weary of war and crushed under heavy debt, was ready to end the wars in Europe and America. Besides, the cause of the War of the Spanish Succession had become a moot point. The 11-year-old Bavarian archduke backed by the Grand Alliance had died, and Louis's grandson Philip of Anjou ascended the Spanish throne by default. The Treaty of Utrecht (July 13, 1713) ended the European and American wars, with Hudson Bay and Acadia becoming English and the St. Lawrence islands becoming French. The Abnakis swore allegiance to the English crown but continued to raid the English settlements of Maine for years.

Tuscarora and Yemasee Wars

About the time that Queen Anne's War was winding down, the Tuscarora Indians in North Carolina were growing tired of being cheated and abused by colonial traders, to whom they continually lost goods and land and at whose hands they even suffered abduction for sale into the West Indies slave trade. Wishing to avoid war, the Tuscaroras, in 1709, obtained permission from the government of Pennsylvania to relocate there. The government of North Carolina refused to furnish the required certificate to make the move possible, however. After all, the North Carolina traders enjoyed making a profit, however dirty, from the Indians. In 1710, a Swiss entrepreneur named Baron Cristoph von Graffenried founded the settlement of New Bern at the confluence of the Neuse and Trent rivers in North Carolina. Graffenried chose not to purchase his land from the Tuscaroras, but instead secured the blessing of North Carolina's surveyor general to "appropriate" the property and drive off the Indians.

That was the final straw for the Tuscaroras. On September 22, 1711, they attacked New Bern, killing 200 settlers, including 80 children. Remarkably, Graffenried, captured and released, managed to negotiate peace, only to have it broken by one William Brice, who, thirsting for revenge, captured a local chief of the Coree tribe (allies of the Tuscaroras) and roasted him alive. The war was renewed, and, as though Brice's act had set its tone, was filled with more than the usual quota of atrocities, including the death-by-torture of scores of captive soldiers and settlers.

North Carolina called on South Carolina for help. In 1713, South Carolina's Colonel James Moore combined 33 militiamen and 1,000 allied Indians with the troops of North Carolina to strike all the principal Tuscarora settlements. This force killed hundreds of Tuscaroras and captured some 400 more, whom the governor sold into slavery to defray the costs of the campaign. A peace treaty was signed in 1715, and those Tuscaroras who managed to escape death or enslavement migrated north, eventually reaching New York. In 1722, they were formally admitted into the Iroquois League as its "sixth nation."

No sooner was the 1715 treaty concluded than the Yemasees, a South Carolina tribe, rose up against their white neighbors for much the same reasons that had motivated the Tuscaroras: retaliation for abuse, fraud, and enslavement. The military response, led by South Carolina governor Charles Craven, was swift and terrible. With the aid of Cherokee allies, the Yemasees were hunted to the point of tribal extinction.

Vital Statistics

How much was a human being worth? The whole-sale price for the Tuscaroras sold on the West Indies slave market was £10 each at a time when £100 per year was considered a handsome living.

King George's War

Men have seldom needed to look very hard for a reason to start a war. This one began with the loss of an ear. Following Queen Anne's War (or, if you prefer, the War of the Spanish Succession), England concluded the "Assiento" with France's ally, Spain. This was a license permitting the English to trade with the Spanish colonies in goods and slaves.

When British traders almost immediately abused the privileges granted by the Assiento, Spanish officials responded energetically. One British sea captain, Robert Jenkins, claimed that he had had an ear cut off during an interrogation by Spanish coast guards. Historians doubt his tale (he probably lost his ear in a barroom brawl), but his country-men believed him, and in 1739 England declared on Spain the so-called "War of Jenkins's Ear." Within a year, the War of Jenkins's Ear had been enveloped by a larger conflict. In Europe, it was called the War of the Austrian Succession (1740–1748).

The death of the Holy Roman Emperor Charles VI in 1740 brought several chal-lenges to the succession of daughter Maria Theresa as monarch of the Hapsburg (Austrian) lands. It looked as if the Hapsburg territories were ripe for the plucking, and King Frederick the Great of Prussia moved first to claim his slice by invading Silesia. France, Spain, Bavaria, and Saxony joined Frederick's fold, while Britain came to the aid of Maria Theresa. Once again, the European conflict also appeared in an American export version: King George's War.

It was fought mainly by New Englanders against the French of Nova Scotia and again engulfed the wilderness in flames. Territory changed hands, but only temporarily; for the 1748 Treaty of Aix-la-Chapelle, which ended the War of the Austrian Succession, also ended King George's War, restoring (as the treaty language put it) the *status quo ante bellum:* the way things were before the war.

But treaty language can be misleading, and the *status* was no longer quite *quo*. Enmities and alliances among the French, the Indians, and the English were now not only lines drawn on a map, but scars seared into the souls of all involved. Wait a few more years. There would be a new, far bigger, far more terrible war.

The Least You Need to Know

♦ Wars were fought with the Indians to gain their land.

♦ Colonies often used Indians as pawns in violent struggles with one another.

♦ North America frequently was a theater of wars that originated in Europe.

♦ King Philip's War (1675–1676) was, in proportion to the population at the time, the most destructive war in American history, killing 1 in 16 colonial men of military age and some 3,000 Indians.

Chapter 8

Global War in the Backwoods (1749–1763)

In This Chapter

- ◆ Conflict over the Ohio Valley
- ◆ Braddock's defeat at Fort Duquesne
- ◆ Forbes's victory at Fort Duquesne
- ◆ Wolfe's takeover of Quebec
- ◆ Aftermath: Pontiac's Rebellion

The treaty of Aix-la-Chapelle, which ended King George's War on October 18, 1748, brought no more than momentary peace to the American frontier. On March 27, 1749, King George II granted huge wilderness tracts to a group of entrepreneurs called the Ohio Company, stipulating that, within 7 years, the company had to construct a settlement of 100 families and build a fort for their protection. The grant and the stipulation accompanying it rekindled the hostility of the French and their Indian allies, who feared an English invasion.

Their fears were well grounded. Throughout 1749, an influx of British traders penetrated territories that had been the exclusive trading province of the French. In response, on June 26, 1749, Roland-Michel Galissonière, marquis de La Galissonière, governor of New France, dispatched Captain Pierre-Joseph Céleron de Blainville with 213 men to the Ohio country. By November 20, 1749, Céleron had made a round trip of 3,000 miles, burying at intervals lead plates inscribed with France's claim to sovereignty over the territory. The lines of battle were drawn.

The French and Indian War

La Galissonière was replaced as governor by Jacques-Pierre de Jonquière, marquis de La Jonquière, in August 1749. He decided it would take more than buried lead plates to gain control of North America and therefore began to build forts. He also attacked the Shawnees, the most powerful of the Ohio country tribes who traded with the English. In the meantime, however, an English trader named Christopher Gist negotiated a treaty (1752) at Logstown (Ambridge), Pennsylvania, between Virginia and the Ohio Company on the one hand and the Six Iroquois Nations (plus the Delawares, Shawnees, and Wyandots) on the other. The treaty secured for Virginia and the Ohio Company deeds to the vast Ohio country lands. French-allied Indians responded by driving the English out of this wilderness country by 1752, and yet another governor of New France, Ange Duquesne de Menneville, marquis Duquesne, quickly built a chain of forts throughout the Ohio country that ultimately stretched from New Orleans to Montreal. In response to this, Lord Halifax, in England, pushed the British cabinet toward a declaration of war, arguing that the French, by trading in the Ohio Valley wilderness, had invaded the wilderness of Virginia.

Baptism by Fire for the Father of Our Country

In the heat of war fever, Governor Robert Dinwiddie of Virginia secured authority from the crown to evict the French from the territory under his jurisdiction. He commissioned 21-year-old Virginia militia captain George Washington to carry an ultimatum to the French interlopers: *Get out or suffer attack*. Washington set out from Williamsburg, Virginia's capital, on October 31, 1753, and delivered the message to the commandant of Fort LeBoeuf (Waterford, Pennsyvania) on December 12, 1753. Thirty years Washington's senior, Captain Legardeur responded with polite condescension; he declined to leave. Washington reported to Governor Dinwiddie, who ordered the construction of a fort at the strategically critical "forks of the Ohio," the junction of the Monongahela and Allegheny rivers, site of present-day Pittsburgh.

In the meantime, up in Nova Scotia, British authorities demanded that the Acadians—French-speaking Roman Catholic farmers and fishermen who freely inter-married with the Micmac and Abnaki Indians—swear loyalty to the British crown. The Acadians had the misfortune of living in the midst of the most important fishery in the world, waters coveted by all the nations of Europe. While the British threatened the Acadians with expulsion from Nova Scotia, the French threatened to turn their Indian allies against any Acadians who took the loyalty oath. Thus the Acadians were held hostage between two opposed nations, and tensions rapidly mounted.

Back at the forks of the Ohio, the French, having patiently watched the construction of Dinwiddie's fort, finally attacked. Badly outnumbered, Ensign Edward Ward, in command of the new outpost, surrendered on April 17, 1754, and was allowed to march off with his men the next day. The English stronghold was now christened Fort Duquesne and occupied by the French. Unaware of this takeover—and on the very day that the fort fell—Dinwiddie sent Washington (now promoted to lieutenant colonel) with 150 men to reinforce it. En route, on May 28, Washington surprised a 33-man French reconnaissance party. In the ensuing combat, 10 of the Frenchmen were killed, including Ensign Joseph Coulon de Villiers de Jumonville, whom the French claimed was an "ambassador." This was the first real battle of the French and Indian War.

What's the Word?

Most of the colonial-Indian conflicts of the seventeenth and early eighteenth century (King William's War, Queen Anne's War, and King George's War) are collectively called the French and Indian *wars*. The cataclysmic North American war of 1754 to 1763 is *the* French and Indian *War*.

"Who Would Have Thought It?"

Realizing that the French would retaliate, Washington desperately sought reinforcement from his Indian allies. Imagine the young lieutenant colonel's chagrin when a grand total of 40 warriors answered his call.

It was too late to retreat, so at Great Meadows, Pennsylvania, Washington built a makeshift stockade he aptly named Fort Necessity. On July 3, Major Coulon de Villiers, brother of the man Washington's small detachment had killed, led 900 French soldiers, Delawares, Ottawas, Wyandots, Algonquins, Nipissings, Abnakis, and French-allied Iroquois against Fort Necessity. On July 4, half the outpost's defenders having been killed, Washington judged that honor had been served, and he surrendered. He and the other survivors were permitted to leave, save for two hostages, who were taken back to Fort Duquesne.

With the loss of the Ohio fort and the defeat of Washington, it was the English, rather than the French, who had been evicted from the Ohio country. A desperate congress convened at Albany from June 19 to July 10, 1754, and produced a plan for unity among the English colonies. The plan, however, managed to please no one. In the meantime, from Fort Duquesne, the French and their many Indian allies raided freely throughout Pennsylvania, Maryland, and Virginia. Finally, in December 1754, the British crown authorized Massachusetts governor William Shirley to reactivate two colonial regiments.

These 2,000 men were joined by two of the British army's shabbiest regiments, commanded by one of its bravest but least imaginative officers, Major General Edward Braddock. The French responded by sending more troops as well, and British forces were again expanded, to a total of 10,000 men.

On April 14, 1755, Braddock convened a council of war and laid out a plan of attack. Brigadier General Robert Monckton would campaign against Nova Scotia, while Braddock himself would capture Forts Duquesne and Niagara. Governor Shirley would strengthen and reinforce Fort Oswego and then proceed to Fort Niagara—in the unlikely event that Braddock was delayed in his conquest of Fort Duquesne. Another colonial commander, William Johnson, was slated to take Fort Saint Frédéric at Crown Point.

Monckton and John Winslow (a colonial commander) achieved early success in Nova Scotia, but General Braddock struggled even to get his expedition under way to Fort Duquesne. At long last, Braddock led two regiments of British regulars and a Virginia detachment (under George Washington) out of Fort Cumberland, Maryland. It was an unwieldy, sluggish force of 2,500 men loaded down with heavy equipment. Along the way, French-allied Indians sniped at the column. Washington advised Braddock to detach a "flying column" of 1,500 men to make the initial attack on Fort Duquesne, which Braddock believed was defended by 800 French and Indians. By July 7, the flying column set up a camp 10 miles from their objective.

Spies out of Fort Duquesne made Braddock's forces sound very impressive, and the fort's commandant, Claude-Pierre Pécaudy de Contrecoeur, was prepared to surrender without a fight. But Captain Liénard de Beaujeu talked him into taking the initiative and attacking by surprise.

Liénard de Beaujeu must have been some talker, because all the French had available were 72 marines, 146 Canadian militiamen, and 637 Indians of various tribes. Nevertheless, Pécaudy de Contrecoeur threw this outnumbered mixed force against Braddock's encampment on the morning of July 9, 1755. The result was panic among the inept British troops. They fired wildly—or at each other. It is said that many did nothing more than huddle in the road, awaiting slaughter like so many sheep.

Braddock, dull-witted but valiant, had five horses shot from under him as he vainly tried to rally his troops. At last, mortally wounded, he could do nothing more than look on as the disaster continued to unfold. Of 1,459 officers and men who had engaged in the Battle of the Wilderness, only 462 would return. (George Washington, although unhurt, had two horses shot from under him and his coat pierced by four bullets.) As he lay dying, Braddock, still uncomprehending, remarked: "Who would have thought it?" They were his last words.

Panic, Retreat, Retrenchment

The British defeat at the Battle of the Wilderness drove many more Indians into the camp of the French and laid open to devastation English settlements up and down the entire frontier. To make matters worse, the French had captured Braddock's private papers, which contained his main war plan. French governor Vaudreuil had intended to move against Fort Oswego on the south shore of Lake Ontario; learning from Braddock's papers that Forts Niagara and Saint Frédéric would be the objects of attack, he reinforced these positions, using the very cannon the routed English had left behind.

While the Pennsylvania, Maryland, and Virginia frontiers were convulsed by Indian raids, William Johnson was victorious at the Battle of Lake George and built the strategically important Fort William Henry on the south end of the lake. Washington, returned from the Battle of the Wilderness, persuaded authorities to build more forts, extending from the Potomac and James and Roanoke rivers, down into South Carolina. These forts, Washington said, were the only effective means of combating the widespread Indian raids unleashed by the French.

Remember This

The British so hated and feared the Indians that, on April 10, 1756, the colonial council of Pennsylvania began to offer a "scalp bounty" on Delawares: $50 for a woman's scalp; $130 for the scalp of each man over 10 years of age. How officials were supposed to determine sex and age, let alone tribe, based on the appearance of the scalps was not specified.

By June 1756, British settlers in Virginia had withdrawn 150 miles from the prewar frontier. George Washington complained to Governor Dinwiddie: "the Bleu-Ridge is now our Frontier—there will not be a living creature left in Frederick County: and how soon Fairfax, and Prince William may share its fate, is easily conceived."

Seven Years' Bad Luck

For its first 3 years, the French and Indian War had been strictly a North American conflict. In 1756, it became a world war as Prussia invaded Saxony. The following year, the Holy Roman Empire declared war on Prussia, which then invaded Bohemia. Through a complex web of interests, intrigues, and alliances, the French, British, Spanish, and Russians also joined the war, which eventually encompassed more than 30 major battles in Europe and European colonies in India, Cuba, the Philippines, and North America. The greatly expanded conflict was given the generic title of the Seven Years' War.

France sent the dashing and highly capable Louis Joseph, marquis de Montcalm to take charge of Canadian forces on May 11, 1756. For their part, the British forces suffered defeat after defeat. At last, in December 1756, William Pitt became British secretary of state for the southern department, a post that put him in charge of American colonial affairs. He took command away from inept, politically chosen officers and gave it to those with genuine military skill—colonial commanders included. The result was a gradual reversal of Britain's ill fortune.

Pitt chose Brigadier General John Forbes, one of his best commanders, to assault—for the third time in the war—Fort Duquesne. An army of 5,000 provincials, 1,400 Highlanders, and an ever-diminishing number of Indian allies lumbered toward the stubborn objective at the forks of the Ohio. When the main force became bogged down in mud not far from the fort, one of Forbes's subordinates, Colonel Henry Bouquet, lost patience and, on September 11, ordered 800 Scottish Highlanders to attack. They were cut down by French and Indians, who killed a third of their number.

This triumph, however, proved a Pyrrhic victory for the French. Losses among their Indian allies were so heavy that most deserted the cause. A treaty concluded at Easton, Pennsylvania, in October 1758 brought peace between the French-allied Delaware and the English. Colonel Bouquet, still reeling from defeat, proclaimed with relief that the Treaty of Easton had "knocked the French on the head."

On November 24, Forbes was at last ready to make his advance on Fort Duquesne. Suddenly, a distant explosion was heard. Rather than allow the English to capture the fort, the French had blown it up. Advancing to the smoldering ruin, Forbes beheld the severed heads of Bouquet's Highlanders skewered on upright stakes, the soldiers' kilts tied below them. It was a grisly greeting, yet Forbes knew that the nation in control of the forks of the Ohio—the confluence of the Monongahela, Allegheny, and Ohio rivers—held the gateway to the West. And that gateway was now in British hands.

If the year 1758 marked the turning of the tide in favor of the British, 1759 was the year of French disaster, culminating in the siege, battle, and loss of Quebec on September 18, 1759, following a battle in which the war's two most famous commanders, British general James Wolfe and French general Montcalm, died. The British capture of Quebec effectively brought to an end French power in North America.

Although the war had been decided with the surrender of Quebec, the fighting did not stop. Montreal remained in French hands, and Quebec had to be held. For the next 2 years, however, the British steadily contracted the circle around French Canada. At last into the fray, during its waning months, came Spain, which sided with France. England declared war on the new combatant on January 2, 1762, and crushed Spain with sea power alone. France rushed to conclude in secret the Treaty of San Ildefonso with Spain (November 3, 1762), in which it ceded to that country all of its territory west of the Mississippi and the Isle of Orleans in Louisiana. This offering was intended as compensation for the loss of Spain's Caribbean holdings to the British. On February 10, 1763, the great Treaty of Paris followed, which officially ended hostilities in America and abroad.

The score? France ceded all of Louisiana to Spain and the rest of its North American holdings to Great Britain. Spain recovered Cuba (in compensation for the loss of territories in Florida and in the Caribbean), and France retained the Caribbean islands of Guadeloupe, Martinique, and St. Lucia.

Rebellion of a Chief

In far-off Paris, pens had been put to paper. Within a few days of the Treaty of Paris, on April 27, 1763, Pontiac (ca. 1720–1769), war chief of the Ottawa Indians, called a grand council of Ottawas, Delawares, Senecas, and Shawnees. The chief pushed for an attack on Detroit. This decision ignited a series of bloody assaults on the western outposts that the French had just officially surrendered to the English. Although many Indian war leaders participated, this coda to the French and Indian War is known as Pontiac's Rebellion.

Pontiac's Rebellion tore the white frontier apart, as Indian warriors tortured, mutilated, and killed with exuberance. British general Lord Jeffrey Amherst, in desperation, gave orders to take no prisoners, and he even waged biological warfare, directing one of his officers to deliberately infect the tribes with smallpox. Although this plan was officially abandoned for fear of spreading the infection among the white settlements, Simon Ecuyer, a Swiss mercenary temporarily acting as commander of the besieged Fort Pitt (the former French Fort Duquesne), called a peace conference with his Delaware attackers. As a token of esteem, he presented them with two blankets and a handkerchief furnished by Captain William Trent from the fort's smallpox hospital.

"I hope they will have the desired effect," Trent remarked to Ecuyer.

They did. An epidemic swept through the Delaware tribe, and this misfortune, along with the Indians' realization that the supply of English settlers was apparently inexhaustible, brought Pontiac to the peace table at the end of 1763. By the following year, other disaffected tribal leaders had also surrendered, but not before a band of renegade white settlers had gone on their own rampage.

On December 14, 1763, a mob of 57 Scotch-Irish Presbyterians from Paxton and Donegal, settlements in the heart of the raid-racked Pennsylvania frontier, butchered a party of six Conestoga Indians, notwithstanding that the Conestogas were and had always been peaceful. The magistrates of Lancaster County gathered the surviving Conestogas into a public workhouse for their protection. The "Paxton Boys" raided the building on December 27, killing 14 Indians as they knelt in prayer. The survivors were once more removed, this time to a barren island in the middle of the windswept Delaware River. Safe from the Paxton Boys, the Indians were exposed to a brutal winter. Fifty-six sickened and died. This sordid end to one war would prove but a prelude to another, even more momentous, struggle in the wilderness.

The Least You Need to Know

◆ The French and Indian War was the American phase of the Seven Years' War, which historians consider the first "world" war.

◆ A young Virginia militia colonel, George Washington, destined to become the military leader of the American Revolution and the first president of the United States, initiated the first battle of the French and Indian War and, under General Braddock, played a heroic role in the disastrous Battle of the Wilderness.

◆ Although the English had more colonists, the French had more Indian allies and were far better at wilderness combat tactics than the inflexible British regulars.

◆ Pontiac attempted to unite several tribes in a campaign to stem the tide of English immigration into the Ohio Valley.

Part 2

The World Turned Upside Down

A few years ago, so-called "revisionist" historians set themselves up in the business of "debunking" American history, and it was common to hear talk about how the American Revolution was about economics rather than such "ideals" as freedom and equality. Well, to a colonist struggling to make ends meet, economics *was* freedom and equality. It's true, the roots of the American Revolution were tangled up in money, but they grew into a great tree of liberty that all the world has gazed on with envy and wonder ever since. The chapters in this part discuss the origin and course of the war for independence.

Invitation to a Tea Party (1763–1775)

In This Chapter

- ◆ Proclamation Line of 1763

- ◆ Taxation without representation

- ◆ The Boston Massacre and Boston Tea Party

- ◆ The First Continental Congress

- ◆ The Battles of Lexington and Concord, and the misnamed "Battle of Bunker Hill"

- ◆ *Common Sense* and the Declaration of Independence

Britain finally won the French and Indian War, but in the process started losing its North American colonies. The colonists had seen two very different sides of the mother country during the conflict. On the one hand, they had experienced the incompetence and arrogance of some British officers and administrators. On the other hand, late in the conflict, the colonists had witnessed some examples of inspiring British political and military leadership. Those latter impressions were more recent and left a stronger mark, so that at the start of the 1760s, except in parts of the frontier and in the urban centers of Massachusetts, Americans' loyalty to Great Britain was at its height. Yet it was not a passive loyalty. Participation in the successful war against France and Spain had boosted American self-confidence, and the colonists now felt they deserved to play a more assertive role within the British Empire. The colonies, traditionally competitive with one another, emerged from the crucible of war feeling stronger bonds among themselves than with an increasingly aloof and unfeeling government across the sea.

King George Draws a Line

The Treaty of Easton, concluded in 1758, had helped turn the tide toward the British in the French and Indian War. By formally agreeing to prohibit white settlement west of the Allegheny Mountains, British authorities persuaded the war-weary Indian allies of the French that they no longer needed to fear invasion by the English. But another product of the French and Indian War, the road that General John Forbes had hacked through the Pennsylvania wilderness to transport his unwieldy army to battle at Fort Duquesne, ensured that the treaty would be violated almost immediately. The Forbes Road was the first great avenue into the North American interior. It led to the confluence of the Ohio, Allegheny, and Monongahela rivers—the site of present-day Pittsburgh and the gateway to the trans-Allegheny West. Even before the war was over, settlers began to use the road, and the Easton agreement was breached scarcely before the ink on it was dry.

With the French neutralized in North America, the British crown saw the next and continuing threat of war to be conflict with the Indians. But as long as a buffer zone existed between the Indians and the colonists, peace could be maintained. Accordingly, a royal proclamation was issued forbidding whites from settling beyond the Appalachians. This "Proclamation Line" was not a permanent prohibition of western settlement, but a temporary measure designed to restore stability. Having fought a costly war to gain the trans-Appalachian region, the British were not going to abandon the idea of colonizing it. Nevertheless, many frontiersmen were impatient even of temporary rules. They defied the proclamation, crossed the mountains, and seized land. The Indian response was violent.

British administrators rushed to placate the Indians by negotiating more treaties demarcating Indian and white territory. Sir William Johnson, a New Yorker married to Mary Brant, an Iroquois woman of high rank, was appointed chief negotiator.

Thoroughly versed in Indian culture, he managed to pacify one tribe after another, finally bringing Pontiac's Rebellion to an end in 1766. Almost immediately afterward, he negotiated additional treaties to open up limited sections of the trans-Appalachian West to settlers. From 1768 onward, orderly, treaty-driven settlement began.

This did not please everyone. Wealthy colonists from the well-established coastal regions enthusiastically approved of the policy, but many struggling frontier folk either could not or would not submit to the law and pay for land. These men continued to seize land illegally, often provoking Indian attacks as a result. When the illegal settlers appealed to royal authorities for aid, they were rebuffed, and their alienation from the mother country increased. As the frontier regions became more populous and powerful, the allegiance of many authorities in the Tidewater (as the coastal region was known) turned westward rather than back toward Europe.

Taxation Without Representation

Fighting any war is expensive, and no war is more costly than one fought far away. During the French and Indian War, the English treasury had incurred a huge debt. The English government, led by Chancellor of the Exchequer George Grenville, decided that it was fitting and proper for the colonies to pay their fair share. Grenville pushed through Parliament heavy duties on numerous commodities imported into the colonies, most notably molasses and sugar, and the laws became known collectively as the Sugar Act. Passed in 1764, this was the first act the English Parliament passed for the specific purpose of raising tax revenues in the colonies.

At the same time, Parliament passed the Currency Act, which forbade the colonies from issuing paper money and required the use of gold in all business transactions. This act thereby guaranteed that the colonies would be economically dependent on England forever. Parliament also decided to enforce the Acts of Trade and Navigation, which had been passed during the 1650s but had never been put into effect. England used these acts to raise additional duty revenue.

Reeling from a business recession caused by the French and Indian War, the colonists were stunned and outraged by being taxed without the benefit of parliamentary representation. After a Boston town meeting denounced "taxation without representation," the phrase evolved into a battle cry that spread from that city to the other colonies. Thus, the resentment already stirring in parts of the frontier and quite well established in Boston began to grow in other villages and towns along the coast as well.

The action the Boston meeting proposed was nonviolent. The colonies made a Non-Importation Agreement, pledging to boycott a wide variety of English goods. Parliament, taking little heed of this protest, passed the Quartering Act in 1765, requiring colonial governments to furnish barracks and other provisions for royal troops. The next year, the act was extended to require the billeting of soldiers in taverns and inns at the expense of the colonists. Not only were these measures a further financial hardship on the colonies, they rankled in a way that reached beyond economics. The Quartering Act was seen as an invasion of privacy and an affront to personal liberty. Even colonists who were not directly affected by the revenue acts were enraged by the Quartering Act.

Stamps of Tyranny

Parliament had an even more offensive measure in store. In 1765, it passed the Stamp Act, which required that every paper document—from newspapers, to deeds, to playing cards—bear a revenue stamp purchased from royally appointed colonial stamp agents. Worse, violations of the act were to be tried summarily by vice-admiralty courts, in which there were no juries. Not only did the colonists see the stamps as evil, but denial of trial by jury attacked a right as old as the Magna Carta.

The Stamp Act united the colonies in opposition to the "tyranny" of the mother country. Subversive secret societies, most notably the Sons of Liberty, were formed in many towns, the boycott of English goods was stepped up, and a Stamp Act Congress was called in New York in October of 1765 (eight colonies sent delegates). The Congress drafted a "Declaration of Rights and Grievances," claiming that the colonists were entitled to all the rights of British subjects and that taxation without parliamentary representation was a violation of those rights. Parliament repealed the Stamp Act in March of 1766, but simultaneously delivered a political slap in the face by passing the Declaratory Act, which affirmed Parliament's authority to create laws for the colonies "in all cases whatever."

Act II

Chancellor of the Exchequer Charles Townshend (1725–1767) next pushed through Parliament a bundle of acts intended to raise revenue, tighten customs enforcement, and assert imperial authority in America. Enacted on June 29, 1767, the so-called Townshend Acts levied import duties on glass, lead, paint, paper, and tea. Additional bills in the package authorized "writs of assistance" (blanket search warrants), created additional juryless vice-admiralty courts, established a board of customs commissioners with headquarters in Boston, and suspended the New York assembly for its defiance of the Quartering Act of 1765.

Samuel Adams, of the Massachusetts Sons of Liberty, sent a "circular letter" to the other 12 colonies calling for renewal of the nonimportation agreements. Royal customs officials in Boston were attacked after they seized a ship belonging to the merchant—and political troublemaker—John Hancock. The beleaguered officials requested a contingent of English troops to occupy Boston.

During 1768 and 1769, all the colonies except New Hampshire boycotted English goods, and the Virginia House of Burgesses, led by Patrick Henry, created the Virginia Association to enforce the boycott. At this, the royal governor of Virginia dissolved the House of Burgesses, thereby further inflaming anti-British passions. However, in April 1770, Parliament again bowed to the pressure and repealed all the Townshend duties—except for a tax on tea.

Bloody Boston

The British troops sent to Boston at the request of the beleaguered customs officials were, to put it mildly, not popular. On March 5, 1770, a British redcoat, looking to supplement his meager soldier's pay with a part-time job, got into a brawl with Bostonians out of work in the depressed economy prevailing at the time. The brawl touched off an evening of protests by bands of colonists who roamed the streets. Finally, a small mob gathered in front of the hated Customs House, where they cornered and threatened the soldier whose job hunting had started it all. Captain Thomas Preston arrived on the scene with a squad of redcoats, and a tense standoff developed, in which the mob continually taunted the soldiers, pelting them with icy snowballs, stones, and other missiles. Discipline broke down among the soldiers, one of whom fire into the crowd. Others began firing as well. Three colonists died instantly, and two others were mortally wounded.

Preston had given no order to fire, and only with difficulty did he regain control of his men. Prudently, British authorities immediately withdrew all the troops from town. But the "Boston Massacre" became the focal point of anti-British propaganda and heightened American

Remember This

First to die in the cause of American liberty was a member of the Boston mob, Crispus Attucks (born about 1723). He was almost certainly a black man, probably a fugitive slave, perhaps partly of Indian descent.

fears about standing armies established in the colonies. Committees of correspondence, which had formed during the Stamp Act protest to coordinate action among the colonies, got very busy, and the colonies drew closer together in opposition to the crown.

Despite the efforts of Sam Adams and other Sons of Liberty to fan the flames of the Boston Massacre into a full-scale revolutionary conflagration, cooler heads prevailed. Some of the redcoats and their captain were put on trial in a colonial court and, thanks to the principled defense of attorneys John Adams and Josiah Quincy, they were either acquitted of murder or punished for lesser offenses. Anglo-American relations actually improved—albeit briefly.

Tearing Apart and Coming Together

By 1773, the only tax remaining from the Townshend Acts was the duty on tea. To modern ears, this sounds rather trivial. Don't want to pay a tax on tea? Well then, stop drinking tea!

But going without tea was never a viable option for *English* men and women. More-over, in the eighteenth century, tea was an extremely valuable trade commodity—practically a second currency. The East India Company, England's chief tea producer, was vital to British government interests because it had extensive influence in India. Expenses, however, were high, and the company was poorly run. By the 1770s, it was close to bankruptcy. To bail out the firm, Parliament suspended the tax paid on tea in England but retained the import tax on tea sold in the colonies. Worse, the government ruled that the East India Company could sell the tea directly to agents at a set price rather than through colonial merchants at public auction. Not only was the tax unfair, but colonial merchants, cut out of the profit loop, resented the crown's intrusion into free enterprise.

 Vital Statistics

The protesters dumped 342 chests of tea into Boston Harbor. The cargo weighed 92,616 pounds and was valued at approximately a pound per pound: £92,659. This was a tremendous amount of money in a day when a man earning £100 a year was considered moderately wealthy.

The committees of correspondence worked overtime to spread the word of opposition to the tea duty and to impose an absolute boycott of English tea. On one occasion, the royal governor of Massachusetts refused demands to send recently arrived tea ships back to England. So, on the night of December 16, 1773, a band of Bostonians—rather lamely disguised as Indians—boarded three ships in the Boston harbor and dumped a cargo of tea chests overboard. The act triggered similar "tea parties" in ports up and down the coast.

Some Intolerable Acts

King George III of England (1738–1820) has always gotten a bad rap in American schoolbooks, which traditionally paint him as a tyrant seeking to squeeze out of the colonies not only their cash, but their liberty as well. In truth, George was a popular monarch, as earnest as he was mediocre and incapable of thinking on his own. During the period immediately preceding the American Revolution, he depended entirely on the advice of his prime minister, Lord North, an aggressive autocrat. Following the Boston Tea Party, it was North who sponsored what the colonists called the Intolerable Acts.

The first of these acts, the Boston Port Act (March 31, 1774), closed the harbor to commerce until such time as Boston paid for the destroyed tea. Next, the Massachusetts Government Act (May 20) reserved for the crown the power to appoint members of the upper house of the legislature. The Government Act also increased the royal governor's patronage powers and provided that juries be summoned by royally appointed sheriffs rather than elected by colonists. Most onerous of all, the Government Act banned town meetings not explicitly authorized by law or by the royal governor. At the same time, the Impartial Administration of Justice Act authorized a change of venue to another colony or even to England for crown officers charged with capital crimes while performing official duties.

Intended to restore order to Massachusetts, the Intolerable Acts boomeranged, leading the colonies to recognize their common cause and to convene the First Continental Congress.

Continental Congress

The Congress met in Philadelphia during September 1774, and only Georgia failed to send delegates. The 56 delegates who convened represented the full spectrum of colonial thought, from radicals who wanted instantly to sever all ties with England, to conservatives who wanted to find a way to heal the breach; however, at this point, those favoring independence were decidedly in the minority. The Massachusetts delegation produced the Suffolk Resolves, which the radicals supported, calling for the people to arm, to disobey the Intolerable Acts, and to collect their own colonial taxes. The moderates countered with a plan of union between England and the colonies. With modifications, the Suffolk Resolves were adopted by a margin of six to five. The Intolerable Acts were declared unconstitutional, and the nonimportation boycott was given teeth by the creation of a colonial association to enforce it.

Following the Continental Congress, Thomas Jefferson (in his pamphlet, *Summary View of the Rights of British America*) and John Adams (in a series of published letters he signed "Novanglus," Latin for New Englander) proposed dominion status for the colonies, whereby the colonies would entirely govern themselves, but acknowledge the crown as the head of state. At the time, Parliament rejected this idea as too radical, but liberals in the English government did formulate a plan of conciliation in 1775, which would have granted a considerable degree of self-government to the colonies. The ultra-conservative House of Lords rejected the plan, however, and Parliament as a whole declared Massachusetts to be in rebellion. In a sense, then, it was the British Parliament, not the American rebels, that declared the American Revolution.

The Shot Heard 'Round the World

Massachusetts responded to the Parliamentary declaration by organizing special militia units that could be ready for battle on a minute's notice. They were called—what else?—the *Minutemen*.

General Thomas Gage, commander of British regulars, under Parliamentary and royal orders to use force against the defiant colonials, dispatched Lieutenant Colonel Francis Smith with a column from Boston to seize the gunpowder stored at the Massachusetts Provincial Congress in the town of Concord. On the morning of April 19, 1775, Smith's troops dispersed a company of Minutemen at Lexington, unintentionally killing several in an unauthorized burst of musket fire. Smith reached Concord but found only a small portion of the gunpowder still there. He had not reckoned on the resourcefulness of a small band of swift Patriot riders.

American Echo

By the rude bridge that arched the flood, / Their flag to April's breeze unfurled, / Here once the embattled farmers stood, / And fired the shot heard round the world.

—Ralph Waldo Emerson, "Hymn Sung at the Completion of the Concord Monument, April 19, 1836"

Paul Revere (1735–1818) was a prosperous and highly skilled Charlestown, Massachu-setts, silversmith, who was a leader of the Sons of Liberty and had been a participant in the Boston Tea Party. A courier for the Massachusetts Committee of Correspondence, Revere rode, on the night of April 18, from Charlestown to Lexington, alerting the populace to the approach of British troops. In Lexington, he also warned John Hancock and Samuel Adams, the chief leaders of the Massachusetts rebels, to escape. Accompanied by two other riders, Charles Dawes and Samuel Prescott, Revere rode on to Concord, but was intercepted by a British patrol. Although Prescott was the one who actually managed to reach Concord, it was Revere whom Henry Wadsworth Longfellow celebrated in his famous, if fanciful, poem of 1863, "Paul Revere's Ride."

At Concord, colonial resistance to the redcoats was far more effective than at Lexington. Not only did the British find few arms to capture, they were driven out of town and sent on their way back to Boston. All along the retreat route, the redcoat column was harassed by gunfire from Patriot snipers, resulting in the deaths of 73 British soldiers and the wounding of an additional 200. The pattern would prove typical of the war. British forces, trained to fight European-style, open-field battles, would often win such engagements, only to be cut up piecemeal by colonial guerrilla groups using concealed ambush tactics. Had the Patriots been led in a more orderly and aggressive manner, they could have dealt an even harsher blow to the British troops.

Washington Signs On

Soon after the battles at Lexington and Concord, colonial militia forces from all over New England converged on Boston and laid siege to the city. In May 1775, a Vermont landowner named Ethan Allen led a militia outfit he had organized—the Green Mountain Boys—against Fort Ticonderoga, situated between Lake Champlain and Lake George in New York, and seized it from British regulars. Next, Crown Point, on the western shore of Lake Champlain, fell to rebel forces. Despite these early triumphs, anyone who assessed the situation with a cold eye would have put their money on the Brits. Britain was an established imperial power, with deep pockets, a tested army, and the most powerful navy in the world. Moreover, while the *colonies* had acted in unity, the *colonists* were hardly unanimous in the desire to rebel. Each colony contained a large "Loyalist" population as well as many other colonists who just wanted to be left out of the conflicts.

Then there was the matter of leadership. The English had a king and a prime minister, but the colonies had no king or any other chief executive. In fact, the colonies had no government at all, no treasury, and no regular army. True, a Continental Congress had convened, but 13 separate colonial assemblies vied with it for power and authority.

Forty-three-year-old George Washington, now a prosperous Virginia planter, was accustomed to long odds. He had played them during his militia service in the French and Indian War. Sometimes, he had won. Mostly, he had lost. On June 15, 1775, at the suggestion of John Adams of Massachusetts, the Second Continental Congress asked Washington to lead the as-yet nonexistent Continental Army. Washington accepted.

A Misnamed Battle near Bunker Hill

The colonies' new commander set off for New England to take command of the Minutemen and the rest of the militia. Before Washington arrived, however, British General Thomas Gage (who had been reinforced on May 25 by fresh troops from Britain and additional generals, John Burgoyne, William Howe, and Henry Clinton) offered to call the Revolution quits—no harm, no foul. General Gage would grant an amnesty to everyone except Sam Adams and John Hancock, the two chief trouble-makers. In response to the offer, the Massachusetts Committee of Public Safety ordered General Artemus Ward to fortify Bunker Hill on Charlestown Heights, overlooking Boston harbor. Ward instead sent Colonel William Prescott with 1,200 men to occupy nearby Breed's Hill, which was lower, flatter, and easier to fortify, but also more vulnerable to attack.

Gage opened up on Breed's Hill with a naval bombardment at dawn on June 17, 1775. Then he launched an amphibious attack with 2,500 men under General Howe.

 Vital Statistics

Of the 2,500 British troops engaged at Bunker Hill, 1,000 perished, a devastating casualty rate of 42 percent—the heaviest loss the British would suffer during the long war.

Twice, the superior British force attempted to take the hill, and twice it was repelled. A third assault, with fixed bayonets, succeeded only after the colonials had run out of ammunition. Misnamed for Bunker Hill (the superior position that *should* have been defended), the battle was a tactical defeat for the colonists, but it was a tremendous psychological victory for them. They had been defeated only because of a shortage of ammunition and had inflicted severe casualties on the British.

The Olive Branch Spurned, a Declaration Written

The Second Continental Congress made its own final attempt to stop the revolution by sending to King George III and Parliament the so-called Olive Branch Petition. Meanwhile, Washington formed the first parade of the Continental Army on Cambridge Common in Cambridge, Massachusetts, on July 3, 1775. In September, the crown contemptuously rejected the Olive Branch Petition. Georgia, the final holdout from the Second Continental Congress, joined that assembly and the Revolution. Congress next moved to organize a post office department, a commission for negotiating with Indians, and a Navy. By December 1775, Virginia and North Carolina militia defeated the forces of the royal governor of Virginia and destroyed his base at Norfolk.

With the rebellion in full swing, it was time to create a feeling of historical purpose to catch up with the rush of events. In January 1776, Thomas Paine, a Philadelphia patriot and orator, anonymously published a modest pamphlet called *Common Sense*. In brilliant, even melodramatic prose, Paine outlined the reasons for breaking free from England, portraying the American Revolution as a *world* event, an epoch-making step in the history of humankind.

With the colonies united as never before, the next great document to emerge from the gathering storm was a formal declaration of independence. On July 1, 1776, Richard Henry Lee, one of Virginia's delegates to the Continental Congress, presented a draft proposal for a document asserting that "these United Colonies are, and of a right ought to be, free and independent States." Congress adopted the resolution on July 2, and Thomas Jefferson of Virginia, who had a fine reputation as a writer, was selected to draft a declaration of independence. Like Thomas Paine's *Common Sense*, Jefferson's document cast the American struggle for independence in a noble light as a profound gesture "in the course of human events." Inspired by the great English political philosopher John Locke (1632–1704), Jefferson listed the "inalienable rights" of humankind.

These included life and liberty, but where Locke had listed *property* as the third right, Jefferson specified "the pursuit of happiness." The purpose of government, Jefferson declared, was "to secure these rights," and the authority of government to do so derived "from the consent of the governed." When a government ceased to serve its just purpose, it was the right and duty of "the governed" to withdraw their allegiance from it. And that is precisely what the colonies had done. The Second Continental Congress edited Jefferson's draft, eliminating, among other things, his condemnation of slavery, and then adopted the Declaration of Independence on July 4, 1776. That is the date we celebrate as Independence Day, although the Declaration was not signed by the congressional delegates until August 2.

American Echo

O ye that love mankind! Ye that dare oppose, not only the tyranny, but the tyrant, stand forth! Every spot of the old world is overrun with oppression. Freedom hath been hunted round the globe. Asia, and Africa, have long expelled her … Europe regards her like a stranger, and England hath given her warning to depart. O! receive the fugitive, and prepare in time an asylum for mankind.

—Thomas Paine, *Common Sense*, 1776

The Least You Need to Know

- ◆ Unfair taxation, limits on westward settlement, and the involuntary quartering of British soldiers united the colonies in rebellion.

- ◆ Thomas Paine (*Common Sense*) and Thomas Jefferson (the Declaration of Independence) helped elevate a colonial revolution to the status of a momentous world event.

- ◆ American troops were citizen soldiers, fighting at home and committed to their cause. The British soldiers were a professional army doing a grim job in a distant land.

- ◆ The American Revolution began well before there was general agreement among the colonies that outright independence from Britain should be the goal of the war; many colonists wanted nothing more than relief from taxes and other British laws they believed unjust.

Chapter 10

Fanning the Flames of Liberty (1776–1783)

In This Chapter

- ◆ The Articles of Confederation
- ◆ Early Patriot triumphs and losses
- ◆ Victory at Saratoga
- ◆ Surrender of Cornwallis

Great as it is, the Declaration of Independence, a human document, is imperfect. It failed to deal with the issue of slavery (Congress struck down Jefferson's condemnation of it in the text's first draft), and it failed to specify just how the separate colonies, each with its own government and identity, were to unite as a single nation. Throughout the early years of the Revolution, the Continental Congress struggled with this issue and finally produced, in November 1777, the Articles of Confederation.

A timid and tentative document, the Articles gave the individual states—not the federal government—most of the power, including the authority to levy taxes; after all, "taxation without representation" had triggered the rupture with England. Eventually, the Articles would be scrapped in favor of a brand-new, much bolder Constitution. But the earlier document, the product of agonizing debate, would hold the nation together through a Revolutionary War that, like most wars, went on much longer than either side had any reason to expect.

A Bad Bet

While the framers of the Articles of Confederation in Philadelphia did battle with words and ideas, soldiers in the field fought with powder and lead. Politician and militiaman alike were well aware that, if Parliament and King George III earnestly willed it and if he sent to America everything he had, the colonies would, in all likelihood, be defeated. But during the early years of the war, Britain was surprisingly slow to take the offensive.

Boston Besieged

Most of the "Lobsterbacks" (as the colonials called the British troops, in contemptuous reference to the scars and welts many bore on their backs, betraying harsh discipline enforced by flogging) were bottled up in Boston, to which Washington's forces laid siege. Try as they might, the British were unable to break out of the city. Then, when Washington displayed his artillery on Dorchester Heights, British commanders gave the order to evacuate by sea in March 1776. The British army re-established its headquarters at distant Halifax, Nova Scotia.

Southern Exposure

While His Majesty's forces were being humiliated in New England, Sir Henry Clinton sailed with his troops along the southern coast. His purpose was to rally property-rich Loyalists against the upstart, ragtag rabble of the newly established "American" governments in the Carolinas and Georgia. As he prepared to disembark at Cape Fear, North Carolina, Clinton received news that a Loyalist uprising had been squelched by Patriot forces at the Battle of Moore's Creek Bridge near Wilmington, North Carolina, on February 27, 1776. Clinton pressed southward to Charleston Harbor. Seeking to establish a base for Loyalist resistance, Clinton bombarded Charleston's harbor fortifications as a prelude to capturing the city. A stockade constructed of stout palmetto trunks fended off the British cannonballs—and the flag of South Carolina, a palmetto tree beneath a crescent moon, has commemorated this stubborn resistance ever since. Patriot forces drove off the British by June 28, 1776. It was a valuable triumph, which stalled British activity in the South for more than 2 years.

A Pale Flush of Victory

The first 12 months of the war had gone far better than any self-respecting odds-maker would have predicted. The British had been forced out of New England and the South. However, a key American hope had also been dashed. The Patriots had tried to persuade the French citizens of Quebec to make common cause with them against the British. American strategists understood that, as long as the British conducted the war from far-off London, the Patriot cause would enjoy a great advantage. However, if the British should begin to use nearby Canada as the staging area for an invasion of the colonies, that advantage would evaporate. Unfortunately, the French Canadians were unwilling to initiate any action themselves. But, fortified by successes in defending against the British in New England and the South, the Americans decided to take the offensive into Canada.

An army under General Richard Montgomery marched from upper New York and captured Montreal on November 10, 1775. Simultaneously, troops commanded by Colonel Benedict Arnold advanced through the wilderness of Maine to unite with Montgomery's units in an attack on the walled city of Quebec. The invaders were beaten back, and Montgomery was killed on December 30. American forces maintained a blockade of the Canadian capital through May 1776, but the offensive in Canada petered out. Americans would stay out of the region for the rest of the war— and there was worse, much worse, to come in this war.

The British Lion Roars

Beginning in the summer of 1776, British forces wrested the initiative from the Americans. British general Guy Carleton, the very able governor of Quebec, was ordered to chase the Americans out of Canada and down through the region of Lake Champlain and the Hudson River. This action would sever the far northern tier of colonies from the southern tier. Simultaneously, a much larger army led by General William Howe, who had replaced Gage as supreme commander of Britain's North American forces, was assigned to capture New York City and its strategically vital harbor.

Carleton succeeded handily in driving the remaining Americans out of Canada, but, plagued by supply problems and the approach of winter, he was unable to pursue them below the border. This setback, however, did not stop Howe, who hurled against New York City the largest single force the British would ever field in the Revolution: 32,000 troops, 400 transports, 73 warships (commanded by his vice admiral brother, Richard Howe, with whom he shared the American supreme command). It was all too apparent to General Washington that, militarily, the situation in New York was hopeless. In the course of the war, the American commander would prove highly skilled at the art of the strategic withdrawal, pulling back in a manner that exacted a great price from the attacker and yet left his own forces intact to fight another day. This is precisely what he wanted to do in the case of New York, but Congress, fearing that the loss of a major city would dispirit Patriots throughout the colonies, ordered him to defend the position. Washington met with defeat on Long Island on August 27, 1776.

American Echo

These are the times that try men's souls. The summer soldier and sunshine patriot will, in this crisis, shrink from the service of his country; but he that stands it now, deserves the love and thanks of man and woman. Tyranny, like hell, is not easily conquered.

—Thomas Paine, *The American Crisis* (December 23, 1776)

If Washington and the Continental Congress had weighed the odds more soberly, perhaps they would have raised the white flag. But Washington did not surrender. Instead, he fought a series of brilliant rearguard actions against Howe on Manhattan Island, which cost the British time, money, and energy. It took Howe from August to November to clear Washington's forces from New York City and its environs. Then, instead of moving inland via the Hudson, Howe simply pushed Washington across New Jersey. If he had hoped to corner the Continental Army and fight it to a standstill, Howe was mistaken. The Americans escaped across the Delaware River into Pennsylvania on December 7, 1776.

Recrossing the Delaware

"These are the times that try men's souls," Thomas Paine wrote on December 23, 1776, and they were times that had transformed Washington's men into a determined and disciplined army, even in the depths of the war's first vicious winter. Washington, as General Howe saw the situation, was defeated, crushed. Certainly, he had no business striking back, especially not in this inclement season. Howe was a competent European general. In Europe, the proper times of year for fighting were spring, summer, and fall. In Europe, armies avoided fighting in winter. But Washington understood one very important fact: this was not Europe. Collecting his scattered regulars and militiamen, General Washington reorganized his army and led it back across the Delaware River, from Pennsylvania to New Jersey.

On December 26, 1776, Washington surprised and overran a garrison of *Hessian* mercenaries at Trenton, New Jersey, and then went on to an even bigger victory at Princeton on January 3, 1777. The triumphs were a sharp slap in General Howe's face. Encouraged by these miraculous victories, Congress rejected the peace terms the Howe brothers, in their capacity as peace commissioners, proposed. The fight for independence would continue.

What's the Word?

Following the practice of the day, King George III paid foreign mercenary troops to do much of his fighting in America. The **Hessians** came from the German principality of Hesse-Kassel. Although not all of the German mercenaries employed in the war came from this principality, most of them did. The name, therefore, was applied to all the hired soldiers—about 30,000 in all—who fought in most of the major campaigns, usually answering to British commanders. Some Hessians stayed here after the war and became American citizens.

Saratoga Sunrise

Wearily, the British laid out plans for a new assault on the northern colonies. Major General Burgoyne was in charge of Britain's Canadian-based army, but he and Howe failed to work out a plan for coordinating their two forces. Burgoyne led his army down the customary Lake Champlain-Hudson River route, while Howe was stalled by indecision. Finally, he decided not to support Burgoyne's offensive, but to leave a garrison under Sir Henry Clinton in New York City and to transport the bulk of his army by sea to attack Philadelphia. It was a fatal blunder.

Burgoyne's operation began promisingly, as the American Northern Army, suffering from lack of supplies and disputes among its own commanders, fell back before the British advance. Burgoyne, popularly known as "Gentleman Johnnie," was so confident of victory that he invited officers to bring wives and mistresses on the campaign. He staged sumptuous dinner parties for all engaged in the grand enterprise of teaching the rebels a lesson they would never forget. At his arrogant leisure, Burgoyne advanced against and recaptured Fort Ticonderoga on July 5, 1777, but he moved at such a regal pace that American forces had plenty of time to regroup for guerrilla combat in the wilderness of upstate New York.

The Americans destroyed roads, cut lines of communication and supply, and generally harassed Burgoyne's columns. At Bemis Heights, on the west bank of the Hudson River, Burgoyne was met by the revitalized Northern forces of the Continental Army commanded by Horatio Gates and supported by Benedict Arnold and Daniel Morgan. In the course of the Saratoga Campaign, Burgoyne charged the Americans twice, on September 19 and October 7, 1777, only to be beaten back with heavy losses both times. Blocked to the south and without aid from Clinton, Gentleman Johnnie surrendered 6,000 regulars plus various auxiliaries to the Patriot forces on October 17, 1777.

Trouble in the City of Brotherly Love

Despite the triumphs at Saratoga, the news was not all good for the Americans. Howe transported his army by sea and landed on upper Chesapeake Bay, 57 miles outside of Philadelphia, poised for an assault on that city, which he captured on October 4, 1777. The American capital was in British hands.

But what, really, had Howe gained for the mother country? An entire army, Burgoyne's, was lost, and Howe had paid dearly for the prize he now held. In contrast, the American forces remained intact, and the rebellion continued, administered by a Continental Congress that had safely evacuated Philadelphia and set up in York, Pennsylvania. Most important of all, the French were deeply impressed by the American victory at Saratoga and the resolve with which Washington had fought at Germantown (today a Philadelphia neighborhood, but then a separate village) during the Philadelphia campaign. That Washington had lost Philadelphia and Germantown mattered little to the French. They had seen him fight like a lion.

Vive la France!

As early as 1776, Louis XVI's foreign minister, the Comte de Vergennes, persuaded his king to aid—albeit secretly—the American cause. Prudently, Vergennes withheld recommending an official and overt military alliance until he was confident of the Americans' prospects for victory. He did not want to risk a *losing* war with Britain. The victory at Saratoga, rumors that Britain was going to offer America major territorial concessions to bring peace, and the extraordinary diplomatic skills of Benjamin Franklin (whom Congress had installed in Paris as its representative during this period) finally propelled France openly into the American camp. An alliance was formally concluded on February 6, 1778, whereby France granted diplomatic recognition to the "United States of America." Shortly after the treaty of alliance was signed, Spain, a French ally, also declared war on Britain.

A Hard Forge

Nations may *disagree* and fight one another, and they may *agree* and fight together, but nature takes no notice in either case. The winter of 1778 visited great suffering on the Continental Army, which was encamped at Valley Forge, Pennsylvania. Yet on the cruel, cold anvil of that terrible winter, a stronger army was forged, in large part through the efforts of Baron von Steuben (1730–1794), a Prussian officer who trained American troops to European standards. (A number of Europeans played valiant roles as volunteers in the service of the American Revolution. In addition to Baron von Steuben, these included Johann, Baron de Kalb [1721–1780], a German in the French army, and two Polish patriots, Tadeusz Kosciuszko [1746–1817] and Kasimierz Pulaski [ca. 1747–1779]. Most famous of all was a Frenchman, the Marquis de Lafayette [1757–1834], a brilliant commander fiercely loyal to Washington.)

Spring brought Washington new recruits and the promise of French auxiliary forces, while it brought the British nothing but new pressures. The Howe brothers, having failed to crush the Revolution, resigned their commands and returned to England. Sir Henry Clinton assumed principal command in North America and evacuated his army from Philadelphia (which, surprisingly, proved to be a prize of no military value), concentrated his forces at New York City, and dispatched troops to the Caribbean in anticipation of French action there.

Washington pursued Clinton through New Jersey, fighting him to a stand at Monmouth Courthouse on June 28, 1778. The result, a draw, was nevertheless a moral victory for the Continentals, who had stood up to the best soldiers England could field. If Monmouth was not decisive, it did mark the third year of a war in which the British could show no results whatsoever.

White War, Red Blood

The American Revolution was really two wars. Along the eastern seaboard, it was a contest of one army against another. Farther inland, the fighting resembled that of the French and Indian War. Both sides employed Indian allies, but the British recruited more of them and used them as agents of terror to raid and burn outlying settlements. From the earliest days of the war, the royal lieutenant governor of Detroit, Henry Hamilton, played a key role in stirring the Indians of the Indiana-Illinois frontier to wage ferocious war on Patriot settlers. Hamilton's Indian nickname tells the tale: they called him "Hair Buyer," because he paid a bounty on Patriot scalps. In 1778, young George Rogers Clark (1752–1818), a hard-drinking Kentucky militia leader, overran the British-controlled Illinois and Indiana region and took "Hair Buyer" prisoner. Even more celebrated in the western campaign—albeit less militarily significant—was the intrepid frontiersman Daniel Boone.

Bloody though the Kentucky frontier was, conditions were even worse on the New York–Pennsylvania frontier, which was terrorized by the Iroquois. Washington dispatched Major General John Sullivan into western New York with instructions to wipe out tribal towns wherever he found them. Nevertheless, the Iroquois persisted in raiding, as did the tribes throughout the Ohio country. They were supported and urged on by Loyalist elements in this region, and their combined activity would not come to an end even with the conclusion of the war. Indeed, this western frontier would smolder and be rekindled periodically, bursting into open flame in the form of the War of 1812.

More Action in the South

In the lower South, the British found effective Indian allies in the Cherokees, who, despite suffering early defeats at the hands of the American militia in 1776, continued to raid the frontier. As the war ground on, the British regular army, which had generally neglected the South following early failures there, began to shift attention to the region by late 1778. The British reasoned that the South had a higher percentage of Loyalists than any other part of America and also offered more of the raw materials—indigo, rice, and cotton—valued by the British.

In December 1778, British forces subdued Georgia, and then during 1779, fought inconclusively along the Georgia–South Carolina border. A combined French and American attempt to recapture British-held Savannah, Georgia, was defeated. In February of 1780, Sir Henry Clinton arrived in South Carolina from New York with 8,700 fresh troops and laid siege to Charleston. In a stunning defeat, Charleston was surrendered on May 12 by American General Benjamin Lincoln, who gave up some 5,000 soldiers as prisoners of war. Quickly, Patriot general Horatio Gates led a force to Camden in upper South Carolina but was badly defeated on August 16, 1780, by troops under Lord Cornwallis, whom Clinton, returning to New York, had put in command of the Southern forces.

With the coastal *Tidewater* towns in British hands, the inland *Piedmont* shouldered the task of carrying on the resistance. Such legendary guerrilla leaders as the "Swamp Fox" Francis Marion and Thomas Sumter cost the British dearly. Then, on October

7, 1780, a contingent of Patriot frontiersmen—most from the Watauga settlements in present-day eastern Tennessee—engaged and destroyed a force of 1,000 Loyalist troops at the Battle of King's Mountain on the border of the two Carolinas.

The Triumph at Yorktown

Fresh from his seaboard conquests, Cornwallis was now pinned down by frontier guerrillas. A third American army under Major General Nathanael Greene launched a series of rapid operations in brilliant coordination with the South Carolina guerrillas. Dividing his small army, Greene dispatched Brigadier General Daniel Morgan into western South Carolina, where he decimated the "Tory Legion" of Lieutenant Colonel Banastre Tarleton at the Battle of the Cowpens on January 17, 1781. Breaking free of the guerrillas, Cornwallis pursued Morgan, who linked up with Greene and the main body of the Southern army. Together, Morgan and Greene led Cornwallis on a punishing wilderness chase into North Carolina and then turned about and fought him to a draw at Guilford Courthouse on March 15, 1781.

Cornwallis, effectively neutralized, withdrew to the coast. Greene returned to South Carolina, where he retook every British-held outpost except for Charleston and Savannah. Although the enemy would hold these cities for the rest of the war, their possession was of negligible military value, because the occupying garrisons were cut off from the rest of the British forces.

Cornwallis had withdrawn to Virginia, where he joined forces with a raiding unit led by the most notorious turncoat in American history, Benedict Arnold. Cornwallis reasoned that Virginia was the key to possession of the South. Therefore, he established his headquarters at the port of Yorktown on Virginia's Yorktown peninsula.

General Washington combined his Continental troops with the French army of Comte de Rochambeau and laid siege to Yorktown on October 6, 1781. Simultaneously, a French fleet under Admiral de Grasse prevented Cornwallis's army, bottled up on the Yorktown peninsula, from escaping via the sea. Recognizing the gravity of the situation, General Clinton dispatched a British naval squadron from New York to the Chesapeake, only to be driven off by de Grasse. Washington and Rochambeau relentlessly bombarded Yorktown. At last, the British general surrendered his 8,000 troops to the allies'

> **What's the Word?**
>
> The **Tidewater** is the traditional name for the coastal South. In colonial times, the **Piedmont** (literally, "foot of the mountains") was the region just east of the Blue Ridge Mountains. The Tidewater was the more settled and affluent region, whereas the Piedmont was the poorer, more sparsely settled frontier region.

17,000 men on October 19, 1781. The surrender did not officially end the war—that would not come until 1783—but it marked the end of the British will to continue fighting against colonial independence. That Cornwallis's army saw surrender as the symbolic end of the war is suggested by what happened at the formal surrender ceremony. As Lord Cornwallis presented Washington with his sword, the British regimental band played a popular tune of the time. It was called "The World Turned Upside Down." And so things must have seemed to soldiers of the world's most powerful nation admitting defeat at the hands of a nation so new that it barely even existed.

Remember This _____

Benedict Arnold (1741–1801) was born in Norwich, Connecticut, and, as a teenager, served in the French and Indian War. During the Revolution, he handled himself brilliantly, but became embittered when he was passed over for promotion. When he served as commander of forces in Philadelphia, Arnold was accused of overstepping his authority, and he made matters worse by marrying Margaret Shippen (1779), the daughter of a prominent Loyalist. His new wife, accustomed to affluence, encouraged Arnold to spend freely, and he was soon buried in debt. Arnold saw the British as a means of gaining promotion and cash. He offered them a plan to betray the fortifications at West Point, New York, but his treachery was revealed when British Major John André was captured in September 1780, carrying the turncoat's message in his boot. André was executed as a spy, but Arnold escaped to enemy lines and was commissioned a brigadier general in the British army. In that capacity, he led two expeditions, one that burned Richmond, Virginia, and another against New London in his native Connecticut. However, he never received all of the career advancement and fortune the British had promised. He went to England in 1781, was plagued by a "nervous disease," and died in London in 1801.

The Least You Need to Know

- ◆ George Washington's greatest accomplishments were to hold his armies together during a long, hard war, to exploit British strategic and tactical blunders effectively, and to make each British victory extremely costly.

- ◆ The Revolution did not end in American victory, so much as in the defeat of England's will to continue to fight.

- ◆ The Battle of Yorktown, symbolic (but not official) end of the American Revolution, was as much a French victory as an American one.

- ◆ The Revolution was instantly perceived as a worldwide event—a milestone in the history of humankind.

Part 3

Building the House

With independence achieved, the citizens of the new United States were faced with the task of building a nation, of creating laws without renewing tyranny, of representing the will of the majority without trampling the rights of the minority, and of proclaiming liberty without bringing down upon themselves the curse of anarchy. Then, with a strong Constitution in place, the new nation took its place among the other nations of the world— barely surviving the War of 1812 in the process. Following that conflict, as the United States pushed westward, a new kind of leader emerged, hailing not from the patrician ranks of the Tidewater states, but from the western frontier. The "Age of Jackson" saw the expansion of the nation and the growth of democracy, but also the hard doom of Indian men, women, and children, who were sent marching along a bitter Trail of Tears. Here is a narrative of the years that proved the United States a viable nation.

Chapter 11

From Many, One (1787–1797)

In This Chapter

- ◆ The Treaty of Paris and the end of the Revolution
- ◆ The government of territories by the Northwest Ordinance
- ◆ The creation and ratification of the Constitution
- ◆ The Bill of Rights
- ◆ Hamilton versus Jefferson

Symbolically and strategically speaking, the Battle of Yorktown ended the American Revolution by breaking the will of the British government to keep fighting. Yet triumph here did not mean total victory for the Americans. Sir Henry Clinton still occupied key cities, and Britain continued to skirmish in this hemisphere with France and Spain. Nevertheless, the Yorktown victory put America's treaty negotiators in a powerful bargaining position. They understood that Britain was anxious to pry America free of the French sphere of influence; therefore, they correctly calculated that the British negotiators would be inclined to hammer out generous peace terms. Treaty commissioner John Adams went to Holland, desperately trying to negotiate a loan for the infant republic. John Jay, another commissioner appointed by the Continental Congress, was delayed in Madrid, wrangling with America's difficult Spanish allies; instead of directly helping the

United States, these allies had used the Revolution to expand their North American territories, overrunning much of British Florida by 1781 and launching raids from Spanish Texas across the Mississippi River. While the other treaty commissioners were occupied with Dutch and Spanish affairs, Benjamin Franklin boldly broke with his government's French allies because France had less interest in supporting the new United States than it had in promoting Spanish claims in the New World. Franklin obtained, on his own, not only British recognition of American independence, but also the cession of the vast region from the Appalachians to the Mississippi River as part of the United States. (A fourth American treaty commissioner, Henry Laurens, had been a British prisoner of war since 1780, when he was captured en route to Europe aboard the American brig *Mercury*, and was not present for most of the negotiations.)

The peace agreement was mostly the work of Franklin, who not only gained British acknowledgment of American independence, but also made navigation of the Mississippi free to all signatories—France, Spain, and Holland—and restored Florida to Spain and Senegal to France, and granted to the United States valuable fishing rights off Newfoundland. The Treaty of Paris was signed on September 3, 1783, and ratified by the Continental Congress on January 14, 1784.

Bound by a Rope of Sand

Drafted in 1777 and ratified in 1781, the Articles of Confederation became the first constitution of the United States. As the document was conceived by John Dickinson (1732–1808) in 1776, it provided for a strong national government, a government to make of the several states a single nation—as the Great Seal of the United States would proclaim, *e pluribus unum*, from many, one. But the individual states clamored for more rights, especially the power of taxation, and Dickinson's document was diluted by repeated revision and amendment. Instead of a nation, the revised Articles created a "firm league of friendship" among 13 sovereign states. The Articles did provide for a permanent national congress, consisting of two to seven delegates from each state (yet each state was given one vote, regardless of its size or population), but it did not establish an executive or judicial branch. Congress was charged with conducting foreign relations, declaring war, making peace, maintaining an army and navy, and so on, yet it was ultimately powerless, because it was wholly at the mercy of the states. Congress could issue directives and pass laws, but it could not enforce them. The states, one by one, either chose to comply or not. Miraculously, the Articles held the states together during the Revolution, but it soon became clear that the Articles had created no union, but what various lawmakers called "a rope of sand."

What's the Word?

The eagle on the Great Seal of the United States of America holds in its beak a ribbon on which the Latin motto **e pluribus unum** is inscribed. The words mean "from many, one" and express the formidable nature of the task that faced the Founding Fathers: to forge a single nation from several states and many individuals. The motto was chosen by a committee appointed by the Continental Congress on July 4, 1776, and was officially adopted on June 20, 1782. The phrase is a quotation from "Moretum" by the Roman poet Virgil (70–19 B.C.E.) but was borrowed more immediately from *Gentleman's Magazine,* a popular British periodical on whose cover the phrase had appeared for many years.

Northwest Ordinance

Under the Articles of Confederation, Congress enacted at least one momentous piece of legislation. The Northwest Ordinance (July 13, 1787) spelled out how territories and states were to be formed from the western lands won in the Revolution. What was then called the Northwest—the vast region bounded by the Ohio and Mississippi rivers and by the Great Lakes—was to be divided into three to five territories. Congress was empowered to appoint a governor, a secretary, and three judges to govern each territory. When the adult male population of a territory reached 5,000, elections would be held to form a territorial legislature and to send a nonvoting representative to Congress. When the territorial adult male population reached 60,000, a territory could write a constitution and apply for statehood.

Whereas Britain had refused to make its American colonies full members of a national commonwealth, the Articles ensured that the frontier regions would never be mere colonies of the Tidewater, but equal partners in a common enterprise.

Of equal importance, the Ordinance was the first national stand against slavery. The law prohibited slavery in the territories and also guaranteed in them such basic rights as trial by jury and freedom of religion.

We the People ...

Despite the boldness of the Northwest Ordinance, the weakness of Congress under the Articles of Confederation was demonstrated almost daily. For example, the federal government could do nothing to help Massachusetts, which was faced with its own minor insurrection when a farmer named Daniel Shays led an attack on the state judicial system. Nor could the government intervene when Rhode Island issued a mountain of monumentally worthless paper money. In 1786, a convention was held in Annapolis, Maryland, to discuss problems of interstate commerce. The delegates soon recognized that these issues were only part of a much larger issue that could be addressed by nothing less than a sweeping revision of the Articles. The Annapolis delegates called for a constitutional convention, which met in Philadelphia in May 1787. The projected task of revision rapidly grew into a project of building completely anew. By the end of the month, the delegates agreed that what was required was a genuine national government, not a mere hopeful confederation of states.

Constitutional Convention

Fifty-five delegates convened in Philadelphia and elected George Washington president of the convention. Just as Washington had held the Continental Army together during the long trial of revolution, so now he managed the argumentative delegates with dignity and fairness.

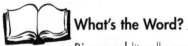

What's the Word?

Bicameral literally means "two-chambered" and refers to a type of legislature consisting of two groups of representatives. In the case of the British Parliament, the two houses are the House of Lords and the House of Commons; in the case of the U.S. Congress, they are the Senate and the House of Representatives.

The Virginia Plan

Although some delegates held out for a simple revision of the Articles of Confedera-tion, the Virginia delegation, led by Edmund Randolph, introduced the Virginia Plan, which proposed the creation of a central federal government consisting of a *bicameral* legislature, an executive branch, and a judicial branch. The executive was to be elected by the members of the legislature, who, in turn, were elected by the citizens. The Virginia Plan further specified that representation in the bicameral legislature would be proportionate to state population—a provision that worried and angered representatives of the smaller states.

The New Jersey Plan

As debate raged over the Virginia Plan, William Paterson of New Jersey introduced a plan labeled with the name of his state. The New Jersey Plan retained most of the

Articles of Confederation, and it gave all the states equal representation in the legislature, but it added a separate and independent Supreme Court. Introduction of the conservative New Jersey Plan set off a protracted, snarled, and often heated debate.

Connecticut Compromise

Into the fray stepped Roger Sherman, a delegate from Connecticut, who proposed a compromise between the two apparently irreconcilable plans. This so-called Great Compromise called for a bicameral legislature; however, the upper house of this body, the Senate, would provide each state with equal representation, whereas representation in the lower house, the House of Representatives, would provide representation proportionate to each state's population. Moreover, the chief executive, the president, would not be elected by the representatives in the legislature, but by an *Electoral College*.

The Connecticut Compromise made possible a strong central government leavened by a system of checks and balances. The legislative and executive branches counterbalanced each other, and, within the legislative branch, the absolute popular representation of the House of Representatives was moderated by the innately more conservative Senate. The full power of the judicial branch was implicit in the Constitution, but it did not come into play until Chief Justice John Marshall introduced the concept of judicial review in the 1803 case of *Marbury* v. *Madison* (see "Supreme Court Reigns Supreme" in Chapter 12).

Three-Fifths of a Person

Any number of additional compromises remained to be made, but the stickiest involved apportioning representation in the House of Representatives. The more representatives a state could claim, the more influential it would be in the federal government. If representation was to be proportional to population, the South wanted its slaves counted as population. The North objected, arguing that slaves could not be both property and people entitled to representation; they should be excluded entirely from the calculation.

A peculiar-sounding solution was reached. Embodied in the Constitution as Article I, Section 2, the "Three-Fifths Compromise" managed delicately to avoid the word *slave* altogether: "Representation and direct taxes will be apportioned among the several states according to respective numbers determined by adding to the whole number of free persons including those bound to service for a set number of years and excluding Indians not taxed three-fifths of all other persons." For purposes of levying taxes and apportioning representatives, slaves were counted as three-fifths of a human being.

Federalist Hard Sell

With the compromises in place, William Johnson (secretary of the Convention), Alexander Hamilton, James Madison, Rufus King, and Gouverneur Morris wrote the actual Constitution document, the product of 3½ months of debate. When 38 of the 55 Convention delegates approved the document, it was sent to Congress, which submitted it to the states for ratification.

Thus began an uphill battle. Those who supported the proposed Constitution were called Federalists; those opposed, Anti-Federalists. Although Delaware, Pennsylvania, and New Jersey instantly ratified the document, a total of nine states had to ratify in order for the Constitution to become law. The process was hotly contested in many states, and nowhere more so than in the key states of Virginia and New York. To convince New York voters to ratify, Alexander Hamilton, James Madison, and John Jay collaborated on a series of essays collectively called *The Federalist Papers*, published during 1787 and 1788 in various New York newspapers under the collective pseudonym "Publius."

Taken together, the *Federalist* essays are a brilliant defense of the Constitution, but perhaps the single most important essay is the tenth, which penetrated to the very heart of the most compelling Anti-Federalist argument: the nation was simply too big and diverse to be regulated by a central government. Madison argued that precisely *because* the nation was so large, it would be *most* effectively governed by a strong central government, which would prevent any single special interest from taking control even as the power of the government would be checked by the multitude of interests and points of view. Essays 15 through 22 dug into the nitty-gritty with a penetrating analysis of the weaknesses of the Articles of Confederation.

 Vital Statistics

Of the 85 *Federalist* essays, most scholars agree that Hamilton wrote 52; Madison, 28; and Jay, 5.

Virginia ratified the Constitution by a close vote of 89 to 79, but only after the framers promised to add a "Bill of Rights" to satisfy the Anti-Federalist argument that the Constitution failed explicitly to address the rights of individuals. In the meantime, *The Federalist Papers* tipped the balance in New York—although just barely. The ratification vote was 30 to 27.

Father of His Country

When New Hampshire became the ninth state to ratify the Constitution on June 21, 1788, the document became law, but it was not put into effect officially until March 4, 1789. The next month, the U.S. Senate convened to count ballots cast by members of the Electoral College for the first president of the United States. The result surprised no one. George Washington had been unanimously elected, and John Adams became his vice president.

It was, in fact, with the implicit understanding that Washington would be elected that the framers of the Constitution entrusted so much power to the chief executive. Washington had amply demonstrated not only a genius for leadership in commanding the Continental Army, but also his skill as a statesman in presiding over the Constitutional Convention. Perhaps most important of all, Washington had made manifest the character of a true republican. The Founding Fathers, most of them, were classically educated and, therefore, well acquainted with the histories of ancient Greece and Rome. They were very familiar with the typical historical pattern in which a revolution is followed by a new tyranny. It was clear to Congress and the people of the United States that Washington was no tyrant.

The new president was inaugurated in New York City on April 30, 1789. Even with a Constitution in place, it was up to Washington to create much of the American government and in particular to shape the office of president. He quickly formulated and installed the key executive departments, naming Thomas Jefferson as Secretary of State, Henry Knox as Secretary of War, Alexander Hamilton as Secretary of the Treasury, Samuel Osgood as head of the Post Office, and Edmund Randolph as Attorney General.

Washington became the model for the presidency, and the chief quality he introduced into the office was restraint. He avoided conflict with Congress, believing it was not the chief executive's duty to propose legislation. He also opposed the formation of political parties, although, by the time of his second term, two opposing parties had, indeed, been formed: the conservative Federalists, headed by John Adams and Alexander Hamilton, and the liberal Democratic-Republicans, headed by Thomas Jefferson. His most eloquent expression of a refusal to become a post-revolutionary tyrant was Washington's decision not to stand for a third term of office. The two-term presidency thereafter became an inviolable tradition until the twin crises of the Depression and World War II prompted the nation to elect Franklin Delano Roosevelt to a third and a fourth term. (Although the nation was grateful to FDR, it also approved the twenty-second amendment to the Constitution on February 26, 1951, restricting future presidents to no more than two elected terms, or in the case of vice-presidential succession, a nearly full term followed by an elected term.)

Washington not only created the office of president, he also signed crucial treaties with England and Spain and approved the creation of a national bank. He wisely proclaimed neutrality in what would become a long series of wars between England and France, and he successfully quelled a spasm of internal rebellion by asserting federal precedence over state and individual authority. More than anything else, this able executive possessed a character that helped establish the United States among the other nations of the world.

The classical Romans reserved one title for their greatest leaders—*Pater Patriae*, Father of His Country—and almost immediately, a grateful nation accorded this epithet to George Washington.

Remember This

George Washington (1732–1799) was born in Westmoreland County, Virginia, to a prosperous planter. After his father died in 1743, he was raised by his half-brother Lawrence at Mount Vernon, Lawrence's Potomac River plantation. Washington became a surveyor—a powerful profession in colonial America—and helped lay out Belhaven, Virginia (now Alexandria). Following the death of his half-brother, Washington inherited Mount Vernon.

He left that beloved home to serve in the French and Indian War, returning afterward to Mount Vernon and service in Virginia's House of Burgesses.

Washington made a happy—and opportune—marriage to a young and wealthy widow, Martha Dandridge Custis, and by 1769 was a prominent leader of Virginia's opposition to Britain's oppressive colonial policies. During 1774 and 1775, Washington was a delegate to the First and Second Continental Congresses, and in June 1775 was unanimously chosen as commander-in-chief of the Continental forces, which he led brilliantly.

After the war, Washington headed the Virginia delegation to the Constitutional Convention and was unanimously elected presiding officer. Upon ratification of the Constitution, he was unanimously elected president in 1789 and was re-elected in 1792. In March 1797, when Washington left office, he left a well-established government and a stable financial system.

Unfortunately, the Father of His Country had little time to enjoy retirement at his beloved Mount Vernon. In mid-December 1799, he fell ill with acute laryngitis, which rapidly worsened. He died on December 14.

Glorious Afterthought: The Bill of Rights

The framers of the Constitution had no desire to deny individual rights, but most believed it unnecessary to provide a special, separate guarantee of those rights because the Constitution states that the government is one of "enumerated powers" only. That is, the government can take no action or assume any authority except those explicitly provided for in the Constitution. As the Anti-Federalists saw it, the concept of enumerated powers was not, however, a sufficient safeguard against the assumption of tyrannical powers by the central government. During the process of ratification, a promise was made to draft a bill of rights for amendment to the Constitution, and in 1789, Congress authorized James Madison to formulate the amendments. He carefully examined, weighed, and synthesized the rights already included in several state constitutions, especially the Virginia Declaration of Rights, which had been adopted in 1776, and produced a set of 12 amendments, 10 of which directly guaranteed individual rights (the other two dealt with different issues and were not offered for ratification at the time). Distilled within the Bill of Rights, an afterthought to the Constitution, is what most Americans consider the very essence of all that is most valuable in the idea of the United States of America.

Hamilton Gets the Credit

Among the most influential members of Washington's cabinet was Secretary of the Treasury Alexander Hamilton. He not only developed a strong financial program for the infant nation, but also used finance to unify the United States and to elevate federal authority over that of the states. He proposed a controversial plan whereby the federal government would assume all debts incurred by the several states during the Revolution and pay them at par value rather than at the reduced rates some states had already negotiated on their own. Hamilton reasoned that this policy would demonstrate the nation's financial responsibility and ultimately improve its standing among other nations and its ability to conduct commerce. Even more important, the plan would demonstrate to the world that the *federal* government, not the individual states, was the responsible contracting party in all international commerce and foreign affairs. Despite great resistance from the Southern states, Hamilton's plan was enacted by Congress.

Equally controversial was Hamilton's proposal to create the Bank of the United States. Fearing that this plan would concentrate far too much power in the central government, Thomas Jefferson led the opposition against the proposal within Washington's cabinet. He argued that the bank was unconstitutional, because the Tenth Amendment granted to the states and the people rights and powers not explicitly given to the United States. If this provision were breached by the creation of the bank, what other powers would the federal government usurp?

Jefferson's view of the Constitution became known as "strict construction." Hamilton, in contrast, supported the constitutional view that became known as "loose construction," arguing in support of the doctrine of "implied powers." Hamilton declared that the framers of the Constitution could not possibly have anticipated all future eventualities and contingencies; therefore, it is impossible to list all the powers the federal government may assume. In the case of the Bank of the United States, Hamilton held, the Constitution does grant the federal government the power to tax, and taxation *implies* the creation of a place to keep the revenue collected—namely, a bank.

Remember This

In 1791, Congress levied a federal tax on corn liquor. In frontier Pennsylvania, farmers distilled whiskey to use up surplus corn, and the product became for them a form of currency. Farmers protested and often refused to pay the tax. In 1794, President Washington sent collectors, who were met by armed resistance in what constituted the first serious test of the new U.S. government's ability to enforce a federal law. Secretary of the Treasury Alexander Hamilton advised the president to call out the militia. In a bold exercise of federal authority, Washington did just that, and the Whiskey Rebellion collapsed.

The disagreement between Jefferson and Hamilton formed the foundation of the American two-party political system, with either party more or less defined and distinguished by its view of the nature of the federal government. Jefferson's Democratic-Republican Party believed in a restrained central government that allowed a great measure of power to individuals and states; Hamilton's Federalist party stood for a powerful and active central government, which claimed for itself the lion's share of authority. The dynamic, shifting balance between these two poles of opinion has defined the lively American political dialogue ever since the days of the first president. Over the years, the running debate has sometimes erupted into ugly argument and even terrible violence—as in the Civil War. Yet the two-party system has also ensured a government and society that is never stagnant and always open to change and challenge.

The Least You Need to Know

- The Treaty of Paris (1783) ended the Revolution and gained British recognition of American sovereignty.

- After the crisis of the Revolution had ended, the weaknesses of the Articles of Confederation became acutely apparent, and a Constitutional Convention was convened.

- In addition to the nation's first president, George Washington, the defining personalities of the early republic were Thomas Jefferson (who favored the forces of liberal democracy) and Alexander Hamilton (who favored a powerful central government).

Chapter 12

Growing Pains (1798–1812)

In This Chapter

- The XYZ Affair and the Alien and Sedition Acts
- *Marbury* v. *Madison*
- The Louisiana Purchase
- Neutralization of the Barbary pirates
- The Embargo and its consequences
- War in the West

When George Washington delivered his Farewell Address in March 1797, the United States was recognized by the world as a nation. That fact was, in large part, *his* greatest accomplishment. In his speech, the outgoing president advised his fellow Americans to avoid "foreign entanglements," to preserve the good credit of the nation, and to beware of the dangers of political parties, which might fragment the nation.

Everyone agreed that the advice was good, but the second presidential election, in 1796, had already shown that political parties were already dividing the nation. John Adams, a Federalist, was elected with 71 votes in the Electoral College. In those days, the runner-up became vice president, and that was Thomas Jefferson, leader of the Democratic-Republican

Party, with 68 electoral votes. Thus, the president and vice president were of different parties and significantly different philosophies of government. As a believer in a strong central government, Adams, although by definition a revolutionary, was significantly less radical than his fellow revolutionary Jefferson, who wanted more authority entrusted to states and individuals rather than to a national government.

Foreign Affairs

During Washington's second term of office, intense friction developed between Britain and the United States. Despite having agreed to do so upon signing the Treaty of Paris that ended the American Revolution, the British refused to evacuate the frontier forts in the Old Northwest—roughly the area corresponding to today's upper Midwest, east of the Mississippi River. Worse, many Americans were convinced that British traders, as well as crown officials, were actively encouraging the Indians to attack settlers. Finally, English naval vessels had begun seizing American merchant ships and *impressing* sailors from them into the British service to fight its war against revolutionary France. The British also complained that Americans had breached the terms of the Paris treaty by failing to pay pre-Revolutionary debts owed British creditors and by refusing to compensate Loyalists for confiscated property during the American Revolution.

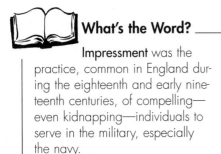

What's the Word?

Impressment was the practice, common in England during the eighteenth and early nineteenth centuries, of compelling—even kidnapping—individuals to serve in the military, especially the navy.

Anxious to avert a new war with Britain, Washington commissioned Chief Justice John Jay to conclude a treaty, signed on November 19, 1794, to secure the British evacuation of the frontier forts and refer debt and boundary disputes to settlement by joint U.S.–British commissions. This amicable solution greatly alarmed the French, who feared that their former ally, the United States, would now unite with Britain against them. Certainly it was true that most Americans, especially the Federalists, recoiled in horror from the excesses of the French Revolution (1789–1799). Just a year before the Jay Treaty was concluded, Washington rebuffed the overtures of Edmond Charles Edouard Genèt (1763–1834), a French diplomat sent to the United States to secure American aid for France in its war with England. "Citizen Genèt" defied Washington by plotting with American privateers (in effect, pirates for hire) to prey on British vessels in U.S. coastal waters. The president asked the French government to recall Genèt.

In France, however, a new, more violently radical revolutionary party, the Jacobins, had replaced the Girondists, the party to which Genèt belonged. In contrast to the United States, where political parties could "disagree without being disagreeable," rival factions in revolutionary France settled their differences with the guillotine. The Jacobin government asked Washington to extradite Genèt, but the president, observing strict neutrality, refused to compel Genèt to return to France, whereupon Citizen Genèt chose to become a citizen of the United States.

As Easy as XYZ

The Genèt episode, combined with the Jay Treaty, brought Franco-American relations to the verge of war. After the French Directory, the body that governed France for a time during the period of the French Revolution, high-handedly refused to receive U.S. minister Charles Cotesworth Pinckney, the new president, Adams, sent a commission consisting of Pinckney, John Marshall, and Elbridge Gerry to attempt to heal the breach by concluding a new treaty of commerce. Incredibly, French prime minister Charles Maurice de Talleyrand-Périgord (1754–1838) sent three agents to greet the American commissioners in Paris in October 1797. The agents told the commissioners that before they could even discuss a treaty, the United States would have to loan France $12 million *and* pay Talleyrand a personal bribe of $250,000.

On April 3, 1798, an indignant President Adams submitted to Congress the correspondence from the commission, which designated the French agents as "X," "Y," and "Z." Congress, equally indignant, published the entire portfolio, and in this way the public learned of the "XYZ Affair." Americans of all political persuasions united in outrage; the nation mobilized for war with its erstwhile ally; and, in fact, an undeclared naval war (often called the Franco-American Quasi-War) was fought sporadically from 1798 to 1800. Fortunately, that conflict was limited to a few naval engagements, and international tempers cooled as the French Revolution and its immediate aftermath came to an end.

The Tyranny of Democracy

Yet something far more sinister than another war was brewing. In the summer of 1798, in response to the Genèt episode, the XYZ Affair, and the escalating war fever, the Federalist-dominated Congress passed the Alien and Sedition Acts, which included the Naturalization Act (June 18, 1798), raising the residence prerequisite for citizenship from 5 to 14 years; the Alien Act (June 25, 1798), authorizing the president summarily to deport, without trial or hearing, all aliens he regarded as dangerous; and the Alien

Enemies Act (July 6, 1798), authorizing the president, in time of war, to arrest, imprison, or deport subjects of any enemy power, again without resort to trial or hearing. Most tyrannical of all, the Sedition Act (July 14, 1798) prohibited assembly "with intent to oppose any measure of the government" and forbade printing, uttering, or publishing anything "false, scandalous, and malicious" against the government. What made the dangerous Alien and Sedition Acts even more insidious in the fledgling democracy was the fact that many of the leading Democratic-Republicans, the political party opposed to the Federalists, were recent refugees from Europe. The acts were aimed directly at neutralizing their power by extending the residency requirement for citizenship.

What's the Word?

Nullification would become a major issue in the decade before the Civil War, when South Carolina's John C. Calhoun echoed Jefferson and asserted that the states could override ("nullify") any federal laws they judged unconstitutional. Nullification attacked the foundation of American nationhood.

In 1798 and 1799, Virginia and Kentucky published resolutions (written by James Madison and Thomas Jefferson, respectively) opposing the Alien and Sedition Acts as unconstitutional and, therefore, not binding on the states. Jefferson maintained that a state had the right to judge the constitutionality of acts of Congress and to *nullify* any it determined to be unconstitutional. Due in significant part to the resolutions, the Alien and Sedition Acts were (for the most part) short-lived.

The Age of Jefferson

Public disgust with the Alien and Sedition Acts helped oust the Federalist Adams in the elections of 1800, but the Electoral College voted a tie between the two Democratic-Republican candidates, Thomas Jefferson and Aaron Burr. As prescribed by the Constitution, the tied election was sent to the House of Representatives for resolution. Hamilton, no friend of Jefferson but very much the implacable enemy of Burr, persuaded fellow Federalists to support Jefferson, who was elected on the *36th* ballot. Runner-up Burr became vice president.

Historians speak of an "Age of Jefferson," but not of an "Age of Adams." Perhaps the reason is that, despite Federalist objections to most of Jefferson's policies, the people made them key elements of the American agenda. Internal taxes were reduced; the military budget was cut; and the Alien and Sedition Acts were repealed, unenforced, or allowed to expire. The greatest triumph of Jefferson's first term was the momentous expansion of the nation through the Louisiana Purchase.

Supreme Court Reigns Supreme

Although Jefferson commenced his first term as president by proposing that the Democratic-Republicans and Federalists bury the hatchet, he was not above manipulating the law to prevent a group of Federalist judges, appointed by John Adams, from assuming office. After his inauguration, Jefferson discovered that, during Adams's final days as president, the former president had signed a number of judicial appointments, but had not "distributed" (formally delivered and activated) them. Not wanting to place Federalists in important circuit court and federal court positions, Jefferson decided, quite simply, never to distribute the signed appointments.

When one of the appointees, William Marbury, failed to receive his commission as justice of the peace for Washington, D.C., he petitioned the Supreme Court for a writ of mandamus—an order to Secretary of State James Madison to distribute the commissions. This order created a critical dilemma for Chief Justice John Marshall; if he issued the writ, he would put the court in direct opposition to the president. If Marshall denied the writ, he would dilute the power of the Supreme Court by appearing to bow to the president's wishes. Refusing to be impaled on the horns of the dilemma, Marshall instead found that Marbury had indeed been wrongfully deprived of his commission, but he also declared that Section 13 of the Judiciary Act of 1789, under which Marbury had filed his suit, was unconstitutional. Section 13 added to the Supreme Court's "original jurisdiction" by improperly allowing into the Supreme Court a case that should have been heard by a lower court. Marbury's suit was thrown out, a political crisis averted, and—most important of all—the powerful Supreme Court function of "judicial review" was established, an extraordinary federal power that made complete the definition of the system of "checks and balances" the framers of the Constitution had created among the executive, legislative, and judicial branches of government.

A Purchase and a Grand Adventure

Jefferson's first term was crowned by an action that added a vast new territory to the United States. This triumph began with a crisis. Following the French and Indian War, France ceded the Louisiana Territory to Spain. However, in 1800, Napoleon Bonaparte reacquired the territory by secret treaty in exchange for parts of Tuscany, which Napoleon pledged to conquer on behalf of Spain. Napoleon also promised to maintain Louisiana as a buffer between Spain's North American settlements and the United States. After the secret treaty was concluded, Napoleon promptly abandoned his Tuscan campaign, and the two nations fell to disputing. During this period, beginning in 1802, Spain held the United States hostage to its dispute with France by closing the Mississippi to American vessels.

Vital Statistics

The Louisiana Purchase added 90,000 square miles of trans-Mississippi territory to the United States. Purchased at a cost of 60 million francs (about $15 million), it was a great real estate bargain at 4 cents an acre.

Jefferson could not tolerate an end to western trade, but neither did he relish the notion of Napoleon at his back door. To resolve the crisis, the president dispatched James Monroe to France to make an offer for the purchase of New Orleans and Florida.

Monroe, it turned out, was in precisely the right place at precisely the right time. One of Napoleon's armies was bogged down in the disease-infested West Indies. Rather than lose his forces to illness, Napoleon decided to withdraw from the hemisphere altogether and focus his conquests exclusively in Europe. Even as Monroe was crossing the Atlantic, Napoleon's minister Talleyrand asked U.S. foreign minister to France Robert R. Livingston how much Jefferson would offer not just for New Orleans and Florida, but for the *entire* Louisiana Territory. Negotiations proceeded after Monroe arrived, and the bargain was concluded for 60 million francs.

The Louisiana Purchase was an overwhelmingly popular move, which helped to catapult Jefferson to a second term. He swept every state except two Federalist bastions—Connecticut and Delaware—in the election of 1804.

Struggle for Sovereignty

Jefferson's second term began with great promise as his administration negotiated a favorable peace in the Tripolitan War, putting an end to intimidation by the Barbary pirates of Tripoli, Algiers, Morocco, and Tunis, who had been extorting protection money in return for safe passage of U.S. merchant vessels through the Mediterranean. Alas, the rest of Jefferson's second administration was marked by a crippling economic crisis resulting from a failure of foreign policy.

In Europe, the Wars of the French Revolution had segued into the Napoleonic Wars. When neither the English nor the French could score a decisive victory, they turned to attacks on the commerce of noncombatant nations, including the United States, in the hope of crippling one another's economy. The English resumed the practice of impressing sailors on American merchant ships and also seized American vessels attempting to enter French ports. Jefferson retaliated with the Non-Importation Act, which prohibited the importation of many English goods.

The simmering crisis came to full boil on June 22, 1807, when the British man-of-war *Leopard*, off Norfolk Roads, Virginia, fired on the U.S. frigate *Chesapeake*. The

British boarded the frigate and seized four men they claimed to be deserters from His Majesty's navy. The incident infected the nation with war fever, but President Jefferson resisted. Instead of resorting to war, he pushed through Congress the Embargo Act of December 22, 1807, prohibiting all exports to Europe and restricting imports from Great Britain.

The embargo was intended as an alternative to war with England or any other European nation, but it was really a self-inflicted wound that severely crippled the American economy and provoked well-founded outrage from American farmers and merchants. Jefferson was a man of tremendous intellect, but even he proved capable of fostering, in the Embargo, a very stupid law.

Tecumseh Raises the Hatchet

While Jefferson was dealing with England and France, the West that he had done so much to "open" with the Louisiana Purchase was erupting into violence. In 1794, the major tribes of the Old Northwest were defeated by General "Mad Anthony" Wayne at the watershed Battle of Fallen Timbers (August 20). After almost a decade of relative peace on that frontier region, President Jefferson in 1803 directed the territorial governor of Indiana, William Henry Harrison (1773–1841), to obtain "legal" title to as much Indian land as possible. Over the next 3 years, Harrison acquired 70 million acres by negotiating with whatever chiefs and tribal leaders were willing to sign deeds. The trouble was that for every Indian leader who claimed authority to sell land, another rose up to repudiate that authority and sale.

The most prominent, brilliant, and charismatic of those who resisted the transfer of Indian lands to the whites was the Shawnee Tecumseh (ca. 1768–1813), who organized a united resistance against white invasion, while cultivating an alliance with British interests. Westerners were fearful of Tecumseh and other British-backed Indians, and they were also angry. Not only did the Indians need a good whipping, but so did the British, who became the focus of concentrated hatred in the new American West, for inciting Indians to war and for disrupting American shipping and commerce. What was bad for the coastal economy was disastrous for the West, which, during this critical phase of its development, was being prevented from shipping out its abundant exports. The West was spoiling for a war, and William Henry Harrison and Tecumseh would give it one.

The Least You Need to Know

- ◆ The liberal "Age of Jefferson" swept away the repressive Alien and Sedition Acts and expanded the United States with the Louisiana Purchase.

- ◆ Chief Justice John Marshall defined the function and power of the Supreme Court through his decision in the case of *Marbury* v. *Madison*.

- ◆ The Shawnee leader Tecumseh emerged with a dream of once and for all uniting Native America in resistance to the expansion of white civilization.

1812: A War for What? (1812–1814)

In This Chapter

- Early disasters and the near-collapse of the West
- Naval triumphs and Western victories
- The burning of Washington and the defense of Baltimore
- The Battle of Lake Champlain and the Treaty of Ghent
- Jackson as the "Hero of New Orleans"

Late in the summer of 1811, Tecumseh left the Ohio country for the South to enlarge his network of alliances by reaching out to the Chickasaws, Choctaws, and Creeks. Except for a militant Creek faction known as the Red Sticks, these groups wanted no part of Tecumseh's enterprise. Worse for Tecumseh, William Henry Harrison used the Indian leader's absence to move against his headquarters at Tippecanoe. Having assembled a rag-tag army of 1,000 men—including 350 U.S. regulars, raw Kentucky and Indiana militiamen, and a handful of Delaware and Miami Indian scouts—Harrison attacked outside Tippecanoe on November 7, 1811. Losses were equally heavy on both sides; about 50 whites and 50 Indians were slain.

But the battle cost Tecumseh's followers their headquarters and prompted many of them to desert Tecumseh. Thus, the settlers of the West had their first taste of a major fight and a significant victory. Of fighting, they were about to get more than their fill during the next 3 years. Victories, however, would be very few in a war some historians have condemned as both destructive and unnecessary, and others have hailed as the nation's "second War of Independence."

The War Hawks Roost

The War of 1812 is one of those historical events few think much about today. However, earlier generations of American schoolchildren were routinely taught that it was nothing less than the "second War of Independence." Over the years, a growing number of historians rejected this notion and criticized the war as not only senseless but extremely hazardous and certainly damaging to the young republic. More recently, some historians have seriously returned to the interpretation of the war as a testing and assertion of the sovereignty of the United States—in effect, a *second* War of Independence.

Outdated schoolbook histories teach that the War of 1812 was fought because the British, at war with Napoleon and in need of sailors for the Royal Navy, insisted on boarding U.S. vessels to impress sailors into His Majesty's service. Actually, the United States declared war on Britain on June 19, 1812, three days *after* the British had agreed to stop impressing seamen. The real cause of the war was not to be found on the ocean, but in the trans-Appalachian West. In Congress, that region was represented by a group of land-hungry "War Hawks," spearheaded by Representative Henry Clay of Kentucky.

The War Hawks saw war with Britain as an opportunity to gain relief from British-backed hostile Indians in the frontier areas and as a chance to gain what was then called Spanish Florida, a "parcel" of land extending from Florida west to the Mississippi River. Spain, which held this land, was allied with Britain against Napoleon. War with Britain, therefore, would mean war with Spain, and victory would result in the acquisition of Spanish Florida, which would complete an unbroken territorial link from the Atlantic, through the recently purchased Louisiana Territory, clear to the Pacific.

The trouble was that President James Madison, elected to his first term in 1808, did not want war. He renewed the diplomatic and economic initiatives Jefferson had introduced (mainly the ineffectual and ultimately self-destructive Embargo) to avoid armed conflict, but, facing a tough re-election battle in 1812, he at last yielded to Clay and the other leading War Hawks, John C. Calhoun of South Carolina and Kentucky's Richard Mentor Johnson. President Madison asked a willing Congress for a declaration of war.

Three-Pronged Flop

Since colonial times, Americans had shunned large, standing armies. Now, having *declared* war, the country had to *fight* it—with an army of only 12,000 regular troops scattered over a vast territory. The troops were led mostly by officers who had achieved their rank through their political connections rather than their military experience, which, in most cases, was nil. As to the nation's navy, its officers were generally of a higher caliber than the army's, but it was nevertheless a very puny force, especially in comparison with the magnificent fleets of the British. Despite these terrible handicaps, U.S. planners developed a three-pronged invasion of Canada: a penetration from Lake Champlain to Montreal; another across the Niagara frontier; and a third into Upper Canada from Detroit.

The sad fact was that the attacks, thoroughly uncoordinated, all failed.

Militia commander William Hull (1753–1825) not only failed to invade Canada, but surrendered Detroit on August 16, 1812, without having fired a shot.

New York militia general Stephen Van Rensselaer led 2,270 militiamen and 900 regulars in an assault on Queenston Heights, Canada, just across the Niagara River. Part of the force, mostly the regulars, got across the river only to be pinned down and quickly overwhelmed.

The principal U.S. force under Major General Henry Dearborn mutinied on November 19, 1812, and refused to invade Canada.

The West in Peril

The surrender of Detroit and the collapse of the Canadian campaign laid the West open to Indian raids and British invasion. Suffering along the frontier was acute, yet neither the British nor their Indian allies were able to capitalize decisively on their advantages. Although most of the Old Northwest soon fell under Indian control, a coordinated British assault on the region, which might have brought the war to a quick and crashing end, never materialized.

British Stranglehold

In frankly miraculous contrast to the dismal American performance on land were the operations of the U.S. Navy. The British brought to bear 1,048 vessels to blockade U.S. naval and commercial shipping in an effort to choke off the nation's war effort. Opposed to this vast armada were the 14 seaworthy vessels of the U.S. Navy and a ragtag fleet of privateers. The U.S. frigates emerged victorious in a series of single-ship engagements, the most famous of which were the battles between the USS *Constitution* ("Old Ironsides") and the British frigates *Guerriere*, off the coast of Massachusetts on August 19, 1812, and *Java*, off the Brazilian coast on December 29, 1812. Despite such American triumphs, the British were able to tighten their blockade into a death grip that wiped out American trade, bringing the U.S. economy to the verge of collapse.

"We Have Met the Enemy, and They Are Ours"

During 1813, renewed American attempts to invade Canada were again unsuccessful. In the West, however, the situation brightened. William Henry Harrison managed to rebuild—and even enlarge—his army, so that by late summer of 1813, he fielded 8,000 men. In the meantime, a dashing young naval officer named Oliver Hazard Perry (1785–1819) cobbled together an inland navy. Beginning in March 1813, he directed construction of an armed flotilla at Presque Isle (present-day Erie), Pennsylvania, while drilling his sailors in artillery technique. By August, he was ready to move his vessels onto Lake Erie. On September 10, Perry engaged the British fleet in a battle so fierce that he had to transfer his flag from the severely damaged brig *Lawrence* to the *Niagara*, from which he commanded nothing less than the destruction of the entire British squadron. He sent to General Harrison a message that instantly entered into American history: "We have met the enemy, and they are ours."

Perry's triumph cut off British supply lines and forced the abandonment of Fort Malden, as well as a general retreat eastward from the Detroit region. On October 5, 1813, Harrison overtook the retreating British and their Indian allies at the Battle of the Thames. The great Indian leader Tecumseh fell in this battle. Although no one knows who killed him, it is certain that, with his death, the Indians' last real hope of halting the northwestward rush of white settlement likewise died.

O, Say Can You See

The American victories in the West, so long in coming, might have turned the tide of the war had it not been for the defeat of Napoleon in Europe and his first exile, to the British-controlled fortress island of Elba. With Napoleon out of the way, the British could now turn their attention to what had become (from their point of view) a very nasty little war in North America. Soon, more ships and more troops, including experienced veterans of the campaigns against Napoleon, sailed across the Atlantic.

The British plan was to attack in three principal areas: New York, along Lake Champlain and the Hudson River, which would sever New England from the rest of the Union (it was the very plan that had failed to come to fruition during the Revolution); New Orleans, which would block the vital Mississippi artery; and Chesapeake Bay, a diversionary maneuver that would draw off U.S. manpower from the New York–New England and southern fronts. The British objective was to bring America to its knees and thereby extort major territorial concessions in return for peace. By the fall of 1814, the situation looked very bleak for the United States. The nation was flat broke, and in New England, some opponents of the war had actually begun talking about seceding from the Union.

Late in the summer of 1814, American resistance to the attack in Chesapeake Bay folded. The British, under Major General Robert Ross, triumphed in Maryland at the Battle of Bladensburg (August 24), when inexperienced Maryland militiamen commanded by the thoroughly incompetent General William H. Winder broke and ran in panic. Ross invaded Washington, D.C., and burned the major public buildings, including the Capitol and the White House, as President Madison and most of the government fled into the countryside.

Ross next set his sights on Baltimore, but at last met stiffer resistance. His forces bombarded Fort McHenry, in Baltimore Harbor, during the night of September 13–14, 1814. The event was witnessed by a young Baltimore lawyer, Francis Scott Key (1779–1843), while he was detained on a British warship. Peering anxiously through the long night, Key saw at dawn that the "Star-Spangled Banner" yet waved; the fort had not fallen to the British, who ultimately withdrew. Key was moved to write a poem that eventually became our national anthem.

Deliverance on Lake Champlain

Even while Washington burned and Baltimore fell under attack, a grim band of 10,000 British veterans of the Napoleonic wars was advancing into the United States from Montreal. On land, nothing more than an inferior American force stood between them and New York City. But on September 11, 1814, American naval captain Thomas MacDonough (1783–1825) defeated and destroyed the British fleet on Lake Champlain. This was disastrous enough to send the British army into retreat; commanders feared the loss of their lines of communication and supply.

The failure of the British offensive along Lake Champlain added some high cards to the hand of American peace negotiators meeting with their British counterparts across the ocean in the Flemish city of Ghent. The war-weary British decided to forego territorial demands, and the United States, relieved to escape without major losses, let up on its demand that Britain recognize American neutral rights. The Treaty of Ghent, signed on December 24, 1814, restored the *status quo ante bellum*—the way things were before the war, and the document was unanimously ratified by the U.S. Senate on February 17, 1815.

What's the Word?

The Latin phrase *status quo ante bellum* is common in treaties and underscores the utter futility of much combat. The phrase means "the way things were before the war."

An American Hero Is Born

The Treaty of Ghent notwithstanding, the *status quo ante bellum* did not prevail in the United States. To begin with, the nation was suffering through a crippling economic depression created by the British blockade, although the economy would, in time, recover. More important, withdrawal of British support for that nation's wartime Indian allies greatly weakened the hostile tribes, making the West that much riper for white expansion. Finally, in 1814, trans-Atlantic communication was anything but instantaneous. Word of the Treaty of Ghent had not reached General Andrew Jackson, who, fresh from victory against the Red Stick Creek Indians in the South, moved on to New Orleans to engage 7,500 British veterans under Major General Edward Pakenham. He had not heard about Ghent either and was now sailing from Jamaica to attack the city.

Jackson's forces consisted of 3,100 Tennessee and Kentucky volunteers, in addition to New Orleans militiamen and a motley mob of locals, which Jackson wisely kept well to the rear. Jackson's numerically inferior forces withstood a fierce artillery bombardment and repulsed two British assaults on their defensive positions. On January 8, 1815, the British, having suffered terrible losses (including the death of Pakenham and his two senior subordinates), withdrew. Although the War of 1812 had actually ended in December 1814, Jackson gave his countrymen their most glorious victory of the war.

To most Americans, it now mattered little that the War of 1812 had been mostly a misery and a disaster. The victory at New Orleans changed everything, making them feel as though they had won the war hands down. All the economic and physical hardships suddenly seemed worthwhile, and the bonds of American nationhood were strengthened. This was not necessarily a case of collective self-delusion. The dubious wisdom of the war aside, the fact is that the United States had stood its ground against the most powerful military force in the world. Moreover, the country also had a brand-new hero, a "Westerner" born and bred far from the traditional seaboard seats of power. As Jefferson had before him, Andrew Jackson would lend his name to an entire era.

The Least You Need to Know

- The War of 1812 was provoked by Westerners, who were eager to expand the territory of the United States.

- During the war, the British relied heavily on Indian allies, who believed a British victory would check the incursion of settlers into Indian lands.

- The War of 1812, ended by the Treaty of Ghent, was effectively a draw, restoring the *status quo ante bellum*.

- Although the war brought great hardship to the United States, it ultimately reinforced the bonds of national unity by demonstrating that America could stand up to the most powerful nation on the planet.

Chapter 14

Fanfare for the Common Man (1814–1836)

In This Chapter

- ◆ President Monroe's misnamed "Era of Good Feelings"
- ◆ The Monroe Doctrine
- ◆ Economic crisis: the Panic of 1819
- ◆ The Missouri Compromise
- ◆ Jacksonian Democracy

Casualties of the War of 1812 included many soldiers, settlers, and Indians, in addition to the U.S. economy, which went into a free fall during the war, bottoming out in the Panic of 1819. Also slain in battle was the British desire to fight any more wars with its erstwhile colonies. Although it is true that Great Britain certainly didn't *lose* the War of 1812, it didn't win it, either, and the British government came away persuaded that fighting the United States just wasn't worth doing. For this reason, the War of 1812 has been called, with at least some justification, America's *second* War of Independence.

A final casualty of the war was the Federalist Party. Federalists, who had bitterly questioned the wisdom of the war and, in some extreme cases, even advocated dissolution of the union because of it, were now seen as unpatriotic and lacking in resolve. In 1816, Democratic-Republican James Monroe, presented to the electorate as the heir apparent of James Madison (himself the protégé of Thomas Jefferson), handily won election to the presidency.

Good Feelings

The history of the American democracy is filled with contradictions, and one of the great misnomers that describes this nation in the years following the War of 1812 is the "Era of Good Feelings." The famous phrase was coined sarcastically by a Federalist newspaper following the re-election of Monroe in 1820, when he ran against his secretary of state, John Quincy Adams, whom he defeated by an electoral vote of 231 to 1. Monroe himself was popular, revered by the people as the last of the "cocked hats," an affectionate name for the Founding Fathers. However, Monroe presided over a country that, although proud of its nationhood after the war, was seriously torn by bitter sectional rivalries and disputes over the interpretation of the Constitution.

Monroe tried to salve sectionalism by appointing a stellar cabinet that included the best political minds of the day, among them John Quincy Adams (Secretary of State), John C. Calhoun (Secretary of War), and William H. Crawford (Secretary of the Treasury). But these leading lights soon disputed with one another, not only over philosophical and sectional issues, but over whom would succeed Monroe as president.

Although he was a Democratic-Republican, Monroe broke with Jefferson and supported the rechartering of the Bank of the United States, which had been the brainchild of Washington's Federalist Secretary of the Treasury Alexander Hamilton. The bank was popular with the East Coast establishment because it effectively gave them control of the nation's purse strings. The bank was bitterly opposed by always-struggling Westerners, however, who needed easy credit to expand and establish themselves.

Those Westerners also argued for a loose interpretation of the Constitution, particularly the phrase in the Preamble, "to promote the general welfare." These words, Calhoun and Henry Clay (powerful Congressman from Kentucky) argued, mandated that the federal government build the roads the West badly needed to develop its commerce and economy. Monroe consistently vetoed road-building bills on Constitutional grounds, but he did support a high *tariff* on imports, which aided the industrialized Northeast at the expense of the rural South and West. The tariff increased sectional strife.

What's the Word?

A **tariff**, as the word was used during the era of Monroe, is a tax on imported goods. Tariffs produce significant revenues for the government, and they "protect" certain domestic industries by giving their goods an artificial price advantage over imports. However, tariffs also result in higher prices to domestic purchasers because the higher costs are ultimately passed on to them.

A Monumental Ditch

Monroe's opposition to federally built roads for the West did not impede—and might even have actually stimulated—development of the nation's first great commercial link between the East Coast and the vast inland realm. Gouverneur Morris, U.S. Senator from New York, proposed in 1800 the construction of a great canal from New York City to Buffalo on Lake Erie. The project was approved by the New York legislature in 1817, and it was completed in 1825. Running 363 miles, the Erie Canal was a spectacular engineering achievement and a testament to American labor. The project was also a stunning commercial triumph, which quickly repaid the $7 million it had cost to build and soon returned an average of $3 million in annual profits—all without the assistance of the federal government.

The success of the Erie Canal, which truly inaugurated the *commercial* opening of the West, touched off a canal-building boom, linking the Northeast with the western system of natural waterways. By 1840, the United States boasted 3,326 miles of canals, which helped carry the nation out of its postwar economic funk. The canals also tied the Northeast more securely to the West, thereby making deeper the growing division between the North and South, which had few east-west connections.

A Place in the Family of Nations

The completion and success of the Erie Canal justifiably puffed the nation's pride, even if its economy was still shaky and the jarring demands of sectionalism were increasingly strident. The United States under Monroe could at least point to growing prestige among the family of the world's nations. Secretary of State John Quincy Adams negotiated the Rush-Bagot Agreement and the Convention of 1818 with Britain. The first document established the U.S. border with Quebec, hitherto a sharp bone of contention and established the enduring precedent of a friendly, open border—without forts or fortification—between the United States and Canada.

The second document, the Convention of 1818, addressed the issue of the disputed Oregon Territory (that is, the land west of the Rocky Mountains, north of the 42nd parallel to the 54°42' line). The Convention specified joint U.S. and British occupation of the area—a temporary solution to a hot dispute, but also a demonstration that England now took American sovereignty seriously.

On February 12, 1819, Adams concluded a treaty with Luis de Onís, Spain's minister to Washington, which secured both western and eastern Florida for the United States. With the acquisition of Florida, a prime objective of the War of 1812 was realized—albeit belatedly. A thornier problem was the establishment of the border between the United States and Mexico, at the time part of the empire of Spain. Adams wanted a border that would pull Texas into American territory. However, to get Florida, he ultimately sacrificed Texas and agreed on a boundary at the Sabine River, the western border of the present-day state of Louisiana, and the United States renounced all claims to Texas. That renunciation was destined to endure during the handful of years before the revolutions by which Mexico won its independence from Spain. After the Texas War for Independence in 1836, U.S. rights to the territory would become a cause of war between Mexico and the United States.

Yet one more treaty was concluded, this one with the czar of Russia, who had asserted a claim to the California coast as far south as San Francisco Bay. Adams managed to talk Czar Alexander I into a position north of the 54°42' line, so that Russia would no longer be a contender for the Oregon Territory. The czar did retain his claim to Alaska, a barren and frozen land, which, at the time, nobody in the United States could imagine wanting anyway.

Monroe Doctrine

Although these foreign agreements were of great importance to establishing American sovereignty, the cornerstone of Monroe's foreign policy was laid in 1823 and has since been stamped with the president's name. The origin of the Monroe Doctrine is found in the turbulent years of the Napoleonic Wars. These wars touched South America, sparking widespread revolution there. After peace was re-established in Europe in 1815, Spain began making noises about reclaiming its South American colonies. President Monroe responded in his 1823 message to Congress with the four principles now known as the Monroe Doctrine:

1. The Americas were no longer available for colonization by any power.

2. The political system of the Americas was essentially different from that of Europe.

3. The United States would consider any interference by European powers in the Americas a direct threat to U.S. security.

4. The United States would not interfere with existing colonies or with the internal affairs of European nations, nor would the United States participate in European wars.

Bad Feelings

The so-called Era of Good Feelings was filled with plenty of distinctly *bad* feelings, a mixture of present financial hardships and an anxiety-filled foreboding of political and civil calamity just over the horizon.

A Panic

Economic conditions in the wake of the War of 1812 read like a recipe for disaster:

- Start with a grinding war debt.
- Add high tariffs to create commodity inflation.
- Stir in wild speculation on western lands opened by the war.
- Overextend manufacturing investments.
- Pour the whole thing down the drain.

From 1811, when constitutional challenges prevented the rechartering of the Bank of the United States, until 1816, the year the bank was revived under Monroe, a host of shabby state banks rushed to provide credit to practically all comers. Then, when the War of 1812 broke out, all the state banks (except for those in New England) suspended the practice of converting paper bank notes to gold or silver (*specie*) on demand. The value of all that paper money so recklessly loaned now plummeted. Banks failed; investors collapsed; businesses went belly up.

Monroe's Second Bank of the United States stepped in with a plan to stabilize the economy by sharply curtailing credit and insisting on the repayment of existing debts in specie. This plan preserved the Bank of the United

What's the Word?

Specie payments are payments in gold and silver, rather than paper money.

States, but it hit the nation hard. "The Bank was saved," one pundit of the day observed, "but the people were ruined." In the West and South, individuals were particularly hard hit, and these states passed laws to provide debt relief, but not before 1819, when the panic peaked.

The nation ultimately weathered the Panic of 1819, but the crisis created lasting resentment against the Bank of the United States (called "The Monster" by Missouri senator Thomas Hart Benton). The West and the South resented what they felt was the economic and political stranglehold of the Northeast.

A Compromise

The deepening gulf between the northern and southern states gaped its widest thus far in 1818 and 1819. At that point, the U.S. Senate consisted of 22 senators from northern states and 22 from southern states. Since the era of the Revolution, the balance between the nonslave-holding North and the slave-holding South had been carefully and precariously preserved with the addition of each state, a slave state always balancing a free state. Now, the territory of Missouri petitioned Congress for admission to the Union as a slave-holding state. The balance threatened suddenly to shift.

Representative James Tallmadge of New York responded to Missouri's petition by introducing an amendment to the statehood bill calling for a ban on the further introduction of slavery into the state (but persons who were slaves in the present territory would remain slaves after the transition to statehood). The amendment also called for the emancipation of all slaves born in the state when they reached 25 years of age. Thus, gradually, slavery would be eliminated from Missouri. The House passed the Tallmadge amendment, but the Senate rejected it and then adjourned without reaching a decision on Missouri statehood.

When the Senate reconvened, a long and tortured debate began. Northern senators held that Congress had the right to ban slavery in new states, whereas the Southerners asserted that new states had the same right as the original 13, to determine whether they would allow slavery or not. Not until March 1820 was a complex compromise reached on this issue, which, in reality, could admit of no satisfactory compromise. Missouri, it was agreed, would be allowed to join the Union as a slave state, but simultaneously, Maine (hitherto a part of Massachusetts) would be admitted as a free state. By this means, the slave state/free state balance was maintained. Then, looking toward the future, the Missouri Compromise drew a line across the Louisiana

Territory at latitude 36°30'. North of this line, slavery would be forever banned, except in the case of Missouri.

The Missouri Compromise held the fragile Union together for another three decades.

The Age of Jackson

The single strongest candidate in the presidential election of 1824 was Andrew Jackson (1767–1845), "Old Hickory," "The Hero of New Orleans," the candidate of the people. However, Jackson did not win the election.

As the facade of the Era of Good Feelings crumbled away, no party had risen to replace the Federalists in opposition to the Democratic-Republicans. Within the Democratic-Republican camp, however, a host of candidates emerged, each reflecting deep regional divisions. The Tennessee and Pennsylvania state legislatures nominated Jackson;, Kentucky nominated Henry Clay; Massachusetts nominated John Quincy Adams (who had left the defunct Federalist fold to become a Democratic-Republican); and Congress presented William H. Crawford.

In the subsequent election, Jackson received 99 electoral votes, Adams 84, Crawford 41, and Clay 37. Because none of the candidates had a majority, the election was sent to the House of Representatives to choose from among the top three. Illness forced Crawford out of the running, and the choice was between Adams and Jackson. The House voted Adams into office over Jackson, who had received the greater number of electoral votes. Charging that a corrupt bargain had been made, Jackson's supporters split from the Democratic-Republican Party and became simply Democrats.

Adams had a tough time as a "minority president." His support of canals and other internal improvements, his call for the establishment of a national university, and his advocacy of scientific explorations were largely rejected by Congress, which focused on expansion and frontier individualism. This attitude swept Jackson into office in his second bid for the presidency in 1828.

Common Man or King Andrew?

Jackson, seventh president of the United States, was the first who had not been born in patrician Virginia or New England. Although he was, in fact, a wealthy man who lived in a magnificent mansion, the Hermitage, outside of Nashville, Tennessee,

Jackson was also a self-made son of the Carolina backcountry. By the political geography of the day, he was a "Westerner" as well as one of the common folk.

There can be no doubt that Andrew Jackson's two terms as president—from 1829 to 1837—brought a greater degree of democracy to American government. Jackson's contemporaries, as well as subsequent generations of historians, have debated whether the *kind* of democracy his administration fostered was always a good thing. During the Jackson years, most states abandoned property ownership as a prerequisite for the right to vote. This move broadened the electorate and made elected officials act in a way that was more fully representative of the people who had put them in office. Although this transformation nurtured democracy, it also encouraged demagoguery.

Jackson reserved his most potent venom for the Second Bank of the United States. When the bank's charter came up for renewal, Jackson vetoed the recharter bill. After winning re-election in 1832, he issued an executive order withdrawing all federal deposits from the bank. That was the fatal blow, and the bank fizzled, finally closing its doors when its charter expired in 1836. With the demise of the Second Bank of the United States, credit became more plentiful, and westward settlement proceeded more rapidly. But for the rest of the nineteenth century, the American economy was doomed to a punishing ride over tumultuous seas, riding the crest of each boom, only to be nearly drowned in the trough of every bust.

The Least You Need to Know

◆ Monroe was a popular leader, who nevertheless presided over a period of great economic hardship and bitter sectional rivalries.

◆ Andrew Jackson was perceived by the electorate as the champion of "Westerners" and the common man.

◆ The "Age of Jackson" brought with it a vast expansion of the concept of democracy. However, this period also sacrificed some of the reason and restraint that had characterized the nation under the "Founding Fathers."

◆ Jackson's destruction of the Second Bank of the United States freed up credit in a democratic manner, but also ushered in an era of financial instability that would endure throughout the nineteenth century.

Trails of Tears (1817–1842)

In This Chapter

- ◆ The Nullification Crisis
- ◆ The Seminoles refuse to cede their lands
- ◆ Black Hawk leads an uprising against the expansion of white settlement
- ◆ The Indian Removal Act of 1830 and its consequences

Democracy seems logical and sounds simple—a matter of giving the people what they want. But just who are the American people? In Andrew Jackson's time, they were rich and poor, Easterners and Westerners, Northerners and Southerners, whites and blacks, slaves and masters, Indians, and everyone else. All, of course, are people, but most of them had diverse needs and desires. The "Age of Jackson," like Jackson the man, was full of contradiction and paradox. Bringing to the United States its first full measure of undiluted democracy, "Old Hickory" was also derided as "King Andrew," a tyrant. A believer in individual rights, Jackson made the federal government more powerful than ever. A frontier Southerner, he didn't want to disturb the institution of slavery, yet he turned against the South when that region threatened the authority of his government. A military hero who had built his reputation in large part by killing Indians, he espoused what was considered, in his day, the most enlightened approach to the so-called "Indian problem"—relocation from the East ("removal") to new lands in the West. *Enlightened?* The great "removal" opened the darkest chapter of Indian-white relations in the United States and forever stained the administration of Andrew Jackson.

Liberty and Union, Now and Forever

In 1828, as the administration of John Quincy Adams drew to a close, Congress passed the latest in a long series of tariff laws designed to foster American manufac-turing industries by levying a hefty duty on manufactured goods imported from abroad. These laws were warmly embraced by the rapidly industrializing Northeast, but they were deeply resented in the South. The southern economy thrived on trade in raw materials, such as rice, indigo, and cotton. Among the South's best customers were the nations of Europe, especially England, which would buy the raw goods, turn them into manufactured products (such as fine fabric), and export them to the United States. If tariffs made it too costly for Americans to buy European goods, then Europe would have a reduced need for the South's raw materials, and the region's export business would suffer accordingly.

Southerners denounced the 1828 measure as the "Tariff of Abominations." Led by South Carolinian John C. Calhoun, vice president under both Adams and Jackson, Southerners charged that the act was both discriminatory in economic terms *and* unconstitutional. Calhoun wrote the *South Carolina Exposition and Protest* in 1828, arguing that the federal tariff could be declared "null and void" by any state that deemed it unconstitutional.

Calhoun could point to an impressive precedent for his bold position. Two Founding Fathers, Thomas Jefferson and James Madison, had introduced the concept of nullifi-cation when they wrote, respectively, the Kentucky and Virginia Resolutions of 1798, which declared that the Alien and Sedition Acts violated the Bill of Rights. But a major showdown over the Tariff of Abominations was temporarily deferred by the 1828 election of Andrew Jackson, who pledged tariff reform. Southerners, however, were soon disappointed by the limited scope of Jackson's reforms, and when the Tariff Act of 1832 was signed into law, South Carolina called a convention. On November 24, 1832, the convention passed an Ordinance of Nullification forbidding collection of tariff duties in the state.

Calhoun gambled that Jackson's loyalty as a "son of the South" would prompt him to back down on the tariff. But, instead, Jackson responded on December 10 with a dec-laration upholding the constitutionality of the tariff, denying the power of any state to block enforcement of any federal law, and threatened armed intervention to enforce the collection of duties. To show that he meant business, Jackson secured from Congress passage of a Force Act, authorizing the use of federal troops, which might well have ignited a civil war right then and there. However, the same year that the Force Act was passed, 1833, also saw passage of a compromise tariff. Although Calhoun's South Carolina stubbornly nullified the Force Act, it did accept the new tariff, which rendered nullification moot. Civil war was averted—for the time being—but the theory of nullification remained a profound influence on southern political thought and provided a key rationale for the breakup of the Union less than 3 decades later.

The Seminoles Say No

The political fabric was not the only aspect of the Union showing signs of wear during the Age of Jackson. Violence between settlers and Indians had reached epidemic proportions during the War of 1812 and never really subsided thereafter. During the war, General Jackson had scored a major triumph against the Red Stick Creeks in the lower Southeast, extorting from them the *cession* of vast tracts of tribal lands. Closely allied with the Creeks were the Seminoles, who lived in Florida and Alabama. The Creek land cessions made the Seminoles all the more determined to hold on to their own homelands. When the British withdrew in 1815 from the fort they had built at Prospect Bluff, Florida, it was taken over by a band of Seminoles together with a group of fugitive slaves, and it became known as "Negro Fort." The facility posed a military threat to navigation on key water routes in Florida, Georgia, and Alabama; moreover, slave-holders were angered that the fort sheltered their escaped "property."

In 1816, Jackson, at the time a general, ordered his subordinate Edmund P. Gaines to build Fort Scott on the Flint River fork of the Apalachicola in Georgia. In July of that year, Jackson dispatched Lieutenant Colonel Duncan Lamont Clinch, with 116 army regulars and 150 white-allied Coweta Creeks, to attack Negro Fort. Ordered to recover as many fugitive slaves as possible, Clinch attacked the fort on July 27 and was supported by a pair of riverine gunboats. The skipper of one of these vessels had the bright idea that bombardment

What's the Word?

To **cede** land is to give it up, usually as a condition of surrender or in exchange for something of value (money or other land). **Cession** is the noun form of the word and is not to be confused with "secession," which refers specifically to the breakaway of 11 Southern states that precipitated the Civil War.

would be most effective if he heated the cannonballs red hot and fired them with an extra-heavy charge. The first projectile launched in this way landed in the fort's powder magazine, setting off an explosion so spectacular that it has been described as the biggest bang produced on the North American continent to that date. Three hundred fugitive slaves and 30 Seminoles were blown to bits, and the Indian tribe was propelled to the brink of war.

Late in 1817, a Seminole chief named Neamathla warned General Gaines to keep whites out of his village, Fowl Town. In response, Gaines sent a force of 250 to arrest Neamathla. The chief escaped, but the troops attacked the town, and the First Seminole War was under way.

Andrew Jackson led 800 regulars, 900 Georgia militiamen, and a large contingent of friendly Creeks through northern Florida, bringing destruction to the Seminole villages he encountered and high-handedly capturing Spanish outposts in the process. The taking of Pensacola on May 26, 1818, created a diplomatic crisis, which was resolved, however, when Spain decided to abandon Florida and cede the territory to the United States. With that, many more settlers rushed into the region, overwhelming the battered Seminoles and their remaining Creek allies. A minority of these tribes signed treaties in 1821, 1823, and 1825, turning over 25 million acres to the United States. The Seminoles were ordered to a reservation inland from Tampa Bay; few actually went to it. A majority of the Creeks repudiated the land cessions but were persecuted under the policies of Georgia governor George Troup. When the Creeks appealed to Andrew Jackson (now president) for help, he advised them to move to "Indian Territory" west of the Mississippi. Ultimately, many did just that.

The Defiance of Black Hawk

In the meantime, the so-called Old Northwest was racked with violence as well. The end of the War of 1812 and the death of Tecumseh failed to bring peace as white settlers pushed farther and farther west, through present-day Ohio and Indiana, and into Illinois. A group of determined Indian militants rallied behind Black Hawk (1767–1838), a charismatic chief of the closely allied Sac and Fox tribes.

Throughout 1832, Black Hawk skillfully led resistance against white settlement in Illinois, but by the end of the summer, he and his followers had been defeated.

Indian Removal

As seen by later generations, Andrew Jackson is one of our most controversial chief executives. However, even his most enthusiastic admirers have difficulty justifying his role in the passage of the Indian Removal Act of 1830. This law effectively evicted the major Indian tribes from land east of the Mississippi and consigned them to "Indian Territory" in the West. In fairness to Jackson and Congress, it was reasonably enlightened legislation by the standards of the time. The act, passed on May 28, 1830, did not propose robbing the Indians of their land, but exchanging western for eastern territory and, by way of additional compensation, paying tribal annuities.

Hollow Victory

In theory, and by law, Indian "removal" was a voluntary exchange of eastern lands for western lands. In practice, however, Indians were most often coerced or duped into making the exchange. Typically, government officials would secure the agreement of some Indian leaders deemed—by the government—to speak for the entire tribe, make the exchange, and declare that exchange binding on all members of the tribe. Whether or not a majority of the tribe acknowledged the authority of these leaders hardly mattered. After an agreement was concluded, the government claimed the right to move all the Indians off the land, by force if necessary.

Some individuals and even entire tribes went quietly; others, such as the Seminoles, fought. Still others, including numbers of Cherokees, holed up in the Appalachian Mountains to evade removal. The Cherokees, a politically sophisticated tribe, also took legal action. The tribe's majority party, called the Nationalist Party, appealed to the U.S. Supreme Court in 1832 to protest state-sanctioned seizures of property and prejudicial treatment in state and local courts, all intended to pressure the Indians into accepting the "exchanges" mandated by the Removal Act. In *Worcester* v. *Georgia* (1832), Chief Justice John Marshall declared Georgia's persecution of the Indians unconstitutional. But this judgment proved a hollow victory, because President Jackson refused to use federal power to enforce the high court's decision. The chief executive, who had shown himself quite capable of threatening South Carolina with armed federal intervention during the Nullification Crisis, now claimed that the U.S. government was powerless to interfere in the affairs of an individual state. Jackson advised the Indians to resolve their difficulties by accepting removal.

In the meantime, Jackson's officials were directed to negotiate a removal treaty with the compliant minority faction of the Cherokees (called the Treaty Party), representing no more than a thousand or so out of 17,000 Cherokees living in the South. On December 29, 1835, the Jackson administration concluded the Treaty of New Echota, binding *all* of the Cherokees to remove. To crush resistance, Jackson barred the Cherokee National Party from holding meetings to discuss the treaty or alternative courses of action. Nevertheless, under the leadership of John Ross, the Nationalists managed to delay the major phase of the removal operation until the fall and winter of 1838 and 1839.

A Man Called Osceola

While the Cherokees were being subdued and removed, federal authorities turned their attention to the always-troublesome Seminoles. Like the Cherokees, the Seminoles suffered abuse from state and local governments; their suffering was compounded in 1831 by a devastating drought. Faced with annihilation, Seminole leaders signed a provisional treaty on May 9, 1832, agreeing to removal pending tribal approval of the site designated for resettlement. Accordingly, a party of seven Seminoles traveled westward. But before they returned, an Indian agent named John Phagan coerced tribal representatives into signing a final treaty, binding the Seminoles to leave Florida by 1837. Not only did the tribe rescind the signatures as fraudulent, but even the government acknowledged the wrongdoing by removing Phagan from office. Nevertheless—and despite the fact that the Seminoles' report on the proposed new homeland was negative—President Jackson sent the treaty to the Senate for ratification. With the treaty secured, troops were sent into Florida to begin organizing the removal.

By early in the winter of 1835, the increasing troop strength made it clear to Seminole leaders that war was in the offing. During this period, Osceola (1803–1838), called Billy Powell by the whites, emerged as a charismatic Seminole leader. He negotiated with federal Indian agents to put off removal until January 15, 1836, hoping to buy sufficient time to prepare for the coming combat. Osceola set about organizing Seminole and Red Stick Creek resistance.

Beginning in December 1835, Osceola initiated guerrilla warfare, taking special pains to attack bridges critical for transporting troops and artillery. In every respect, Osceola proved a formidable adversary, a brilliant tactician who made extensive use of effective reconnaissance, and a fierce warrior. Generals Edmund Gaines, Duncan Clinch, Winfield Scott, Robert Call, Thomas Jesup, and Zachary Taylor all failed to bring the Second Seminole War to a conclusion. Osceola himself was finally captured, on October 21, 1837, not through the military skill of the federal troops, but by deception. General

Jesup requested a "truce" conference in Osceola's camp; Osceola complied, and thereupon was treacherously taken captive. Consigned to a prison cell at Fort Moultrie, South Carolina, Osceola contracted "acute quinsy" and died on January 30, 1838.

Despite Osceola's capture and death, the war continued from 1835 to 1842, a period during which 3,000 Seminoles did submit to removal, but at the average cost of one soldier killed for every two Indians "removed." The Second Seminole War never really ended, but petered out through the mutual exhaustion of both sides, only to become reactivated between 1855 and 1858 as the Third Seminole War. The last Seminole holdouts refused to sign treaties with the United States until 1934.

"The Cruelest Work I Ever Knew"

During the summer of 1838, Major General Winfield Scott began a massive roundup of Cherokees. In accordance with the terms of the fraudulent Treaty of New Echota, the Cherokees were to be removed to "Indian Territory," an area encompassing present-day Oklahoma and parts of Nebraska, Kansas, and the Dakotas. Except for those relatively few who found refuge in the Blue Ridge Mountains, the Cherokees were herded into hastily built concentration camps, where they endured the misery of a long, hot, disease-plagued summer.

During the fall and winter of 1838 and 1839, the Indians were marched under armed escort along the 1,200-mile route to Indian Territory. Cold, short of food, subject to abuse at the hands of their military guards (including theft, rape, and murder), 4,000 of the 15,000 who started the journey perished before reaching its end. Many years later, a Georgia soldier recalled: "I fought through the Civil War and have seen men shot to pieces and slaughtered by thousands, but the Cherokee removal was the cruelest work I ever saw." The Cherokees forever afterward called the experience the "Trail of Tears."

Welcome to Indian Territory

What awaited the Cherokees and other native peoples removed from the East was a vast tract of bleak and forbidding western land. Whereas their eastern homelands had been lush and green, the Oklahoma, Kansas, Nebraska, and Dakota region was arid. Much of the stubborn soil was resistant to cultivation and certainly unsuited to the type of agriculture the Indians had pursued in the East. The hardships of soil and climate, combined with the callous inefficiency and general corruption of the federal system that was obligated by treaty to aid and support the "resettled" Indians, killed many. Others, certainly, died of nothing more or less than broken hearts. Yet, over time, many among the removed tribes made the best of their grim situation and, in varying degrees, even prospered.

Contrary to treaty agreements, the Kansas-Nebraska Act of 1854 reduced the area of Indian Territory. During the Civil War, many Cherokees, Creeks, and others allied themselves with the Confederates in the hope of getting a better deal from that government than what the Union had dished out. In 1866, the victorious Union forces punished these Confederate Indians by further reducing the size of Indian Territory, contracting it to the area encompassed by present-day Oklahoma.

The Least You Need to Know

◆ In the Nullification Crisis, "states' rights" confronted federal authority in a prelude to civil war.

◆ Osceola (among the Seminoles) and Black Hawk (among the Sac and Fox) emerged as formidable leaders of Native American resistance against the expansion of white settlement into Indian lands.

◆ The Indian Removal Act was an attempt to separate Indians and whites by means of land exchanges.

Part 4

The House Divided

Just as you can find people to tell you that the Revolution had little or nothing to do with liberty, there are still plenty of folks who'll argue that the Civil War was about states' rights or about the North wanting to achieve economic domination over the South. These things are important and partly true, but the irreducible fact is this: if it hadn't been for slavery in the South, and the opposition to it in the North, there would have been no Civil War. This part of the book tells the story of how the "peculiar institution" of slavery divided the country, and how, finally, the question of whether a "nation conceived in liberty and dedicated to the proposition that all men are created equal can long endure" was answered by the bloodiest, costliest, and most destructive war in American history.

Chapter 16

A Nation in Chains (1724–1857)

In This Chapter

- ◆ A nation divided over the slavery issue
- ◆ Abolition movements, the Underground Railroad, and rebellion
- ◆ Compromises on the slavery issue
- ◆ Bleeding Kansas and the Dred Scott decision

By the early 1700s, slavery had caught on in a big way throughout the Southern colonies. In places like South Carolina, slavery became essential to the economy, and slaves soon outnumbered whites in that colony. The Declaration of Independence declared no slave free, and although the Constitution gave Congress the option of ending the slave trade (that is, importation of slaves) after the last day of 1807, it both sanctioned and protected slavery itself.

Against the American Grain

From the beginning, a significant number of Americans were opposed to slavery. The first organized opposition came from the Quakers, who issued a statement against the institution as early as 1724.

During the colonial periods, slave markets were active in the North as well as the South. However, the agricultural economy of the northern colonies was built upon small family farms rather than vast plantations. Although some people in the North were passionately opposed to slavery on moral grounds, it is also true that the region lacked the economic motives for it. Following independence, various states outlawed the institution altogether. Rhode Island, traditionally a seat of tolerance, abolished slavery as early as 1774, and the Northwest Ordinance of 1787 excluded slavery from the vast Northwest Territory.

A number of the founding fathers, including George Washington and Thomas Jefferson, owned slaves. Nevertheless, Jefferson clearly wanted the institution of slavery to end. He condemned it in his draft of the Declaration of Independence, but Congress deleted this passage from the final document. Jefferson championed a bill to abolish the slave trade, and he signed it into law, effective January 1, 1808, the first day the Constitution allowed such a law to take effect. Recent scholarship shows that Washington engaged in a deep moral struggle with slavery and wrote an eloquent passage in his will stipulating that his slaves were to be freed immediately upon the death of his wife, Martha. Few of Washington's slave-holding contemporaries were willing to relinquish such a valuable legacy as human property.

Eli Whitney's Slave Machine

Even in the South itself, there was reason to believe that slavery would eventually die out. As the free laboring population grew, there was a decreasing need for slaves, and so, it was hoped, the slavery question would ultimately answer itself.

But, just 6 years after passage of the Northwest Ordinance, an invention appeared that changed everything. Eli Whitney (1765–1825) was a New Englander working as a tutor in Georgia. Fascinated by operations on the large Southern plantations, he observed that planters were vexed by a problem with the short-staple cotton raised in the inland region of the lower South. In contrast to the long-staple cotton that grew near the coast, the inland variety of the plant had particularly stubborn seeds that required extensive handwork to remove. Even done by slaves, the labor was so time-consuming that profits from cotton cultivation were sharply diminished, making large-scale production impractical.

Whitney set to work, and by April 1793 he had fashioned a machine that used a toothed cylinder to separate the cottonseed from the cotton fiber. Each *cotton gin* could turn out 50 pounds of cleaned cotton a day—far more than the amount manual labor could produce.

The gin caught on fast, and it suddenly made the cultivation of short-staple cotton extremely profitable. "King Cotton" soon displaced tobacco, rice, and indigo as the primary Southern export crop. With increased production came a greatly increased demand for slave labor to feed the ever-churning cotton gins.

Underground Railroad

As the generation of the late eighteenth century had been fascinated by inventions like the cotton gin, so, by the third decade of the nine-

> **What's the Word?**
>
> **Cotton gin** sounds to us like a peculiar form of booze, but late-eighteenth-century ears would have immediately recognized "gin" as a shortened form of the word "engine." Two hundred years ago, a gin—or engine—was any labor-saving device, particularly one intended to help move heavy objects.

teenth century, Americans were enthralled by another innovation, railroads, which began appearing in the United States during the late 1820s. The railroad seemed nothing less than a miracle of technology, and maybe because abolitionists (those who wanted to *abolish* slavery) were in search of a moral miracle to end slavery, they called the loosely organized, highly stealthy network developed in the 1830s to help fugitive slaves escape to the North or Canada the *Underground Railroad.*

> **Remember This**
>
> The most famous "conductor" on the Underground Railroad was Harriet Tubman, a courageous, self-taught, charismatic escaped slave, single-minded in her dedication to freeing others. Born in Dorchester County, Maryland, about 1821, she escaped to freedom about 1849 by following the North Star. Not content with having achieved her own freedom, she repeatedly risked recapture throughout the 1850s by journeying into slave territory to lead some 300 other fugitives, including her parents, to freedom.
>
> With the outbreak of the Civil War, Tubman volunteered her services as a Union army cook and nurse and then undertook hazardous duty as a spy and guide for Union forces in Maryland and Virginia. Capture would surely have meant death.
>
> Following the war, Tubman operated a home in Auburn, New York, for aged and indigent African Americans. She ran the facility until her death on March 10, 1913. She was buried with full military honors.

The Underground Railroad was a group of committed whites and free blacks (including escaped slaves), called "conductors," and safe houses (called "stations") dedicated to nothing less than the secret delivery and deliverance of slaves ("passengers" or "freight") out of the slave states—or, at least, the slave states bordering the North. In the years prior to the Civil War, 50,000 to 100,000 slaves found freedom via the Underground Railroad.

Southern slave-holders did not suffer the Underground Railroad gladly. "Conductors" were menaced, assaulted, and even killed. Fugitive slaves, when retaken, were often severely punished as an example to others. When the Supreme Court ruled in 1842 (*Prigg* v. *Pennsylvania*) that states were not required to enforce the Fugitive Slave Law of 1793 (which provided for the return of slaves who escaped to free states), opposition to the Underground Railroad turned downright rabid as "conductors" became increasingly bold in moving their charges toward freedom.

The Liberator and the Narrative

William Lloyd Garrison (1805–1879) was a genteel New England abolitionist—a native of Newburyport, Massachusetts—who became co-editor of a moderate periodical called *The Genius of Universal Emancipation.* But the injustice of slavery soon ignited a fiercer fire in Garrison's belly, and on January 1, 1831, he published the first issue of *The Liberator.* This was a radical and eloquent abolitionist periodical that declared slavery an abomination in the sight of God and demanded the emancipation of all slaves, without compromise or delay.

The Liberator galvanized the abolitionist movement. Three years after the first issue was printed, Garrison presided over the founding of the American Anti-Slavery Society. Using *The Liberator* and the society, Garrison embarked on a massive campaign of what he called "moral suasion." He believed that slavery would be abolished when a majority of white Americans experienced a "revolution in conscience," and he meant to move heaven and Earth to bring that revolution about.

Garrison grew increasingly extreme in his views, and by the late 1830s, some more conservative abolitionists broke away from his group. In 1842, he made his most radical stand, declaring that Northerners should disavow all allegiance to the Union because the Constitution protected slavery. A pacifist, Garrison nevertheless hailed John Brown's bloody 1859 raid on Harpers Ferry for the purpose of stealing guns to arm slaves for a general uprising.

If *The Liberator* was the most powerful white voice in support of abolition, a gripping account of slavery and liberation by an escaped Maryland slave named Frederick Douglass was the most compelling African American voice. Published in 1845, *Narrative of the Life of Frederick Douglass* was widely read and discussed. Not only did the book vividly portray the inhumanity of slavery, it also made manifest the intense humanity of the slaves, especially as evidenced in the author himself, the brilliant, self-educated Douglass. Active as a lecturer in the Massachusetts Anti-Slavery Society, Douglass parted company with Garrison over the issue of breaking with the Union. Douglass wanted to work within the Constitution.

The Tortured Course of Compromise

Awkward and strained, the Missouri Compromise, negotiated in 1820, began to buckle and break in 1848. In that year, California was officially transferred to the United States by the Treaty of Guadalupe Hidalgo, which ended the U.S.–Mexican War on February 2, 1848. On January 24, 1848, just a few days before the treaty was signed, gold was discovered in the run (watercourse) of a sawmill on the south fork of the American River. During the height of the gold rush, in 1849, more than 80,000 fortune seekers poured into the territory. This event suddenly made statehood for the territory an urgent issue.

But would California be admitted as a slave state or free?

In 1846, Congress, seeking a means of bringing the war with Mexico to a speedy conclusion, had debated a bill to appropriate two million dollars to compensate Mexico for "territorial adjustments." Pennsylvania congressman David Wilmot introduced an amendment to the bill, called the Wilmot Proviso, which would have barred the introduction of slavery into any land acquired by the United States as a result of the war. As usual, Southern opposition to the limitation of slavery was articulated by John C. Calhoun, who was by this time a South Carolina senator. He proposed four resolutions:

1. Territories, including those acquired as a result of the war, were the common and joint property of the states.

2. Congress, acting as agent for the states, could make no law discriminating between the states and depriving any state of its rights with regard to any territory.

3. The enactment of any national law regarding slavery would violate the Constitution and the doctrine of states' rights.

4. The people have the right to form their state government as they wish, provided that its government is republican.

As if Calhoun's resolutions were not enough, he warned that failure to maintain a balance between the demands of the North and the South would surely lead to "civil war."

1850: A New Compromise

Over the next 3 years, Congress labored to bolster the 1820 compromise. Thanks to abolitionists such as Garrison and Douglass, most Northerners were no longer willing to allow slavery to extend into any new territory, whether it lay above or below the line drawn by the Missouri Compromise. To break what had become a very dangerous stalemate, Senator Lewis Cass of Michigan advanced the doctrine of "popular sovereignty," proposing that new territories would be organized without any mention of slavery one way or the other. When the territory wrote its own constitution and applied for admission as a state, the people of the territory would vote to be slave or free. As to California, it would be admitted to the Union directly instead of going through an interim of territorial status.

Southerners cringed. They assumed that California would vote itself free, as would, down the line, New Mexico. Senators Henry Clay and Daniel Webster worked out a new compromise. California would indeed be admitted to the Union as a free state. The other territories acquired as a result of the U.S.–Mexican War would be subject to "popular sovereignty." In addition, the slave auction market in the District of Columbia (long an embarrassment in a city that hosted foreign diplomats) would be closed. To appease the South, a new ironclad Fugitive Slave Law was passed, strictly forbidding Northerners to grant refuge to escaped slaves. Additionally, the federal government agreed to assume debts that Texas (admitted as a slave state in 1845) incurred before it was annexed to the United States.

As with the Missouri Compromise, the Compromise of 1850, passed but thoroughly pleased no one. Abolitionists were outraged by the Fugitive Slave Law, and states' rights supporters saw the slave-free balance in Congress as shifting inexorably and intolerably northward.

Kansas-Nebraska Act

In the Compromise of 1850, many observers saw the flaming handwriting on the wall: the Union was coming apart, and its dissolution would be bloody. In 1854, the territories of Nebraska and Kansas applied for statehood. In response, Congress repealed the Missouri Compromise and passed the Kansas-Nebraska Act, which left the question of slavery entirely to "popular sovereignty." There was never any doubt that Nebraskans would vote themselves a free state, but Kansas was very much up for grabs. Pro-slavery Missourians suddenly flooded across the border, elected a pro-slavery territorial legislature, and then, mission accomplished, returned to Missouri. Anti-slavery Iowans likewise poured in, but they decided to settle permanently. Soon a chronic state of civil warfare developed between pro- and anti-slavery factions in Kansas. The situation became so ugly that the territory was soon called "Bleeding Kansas."

The anti-slavery faction set up its headquarters in the town of Lawrence. In 1856, pro-slavery "border ruffians" raided Lawrence, setting fire to a hotel and a number of houses and destroying a printing press. In the process, several townspeople were killed. During the night of May 24, John Brown, a radical abolitionist who had taken command of the territory's so-called Free Soil Militia, led four of his sons and two other followers in an assault on pro-slavery settlers along the Pottawatomie River. Five defenseless settlers were hacked to death with sabers. Proudly claiming responsibility for the act, Brown pronounced it payback for the sack of Lawrence. The incident was just one jarring passage in a grim overture to the great Civil War.

The Dred Scott Disaster

In 1857, at the height of the Kansas bloodshed, the U.S. Supreme Court weighed in with a decision in the case of one Dred Scott, a fugitive slave, who had belonged to John Emerson of St. Louis. An army surgeon, Emerson had been transferred first to Illinois and then to Wisconsin Territory, with his slave in tow. When Emerson died in 1846, Scott returned to St. Louis and sued Emerson's widow for his freedom, arguing that he was a citizen of Missouri, now free by virtue of having lived in Illinois, where slavery was banned by the Northwest Ordinance, and in Wisconsin Territory, where the terms of the Missouri Compromise made slavery illegal. The Missouri state court decided against Scott, whereupon his lawyers appealed to the Supreme Court.

The high court was divided along regional lines. The anti-slavery Northern justices sided with Scott, but the pro-slavery Southerners upheld the Missouri state court decision. Chief Justice Roger B. Taney, son of wealthy Maryland slave-holders, had the final word. He ruled, in the first place, that neither free blacks nor enslaved blacks were citizens of the United States and, therefore, neither could sue in federal court. That ruling would have been enough to settle the case, but Taney went further. He held that the Illinois law banning slavery had no force on Scott after he returned to Missouri, a slave state. The law that stood in Wisconsin was likewise null and void, Taney argued, because the Missouri Compromise was (he declared) unconstitutional. According to Taney, the law violated the Fifth Amendment, which bars the government from depriving an individual of "life, liberty, or property" without due process of law.

The Dred Scott decision outraged abolitionists and galvanized their cause. Here was the spectacle of the U.S. Supreme Court using the Bill of Rights to deny freedom to a human being! Here was the federal government saying to slave owners that their ownership of human beings would be honored and protected everywhere in the nation! No longer was the slavery issue a question of how the nation could expand westward while maintaining a balance in Congress. It was now an issue of property. Justice Taney's decision had put slavery beyond compromise. A constitutional amendment abolishing slavery would resolve the issue to the satisfaction of the abolitionists, but that required ratification by two thirds of the states—an impossibility. The only alternative, it seemed, was war.

The Least You Need to Know

- ◆ Opposition to slavery in America came early; the first organized efforts to abolish it began in 1724.

- ◆ The labor-intensive cultivation of cotton made the Southern economy dependent on slavery, especially after the invention of the cotton gin.

- ◆ A series of compromises staved off civil war for three decades, as Northern opposition to slavery grew stronger and Southern advocacy of it became increasingly strident.

- ◆ The Dred Scott decision made slavery an issue transcending individual states; therefore, it made compromise impossible and civil war inevitable.

Chapter 17

Westward the Course (1834–1846)

In This Chapter

- ◆ Land: the great American asset
- ◆ McCormick's reaper and Deere's plow
- ◆ Independence for Texas
- ◆ Development of the western trails and the telegraph

Two cancers consumed the American body politic: chronic war between whites and Indians, and the continued existence of slavery. Symptoms of these diseases were violent. Add to this picture two major wars with foreign powers—the War of 1812 and the U.S.–Mexican War—and America, in the years leading up to mid-century, seemed a highly volatile place.

Yet as the cliché has it, everything's relative. Between 1800 and the 1850s, Europe was in a virtually continuous state of war, so that, despite their own problems, Americans looked across the sea and counted themselves lucky.

Americans understood that they had one powerful peace-keeping asset Europe lacked: space. Seemingly endless space stretched beyond the

Appalachian Mountains and the Mississippi River, across plains and deserts, over more mountains, to the Pacific Ocean itself. Surely, America had room enough for everybody.

The Plow and the Reaper

Of course, land aplenty was one thing; actually *living* on it and making a living *from* it could be quite another matter. In the Northeast, the American farm of the early nineteenth century was a family affair, providing enough food to feed the family, with something left over for market. Farm life wasn't easy, but it was manageable. In the South, farms often expanded into vast plantations, which grew rice, indigo, tobacco, and, above all, cotton. These crops were all commercial, and slaves were the cheap source of labor used to produce them profitably.

The West also offered the prospect of large-scale farming, but most of the western territories and states barred slavery. In any event, the *emigrants* who settled on the western lands were culturally and morally disinclined to keep slaves. However, without slaves, how would a big piece of land be worked? No matter how vast, property was worth nothing if you couldn't work it profitably.

And that wasn't the only problem. In most of the new territories prairie soil was hard, breaking, when it finally did break, into rocklike clods. It did not yield to the plow, but clogged it, making cultivation all but impossible. Was the nation destined to cling to its east coast, leaving vast western tracts useless, desolate, and empty?

As would happen time and again in American history, technology changed everything.

What's the Word?

The dictionary will tell you that an **emigrant** is one who emigrates—that is, leaves one place to settle in another—whereas an **immigrant** immigrates: he or she comes into a place. The emphasis is on arrival rather than departure. Be that as it may, those who made the westward trek were almost always called "emigrants" by their contemporaries.

Cyrus McCormick

Cyrus McCormick (1809–1884) was born and raised on a Rockbridge County, Virginia, farm where his father, Robert, gave him the run of his well-equipped workshop. There, Cyrus began to redesign a mechanical reaper that the elder McCormick had been tinkering with. By the time he was 22, Cyrus McCormick had come up with a practical prototype of a horse-drawn reaper. It was equipped with a cutting bar, a reel, divider, guards over reciprocating knives, and a platform on which the grain was deposited after having been cut. Everything was driven and synchronized by a gear wheel. Perfected and patented in 1834, the device was an important step toward making large-scale farming possible with a minimal labor force.

 Vital Statistics

Before the advent of the reaper, it took 20 hours to harvest an acre of wheat. By the time the McCormick device was fully perfected, about 1895, the same task consumed less than an hour.

John Deere

The reaper solved only half the problem of large-scale farming on the stubborn prairies of the Midwest and West. John Deere (1804–1886) was a young man who left his native Rutland, Vermont, for Grand Detour, Illinois, in 1837 to set up as a blacksmith. While McCormick was perfecting his reaper, Deere hammered out a new kind of plow. Made of stout steel, the plow was beautifully shaped, calling to mind the prow of the graceful clipper ships of the period. And it was sturdy, much stronger than a conventional plow. The combination of sleek, shiplike design and steely strength made the plow ideal for breaking up and turning over the tough prairie soil.

The McCormick reaper and the John Deere plow came in the nick of time to open the West to agriculture. Armed with these implements, more and more emigrants pushed the frontier farther west with each passing year.

Martyrdom in Texas

As the prairie voids of the northern Midwest and West began to fill in, the Southwest, still territory belonging to the Republic of Mexico, was being settled by an increasing number of American colonists.

That colonization had started in 1820, when Moses Austin secured a grant from the Spanish government to establish an American colony in Texas. He fell ill and died in 1821, before he could begin the project of settlement. On his deathbed, Austin asked his son, Stephen F. Austin, to carry out his plans. Mexico, in the meantime, had won independence from Spain in the revolution of 1821. Under terms established by a special act of the new Mexican government in 1824 (as well as additional agreements negotiated in 1825, 1827, and 1828), Austin brought more than 1,200 American families to Texas. Colonization was so successful that by 1836 the American population of Texas was 50,000, and that of the Mexicans was a mere 3,500.

Throughout the 1830s, the American majority chafed under Mexican rule—especially Mexican laws forbidding slavery. Violent conflicts between settlers and military garrisons became frequent. Feeling that his colony was not ready for a full-scale war of independence, Austin repeatedly negotiated peace with the increasingly unstable Mexican government. He drew up a proposed constitution to make Texas a Mexican state, with all the self-governing rights of a state, and in 1833, traveled to Mexico City to seek an audience with Antonio López de Santa Anna, the country's new president. For 5 months, Austin tried in vain to see the president; at last, he gained an audience, only to have Santa Anna reject the statehood demand, although Santa Anna did agree to address a list of Texas grievances. Austin began his ride back to Texas, feeling that he had at least gained something. En route, however, he was arrested, returned to Mexico City, and imprisoned there on a flimsy pretext for the next 2 years.

When Austin was finally released in 1835, he returned to Texas embittered and broken in health. He urged Texans to support a Mexican revolt against Santa Anna, and this effort triggered the Texas Revolution or Texan War of Independence.

Seeking to put down the Texas rebellion, Santa Anna led troops into Texas during January 1836 and reached San Antonio in February. There, against the advice of independence leader Sam Houston (1793–1863), a force of 187 Texans under militia colonel William B. Travis resolved to make a defensive stand behind the walls of a decayed Spanish mission formally called San Antonio de Valero but nicknamed "the Alamo" because it was close to a grove of cottonwoods (*alamos* in Spanish).

The tiny Texas band, which included such renowned frontier figures as Jim Bowie and Davy Crockett, held off some 2,000 of Santa Anna's troops for 10 days. The band hoped desperately that the American nation somehow would rally and rush to its aid. But that didn't happen. On March 6, the Mexican troops finally breached the mission's wall and slaughtered almost everyone inside, allowing only the handful of women and children there to leave. Crockett and a few others were made prisoners of war and then summarily executed by order of Santa Anna.

This Mexican "victory" turned out to be a disaster for Santa Anna. Sam Houston rallied Texans under the battle cry "Remember the Alamo!" and brilliantly led his ragtag army against the Mexican leader at the Battle of San Jacinto on April 21. Defeated in a mere 15 minutes, Santa Anna was subsequently captured and given a choice of signing the hastily drawn up Treaty of Velasco, which granted Texas independence or being shot. He signed, and Texas became an independent republic.

Rolling West

During the 1830s and well into the 1840s, before the McCormick reaper and the Deere plow had worked their act of transformation, the western plains were known as the Great Desert, and they remained largely unsettled as settlers set their sights on the Far West beyond. By the early 1830s, Americans were beginning to settle in California, many of them "mountain men"—fur trappers—who turned from that profession to ranching and mercantile pursuits.

These pioneers made their way into the territory via the brutally punishing southwestern deserts until 1833, when Joe Walker, a mountain man from Tennessee, marched due west from Missouri. Walker took the so-called South Pass through the Great Divide, went west across the Great Basin, climbed the Sierra Nevada, and entered California. This path became the California fork of what would be called the Overland Trail. It opened California to the rest of the nation. By 1840, 117 mountain men were settled in Mexican California, bringing the American population there to about 400.

Overland Trail

The mountain men and other explorers carried back to the East tales of the wondrous and potentially bountiful lands that lay toward the sunset. Through the decade of the 1830s, America's westward dreams simmered. At last, on February 1, 1841, 58 men—settlers living in Jackson County, Missouri—met at the town of Independence to plan the first fully organized emigrant wagon train to California. By the time it assembled across the Missouri River, at Sapling Grove, the party had grown to 69, including more than 20 women and children, under the leadership of John Bartleson. The prominent Catholic missionary Father Pierre-Jean de Smet and the mountain man Thomas Fitzpatrick also joined the train of 15 wagons and 4 carts.

The trek consumed 5 months, 3 weeks, and 4 days. It was marked by a single death, a single birth, and a single marriage. The following year, some 20 wagons carrying more than 100 persons made the trip. Other journeys followed each year thereafter until the completion of the transcontinental railroad in 1869 made the Overland Trail and the other trans-West routes obsolete.

Surviving the 3- to 7-month journey across a grueling and unforgiving landscape took discipline, strength, and luck. Yet most who undertook the trek lived—albeit transformed by the ordeal: haggard, even reduced to skin and bones. Such hardship was sufficient to convince many emigrants to make an expensive and often storm-tossed journey by sea—either all the way around Cape Horn at the tip of South America or to the Isthmus of Panama. The Panama Canal would not be completed until 1914, so travelers bound for the West Coast had to disembark on the Atlantic side of the isthmus, make a disease-ridden overland journey through a steaming jungle, and then board a California-bound ship on the Pacific side.

Oregon Fever

Until gold was discovered in California during 1848 and 1849, Oregon was the strongest of the magnets drawing emigrants westward. In 1843, a zealous missionary named Marcus Whitman led 120 wagons with 200 families in what was called the "Great Migration" to Oregon. Soon, stories of a lush agricultural paradise touched off "Oregon fever," which brought many more settlers into the Northwest.

Oregon was a very hard paradise. The elements could be brutal, and diseases ranged from endemic to epidemic. Whitman worked tirelessly as a missionary and physician, ministering in both capacities to the Cayuse Indians in the vicinity of Walla Walla (in present-day Washington state). An overbearing man who insisted that the Indians accept none other than the Christian God (and *his* version of that God at that), Whitman fell afoul of the Cayuse during a measles epidemic that killed half their number. Blamed for the sickness, he and his pretty blonde wife, Narcissa, were massacred on November 29, 1847.

"What Hath God Wrought?"

Historians often refer to the emigrant trails as "avenues" of civilization as if they were neatly constructed highways. In fact, the trails were often nothing more than a pair of wheel ruts worn by the passage of one wagon after another. Yet, even as ox hooves and iron-rimmed wheels crunched through the dust of rudimentary trails, a very different, very modern means of linking the continent appeared.

In 1819, the Danish scientist Hans C. Oersted (1777–1851) discovered the principle of induction when he noticed that a wire carrying an electric current deflected a magnetic needle. After this discovery, a number of scientists and inventors began experimenting with deflecting needle *telegraphs*. Two scientists, William F. Cooke and Charles Wheatstone, installed a deflecting-needle telegraph along a railway line in England in 1837, but it proved too delicate to be practical. In 1825, William Sturgeon invented the electromagnet, and the experiments of Michael Faraday and Joseph Henry on electromagnetic phenomena in 1831 excited an American painter, Samuel F. B. Morse, to begin working on a new, more robust telegraph receiver.

Morse developed a device in which an electromagnet, when energized by a pulse of current from the line—that is, when the remote operator pressed a switch ("telegraph key")—attracted a soft iron armature. The armature was designed to inscribe, on a piece of moving paper, dot and dash symbols, depending on how long the key was held down. Morse developed "Morse Code" to translate the alphabet into combinations of dots and dashes.

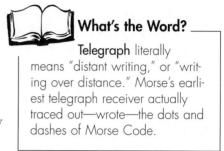

What's the Word?

Telegraph literally means "distant writing," or "writing over distance." Morse's earliest telegraph receiver actually traced out—wrote—the dots and dashes of Morse Code.

Morse successfully lobbied Congress to fund a 40-mile telegraph line between Baltimore and Washington, D.C., and, on March 4, 1844, he demonstrated his magnetic telegraph by sending the message "What hath God wrought?" from the capital to a remote station in Baltimore.

Morse's transmitter, receiver, and code system were widely adopted, although the cumbersome graphic device was soon abandoned. The difference between the dot and dash signals was quite audible, and a well-trained operator could translate and transcribe them by ear more quickly and reliably than any mechanical printing device. Within a span of only 10 years, the single 40-mile line from Baltimore to Washington had multiplied into 23,000 miles of wire connecting the far-flung corners of the nation. In a burst of keystrokes, Morse compressed vast distance and gave the nation a technology that would help bind East to West.

The Least You Need to Know

- Vast spaces were always America's greatest resource as well as heaviest burden; a large nation was difficult to unify and govern.

- A group of American entrepreneurs colonized the Mexican frontier state of Texas, and then fought a brief, decisive war to achieve independence.

- Most Texans were eager for annexation to the United States, but fears of adding another slave state to the Union and of provoking war with Mexico delayed the process for almost a decade—from 1836 to 1845.

- Technology played a key role in westward expansion. The McCormick reaper and Deere plow made farming the plains practical, and Morse's telegraph made the vastness of the West less daunting.

Chapter 18

Destiny Manifested (1846–1860)

In This Chapter

- ◆ California's Bear Flag Rebellion
- ◆ War with Mexico
- ◆ The Mormon Trek
- ◆ The Gold Rush of 1849

Phrases enter and exit the American language as through a revolving door, but one phrase used in 1845 by *New York Post* editor John L. O'Sullivan to describe America's passion for the new lands of the West, arrived and lingered. "It is our *manifest destiny*," O'Sullivan wrote, "to overspread and to possess the whole of the continent which Providence has given us for the development of the great experiment of liberty and federated self-government entrusted to us." Under the banner of "manifest destiny," the American West would be won—the obstinacy of prairie soil, the harshness of the elements, the lives and culture of the Indians, and the claims of Mexico notwithstanding.

After Texas gained its independence, the United States was reluctant to accept the newborn republic's bid for annexation. To accept Texas into the Union would not only add a slave state, but would surely also ignite war with Mexico. However, when France and England made overtures of alliance to the young Republic of Texas, outgoing President John Tyler urged Congress to adopt an annexation resolution. It was under Tyler's successor, James K. Polk, that Texas was admitted into the Union on December 29, 1845.

In the meantime, England and France also seemed to be eyeing California, held so feebly by Mexico that it looked to be ripe and ready to fall into whatever hands were there to catch it.

Halls of Montezuma

Polk was moved to action. He offered Mexico $40 million for the California territory. The Mexican president not only turned down the offer, but refused even to see President Polk's emissary. Thus rudely rebuffed, Polk authorized the U.S. consul at Monterey (California), Thomas O. Larkin, to organize California's small but powerful American community into a separatist movement sympathetic to annexation by the United States. In the meantime, John Charles Frémont, a military officer and intrepid western explorer surveying potential transcontinental railroad routes for the U.S. Bureau of Topographical Engineers, marched onto the stage of action with the so-called Bear Flag Rebellion, in which California's independence from Mexico was proclaimed.

As far as Mexico was concerned, the independence of California merely added insult to injury. Mexico's most intense dispute with the United States was over the boundary of the new state of Texas. President Polk dispatched troops to defend the new state and its boundary on the Rio Grande, and, on May 13, 1846, after Mexican troops advanced across the river, the president asked Congress for a declaration of war on Mexico. By this time, Mexican forces had already laid siege against Fort Texas— present-day Brownsville.

General Zachary Taylor, marching to the relief of the fort, faced 6,000 Mexican troops with a mere 2,000 Americans, but he nevertheless emerged victorious in the May 8 Battle of Palo Alto. The battle set the pattern for the rest of the conflict. Usually outnumbered, the Americans almost always outmatched the poorly led and poorly armed Mexican forces.

In the meantime, early in June, official U.S. action commenced against the Mexicans in California as Stephen Watts Kearny led the "Army of the West" from Fort Leavenworth, Kansas, to California via New Mexico. Near Santa Fe, at steep-walled Apache Canyon, New Mexico's governor Manuel Armijo set up an ambush to destroy Kearny's column, but the governor's ill-disciplined and ill-equipped troops panicked and dispersed without firing a shot. Kearny passed through the canyon unopposed; Santa Fe was taken; and on August 15, New Mexico was annexed to the United States.

General Taylor attacked Monterrey (Mexico) on September 20, 1846, taking the city after a 4-day siege. Always cautious, Taylor chose not to capitalize on what he had gained and allowed Mexican forces to withdraw. In the meantime, the remarkably resilient Antonio López de Santa Anna, who had been living as an exile in Cuba after a rebellion had ended his dictatorship of Mexico, made a proposal to the government of the United States. He pledged to help the nation win the war, to secure a Rio Grande boundary for Texas, and to secure a California boundary through San Francisco Bay. In return, Santa Anna asked for $30 million and safe passage to Mexico. American officials were prudent enough not to pay him, but Santa Anna was allowed to return to his homeland. No sooner did he arrive than he began assembling an army to defeat Zachary Taylor.

By January 1847, Santa Anna had gathered 18,000 men, about 15,000 of whom he hurled against Taylor's 4,800-man force at Buena Vista. After 2 days of bloody battle, Taylor—incredibly—forced Santa Anna's withdrawal on February 23. Despite this brilliant victory, President Polk was distressed by Taylor's continued reluctance to pursue the defeated enemy. The president was even more worried that Taylor's victories would transform him into a military celebrity and, therefore, a potential political rival. So, for both military reasons and political reasons, Polk replaced Taylor with General Winfield Scott, hero of the War of 1812.

Scott was a much bolder commander than Taylor, and, on March 9, he launched an invasion of Veracruz, which commenced with the first-ever amphibious assault in U.S. military history. He laid siege against the fortress at Veracruz for 18 days, forcing Santa Anna to withdraw to the steep Cerro Gordo Canyon with 8,000 of his best troops.

Scott cannily declined the frontal attack the Mexicans expected. Instead, he sent part of his force to cut paths up either side of Cerro Gordo and attacked in a pincers movement, sending Santa Anna's troops into headlong retreat all the way to Mexico City.

Now Scott showed himself willing to take the kind of gamble Taylor would have found unthinkable. He deliberately severed his rapidly pursuing army from its slower-moving supply lines, so that he could press the pursuit of Santa Anna's force. On September 13, Chapultepec Palace, the seemingly impregnable fortress guarding Mexico City, fell to Scott. (The Palace had been defended by a force that included teenage cadets from the Mexican Military College. These cadets are celebrated in Mexican history as "Los Niños," the children.) On September 17, Santa Anna surrendered.

The Mexican War ended with the hastily concluded Treaty of Guadalupe Hidalgo, which was ratified by the U.S. Senate on March 10, 1848. By this treaty, Mexico ceded to the United States New Mexico (which also included parts of the present states of Utah, Nevada, Arizona, and Colorado) and California. The Mexicans also renounced claims to Texas above the Rio Grande. In return, the Mexican government received a payment of $15 million and an American promise that the federal government would assume the financial claims of all Texans against the Mexican government.

Of God and Gold

The Mexican War was controversial. Citizens in the Northeast, especially in New England, saw it as unjust to Mexico and, even worse, little more that a Southern-backed effort to gain more territory that could be divided up into slave-holding states. In contrast, Southerners and Westerners were thrilled by the war and even more excited by its outcome, which added vast lands to the nation.

The Mormons' Trek

The force of war was not the only engine that drove "manifest destiny." The West likewise lured seekers of God and those who lusted after gold. In March 1830, young Joseph Smith Jr. published something he called *The Book of Mormon*. One month later, he started a religion based on the book, which relates how, in 1820, the 15-year-old Smith had been visited by God the Father and Jesus Christ near his family's farm in upstate New York. Three years after this, Smith was visited by an angel named Moroni, who instructed him to dig in a certain place on a nearby hill. There Smith unearthed a book consisting of thinly beaten gold plates engraved with the words of Moroni's father, the angel Mormon. The book told of a struggle between two tribes, one good, the other evil, which took place in the New World long before the arrival of Columbus. Moroni emerged as the sole survivor of the tribe of the good. Whoever dug up *The Book of Mormon* would be charged with restoring to the world the true Church of Christ.

The church Smith founded in April 1830 consisted of six members. By 1844, 15,000 members of the Church of Jesus Christ of Latter-day Saints—popularly called Mormons—were settled in Nauvoo, Illinois, the beautiful community they had built. Persecuted wherever they went, the Mormons always lived apart in such separatist villages.

Particularly distasteful to "gentiles" (as Mormons called those outside of the faith) was the Mormon practice of polygamy (multiple wives). Opposition to polygamy often grew violent, and on June 27, 1844, a "gentile" mob murdered Joseph Smith and his brother. Smith's second-in-command, the dynamic Brigham Young, realized that the Mormons would have to move somewhere so remote that no one would ever bother them again. Over the next 2 years, under his direction, a great migration was organized. The destination, which Young had read about in an account by John C. Frémont, was near the Great Salt Lake in the present-day state of Utah.

Young planned and executed the Mormon Trek with the precision and genius of a great general in time of war. Hundreds of wagons were built, and a staging area, called Camp of Israel, was set up in Iowa. Emigrant parties were deployed in groups of a few hundred at a time and sent 1,400 miles across some of the least hospitable land on the face of the planet. During the 1840s and 1850s, Saints—as Mormons called themselves—poured into the Salt Lake region. Young oversaw the planning and construction of a magnificent town, replete with public squares, broad boulevards, and well-constructed houses, all centered on a great Temple Square. In addition, Young and his followers introduced into the arid Salt Lake Valley irrigation on a scale unprecedented in American agriculture. By 1865, 277 irrigation canals watered 154,000 square miles of what had been desert.

Chasing the Glitter

Johann Augustus Sutter had consistently rotten luck with money. Born in Kandern, Germany, in 1803, he went bankrupt there and, to escape his many creditors, fled to the Mexican Southwest, where he tried his hand in the Santa Fe trade. Twice more Sutter went bust, before finally settling in Mexican California in 1838, where he managed to build a vast ranch in the region's central valley.

Presumably, January 24, 1848, started like any other day on the ranch. James Wilson Marshall, an employee of Sutter's, went out to inspect the "race" (water course) of a new mill on the property. He was attracted by something shiny in the sediment collected at the bottom of the mill race. It was gold.

Within a month and a half of the discovery, all of Sutter's employees had deserted him in the quest of gold. Without anyone left to run it, Sutter's ranch faltered. Worse for him, his claims to the land around the mill were ultimately judged invalid. Although everyone around Sutter (it seemed) grew instantly rich, Sutter himself was, yet again, financially ruined. He would die, bitter and bankrupt, in 1880.

It was neither Marshall nor Sutter, but a Mormon entrepreneur who did the most to stir up the great Gold Rush of 1849. Sam Brannon was one of a very few Mormon men brash enough to challenge the authority of Brigham Young. In defiance of Young, Brannon had set up his own Mormon community in the vicinity of San Francisco—then called Yerba Buena (literally "good herb," the name of an aromatic plant that grew in the vicinity). Brannon saw in the discovery of gold a chance to profit from serving the needs of hopeful prospectors and other settlers. Fresh from a trip to Salt Lake City, where Young had excommunicated him from the church, Brannon took a quinine bottle, filled it with gold dust, and ran out into the streets of his town.

"Gold!" he yelled. "Gold! Gold from the American River!"

For good measure, he covered the gold story in *The California Star*, a newspaper he owned. Within 2 weeks, the population of Yerba Buena plummeted from a few thousand to a few dozen, as men dropped their tools and left their jobs to prospect on the south fork of the American River.

What's the Word?

People who participated in the great California Gold Rush of 1849 earned the name **'49er** or **Forty-niner.** The 1849 rush was not the country's first, however; nor would it be the last. Western Georgia was the scene of the first rush in the late 1830s, and gold rushes would occur elsewhere in California and throughout the West during much of the nineteenth century. In 1896, the Klondike drew thousands of prospectors, and 2 years after this, more came to Alaska in search of the yellow ore.

From the West Coast, word of the gold strike spread east. The scene played out in San Francisco was repeated in city after city. Employment was unceremoniously terminated; wives and children were left behind; and seekers set out on the long trek to California. The journey was characteristically filled with hardship and heartbreak, whether the traveler chose the tedious overland route, the treacherous sea passage around stormy Cape Horn, or the boat to Panama (and a dreary trudge across the disease-ridden Isthmus to meet another ship for the voyage to the California coast). For a very few, the trip was worthwhile; great fortunes were made. The vast majority of prospectors, however, found only hard lives, mean spirits, and barely enough gold to pay for meals, shelter, and clothing. Many didn't even find that much.

The fact was that most men made the mistake of looking for their fortune on the ground, while the real money was made by those, like Brannon, who sold groceries, hardware, real estate, liquor, and other necessities to the '49ers. Collis Huntington and Mark Hopkins, small merchants, made a fortune in mining supplies. Charles Crocker used the profits from his dry goods store to start a bank. Leland Stanford parlayed his own modest mercantile pursuits into a political career culminating in the governorship of California. Together—as the "Big Four"—Huntington, Hopkins, Crocker, and Stanford provided the major financing for the Central Pacific Railroad, the western leg of the great transcontinental railroad completed in 1869.

The California Gold Rush lasted through the eve of the Civil War. The rush populated much of California, and then, as gold was discovered farther inland in Nevada, Colorado, and the Dakotas, even more of the frontier West was settled. But as the bonds of union grew stronger between East and West, those uniting North and South frayed and fell apart. Still basking in the reflected glory of western gold, the American nation was about to enter its darkest hours.

The Least You Need to Know

- ◆ Although controversial, the war with Mexico greatly expanded the western territory of the United States.

- ◆ In addition to agriculture, the promise of religious freedom and the promise of gold lured many thousands out west in the years between the Mexican War and the Civil War.

- ◆ The Mormon Trek, begun in 1847, was both the most spectacular and best-organzied mass migration to the vast lands of the American West.

- ◆ The lure of gold brought unprecedented numbers of fortune seekers to California beginning in 1849.

Chapter 19

A Strange Flag over Sumter (1859–1862)

In This Chapter

- ◆ Lincoln's rise
- ◆ John Brown's raid on Harpers Ferry
- ◆ The fall of Fort Sumter and the early battles
- ◆ Union military failures
- ◆ Antietam and the Emancipation Proclamation

Abraham Lincoln was born on February 12, 1809, in a log cabin in Hardin (now Larue) County, Kentucky. In 1816, the family moved to Indiana and, finally, to Illinois in 1830. Largely self-taught, Lincoln tried various occupations and served as a militiaman in the Black Hawk War (1832). Although he had little appetite for military life, Lincoln took "much satisfaction" (his phrase) in having been elected captain of his militia company. That position opened new horizons for the young backwoodsman. He ran for the Illinois state legislature, losing his first bid, but subsequently gaining election to four consecutive terms (1832–1841). After setting up a successful law practice in Springfield, the state capital, he served a term (1847–1849) in the U.S. House of Representatives, but then returned to his law practice.

At this point, by his own admission, Lincoln "was losing interest in politics." Then came the Kansas–Nebraska Act in 1854. Its doctrine of popular sovereignty potentially opened vast new territories to slavery. Although he believed that the Constitution protected slavery in states where it already existed, he also thought that the Founding Fathers had put slavery on the way to extinction with the Northwest Ordinance, which barred its spread to new territories. Moreover, he found slavery personally repugnant. Lincoln ran unsuccessfully for the U.S. Senate in 1855, and then, the following year, left the Whig Party to join the newly formed Republicans.

In 1858, Lincoln ran for the Senate against the Illinois incumbent, Stephen A. Douglas. Lincoln accepted his party's nomination (June 16, 1858) with a powerful speech suggesting that Douglas, Chief Justice Roger B. Taney, and Democratic presidents Franklin Pierce and James Buchanan had actually conspired to nationalize slavery. Declaring that the Kansas-Nebraska Act was a compromise doomed to fail and that the nation would become either all slave or all free, he paraphrased the Bible: "A house divided against itself cannot stand." For the fate of the country, it was as if he spoke truest prophecy.

John Brown's Body

Lincoln, a highly principled moderate on the issue of slavery, soon found himself transformed from an obscure Illinois politician to the standard bearer of his party. He challenged Douglas to a series of debates that captured the attention of the national press. Although Lincoln failed to win a seat in the Senate, he emerged as an eloquent, morally upright, yet thoroughly balanced embodiment of prevailing sentiment in the North. Radical Southerners warned that the election of any Republican, even the relatively moderate Lincoln, would mean civil war.

While Lincoln and other politicians chose the stump and the rostrum as forums suited to decide the fate of the nation, others took more direct action.

John Brown was born on May 9, 1800, in Torrington, Connecticut, but he grew to adulthood in Ohio, drifting from job to job, always dogged by bad luck and bad business decisions. By the 1850s, however, Brown's life began to assume definite direction, as he became profoundly involved in the slavery question.

Brown and his five sons settled in "Bleeding Kansas," where they became embroiled in the violence between pro-slavery and anti-slavery forces for control of the territorial government. Brown assumed command of the local Free-Soil militia, and after pro-slavery forces sacked the Free-Soil town of Lawrence, Brown, four of his sons, and two other followers retaliated by wielding sabers to hack to death five unarmed settlers along the Pottawatomie River during the night on May 24, 1856.

Although he claimed full responsibility for the act, Brown was not arrested, and he became increasingly obsessed with the idea of emancipating the slaves by inciting a massive slave revolt. The charismatic Brown persuaded a group of Northern abolitionists to back his scheme financially. He chose Harpers Ferry, Virginia (present-day West Virginia), as his target, planning to capture the federal small-arms arsenal there. Using arms liberated from the arsenal, Brown planned to establish a base of operations in the mountains, from which he would direct the slave rebellion, as well as offer haven to fugitives. On October 16, 1859, with 21 men, Brown seized the town of Harpers Ferry and broke into the arsenal. The local militia responded, and within a day, U.S. Marines under the temporary command of a U.S. Army colonel, one Robert E. Lee, arrived, attacked, and killed 10 of Brown's band. Brown himself, wounded, was taken prisoner.

Yet the battle was hardly over. Arrested and tried for treason, Brown conducted himself with impressive dignity and courage. It was, in fact, his finest hour, and he succeeded in arousing Northern sympathy, eliciting statements of support from the likes of William Lloyd Garrison and Ralph Waldo Emerson. As many Northerners saw it, Brown's execution by hanging, on December 2, 1859, elevated him to the status of martyr. To these onlookers, the raid on Harpers Ferry seemed a harbinger of the great moral contest to come.

Bleak Transition

The brand-new Republican Party, with Lincoln as its presidential candidate, united remnants of the Free-Soil Party and the Liberty Party, as well as the old Whigs and other anti-slavery moderates and radicals. Stephen A. Douglas, who had defeated Lincoln in the race for the Senate, sought the Democratic nomination in 1860. But having denounced the pro-slavery constitution adopted by Kansas, Douglas alienated the pro-Democratic South. Although Douglas was finally nominated, he was the choice of what was now a fatally splintered party; a breakaway Southern Democratic party emerged, with outgoing vice president John C. Breckinridge as its candidate. Yet another splinter group, the Constitutional Union Party, fielded a candidate, further dividing the Democrats and propelling Lincoln to

 Vital Statistics

The popular vote was much closer than the electoral vote. Lincoln received only 1,866,452 votes against 2,815,617 votes for his combined opponents.

victory with 180 electoral votes against 123 for his combined opponents. Lincoln earned a *plurality* of the popular votes (more than any other candidate), but not an outright majority (more than all combined).

News of the victory of a "black Republican" pushed the South to secession. First to leave the Union was South Carolina, on December 20, 1860; Mississippi followed on January 9, 1861; Florida on January 10; Alabama on January 11; Georgia on January 19; Louisiana on January 26; and Texas on February 1. Four days later, delegates from these states met in Montgomery, Alabama, where they wrote a constitution for the Confederate States of America and named Mississippi's Jefferson Davis provisional president. As the Union crumbled about him, lame duck president James Buchanan temporized and fretted, feebly protesting his powerlessness.

Prior to his inauguration, President-elect Lincoln discovered that Jefferson Davis, far from spoiling for war, was offering to negotiate peaceful relations with the United States. And Senator John J. Crittenden (1787–1863) of Kentucky proposed, as a last-ditch alternative to bloodshed, the Crittenden Compromise—constitutional amendments to protect slavery while absolutely limiting its spread. Lincoln, determined to avoid committing himself to any stance before actually taking office, nevertheless let others attribute positions to him. The fact was that Lincoln's prime objective was to preserve the Union, and, despite his earlier "house divided" speech, Lincoln was actually willing to consider protecting slavery where it existed, even by constitutional amendment, if necessary. Lincoln also thought the Fugitive Slave Act should be enforced. Yet by remaining silent during the period between his election and inauguration, he conveyed the impression that he fully shared the Radical Republican opposition to *any* kind of compromise on the subject of slavery.

April 12, 1861, 4:30 A.M.

With Lincoln in office and all hope of compromise extinguished (as far as the South was concerned), the Confederate president and Confederate Congress authorized the creation of an army and navy and set about taking control of federal civil and military installations throughout the South. Fort Sumter, which guarded Charleston harbor, was especially important. If the Confederacy could not control the key international port on the coast of South Carolina, it could not effectively claim sovereignty. Throughout March 1861, the Confederate government attempted to negotiate the peaceful evacuation of the Union garrison at Fort Sumter, but Lincoln remained adamant that the United States would not give up the fort. Yet, not wanting to provoke the Southerners, Lincoln also delayed sending reinforcements.

Faced with South Carolina "fire-eaters" (ardent secessionists) who threatened to seize the fort on their own, Jefferson Davis decided that he had to take action. He assigned the mission of capturing the fort to Brigadier General Pierre Gustave Toutant Beauregard, who laid siege to Sumter, hoping to starve out post commandant Major Robert Anderson and his men. In the meantime, Lincoln and the rest of the federal government seemed to be sleepwalking. With great deliberation and delay, a ship was finally loaded with reinforcements and supplies, bound for the fort. But it was too late. Just before he was prepared to open fire, Beauregard offered Anderson, his former West Point artillery instructor, generous surrender terms: "All proper facilities will be afforded for the removal of yourself and command, together with company arms and property, and all private property, to any post in the United States which you may select. The flag which you have upheld so long and with so much fortitude, under the most trying circumstances, may be saluted by you on taking it down."

Anderson politely refused, and the first shot of the Civil War was fired at 4:30 A.M. on April 12, 1861. Edmund Ruffin (1794–1865), a 67-year-old "fire-eater," claimed credit for having pulled the lanyard on that initial volley, although the truth is that Captain George S. James fired a signal gun first. It matters little. The ensuing bombardment lasted a stupefying 34 hours before Anderson, satisfied that he had done his duty, surrendered. Incredibly, this first engagement of the war, in which some 4,000 rounds had been fired, resulted in no casualties.

It would be the last bloodless battle of the Civil War.

From Bull Run to Antietam

During the spring of 1861, Virginia, North Carolina, Tennessee, and Arkansas joined the seven original Confederate States. Yet even that number put the odds at 11 versus 23 Northern states. The North had a far more extensive industrial base than the South and more than twice as many miles of railroad. As far as the production of foodstuffs was concerned, Northern agriculture was also better organized. Although the North was just recovering from an economic depression, the entire South could scrape together no more than $27 million in specie (gold and silver). The North not only commanded far more wealth, it also had diplomatic relations with foreign powers and, therefore, could secure international credit.

 Vital Statistics

The population of the South in 1861 was about nine million people, including three million slaves (who were not military assets). The North had 22 million people.

Yet the South did have more of the American military's best officers, who, at the outbreak of hostilities, had resigned their commissions in the U.S. Army and joined the "provisional army" of the Confederate States. Mindful of the economic, demographic, and industrial might of the North, Confederate leaders knew that their only chance was to score swift military victories that would sap the Yankees' will to fight.

The first major engagement of the war, after the fall of Fort Sumter, proved just how effective the Confederate officers and men were. When it began, the battle the South would call First Manassas and the North would call First Bull Run was a picnic. On July 21, 1861, Washington's fashionable folk rode out to nearby Centreville, Virginia, in carriages filled with picnic baskets of food and bottles of wine. Through spy glasses, they viewed the action three miles distant. The Union troops seemed similarly carefree; as they marched to battle, they frequently broke ranks to pick blackberries. Remarkably lax, too, was military security. Newspapers published the Union army's plan of action, and what information the papers didn't supply, rebel sympathizers, such as the seductive Rose O'Neal Greenhow, merry widow of the District of Columbia, secured by means of espionage.

Thus, General Beauregard was well prepared for the Union advance and had erected defenses near a railroad crossing called Manassas Junction. There, across Bull Run Creek, his 20,000 rebels (later augmented by reinforcements) faced the 37,000 Yankees under the command of the thoroughly mediocre Irvin McDowell.

The battle began well for the North, as General McDowell managed to push the rebels out of their initial positions. But then the Southern forces rallied when they beheld the spectacle of a Virginia brigade led by General Thomas J. Jackson hold its ground against the Yankee onslaught like a "stone wall." Thereafter, Thomas Jackson was best known by the name his soldiers gave him: Stonewall. Inspired by Jackson and his Virginians, the entire Confederate force now rallied and, ultimately, broke through the Union lines. Suddenly, panicked Northern troops retreated. And they kept retreating, all the way to Washington.

The First Battle of Bull Run stunned the capital, which trembled in anticipation of a Confederate invasion that never came, and it stunned Union loyalists all across the nation. Even the picnickers ran for their lives. It would be a long, hard war.

Seven Days

Justifiably dismayed by McDowell's performance at Bull Run, President Lincoln called Major General George B. McClellan to take command of the main Union force.

Jefferson Davis combined Beauregard's troops with those of General Joseph E. Johnston, who was given senior command of the Confederate forces in Virginia. Now the major action centered in Virginia as McClellan set about building a large army with which to invade Richmond, which had been proclaimed the Confederate capital in May.

Despite the triumph at First Bull Run, the outlook seemed grim for the Confederates. Richmond could not withstand a massive assault, and McClellan, a popular commander who the Northern press dubbed the "young Napoleon," succeeded admirably in transforming the Union army from an undisciplined rabble into a cohesive body of highly credible soldiers. McClellan was a skilled organizer and trainer, a thorough professional, who, however, suffered from a Hamlet-like tendency to fret, ponder, and delay rather than force an issue by combat. Lincoln, in his calculatedly homespun way, later complained that McClellan suffered from a "bad case of the slows."

Timing is everything in war, and McClellan repeatedly put off his big assault on Richmond, delaying so often and so long that he lost the initiative altogether, so that, finally, he was compelled to settle into an arduous campaign on the Virginia peninsula. In that campaign's principal series of battles, called the Seven Days (June 26 through July 2, 1862), more men were killed or wounded than in all the Civil War battles fought elsewhere during the first half of 1862, including another encounter that became a veritable byword for slaughter, Shiloh (April 6 and 7, 1862). Shiloh pitted General Ulysses S. Grant's 42,000-man Union force against 40,000 Confederates under General Albert S. Johnston. Grant lost 13,000 men, and the Confederates lost more than 10,000 in a battle that resulted in a strategic stalemate on the war's western front.

Back in Virginia, the Seven Days saw the placement of Robert E. Lee at the head of the South's major army, which he renamed the Army of Northern Virginia. Lee led his forces in a brilliant offensive against the always-cautious McClellan, launching daring attacks at Mechanicsville, Gaines Mill, Savage's Station, Frayser's Farm, and Malvern Hill. In fact, Lee lost twice as many men as his adversary, but he won a profound psychological victory. McClellan retreated back up the peninsula all the way to the James River.

Back to Bull Run

Appalled and heartbroken by McClellan's repeated failure to seize the initiative, Lincoln desperately cast about for a general to replace him. On July 11, the president appointed Henry W. Halleck. It was not a good choice. Halleck, whose unflattering nickname among the troops was "Old Brains," dispatched a regrouped army into

Virginia under John Pope, but Lee met him with more than half the Army of Northern Virginia. At Cedar Mountain on August 9, "Stonewall" Jackson drove Pope back toward Manassas Junction, then Lee sent the "Stonewall Brigade" to flank Pope and outmarch him to Manassas. After destroying the Union supply depot, Jackson took a position near the old Bull Run battlefield. Pope lumbered into position to attack Jackson on August 29, just as Lee sent a wing of his army, under James Longstreet, against Pope's left on August 30.

The action at this Second Battle of Bull Run was devastating. Pope reeled back across the Potomac. At this point, the "invading" Union army had been effectively swept out of Virginia, and the Confederates went on the offensive. For the North, it was the low point of the war.

Perryville and Antietam

Lee was a keen student of Napoleonic strategy and tactics, the key to which was the principle of acting always with audacity and boldness. Thus, Lee boldly and audaciously conceived a double offensive: in the West, an invasion of Kentucky; in the East, an invasion of Maryland. Neither of these so-called "border states" had seceded, yet both were slave states, and capturing them would significantly expand the Confederacy. Moreover, if Louisville, Kentucky, fell to the Confederates, Indiana and Ohio would be open to invasion, and control of the Great Lakes might pass to the rebels. For the Union, the war could be lost.

But things didn't happen this way. Confederate general Braxton Bragg delayed, lost the initiative, and was defeated at Perryville, Kentucky, on October 8, 1862. In Maryland, Lee's invasion went well—until a copy of his orders detailing troop placement fell into the hands of George McClellan (restored to command of the Army of the Potomac after Halleck's disastrous performance at Second Bull Run). The Union general was able to mass 70,000 troops in front of Lee at Sharpsburg, Maryland, along Antietam Creek. On September 17, in the bloodiest single day of fighting up to that time, McClellan drove Lee back to Virginia. Indeed, only the belated, last-minute arrival of a division under A. P. Hill saved Lee's forces from total annihilation.

Vital Statistics

Although Antietam was a Union victory, McClellan lost more troops than Lee: 12,000 versus 10,000.

Emancipation Proclaimed—More or Less

Bloody and nearly a draw, Antietam was hardly the military turning point of the war, but it was nevertheless a momentous battle. Lincoln seized it as the platform from which to issue his "preliminary" Emancipation Proclamation.

The fact is that Lincoln had never been a committed, enthusiastic advocate of emancipation. To be sure, he personally hated slavery ("As I would not be a slave, so I would not own slaves," he once declared), but as president, he was sworn to uphold the Constitution, which clearly protected slavery in the slave states. More pragmatically, Lincoln feared that declaring the slaves immediately and universally free would propel the four slave-holding border states into the Confederate fold. For many Northerners, the moral basis of the Civil War *was* the issue of emancipation, but Lincoln moved cautiously.

In August 1861, Lincoln prevailed on Congress to declare slaves in the rebellious states "contraband" property. As such, they could be seized by the federal government, which could then refuse to return them. Congress, dominated by abolitionist Radical Repub-licans, was always several jumps ahead of the president when it came to emancipation. In March 1862, Congress passed a law *forbidding* army officers from returning fugitive slaves. In July, it enacted legislation freeing slaves confiscated from owners "engaged in rebellion." In addition, the Militia Act authorized the president to use freed slaves in the army. With these acts, Lincoln's government edged closer to emancipation.

Secretary of State William H. Seward warned that a proclamation of emancipation would ring hollow down the depressingly long corridor of Union defeats. It was not until Antietam that Lincoln felt confident enough to issue the preliminary proclamation on September 23, 1862. This document did not free the slaves, but rather, warned slave owners living in states "still in rebellion on January 1, 1863," that their slaves would be declared "forever free." When that deadline came and passed, Lincoln issued the "final" Emancipation Proclamation, which set free only those slaves in areas of the Confederacy that were not under the control of the Union army (areas under Union control were no longer, technically, in rebellion); slaves in the border states were not liberated.

Timid, even disappointing as the Emancipation Proclamation may seem from a modern perspective, it served to galvanize the North by explicitly and officially elevating the war to a higher moral plane: slavery was now the central issue of the great Civil War.

The Least You Need to Know

◆ John Brown's October 16, 1859, raid on Harpers Ferry galvanized the abolitionist movement and suggested that war between the North and the South was inevitable.

◆ Plagued by cautious or inept commanders, the Union army performed poorly in the first months of the war.

◆ The Emancipation Proclamation was a fairly timid document, which reflected Lincoln's first priority: to preserve the Union, not necessarily to free the slaves.

Chapter 20

Bloody Road to Appomattox and Beyond (1863–1876)

In This Chapter

- ◆ Gettysburg and Vicksburg: turning point of the war
- ◆ Lincoln's ultimate commander: Ulysses S. Grant
- ◆ "Total war": Sherman's March to the Sea
- ◆ The assassination of Lincoln
- ◆ Reconstruction and bitterness in the South
- ◆ Andrew Johnson's impeachment; election of Rutherford B. Hayes

No face in American history is more familiar, better loved, or more terrible than that of Abraham Lincoln. Fortunately for us, famed Civil War photographer Mathew Brady was there to photograph it. Written into the face of the sixteenth president is a hard early life in the backwoods, an infinite gentleness, and an infinite sorrow. Lincoln's burden is unimaginable; he had a mission to save the Union, even if doing so cost more than half a million lives.

Through the long, murderous summer of 1862, the president despaired. Lincoln was no military man, but he had a sound and simple grasp of strategy, and he saw that Generals Don Carlos Buell and George B. McClellan failed to press their gains toward decisive victories. Frustrated, Lincoln removed Buell from command of the Army of the Ohio and replaced him with William S. Rosecrans in late October 1862. The next month, he put Ambrose E. Burnside in McClellan's place as commander of the Army of the Potomac. Rosecrans scored a very costly victory at Murfreesboro, Tennessee (December 31, 1862–January 3, 1863), forcing Braxton Bragg out of Tennessee, but Burnside suffered a terrible defeat at Fredericksburg, Virginia. He had tried to regain the initiative for the Union forces by renewing a drive on Richmond, but faltered at the Rappahannock River and was mauled by Lee's army. On December 13, Burnside hurled a series of assaults against the Confederate defenses at Fredericksburg. He not only failed to penetrate the Confederate lines, but lost more than 12,000 men in the process.

American Echo

Gone are the proud hopes, the high aspirations that swelled our bosoms a few days ago. Once more unsuccessful, and only a bloody record to show our men were brave.

—New York soldier William Lusk, letter to his mother, December 16, 1862, after Fredericksburg

A month after Fredericksburg, Lincoln replaced Burnside with "Fighting Joe" Hooker, who led the Army of the Potomac at Chancellorsville (May 1 through 3, 1863) in the wilderness of northern Virginia, again aiming to take Richmond. Hooker was defeated—brilliantly—by Stonewall Jackson (who, however, lost his life in the campaign, accidentally shot by one of his own troops). Lincoln replaced Hooker with George Gordon Meade on June 29, 1863, just 2 days before Union and Confederate forces clashed at an obscure Pennsylvania hamlet called Gettysburg.

Four Score and Seven

Anxious to move the war into Union territory and thereby undermine the Northern will to continue the fight, Lee invaded Pennsylvania with an army of about 75,000. He had not planned to do battle with the forces of the North in the vicinity of Gettysburg, a village distinguished only in that it was positioned at an important crossroads, but the fact is that Lieutenant General A. P. Hill's corps of Confederates needed shoes. Short of manufacturing capability, the South always had a difficult time keeping its soldiers shod. On June 30, while marching toward Gettysburg in search of shoes, Hill came under fire by cavalry under Union Brigadier General John Buford. The battle began in earnest on the next day, July 1.

At first, the encounter did not go well for the Union. Hill's troops killed the dashing and much-loved Major General John F. Reynolds, commander of the Union I Corps, almost as soon as he came onto the field. Despite shock and confusion, his troops held their ground until reinforcements arrived. But in the afternoon, Hill and Lieutenant General R. S. Ewell joined forces in an attack that routed the Federals through the town of Gettysburg. The forces regrouped and rallied on Cemetery Ridge, where they were joined by fresh troops from the south and east. The Confederates arrayed their forces in an encircling position, encompassing Seminary Ridge, parallel to Cemetery Ridge.

Vital Statistics

Of 88,289 Union troops engaged at Gettysburg, 3,155 died on the field, 14,529 were wounded (many of these subsequently died), and 5,365 were listed as "missing." Confederate figures are less reliable. Of approximately 75,000 troops engaged, 3,903 were killed outright, 18,735 were wounded (a large percentage mortally), and 5,425 were missing.

Thus, the field was set for the second day. Robert E. Lee attacked on July 2, but was unable to achieve the tactician's Holy Grail, a double envelopment of the Union forces, although he did inflict heavy casualties. Nevertheless, on July 3, Lee still held the initiative, and this being the case, he was unwilling to withdraw. Pressured to achieve a decisive victory, Lee committed what was for him a rare tactical error. Persuaded that a triumph here and now, at Gettysburg, well into Northern territory, would turn the war decisively in favor of the Confederacy, he ordered a direct attack—across open country—on the Union's center.

Fifteen thousand Confederate troops advanced against the Union position on Cemetery Ridge. Exploiting the advantages of high ground, the Union pounded the advancing rebels with heavy artillery and musket fire. Major General George Pickett's division pressed the attack up to the Ridge. The division was decimated: Two brigadiers fell; the third was severely wounded; and all 15 of Pickett's regimental commanders were killed or wounded. Briefly, 150 men from the division, led by Brigadier General Lewis Armistead (who perished in the effort), raised the Confederate banner above Cemetery Ridge—only to be cut down or captured. In the end, "Pickett's Charge," perhaps the single most famous military action in the American Civil War, resulted in the death or wounding of 10,000 of the 15,000 men in Pickett's division.

Watching the survivors return from the failed assault that third awful day, Lee said to a subordinate: "It is all my fault." Hoping, in effect, to win the war at Gettysburg, Lee had suffered a terrible defeat.

Although the losses on both sides were staggering, they were hardest on the Confederates. One very simple fact was at the foundation of this very complex war: the North, with more men and hardware and money than the South, could spend more of all three and still go on fighting. Lee was right. The Battle of Gettysburg *was* a turning point, but it did not turn the war in his favor. From here to the end, despite more Union defeats to come, it became increasingly clear that the North would ultimately prevail.

Vicksburg and Chattanooga

Northern attention focused most sharply on Gettysburg as the battle that foiled the Confederate invasion of the North. However, while that battle was being fought, Union forces under General Ulysses S. Grant were bringing to a conclusion a long and frustrating campaign against Vicksburg, Mississippi, the Confederacy's seemingly impregnable stronghold on the Mississippi River. The prize here was not just a fortress, but control of the great river. When the South lost the Mississippi, the Confederacy would be split in two, the western states unable to communicate with the East or to supply reinforcements to it. Grant had campaigned—in vain—against Vicksburg during the fall and winter of 1862 to 1863. On July 4, 1863, after a long siege that inflicted great suffering on the people of the town, he took the prize.

Grant next turned his attention to Chattanooga, which occupied a critical position in a bend of the great Tennessee River. Union forces under William S. Rosecrans had ousted Braxton Bragg from Chattanooga in early September 1863, but, reinforced, Bragg returned to engage Rosecrans at the Battle of Chickamauga on September 19 and 20. Bragg fielded 66,000 men against Rosecrans's 58,000. By the second day of this bloody struggle along Chickamauga Creek in northwestern Georgia, the Confederates had driven much of the Union army, in disarray, from the field.

Complete disaster was averted by General George H. Thomas, who heroically held the Union left flank and for this was dubbed the "Rock of Chickamauga." Moreover, Bragg failed to press his advantage, laying incomplete siege around Chattanooga while also detaching troops to attack Knoxville. By failing to act with sharper focus, Bragg allowed Grant sufficient time to arrive, on October 23, and reinforce the Army of the Cumberland (now under Thomas's command). Sixty thousand Union troops now faced Bragg's reduced forces, about 40,000 men, in two battles set in the rugged terrain overlooking Chattanooga.

The Battle of Lookout Mountain (November 24) was called the "Battle Above the Clouds" because it was fought at an elevation of 1,100 feet above the Tennessee River and above a thick blanket of fog. The Battle of Missionary Ridge followed (November 25). In these two engagements, Thomas and Grant decisively defeated Bragg, with the result that Tennessee and the Tennessee River fell into Union hands.

To Richmond

To many Americans, George Meade was the hero of Gettysburg—the great turning-point battle of the war. However, President Lincoln observed that Meade, like so many of his other generals, failed to capitalize on victory. Meade could have pursued Lee's defeated army out of Gettysburg and into the South. Had he been sufficiently aggressive, he might have destroyed the Army of Northern Virginia right then and there. But, citing the exhaustion of his men, he refused to drive them any farther. Lee, defeated, was permitted to slip away, his army battered and reduced, but still intact.

In contrast to Meade and so many other Union commanders, Ulysses S. Grant had demonstrated a willingness to fight and then fight some more. Thus, with the war entering its fourth year, Lincoln finally found his general. In March 1864, the president named Grant general in chief of all the Union armies.

The new commander's strategy was starkly simple: exploit the North's superiority in industrial strength and in population. This meant that Grant and his subordinate commanders could not afford to be fearful of sacrificing men and material. Grant was so single-minded in pursuing this strategy that some men within his own ranks cursed him as "The Butcher."

Grant put the Union's fiercest warrior, William Tecumseh Sherman, in command of the so-called western armies (which actually fought in the middle South). Meade retained command of the Army of the Potomac—albeit under Grant's watchful eye. Using these two principal forces, Grant relentlessly kept pressure on the South's Army of Tennessee and the Army of Northern Virginia.

> **American Echo**
>
> I propose to fight it out on this line, if it takes all summer.
>
> —Ulysses S. Grant, telegram to the War Department, May 11, 1864, from Cold Harbor

The Wilderness Campaign (May through June 1864) was the first test of the strategy of *attrition*. Grant directed Meade, leading a force of 100,000, to attack 70,000 men of Lee's Army of Northern Virginia in the tangled woodlands just 50 miles northwest of Richmond. The Battle of the Wilderness (May 5 and 6) cost some 18,000 Union lives. Undaunted, "The Butcher" then ordered Meade southeast to Spotsylvania

What's the Word?

A *war of attrition* is waged by a numerically stronger force against one that is numerically weaker. The assumption is that, by the application of constant stress, the weaker force will crumble, while the stronger force, despite losses, will endure. This theory was the foundation of Grant's strategy.

Courthouse, where more than 14,000 Union soldiers were killed between May 8 and 18. Still Grant pushed, attacking Lee's right at Cold Harbor, just north of Richmond. Thirteen thousand Union troops fell between June 3 and June 12.

Following Cold Harbor, Grant marched south of the James River and began the Petersburg Campaign, laying siege to this important rail center just south of Richmond. The siege was costly and consumed nearly a year, from June 1864 to April 1865, but it succeeded in hemming in Lee, who was forced into a desperate, static defense in an effort to stave off the final assault on Richmond.

In order to restore maneuverability to his army, Lee attempted to draw off some of Grant's strength by detaching Jubal Early, with the late Stonewall Jackson's old corps, in a surprise assault against Washington, D.C., in mid-June. Although the capital was briefly menaced, the attack could not be sustained, and Union general Philip Sheridan pursued Early into the Shenandoah Valley, defeating him at Cedar Creek on October 19.

Just 3 weeks later, Lincoln was elected to a second term by a comfortable margin. Clearly, the North was prepared to continue the fight, and the defenders of Petersburg—starving, sick, and exhausted— at last broke in March 1865. On April 2, Lee evacuated Richmond. Jefferson Davis and the entire Confederate government fled the Southern capital.

The March to the Sea

While Grant concentrated on taking Richmond, William Tecumseh Sherman, after leaving Chattanooga in early May 1864, invaded Georgia with 100,000 men. Sherman was opposed by Joseph P. Johnston's army of 60,000, which repeatedly fell back during the onslaught, although Johnston scored a victory at Kennesaw Mountain on June 27 when a headstrong Sherman made the mistake of launching an assault uphill. By early July, Johnston had assumed a position defending the key rail center of Atlanta. However, President Jefferson Davis, disappointed by Johnston's many retreats, brashly replaced him with General John B. Hood. A heroic but utterly reckless commander, Hood attacked Sherman and lost. By September, Hood abandoned Atlanta, and the Northern army's occupation of this major city greatly boosted Union morale even as it deprived the South of a key industrial and rail center.

After the fall of Atlanta, Hood played a desperate gambit by invading Tennessee, hoping that Sherman would pursue him there and turn away from the Southern heartland. But Sherman had his own strategy. Later generations would call it "total war"—war waged against not only an enemy army, but against "enemy" civilians—men, women, and children. Instead of pursuing Hood himself, Sherman detached General George H. Thomas to do that. With the main force of his army, Sherman then marched from Atlanta to the Atlantic coast. The "March to the Sea" burned a broad, bitter swath of destruction all the way to Savannah.

American Echo

War is at best barbarism …. Its glory is all moonshine. It is only those who have neither fired a shot, nor heard the shrieks and groans of wounded who cry aloud for blood, more vengeance, more desolation. War is hell.

—William Tecumseh Sherman, address to the graduating class of the Michigan Military Academy, June 19, 1879

In the meantime, General Hood did win a battle at Franklin, Tennessee, on November 30, but General Thomas triumphed at Nashville on December 15 and 16, 1864, sending the ragged remnants of Hood's army back toward Georgia. Confederate General Joseph P. Johnston, now in command of the greatly reduced Army of Tennessee, engaged Sherman several times as the Union army stormed through the Carolinas in the spring of 1865. On April 13, 1865, Sherman occupied Raleigh, North Carolina, and on April 26 at Durham Station, Johnston formally surrendered his army.

Mr. McLean's House

Although sporadic fighting would continue west of the Mississippi until the end of May, the principal land campaign of the Civil War ended at Durham Station on April 26. However, an earlier event is traditionally considered the symbolic end of the Civil War.

Following the collapse of Petersburg and the evacuation of Richmond, Robert E. Lee's Army of Northern Virginia desperately foraged for food and arrived at Appomattox Courthouse, about 25 miles east of Lynchburg, Virginia. Lee's forces, which now stood at perhaps no more than 9,000 effective troops, were surrounded by the Army of the Potomac under General George Meade.

After heavy skirmishing on the morning of April 9, Lee concluded that his was a lost cause. He met Ulysses S. Grant, who pressed him to surrender all the Confederate armies, which were nominally under his command. Lee refused to do that, but his surrender of the Army of Northern Virginia, over which he had direct command, signaled the inevitable end of the war.

With Malice Toward Some

Confident now of ultimate victory, President Lincoln delivered a gentle, healing message in his Second Inaugural Address on March 4, 1865, calling for a consummation of the war with "malice toward none" and "charity for all" in an effort to "bind up the nation's wounds." Weary, careworn beyond imagining, Lincoln nevertheless looked forward to peace. On the evening of Good Friday, April 14, 1865, he and his wife, Mary Todd, sought a few hours of diversion in a popular comedy called *Our American Cousin*. The play was being presented at Ford's Theatre, a short distance from the White House.

The President Attends a Comedy

John Wilkes Booth was the popular young scion of America's foremost theatrical family. Although he had no part in *Our American Cousin*, Booth was desperate to play a role in the drama of the great Civil War, which was now rushing to its conclusion. Back in 1864, the Maryland-born white supremacist had concocted a plot to kidnap Lincoln and ransom him in exchange for Confederate prisoners of war. That plan came to nothing, and now, with surrender in the air, there was no point in simply kidnapping the Union president. Booth wanted raw revenge. He conspired with a small band of followers, George A. Atzerodt, David Herold, and a former Confederate soldier called Lewis Paine (real name Louis Thornton Powell). They plotted to murder Lincoln and also to kill Vice President Andrew Johnson and Secretary of State William H. Seward.

On April 14, Atzerodt suddenly backed out of his assignment to kill Johnson. In the meantime, Herold held Paine's horse while Paine broke into Seward's residence. He stabbed and clubbed Seward, an aged man who was recuperating from injuries suffered in a carriage accident. It was a bloody scene: Seward, his son Augustus, and his daughter Fanny were all injured, as were a State Department messenger and a male nurse. Yet none of them died.

Booth was more efficient.

He simply walked into the Ford's Theatre, entered the president's box, raised his derringer, pointed it between Abraham Lincoln's left ear and spine, and then squeezed off a single shot. Booth leaped from the box onto the stage, shouting "Sic semper tyrannis!"—Thus ever to tyrants—the state motto of Virginia. But Booth's right spur had caught on the Treasury Regiment banner festooning the president's box, and he hit the stage full force with his left foot, which snapped just above the instep. As audience and actors stood in stunned silence, Booth limped across the boards and made a clean getaway into Maryland and then Virginia. He was not found until April 26, when he was cornered in a barn near Fredericksburg. Union soldiers set fire to the barn and then, seeing the actor's form silhouetted by the flames, a sergeant named Boston Corbett fired a shot that fatally wounded the assassin.

Reconstruction Deconstructed

The mortally wounded president was carried, comatose, to a house across the street from the theater. There Lincoln died at 7:22 the next morning. With him died any hope of "malice toward none" and "charity for all." Booth murdered Lincoln to avenge the South. In fact, the South became the most thoroughly brutalized victim of the assassination.

As the war was winding down, President Lincoln had formulated plans to set up loyal governments in the Southern states as quickly as possible. New governments had already been formed in Louisiana, Tennessee, and Arkansas, but Congress refused to recognize them. Radical Republicans, wishing to delay the restoration in part to keep Democrats out of Washington, passed the Wade-Davis Reconstruction Bill, which would have put off the process of readmission to the Union pending the signature of loyalty oaths. Lincoln had "pocket vetoed" the measure—declining to sign it before the end of the congressional session, thereby effectively killing it, at least until it might be introduced in the next session of Congress.

After Lincoln was assassinated, his vice president, Andrew Johnson, modified the Wade-Davis plan by issuing amnesty to anyone who took an oath pledging loyalty to the Union now and in the future. Johnson also required that the states ratify the Thirteenth Amendment (which freed the slaves), explicitly abolish slavery in their own state constitutions, repudiate debts incurred while in rebellion, and formally declare secession null and void. By the end of 1865, all of the secessionist states, except for Texas, had complied.

Congress, however, was not satisfied with Johnson's program, which, representatives and senators feared, restored power to the very individuals who had brought rebellion in the first place. Moreover, the readmitted states persisted in keeping former slaves in subservience. To correct this problem, Congress passed in 1866 the Freedman's Bureau Act and the Civil Rights Act, both intended to ensure African American equality under the law. When Johnson vetoed these acts, Republicans responded by refusing to recognize the legitimacy of the Southern states and overrode the veto.

Republicans also introduced the Fourteenth Amendment, declaring African Americans to be citizens and prohibiting states from discriminating against any class of citizen.

When the Southern state governments created under Johnson's plan refused to ratify the Fourteenth Amendment, Congress passed a series of Reconstruction Acts in 1867, effectively placing the South under military occupation.

The military governments quickly enfranchised African Americans, and Congress forced acceptance of the Fourteenth Amendment by refusing to recognize new state governments until those governments had ratified it. Former Confederate leaders were explicitly barred from participating in the creation of the new governments.

Articles of Impeachment

In defiance of Congress, Johnson deliberately interfered with the enforcement of the reconstruction laws, which he considered harsh and unjust. When, at last, in 1868, Johnson dismissed Secretary of War Edwin M. Stanton, House Republicans charged him with having violated the Tenure of Office Act. Passed in 1867, this act (later found unconstitutional by the Supreme Court) barred a president from removing, without the Senate's approval, any officeholder who had been appointed with the Senate's consent. The House impeached Johnson, but after a trial spanning March through May 1868, the Senate acquitted him by a single vote.

No other president would ever again be impeached until 1998, when, amid a banal sexual scandal, the Republican-controlled House brought impeachment proceedings against Democrat Bill Clinton.

Enter "His Fraudulency"

With Andrew Johnson neutralized, the Radical Republicans visited a harsh reconstruction program on the South. Intentions of great nobility were tainted by a spirit of vengeance and motives of political advantage. Under Reconstruction, African Americans were given equal rights; state-supported free public school systems were established; labor laws were made fairer to employees; and tax laws were more generally equitable. Laudable as these objectives were, however, radical reconstruction also exacted a heavy tax burden and led to widespread, ruinous corruption. In many places, uneducated former slaves were thrust into high-level government positions for which they were wholly unprepared. Northern white opportunists took advantage of the South's prostration through loan sharking and buying up distressed properties on the cheap.

Deprived of power by the federal government, Southern whites set up shadow governments and established the Ku Klux Klan and other white-supremacist vigilante groups. During the early 1870s, white resistance to reconstruction often turned violent. Blacks were terrorized by white-hooded Klansmen, "night riders," who administered beatings, burned down black homes, and even murdered, by means of especially brutal lynchings, any blacks deemed "trouble makers."

In this tumultuous atmosphere, the presidential election of 1876 resulted in a majority of popular votes going to Democrat Samuel J. Tilden. However, the Republicans challenged and reversed the *electoral* vote tally in the three Southern states they still controlled under Reconstruction legislation. The Republicans effectively stole the election from Tilden and gave it to their candidate, Rutherford B. Hayes.

After months of wrangling, both sides agreed to send the votes to a special congressional commission. It ruled Hayes the winner after a secret bargain was struck with Democrats, whereby the Republicans pledged to end Reconstruction in exchange for the White House. Southern blacks were now entirely at the mercy of Southern whites, and, freed from slavery, they entered a new period of oppression. As for Hayes, he was dubbed by a cynical press "His Fraudulency" and served a single term as best he could, but was doomed to be regarded as one of the nation's least popular and least effective presidents.

The Least You Need to Know

- ◆ Victory in the Civil War was the result of numbers: the North had more men, money, and manufacturing capacity than the South.

- ◆ The impeachment of Lincoln's successor, President Andrew Johnson, in 1868 was a measure of how bitterly divided the nation remained after the Civil War.

- ◆ Republicans and Democrats struck a backroom deal that elevated Rutherford B. Hayes to the presidency in 1876 in exchange for Republican abandonment of Reconstruction.

Part 5

Rebuilding the House

The years following the Civil War saw the full-scale settlement of the American West and increased pressure on the Indians, whose tribes were broadcast across the plains and mountains. War between settlers and Native Americans, more or less chronic since the days of Columbus, now became acute, and the U.S. Army was called upon to fight three decades of "Indian Wars." Against this background, the West produced real-life legends: cattle barons, cowboys, outlaws, and fortune seekers, as well as fortune makers. The late nineteenth century was an era marked by technological triumphs, by the creation of financial empires, and by the corruption of crooked politics. Good and bad, all seemed bigger than life, as you'll see in the chapters that follow.

Chapter 21

Sea to Shining Sea (1862–1878)

In This Chapter

- The Homestead Act of 1862
- Sodbusters settle the prairies and plains
- Expansion of overland mail and freight operations
- The transcontinental railroad

Armies, money, and the will to continue the fight won the Civil War and restored the Union. There was something else as well; call it the "American Dream."

The phrase rings hollow to some jaded ears today, but in the mid-nineteenth century, the American Dream had a foundation as solid as it was vast. Even amid the awful carnage of a war that tore them apart, Americans looked west. There, it seemed, was refuge from the war. There was a place for new beginnings. There was the future. And what is the future, if it is not a dream?

Home Sweet Home

At least as early as the 1830s, various groups clamored for free distribution of the vast public lands of the West. In 1848, the Free-Soil Party was organized to oppose the extension of slavery into the territories newly acquired as a result of the Mexican War. The party failed to carry a single state in the presidential election that year, but its idea of regulating federal distribution of public lands was one means of stopping the spread of slavery into the territories.

When the Republican Party was founded in 1854, most of the "Free-Soilers" abandoned their dead-end party and joined the new one, which adopted distribution of federal lands as a plank of its 1860 platform. This issue fanned the flames of Southern secession; the slave states were always opposed to any policy that would bring more free states into the Union. But when the Civil War broke out, Southern opposition became a moot point.

On May 20, 1862, President Lincoln signed into law the Homestead Act, which granted 160 acres of public land in the West as a homestead to "any person who is the head of a family, or who has arrived at the age of 21 years, and is a citizen of the United States, or who shall have filed his declaration of intention to become such."

This was no *free* gift. Although the homesteader had only to pay a modest filing fee, he did have to live on the land for 5 years and make certain improvements—the most important of which was the construction of a dwelling. After these conditions had been satisfied, the homesteader received clear title to the land. Alternatively, a homesteader could "pre-empt" the land after only 6 months' residence by purchasing it at the rate of $1.25 per acre. If the settler could scrape together $50—a very substantial sum in the 1860s and beyond the means of many homesteaders—he could augment his original grant with an additional 40 acres.

The Homestead Act was a bold experiment in public policy and was shaped by years of hard experience with the distribution of unsettled land. Traditionally, such territories had drawn unscrupulous speculators, who figured out ways to come into control of vast acreage and make quick fortunes. The new law sought to avoid such abuses and aspired to a high degree of democracy. For the most part, it succeeded, although there were plenty of scoundrels and con artists eager to burrow through legal loopholes. The greatest culprits in fraud were big railroads and big mining companies seeking to acquire large tracts of land at the public expense.

Despite the abuses, however, the Homestead Act opened the West to hundreds of thousands of Americans. The new settlers were different from the first waves of

Westerners. The solitary trapper and mountain man, the bachelor soldier, the grizzled prospector now made way for the farmer and the family, and with the family came stable, permanent communities.

Timber was a scarce commodity on the tree-less plains, but sod was abundant. The very soil that posed such a formidable obstacle to farming—at least until the manufacture of John Deere's "Grand Detour Plow"—was a durable, dense, and (quite literally) dirt-cheap building material.

 Vital Statistics

By the end of the nine-teenth century, some 600,000 farmers had received clear title under the Homestead Act to approximately 80 million acres of formerly public land.

The work of the sod frontier was back breaking. Even using the Deere plow, "busting" the sod into viable crop rows was no easy task. For the many homesteaders who had the misfortune to stake claims at a distance from creeks and streams, there was the added burden of digging a well. Few *sodbusters* could afford to hire a drilling rig, so this work, like most of the work on the prairie farm, had to be done by hand. With nothing more than pick and spade, homesteaders dug to depths of as much as 300 feet, where they were exposed to the dangers of cave-in as well as asphyxiation from subterranean gases such as methane and carbon monoxide. Not that breaking your back and risking your life even guaranteed you'd find water. If you came up dry by the time you hit bedrock or shale, you had no choice but to start digging somewhere else.

Water in a well goes nowhere unless you take it somewhere. As the prairie earth yielded an abundance of natural building material, so the winds that fiercely scoured the prairie afforded a natural source of energy. In 1854, a Connecticut tool-shop tin-kerer named David Halladay invented a windmill with a vane that allowed it to pivot into the wind; moreover, the centrifugal force of the turning blades adjusted the pitch of the mill blades so that the gusty, often vio-lent winds would not tear them apart. A crankshaft transformed the rotary motion of the mill into the up-and-down action needed to operate a pump. Using wind power, hun-dreds of gallons of water could be moved each day to irrigate crops and quench the thirst of livestock.

 **What's the Word?**

Plains homesteaders who built sod houses were called **sodbusters**. The houses them-selves were often referred to as **soddies**.

The sodbusters turned stubborn soil and fierce winds into assets. They also found strength in another, less tangible, but no less harsh, reality of prairie life. Limitless spaces and howling winds were a trial for the spirit. The emotional demands of the wide-open spaces served to reinforce the solidarity of the family as a bulwark against loneliness, despair, and danger. Until recently, historians of the West have largely ignored the role of women in settling the region. For the traditional chroniclers, the western story has been overwhelmingly dominated by men. With the coming of the homesteaders, however, particularly those who settled the bleak sod frontier, women increasingly figured as sources of sustenance and civilization, as secure anchors in a sea of prairie grass. Around them and because of them, the family grew, and the West was no longer the exclusive province of the lone trapper, hunter, prospector, soldier, or cowboy.

Beyond the family, the uncompromising conditions of the prairie lands helped bond neighbor with distant neighbor, gradually forging communities where there had been none before. Neighbors were a new phenomenon in the West; for the trapper, the hunter, the prospector, the cowboy, and the soldier had little need for a traditional community.

Ruts and Rails

Transportation and westward movement have always been a chicken-and-egg proposition in this country. Farmers and others clamored for better and cheaper transportation, while freight carriers did what they could to promote a level of settlement that would make service to the outlying regions profitable. The earliest western transportation was river-borne, with shallow-draft flatboats abounding on the muddy Missouri and its tributaries. Then, spurred by the discovery of gold in California, stagecoach and freight entrepreneurs took the plunge, investing in coaches, livestock, and road improvements.

By the 1850s, Adams Express Company and Wells, Fargo & Company were engaged in cutthroat competition for California freighting. The success of California overland operations prompted others to establish routes elsewhere in the West, often with government subsidy in the form of postal contracts. By 1854, William H. Russell and William B. Waddell merged with their principal competitor, Alexander Majors, to create a freighting empire that endured until the Civil War.

The other giants of freighting in the West included George Chorpenning, John Butterfield, John M. Hockaday, and Ben Holladay (who was so successful that he was dubbed the "Napoleon of the Plains"). Yet if the opportunity for profit was great, the overhead—in livestock, personnel, and maintenance of routes—was staggering. Moreover, stage and freight lines were preyed upon by robbers (popularly called road agents), including the likes of Henry Plummer, Black Bart, the James Gang, and many others who entered into Western legend and lore. Sooner or later, most overland freighters went belly up. Those who survived for any length of time were either wiped out by the advancing railroads or learned to coordinate their service with the new rail lines, serving the widely dispersed stations with feeder routes.

The Great Iron Road

After the success of the Erie Canal, completed in 1825 and linking New York City with the Great Lakes, other eastern seaport cities rushed to build systems of canals. Baltimore was an exception and chose to invest not in a canal, but in a brand-new technology: the railroad. Begun in 1828, the Baltimore and Ohio Railroad reached the Ohio River, principal artery to the West, by 1852. At about this time, railroads were also being built in the Midwest. The Chicago and Rock Island (the "Rock Island Line") became the first rail route to the Mississippi River in 1854. By 1856, the route bridged the river and penetrated the fertile farmlands of Iowa. Other midwestern lines soon followed.

Practically from the start of all this rail activity, in 1832, a Dr. Hartwell Carver published articles in the *New York Courier & Enquirer* proposing a transcontinental railroad to be built on eight million acres of government land from Lake Michigan to Oregon (then the only coastal territory to which the United States had any legitimate claim). Carver's scheme came to nothing, and 10 years later, Asa Whitney, a New Yorker engaged in the China trade, proposed to Congress that the United States sell him nearly 80 million acres, from Lake Michigan to the Columbia River, at 16 cents per acre. Whitney planned to resell parcels of the land to settlers and farmers, using the profits to push a railroad farther and farther West in a pay-as-you-go fashion.

Whitney butted heads with Missouri senator Thomas Hart Benton, who wanted a transcontinental railroad with an eastern terminus at St. Louis rather than Chicago, as Whitney proposed. Benton got Whitney's plan permanently tabled and, in 1848, persuaded Congress to fund a railroad survey led by his son-in-law, John C. Frémont. The recklessly conducted survey resulted in the deaths of 10 of Frémont's party, frozen or starved in a Rocky Mountain blizzard, and ultimately proved inconclusive.

While arguments over routes raged, the means of financing a transcontinental railroad were being negotiated. Railroad lobbyists proposed a system of government land grants alternating checkerboard fashion north and south of the proposed right-of-way. The railroads would sell their land to finance construction, and the presence of the railroad would greatly increase the value not only of the purchasers' land, but of the alternate sections retained by the government. A series of such grants was immediately apportioned to a number of western rail lines.

In 1853, Congress authorized Secretary of War Jefferson Davis to conduct detailed surveys of potential transcontinental rail routes. The result of the hasty surveys was, again, inconclusive (although they added significantly to the general knowledge of the West). It soon became apparent that Davis—the Mississippian who would become president of the Confederacy with the outbreak of civil war—stacked the deck in favor of a southerly route.

Remember This

In 1857, Russell, Majors & Waddell secured a big government contract to supply the army to fight what threatened to become a war against rebellious Mormons in Utah. The firm paid top dollar to buy additional wagons and hire additional crews, but the operation became the target of Mormon guerrilla attacks, a devastating winter, and ultimately, federal default on contracts. Facing financial collapse, William H. Russell saw his company's salvation in making a rapid transition from slow freighting to express mail service.

To make a dramatic demonstration of the speed and efficiency of his company, Russell invented what he called the Pony Express. He promised to deliver mail from St. Joseph, Missouri, to Sacramento, California—a distance just 44 miles shy of an even 2,000—in 10 days.

The unit would have no passengers and no coaches. Instead, the Express would achieve speed by a relay of ponies and riders stretched across the continent.

Russell had purchased 500 semi-wild outlaw horses and had 80 riders continuously en route, 40 westbound, 40 eastbound, who had answered his ads calling for "daring young men, preferably orphans."

Financially, the Pony Express was a failure, charging a staggering $5 per half ounce (soon lowered to $2) of mail that actually cost the company an even more staggering $16 to deliver. Within 19 months, the Pony Express was out of business, rendered obsolete by the completion of transcontinental telegraph lines. But in 650,000 miles of travel, the company lost only one consignment and managed to capture the nation's imagination.

The wrangling might have gone on forever had it not been for one remarkable man. Theodore Dehone Judah (1826–1863), son of an Episcopal clergyman in Bridgeport, Connecticut, was a civil engineer with a genius for building railroads. In 1854, Colonel Charles Wilson, president of California's Sacramento Valley Railroad, commissioned Judah to survey a right-of-way from Sacramento to the gold-mining town of Folsom. Judah reported to Wilson that this stretch of track could serve as something far more significant than a link to little Folsom. The track was ideally suited to be the Pacific end of a transcontinental railroad. Wilson and other backers were very excited, but then the gold petered out at Folsom, and the rail line went no farther.

Judah did not stop, however. He lobbied Washington, even as he continued searching for a viable pass across the Sierra Nevada. A frontier pharmacist, Daniel "Doc" Strong, pointed out a likely route, and right then and there, he and Judah drew up a rough-and-ready agreement to incorporate a Pacific railroad association. All that was lacking now was money. Lots of money. Undaunted, Judah rounded up seven backers, including four whose fortunes were destined to be made by the railroad: Collis P. Huntington and Mark Hopkins, partners in a hardware store; Leland Stanford, wholesale grocer; and Charles Crocker, dry goods merchant. Returning to Washington, D.C., Judah successfully lobbied for passage of the Pacific Railway Act of 1862, authorizing the Central Pacific and the Union Pacific railroads to begin construction of a transcontinental railroad. The Central Pacific would build from the West Coast eastward, and the Union Pacific would build westward from Omaha, Nebraska.

With the North and South torn apart by war, President Lincoln and Congress were eager to bind the northern part of the nation together along its east-west axis. They were so eager, in fact, that they provided railway entrepreneurs with unprecedented amounts of government subsidy. The Railway Act granted huge tracts of land to the railroad, along with massive construction loans, and, at the behest of Abraham Lincoln, multimillionaire congressman Oake Ames and his brother Oliver created one corporation to build the railroad and another corporation to finance the construction. The latter was named Crédit Mobilier, after the company that had successfully financed the French railway system 10 years earlier. The Ames brothers made investors an offer they couldn't refuse: Crédit Mobilier, run by the directors (principal investors) of the Union Pacific, was paid by the Union Pacific to build the Union Pacific. The directors made a profit on the railroad as well as on the cost of building it. The scheme was an open door to fraud, and construction bills were routinely padded.

In the end, scandal and greed could take nothing away from the heroism and wonder of what it meant actually to build a transcontinental railroad, especially in an age when earth was moved and iron rails laid not by machines, but by human muscle.

Under the leadership of Grenville Mellon Dodge and another ex-army general, John Stephen Casement, the Union Pacific began laying prodigious lengths of track—266 miles in 1866 alone. The tracks were set into place mostly by unskilled Irish immigrants, who received, in addition to their pay, room and board. On the Central Pacific, the bulk of the work force was Chinese, who were paid at about the same rate as the Irish but had to furnish their own tent accommodations and their own food.

Laying and spiking 500-pound rail sections was difficult enough, but these men—some 25,000 in all—faced other perils as well. They encountered brutal weather on the prairies and in the mountains, including summer floods, winter blizzards, and the ever-present danger of avalanche; attack from Sioux and Cheyenne, as the rails penetrated Indian hunting grounds in western Nebraska and southeastern Wyoming; and unceasing pressure from bosses, who had little love for Irish immigrants and even less for Chinese "coolies."

Taskmasters drove the laborers relentlessly, heedless of life and limb, because the Central Pacific and Union Pacific, although they would be joined, were actually in fierce competition with one another. The volume of their government land grants was directly proportional to the amount of track that was laid. In fact, in the absence of an officially predetermined meeting point for the converging tracks, survey parties laid out some 200 miles of overlapping, parallel, entirely redundant right-of-way. After parties of roadbed graders, called *roustabouts* (bridge workers were christened *bridge monkeys* and rail layers, *gandydancers*), passed each other—blasting away at hard rocks and almost at one another—U.S. secretary of the interior Orville H. Browning intervened by naming Promontory Summit, 56 miles west of Ogden, Utah, as the meeting point. (Many histories of the West confuse Promontory Summit with nearby Promontory Point.)

What's the Word?

Laborers included **roustabouts,** who graded roadbeds; **bridge monkeys,** who hastily cobbled together trestles over rivers and streams; and **gandydancers,** who actually laid and spiked the rails.

Golden Spike at Promontory

The ceremonial union of the two lines at Promontory Summit was set for May 8, 1869. Leland Stanford of the Central Pacific almost failed to arrive because of a train wreck. Thomas C. Durant of the Union Pacific was kidnapped en route and held hostage by tie cutters his company had not paid for months. Durant telegraphed for money and was released, delaying the ceremony by 2 days.

On May 10, 1869, workers and executives alike were at last prepared to savor their finest moment. But the event did not go quite as planned.

Chinese laborers, acutely aware of how Caucasians felt about them, were lowering the last rail into place when a photographer hollered, "Shoot!" The laborers dropped the quarter-ton rail and ran.

Then there was elegantly frock-coated Leland Stanford, who took upon himself the honor of joining the last eastbound and westbound rails with a single commemorative Golden Spike. It was wired to the telegraph, so that each blow would be transmitted across the nation.

Stanford raised the heavy sledge, brought it on down—and clean missed. After another embarrassing try, laborers in shirtsleeves lent a hand, and the deed was done. From sea to shining sea, the United States was bound by bands of iron.

The Least You Need to Know

- The Homestead Act of 1862 filled in the space between the Mississippi and the Pacific and brought to the West an unprecedented degree of family and community-based settlement.

- Construction of the great transcontinental railroad was an epic task compounded of bold imagination, limitless resolve, and great heroism, as well as rampant political and financial corruption.

- Technology, in the form of the transcontinental railroad, did more than politics to bind East and West into a single nation.

Chapter 22

The Warpath (1862–1891)

In This Chapter

- Indian roles in the Civil War
- The Santee Sioux uprising
- The victory of Red Cloud
- Futile campaigns, the War for the Black Hills, and Custer's Last Stand
- The defeat of the Nez Perce and Geronimo
- The massacre at Wounded Knee

The West was a land of many dreams, but what we seem to remember most vividly today are the nightmares. On the vast stage of prairie and mountain, the last act of a four-century tragedy was played out. The curtain had been raised by the crew of Christopher Columbus, who clashed with the people they called Indians on an island they called Hispaniola. From then on, warfare between Native Americans and European Americans was chronic and continuous. When whites and Indians did not start wars between themselves, Indians became embroiled in wars between whites: the French and Indian War, the Revolutionary War, the War of 1812, and finally, the Civil War.

Read any standard history of the Civil War, and you will learn that this epic struggle was mainly an eastern conflict. In the West, battles were smaller and less frequent—yet often, they were uglier.

Blue, Gray, and Red

The great fear of Union loyalists in the West was that Confederates would readily recruit Indian allies on the promise of securing for them land and other rights. To a limited extent, Confederate officials and sympathizers did drum up support from members of some eastern tribes, but both the North *and* South recruited troops from among tribes that had been "removed" west to Indian Territory: the Cherokees, Chickasaws, Choctaws, Creeks, and Seminoles. Among the *indigenous* western tribes, however, virtually no warriors served either the Union or the Confederacy. Nevertheless, they played a significant role in the war. To begin with, their presence drew off some Union troops who otherwise would have been used against Confederates. Far more important, however, were the demands of the war, which meant that fewer troops were available to occupy the western posts. The absence of the army gave the Indians free rein to raid settlers with relative impunity.

Terror in the Southwest

The entire Southwest was seared by violence. The outbreak of the Civil War stripped the U.S. Army's western outposts of 313 officers—one third of the *entire* officer corps—who resigned their commissions to fight on the side of the Confederacy. Confederate lieutenant colonel John Robert Baylor exploited the Union's weakened position to take possession of Arizona Territory for the Confederacy. Baylor was able to roll over the greatly diminished Union presence, but he didn't count on the hostility of the Chiricahua and Mimbreño Apaches, who terrorized the region. Baylor hastily formed the Arizona Rangers in August 1861 and ordered them to "exterminate all hostile Indians."

In the meantime, hoping to retain New Mexico, Union general Edward R. S. Canby negotiated a treaty with the Navajo, pledging to distribute rations to the Indians. At Fort Fauntleroy, designated site of the distribution, an ostensibly friendly series of horse races was run between Navajos and a regiment of New Mexico volunteers. The featured event was a race between a volunteer lieutenant and Chief Manuelito (ca. 1818–1894). Heavy wagers were laid, and from the beginning, it was apparent that Manuelito—an expert horseman—was not in control of his mount. After he came in a poor second, Manuelito protested that his bridle had been slashed, and he demanded a rematch. The soldiers refused, a fight broke out, and the troops began firing indiscriminately. "The Navahos, squaws, and children ran in all directions and were shot and bayoneted," according to a white civilian eyewitness who testified before a subsequent congressional inquiry. Forty Indians were killed, and the Navajos retaliated. Through August and September, Kit Carson, leading the First New Mexico Volunteer Cavalry, relentlessly counterattacked against the vengeance seekers.

The result, by the end of 1863, was total defeat of the Navajos, who were exiled to a desolate reservation called the Bosque Redondo. Eventually, 8,000 Navajos jammed the reservation, under conditions so intolerable that, after the Civil War, in an all-too-rare act of humanity, a U.S. peace commission granted Navajo pleas to be returned to their homelands.

Massacre in Minnesota

While the Southwest erupted, storm clouds also gathered far to the north. Unlike the Navajos, the Santee Sioux of Minnesota seemed willing to accept "concentration" on a reservation. But as increasing numbers of German and Scandinavian immigrants moved into the region, the Santee found themselves confined to a diminishingly narrow strip of land along the Minnesota River. Worse, provisions and annuity money guaranteed them by treaty were routinely withheld. In June of 1862, Chief Little Crow led the Santee to the Yellow Medicine Indian Agency to demand release of provisions and funds. When these items were not forthcoming by August, warriors broke into the agency warehouse. Local troops responded and repulsed them.

Still hungry and desperate, the Santee appealed to a local trader, Andrew J. Myrick, on August 5 and 6. His heartless reply—"let them eat grass"—enraged the warriors, and on August 18, they ambushed Myrick in his store, killed him, and stuffed *his* mouth with grass. From this point on, raiding became chronic in and around the town of New Ulm. By the end of August, 2,000 Minnesotans were refugees, and the Sioux had killed between 350 and 800 others. Governor Alexander Ramsey telegraphed Abraham Lincoln, requesting an extension of a federal deadline for meeting his state's military draft quota. The president replied: "Attend to the Indians. If the draft cannot proceed of course it will not proceed. Necessity knows no law."

Through the balance of August and most of September, fighting in Minnesota was brutal. On September 26, 2,000 Santee hostiles surrendered to General Henry Hopkins Sibley (not to be confused with the Confederate general, Henry Hastings Sibley), and the deadliest Indian uprising in the history of the West was at an end.

In November, a military tribunal sentenced 303 warriors to hang. Questioning the justice of these mass proceedings, President Lincoln personally reviewed the convictions and reprieved all but 39 of the convicted. In the end, 38 men were hanged (another Indian received a last-minute reprieve), but administrative error resulted in the hanging of two Indians who were not on Lincoln's list of the condemned. As for Chief Little Crow, he fled the final battle, was refused refuge in Canada, and was ambushed and killed in Minnesota on July 3, 1863, while picking raspberries with his 16-year-old son.

War for the Bozeman Trail

Throughout the Civil War, fighting with the Apaches continued. Wars also broke out with the Shoshonis, Bannocks, Utes, and Northern Paiutes—also called the Snakes—in parts of Wyoming, Nevada, Utah, and Idaho. Wars erupted with the Navajos in the Southwest and with the combined forces of the Cheyenne and Arapaho tribes in Colorado. All of these wars ended badly for the Indians, although, as one officer observed, "Ten good soldiers are required to wage successful war against one Indian."

One of the few conflicts from which the Indians emerged unquestionably victorious broke out just after the end of the Civil War. Military authorities had anticipated that the collapse of the Confederacy would free up many troops for service in the West. What actually happened is that the Union army rushed to demobilize, and the post-Civil War army of the West shrunk, rather than expanded. A modest force under Colonel Henry B. Carrington was sent to protect the Bozeman Trail, a major route of western migration through Wyoming and Montana. The trail was being menaced by Oglala Sioux led by Red Cloud, who was determined to resist white invasion of his people's land. Carrington was not popular with his officers, who felt that he devoted too much time to building forts and not enough to fighting Indians.

One subordinate, Captain William J. Fetterman, boasted that with just 80 men, he could ride through the entire Sioux nation. On December 21, 1866, Fetterman was given his chance to make good on the boast. Sent with a detachment of 80, his mission was to relieve a wood-hauling wagon train that was being harassed by Indians. Fetterman found himself up against 1,500 to 2,000 warriors led by Crazy Horse, and his command was wiped out in what came to be called the Fetterman Massacre.

Appalled by the Fetterman disaster, a peace commission concluded a treaty with Red Cloud on April 29, 1868, promising (among other things) to abandon the Bozeman Trail—which, in any case, the commissioners well knew, was about to be rendered obsolete by the transcontinental railroad.

Hancock's War and Sheridan's Campaign

General William Tecumseh Sherman, in charge of western operations, found the peace with Red Cloud humiliating. Sherman advised army General-in-Chief Ulysses S. Grant that "we must act with vindictive earnestness against the Sioux, even to their extermination, men, women, and children." But the mood among politicians in Washington drifted toward conciliation, and Sherman continued to prosecute "punitive campaigns" in the West with little support from Washington and, ultimately, to little purpose.

From April through July of 1867, one of Sherman's best commanders, the Civil War hero Winfield Scott Hancock, fruitlessly pursued the Cheyenne and Sioux through Kansas. The following year, Sherman's most able lieutenant, another great commander in the Civil War, General Philip Sheridan, conducted a harrowing winter campaign against the Sioux and Cheyenne. This campaign proved as punishing to the pursuers as to the pursued, who suffered bitterly in relentless cold.

The colorful colonel of the 7th Cavalry, George Armstrong Custer, laid claim to the biggest victory of "Sheridan's Campaign," when he attacked a peaceful Cheyenne camp on the Washita River. Among the 103 Indians he and his men killed were 93 women, old men, and children. Chief Black Kettle, actually a leading advocate of peace, was slain along with his wife.

Struggle for the Black Hills

The futility and tragedy of Hancock's and Sheridan's campaigns were typical of the so-called "Indian Wars." The usual pattern was this: weeks and months of fruitless pursuit culminated in brief and wanton spasms of violence that resulted in the deaths of innocent victims alongside militant "hostiles." In 1873, the short but intense Modoc War broke out in California because a tiny tribe stubbornly refused to leave an utterly worthless volcanic wasteland, which, despite its lack of value, was coveted by the government. In 1874, the Red River War was launched to punish the Comanches and Cheyennes for attacking a group of white hunters at Adobe Walls, Texas. At about the same time, an expedition led by George A. Custer discovered gold in the Black Hills, the land most sacred to the Sioux. When government attempts to persuade the Indians to sell or lease the Black Hills failed, they were simply ordered to vacate. The Sioux refused, and war erupted.

The army never had an easy time fighting the Indian Wars, but now they found themselves up against an enemy equipped with formidable riding and warrior skills,

American Echo

Fortunately, genocidal phrases rarely enter folklore, but everybody knows the expression "The only good Indian is a dead Indian." It originated with General Philip Sheridan, when a Comanche named Tosawi came to him to sign a treaty after Custer's "victory" at Washita. "Tosawi, good Indian," said Tosawi. Sheridan replied: "The only good Indians I ever saw were dead." The phrase was subsequently modified through repetition.

motivated by religious fervor in defense of a sacred land, and led by the charismatic Tatanka Iyotake, better known as Sitting Bull. On June 17, Sitting Bull mounted a pounding attack against General George Crook's column at the Rosebud Creek in southern Montana. This event made George Armstrong Custer more determined to pursue and destroy the "hostiles."

On the morning of June 22, 1876, to the strains of its regimental tune, "Garry Owen," the 7th Cavalry passed in review before Generals Alfred Terry and John Gibbon. They were embarking on what the commanders conceived as a final, coordinated pincers campaign against the Sioux. As Colonel Custer rode off to join his men, Gibbon called after him: "Now, Custer, don't be greedy, but wait for us."

Custer answered, "No, I will not."

Remember This

Sitting Bull (Tatanka Iyotake, 1831–1890) made an early reputation as a warrior and was revered for his great bravery, strength, generosity, and wisdom. His fame and influence spread far beyond his own Hunkpapa Sioux people. With chiefs Crazy Horse and Gall, Sitting Bull led resistance against the white invasion of the sacred Black Hills after gold was discovered there in 1874. Following the annihilation of Custer at the Little Bighorn in 1876, Sitting Bull and his closest followers fled to Canada. Upon his return to the United States in 1881, Sitting Bull was imprisoned for 2 years and then sent to Standing Rock Reservation. In 1883, he traveled as a performer with Buffalo Bill Cody's Wild West Show. Buffalo Bill was perhaps the only white man Sitting Bull ever trusted.

In 1890, Sitting Bull was identified with the anti-white religious movement known as the Ghost Dance. He was killed during a scuffle when reservation police (who were Indians) attempted to arrest him on December 15, 1890.

Frustrated by long, futile pursuits, Custer, ever ambitious for martial glory, was determined to fight it out whenever and wherever he could. That is why, on June 25, when his scouts discovered a Sioux camp and warriors near the Little Bighorn River, Custer decided not to wait until the next day, when he was supposed to rendezvous with the others. Instead, he resolved to attack immediately. First, Custer sent Captain Frederick

Benteen with 125 men south, to make sure the Sioux had not moved to the upper valley of the Little Bighorn. Then he sent another 112 men under Major Marcus A. Reno in pursuit of a small body of warriors he had sighted. With his remaining troops, Custer planned to charge the Sioux village. But it was soon apparent that Reno and his men were being overwhelmed, and Custer dispatched his bugler, Giovanni Martini, to recall Benteen. Custer then entered the fray, leading his men against the warriors. Almost immediately, he and his troopers were engulfed by huge numbers of Sioux warriors, who killed Custer and 250 cavalrymen. Reno, joined by Benteen—368 officers and men total—held off a relentless siege for the next 2 days.

"I Will Fight No More Forever"

The Battle of the Little Bighorn was the last major Indian victory of the Indian Wars. In subsequent engagements, the Sioux were defeated by the army's two most successful Indian fighters, Ranald Mackenzie and Nelson A. Miles. It was Miles who finally subdued the Nez Perces at the 5-day Battle of Bear Paw Mountain (September 30 through October 5, 1877) in Montana.

Led by Chief Joseph the Younger, a faction of the Nez Perces refused to abide by a characteristically flawed and prejudicial treaty. He and his followers defiantly refused to leave their homeland in the Wallowa Valley of Oregon. Troops under the command of General Oliver O. Howard and Colonel Miles pursued and battled some 800 Indians over 1,700 miles of the most inhospitable terrain on the continent. When it was over, Joseph and his people, having suffered intensely, had also earned the respect of their pursuers. Both Howard and Miles joined in Joseph's petition to the White House to return his people to the Wallowa Valley. The petition was denied—for the valley was rich in minerals—and Joseph lived out the remainder of his long life on a reservation near Colville, Washington in company with about half of his followers, the rest having been assigned to another reservation.

American Echo _____

I am tired of fighting .... It is cold and we have no blankets. The little children are freezing to death. My people, some of them, have run away to the hills, and have no blankets, no food; no one knows where they are—perhaps freezing to death. I want to have time to look for my children and see how many of them I can find. Maybe I shall find them among the dead. Hear me, my chiefs! I am tired; my heart is sick and sad. From where the sun now stands I will fight no more forever.

—Chief Joseph, in surrender to General Nelson A. Miles, October 5, 1877

After Geronimo

The pursuit of the Nez Perces involved a concerted military operation focused on a small band of fugitives. Down in the Mexican border region, an entire army task force was devoted to the pursuit of a *single* Indian. His Apache name was Goyathlay (One Who Yawns), but he was better known by the name the Mexicans had given him: Geronimo (1829–1909).

In 1850, Mexican settlers had ambushed and killed Geronimo's first wife and his children, after which the warrior devoted his life to raiding the borderlands along with his brother-in-law, Juh, a Chiricahua chief.

In 1875, U.S. authorities branded Geronimo a troublemaker because he opposed military plans to "concentrate" all the Apaches at the desolate San Carlos reservation in eastern Arizona. Geronimo fled with a band of followers into Mexico but was soon arrested and returned to the reservation. Not to be contained, Geronimo used the reservation as a base from which he staged raids throughout the decade.

In 1881, authorities killed another "troublemaker," Nakaidoklini, revered by the Apaches as a prophet. His death incited Geronimo to abandon the reservation altogether for a secret stronghold in the Sierra Madre, which became the staging area from which he terrorized the entire border region.

In May 1882, Apache scouts working for the army discovered Geronimo's sanctuary and persuaded him and his followers to return to the reservation. But he fled again on May 17, 1885, with 35 warriors and 109 women and children. In January 1886, a small army unit, together with Apache scouts, penetrated deep into Mexico, where they found Geronimo, who surrendered to General George Crook. Geronimo escaped one more time, but ultimately surrendered to Nelson Miles on September 4, 1886. Geronimo and some 450 other Apaches were sent to Florida for confinement in Forts Marion and Pickens. In 1894, the Apaches were removed to Fort Sill, Indian Territory (present-day Oklahoma), and Geronimo quietly lived out the rest of his life as a rancher.

Wounded Knee Ending

In 1886, when Geronimo surrendered to General Miles, 243,000 Native Americans were confined to 187 reservations. With Geronimo's last resistance extinguished, the Indian Wars were practically at an end.

Yet if the body of defiance was dead, its spirit lingered. Wovoka was the son of a Paiute shaman, but he had spent part of his youth with a white ranch family, who leavened his Paiute religious heritage with the teachings of their own Christianity. By the 1880s, Wovoka began to preach to the reservation Indians, foretelling a new world in which only Indians dwelled, generations of slain braves came back to life, and the buffalo (nearly hunted to extinction during the first two-thirds of the nineteenth century) were again plentiful. To hasten this deliverance, Wovoka counseled, all Indians must dance the Ghost Dance and follow the paths of peace.

Among a people who had lost all hope, the Ghost Dance religion spread rapidly. Soon, many western reservations were alive with what white overseers regarded as "frenzied" dancing. And it is true that, in some places, the Ghost Dance was associated with a renewed militancy. At Pine Ridge, South Dakota, leaders among the Teton Sioux called for armed rebellion against the whites. Hearing this, reservation agent Daniel F. Royer frantically telegraphed Washington, D.C., in November 1890: "Indians are dancing in the snow and are wild and crazy. We need protection and we need it now." But the arrival of troops under Nelson A. Miles seemed only to make matters worse. As a precaution, Indian reservation police were sent on December 15, 1890, to arrest Sitting Bull, domiciled at Standing Rock Reservation. A scuffle broke out, and the most revered chief of the Plains tribes was slain.

In the meantime, another chief, Big Foot of the Miniconjou Sioux, was making his way to Pine Ridge. Miles assumed that his purpose was to bring to a boil the simmering rebellion, and he dispatched the 7th Cavalry to intercept Big Foot and his followers. The troops caught up with the Indians on December 28, 1890, at a place called Wounded Knee Creek, on the Pine Ridge Reservation.

Not only did Big Foot lack hostile intentions, he was, although desperately ill with pneumonia, traveling to Pine Ridge to try to persuade the rebellion leaders to surrender. Neither Miles nor Colonel James W. Forsyth, commander of the 7th Cavalry, were aware of the nature of Big Foot's mission, and Forsyth quietly surrounded the chief's camp, deploying four Hotchkiss guns (rapid-fire howitzers) on the surrounding hills. On December 29, the soldiers entered the camp and began to confiscate the Indians' weapons. A hand-to-hand fight developed, shots were fired—it is unclear whether these came from the Indians or the soldiers—and then the Hotchkiss guns opened up, firing almost a round a second at men, women, and children.

Nobody knows just how many died at Wounded Knee. The bodies of Big Foot and 153 other Miniconjous were found, but many more limped or crawled away. It is likely that some 300 of the 350 camped beside the creek ultimately lost their lives.

Another group of Indians ambushed the 7th Cavalry on December 30, but quickly withdrew. Two weeks later, on January 15, 1891, the entire Sioux nation formally surrendered to U.S. Army officials. It was a miserable end to 400 years of racial warfare on the American continent.

The Least You Need to Know

- ◆ Few Indians participated directly in the Civil War, but some did take advantage of a reduced military presence in the West to raid and plunder.

- ◆ The Indian Wars in the West, spanning the Civil War years to 1891, consisted mainly of long, exhausting pursuits and relatively few battles.

- ◆ The strategy used was to fight a "total war" against women, children, and old men as well as warriors, in order to force the Indians onto reservations.

- ◆ The massacre—some insist on calling it a battle—at Wounded Knee (December 29, 1890) ended the Indian Wars but has remained as a shameful symbol of the long clash between the European Americans and Native Americans of North America.

Chapter 23

Exploitation and Enterprise (1869–1908)

In This Chapter

- ◆ Western agriculture and the day of the cowboy
- ◆ Outlaw legends of the West
- ◆ The triumph of capitalism and the rise of philanthropy
- ◆ The technological revolution

The phrase *Wild West* has become so worn with use that it's hard to say the second word *without* adding the first to it. The spirit that marked the West pervaded national life during the years following the Civil War. If the West had its cowboys and its outlaws, so did the world of big business and power politics in such eastern cities as New York and Washington. Fortunes were made and lost, it seemed, overnight. A wealth of new inventions suddenly materialized, accelerating American life to a pace many found increasingly frenzied. And if tycoons and inventors were pulling the strings, working men and women were often the ones being jerked around.

An Empire of Cows

The West equaled space, but the equation came out differently for different people. To the homesteader, space meant a place to live. To the cattleman, space meant grass and water to fuel the beef herds that made his fortune.

Before the U.S.–Mexican War, even *Texas* ranches were relatively modest in size, but the war brought a tremendous demand for beef to feed the U.S. Army. After the cattle industry geared up for this need, it never pulled back. Texans started to drive cattle beyond the confines of the ranch, pushing herds northward to fatten on the grass of public lands before being shipped east. This period was the start of the range cattle industry, which the Civil War threatened to bring to an untimely end. Union blockades kept Texans from shipping their beef to market, and the cattle were left to run wild on the Texas plains, the ranchers and ranch hands having gone off to fight the war. When the sons of Texas returned after Appomattox, the only visible assets left to many of them were some five million free-ranging animals. Ex-Confederate soldier boys now set themselves up as cowboys, rounding up and branding as many cattle as they could, then "trailing" the herds to grazing lands, marketplaces, and railheads.

The range cattle industry didn't just make beef; it also created the single most beloved, celebrated, talked about, and sung about worker in American history. If generations of little boys and girls across the Atlantic grow up on tales of knights in shining armor, American children have long been raised on tales, songs, and images of the noble riders of the range. Cowboys embody a very powerful—very American—myth of freedom and self-sufficiency. From the cold, hard perspective of economic reality, however, cowboys were not figures of romance, but the poorest of the poor. Dirty, dangerous, lonely, and poorly paid, "cowboy" was a job for desperate men: down-and-out ex-Confederates who had lost all they owned; liberated black slaves who, suddenly masterless, found themselves at loose ends; Indians who struggled at the bottom of the socioeconomic ladder; and Mexicans, who shared that bottom rung.

On the ranch, the cowboy's principal job was to ride over an assigned stretch of range and tend the cattle, doing whatever needed to be done. The most demanding labor was the trail drive, in which cowboys moved a herd of cattle—perhaps as small as 500 head or as large as 15,000—to northern ranges for maturing or to market at railhead cattle towns like Abilene, Ellsworth, and Dodge City, Kansas; Pueblo and Denver, Colorado; and Cheyenne, Wyoming. Distances were often in excess of 1,000 miles over any of four main cattle trails. Hazards of those trails were almost as numerous as the herds themselves: storms, floods, drought, stampede, rustlers, hostile Indians. Pay was about $100 for 3 or 4 months' work.

Law and Disorder

It was not unusual for a cowboy to blow his whole $100 stake during a few nights in the cattle town that lay at the end of the trail. The towns served as points of transfer from the trail to the rails. Here beef brokers shook hands on deals, and the cattle were loaded into stock cars bound for the cities of the East. For the cowboy, a stay in town meant a bath, a shave, a woman (300 prostitutes plied their trade in the small town of Wichita), and plenty to drink (in many towns, saloons outnumbered *all* other buildings two to one). Such towns were also home to professional gamblers who were ready, willing, and able to separate a cowboy from his cash. Like the mining camps of California in the 1850s, the cattle towns of the latter part of the century were rowdy, violent places. Gunfights became commonplace, although, alas, neither so frequent nor so violent as they are on the streets of some American cities today.

Arising from the welter of casually violent men in the West were more than a handful of determined and deliberate career criminals. A few have entered into American legend. Jesse James was born in Clay County, Missouri, on September 5, 1847, and, with his older brother Frank (born 1843), was caught up in the amoral chaos of the Civil War in Missouri. The brothers joined the fierce Confederate guerrilla band of William Quantrill and his lieutenant, "Bloody Bill" Anderson. In the guise of carrying out military operations, these guerrillas were no better than vicious gangsters, and their units became the schools of a generation of accomplished criminals. Cole Younger and Arch Clement, who would become principal members of the James Gang after the war, were also Quantrill–Anderson alumni.

The gang robbed its first bank in February 1866 and continued to prey upon banks, stagecoaches, and trains until 1876. At that time, determined citizens ambushed and decimated the gang during a robbery attempt in Northfield, Minnesota. The James brothers escaped and formed a new gang, which now included a recruit named Robert Ford. On April 3, 1882, eager to claim a bundle of reward money, the newcomer shot and killed Jesse, who was living in St. Joseph, Missouri, under the alias of Thomas Howard. Ford's deed was popularly greeted as anything but a public service. Although they were clearly cold-blooded armed robbers, the "James boys" had acquired a glamorous reputation as latter-day Robin Hoods. In a popular ballad, Ford was reviled as the "dirty little coward who shot Mr. Howard and laid poor Jesse in his grave." As for brother Frank, he later surrendered, was twice tried and twice acquitted by friendly juries (an unfriendly, let alone impartial, jury could not be found). Frank James died, in bed, of natural causes in 1915.

Contemporary legend, dime novels, and, later, movies and television transformed another outlaw into a modern Robin Hood. Billy the Kid was born Henry McCarty in 1859 (either in Marion County, Indiana, or possibly New York City). Raised in Kansas, the Kid was orphaned early and embarked on a life of petty crime that escalated to murder when, aged 17, he killed a man in a saloon brawl. A year later, in 1878, the Kid became embroiled in the so-called Lincoln County War, a New Mexico range war between one set of cattlemen and another. During the conflict, on April 1, 1878, he ambushed and murdered the Lincoln County sheriff and his deputy. As a fugitive, Billy the Kid supported himself with robbery, all the while pursued by the new sheriff, Pat Garrett, to whom he finally surrendered in December 1880. Four months later, the Kid escaped the noose by killing his two jailors and taking flight. When the Kid stopped at Fort Sumner, New Mexico (some say it was to see his sweetheart), Garrett again caught up with him and, this time, gunned him down.

 Vital Statistics _____

For all their notoriety, neither Jesse James nor Billy the Kid holds any Wild West record for gun fighting. In terms of the number of men slain, Billy the Kid comes in at tenth place (4 murders), behind Jim Miller (12), Wes Hardin (11), Bill Longley (11), Harvey Logan (9), Wild Bill Hickok (7), John Selman (6), Dallas Stoudenmire (5), Cullen Baker (5), and King Fisher (5). Jesse James doesn't even come close to the top 10. In nine gunfights, only one killing is confirmed, although James may have assisted in the slaying of three more men.

Cornering the Market

Jesse James, Billy the Kid, and a host of lesser figures were unquestionably criminals. But who were their victims? As many Americans saw it at the time, Jesse, Billy, and the rest did not victimize innocent citizens, but attacked big banks, big railroads, and big money—the very forces that were daily robbing the "common man." If you wanted to talk about victims, well, the _real_ victims were those who weren't lucky enough to have been born a Gould or a Rockefeller. In the popular logic of the day, capitalists such as these were the robber barons, whereas the Western outlaws were the Robin Hoods.

And what about government? In the popular view, lawmakers and police could be counted on to go with the money, making and enforcing laws to serve the Goulds, the Rockefellers, and their kind. People who lived during the years following the

Civil War took to calling their era the Gilded Age—after the title of a satiric novel written in 1873 by Mark Twain and Charles Dudley Warner and depicting a society glittering with showy wealth but corrupt to the core.

The railroads boomed, transporting the raw ores of the West to the industrial machines of the East. With hundreds of thousands of discharged veterans flooding the job market, labor was dirt cheap, and the government was, well, quite pliant to the will of big business. Andrew Johnson, having narrowly escaped removal from office, was succeeded in the White House by Ulysses Simpson Grant in 1869. Grant had proven to be one of the nation's greatest generals, but in two terms as president, he presided over the most thoroughly corrupt administration in American history. He was personally above reproach, but, naively, he surrounded himself with scoundrels who administrated, legislated, and operated hand in hand with the interests of big business, and (in the infamous phrase of railroad magnate William H. Vanderbilt), "The public be damned!"

Gould and Gold

Jay Gould was born in Roxbury, New York, on May 27, 1836, the son of a poor farmer. By 21, Gould had saved up $5,000, which he invested in the leather business and railroad stocks. Within a decade, Gould was a director of the Erie Railroad and, by means of illegal stock manipulation and bribery, clawed his way to a controlling interest in a number of railroads. With fellow tycoon James Fisk (1834–1872), Gould hatched a scheme to corner the U.S. gold market. He persuaded President Grant to suspend government gold sales, thereby driving up the price of gold—which Gould and Fisk held in great quantity. Rousing momentarily from his naive stupor, Grant realized what was going on and ordered the Treasury to release $4 million of its own gold to checkmate Gould. The result was Black Friday, September 24, 1869, which precipitated a major financial panic followed by a severe economic depression as the inflated price of gold tumbled.

Many of the nation's railroads, already reeling from cutthroat competition, now tottered on the verge of bankruptcy. John Pierpont Morgan (1837–1913), who had multiplied his family's already Croesus-like fortune by loaning money to France during the Franco-Prussian War of 1871, now rushed in to pick up the pieces. By 1900, Morgan had acquired *half* the rail track in the nation. Most of the rest of the railroads were owned by Morgan's friends, and, together, they fixed freight prices at exorbitant levels. There was little that shippers, ranging from major manufacturers to poor farming families, could do but pay.

Rockefeller and Oil

The years immediately following the Civil War ran on rails and were fueled by gold. People who controlled either or both interests drove the nation, regardless of who occupied the White House, Congress, or the courts.

There was gold, and then there was *black* gold. In 1859, oil was struck in western Pennsylvania. This event gave a young Ohioan—his gaunt visage and thin lips lending him the air of an undertaker—an idea. John Davison Rockefeller (1839–1937) decided that oil would become a big business and that his hometown of Cleveland was ideally situated to refine and distribute it to the nation. Rockefeller built a refinery there in 1862, then put together the Standard Oil Trust, an amalgam of companies by which he came to control all phases of the oil industry, from extraction, through refining, through distribution. Standard Oil was the first of many vertically integrated trusts formed in various industries during the post–Civil War period.

The Gospel of Wealth

The Gilded Age was an epoch of naked greed, the like of which would not be seen until the merger-crazy 1980s and the scandal-ridden opening years of the twenty-first century. Those few capitalists who bothered to defend their motives turned to the science of the day. In 1859, the great British naturalist Charles Darwin (1809–1882) published *On the Origin of Species by Means of Natural Selection.* This book set forth the theory of evolution, arguing that in nature, only the fittest—the strongest, the most cunning, and the ablest—creatures survive to reproduce their kind. Taking their cue from the British philosopher Herbert Spencer (1820–1903), capitalists translated nature into economics, arguing that the state should not interfere in economic life because people at the top of the socioeconomic heap were there because they were the fittest, having survived the battles of the marketplace. This concept was Social Darwinism.

Yet the era was not entirely heedless and heartless. Andrew Carnegie (1835–1919) came to the United States with his impoverished family from Scotland in 1848. As a youth, Carnegie worked in a cotton factory, then in a telegraph office, and finally for the Pennsylvania Railroad, rising quickly through the executive ranks until he became head of the western division in 1859. Carnegie resigned from the railroad in 1865 to form the Keystone Bridge Company, the first in a series of iron and steel concerns he owned. He consolidated his holdings in 1899 as the Carnegie Steel Company and then sold it to J.P. Morgan's United States Steel Company in 1901 for $492 million—roughly the equivalent of five billion of today's dollars. (And income tax wouldn't come into existence until ratification of the Sixteenth Amendment in 1913!)

Carnegie was as ruthless as any of his fellow robber barons, wielding his steel company like a club, knocking out all competition and (for a time) knocking out the American industrial union movement as well. But in 1889, Carnegie delivered a speech titled "The Gospel of Wealth," in which he reeled out the familiar Social Darwinist line that wealth was essential for civilization and that the natural law of competition dictated that only a few would achieve wealth. Yet Carnegie added a unique twist. The rich, he proclaimed, had a moral responsibility to use their money for the clear benefit of society. "The man who dies rich," Carnegie proclaimed, "dies shamed."

As the Gilded Age drew to a close, from 1901 until his death, Carnegie dedicated himself to philanthropy, donating more than $350 million to a wide spectrum of causes. He founded more than 2,500 public libraries throughout the United States; he established the Carnegie Institute of Pittsburgh, the Carnegie Institution at Washington, the Carnegie Foundation for the Advancement of Teaching, the Carnegie Endowment for International Peace, and the Carnegie Corporation of New York. The truly remarkable thing is that many other robber barons took the Gospel of Wealth to heart. Rail magnate Leland Stanford founded and endowed Stanford University. Rockefeller endowed the University of Chicago, created the Rockefeller Institute of Medical Research, established the Rockefeller Foundation, and bought vast tracts of land that became national parks. Many other wealthy individuals did similar deeds and continue to do so today.

An Age of Invention

If, blooming among the uncut weeds of wild greed, the Gospel of Wealth seemed miraculous, so did the incredible series of inventions that burst forth during what otherwise might have been a dull, hard Age of the Machine. Americans of the post–Civil War era were extraordinarily industrious and inventive.

"Mr. Watson, Come Here!"

Alexander Graham Bell was born in 1847 in Scotland and grew up in England. His grandfather and father earned fame as teachers of the deaf, and Alexander likewise followed this career, continuing in it after the family immigrated to Canada in 1870. In 1872, Alexander Graham Bell became a professor of vocal physiology at Boston University. His profound interest in the nature of speech and sound was combined with a genius for things mechanical, and he began working on a device to record sound waves graphically in order to *show* his deaf students what they could not hear.

Simultaneously, Bell was also trying to develop what he and other inventors independently laboring on the problem called the "harmonic telegraph," a device capable of transmitting multiple telegraph messages simultaneously over a single line.

About 1874, the two concepts suddenly merged in his mind. Bell wrote in his notebook that if he could "make a current of electricity vary in intensity precisely as the air varies in density during the production of sound," he could "transmit speech telegraphically."

The insight was staggering: convert one form of intelligible energy (sound) into another (modulated electric current). With his tireless assistant, Thomas Watson, Bell worked on the device for the next 2 frustrating years. One day, in 1876, while Watson maintained what he thought would be another fruitless vigil by the receiver unit in the next room, Bell made adjustments to the transmitter. In the process, Bell upset a container of battery acid, which spilled on his lap. Painfully burned by the sulfuric acid, he inadvertently made the world's first phone call—a call for help: "Mr. Watson, come here, I want you."

The telephone caught on quickly, and the Bell Telephone Company, founded by Alexander's father-in-law, Gardner G. Hubbard, became a utility of vast proportions and incalculable importance.

One Percent Inspiration

Bell was a teacher of the deaf who taught the world to hear over unlimited distances. Thomas Alva Edison, nearly completely deaf because of a childhood illness and accident, helped the world to see. Born in Milan, Ohio, in 1847, Edison had little education and less money when, as a youth, he started selling candy and newspapers on trains of the Grand Trunk Railroad. What Edison did have was a passion for tinkering and a fascination with an invisible force called electricity. His first commercially successful invention was an electric stock ticker, which delivered stock quotations almost instantaneously and which J. P. Morgan eagerly snatched up. Edison plowed his profits into creating a state-of-the-art laboratory/workshop first in Newark, then in Menlo Park, New Jersey. By the end of his long, creative life, Edison had more than 1,000 patents to his name, a record that has yet to be broken by any individual.

Edison's greatest single invention was undoubtedly the incandescent electric lamp, which he publicly demonstrated on December 31, 1879, after many tedious months of trial and error. ("Genius," Edison once declared to a reporter, "is one percent inspiration and 99 percent perspiration.") By 1881, Edison had built the world's first central generating plant, on Pearl Street in lower Manhattan. Within a very short time, electricity became a fixture not only of American life, but of life throughout the world. The incandescent lamp and the electric power industry associated with it spawned in turn many more industries dedicated to producing an array of devices driven by electric current. It is hardly necessary to point out how much our civilization now depends on what Edison began, but it is significant that, after he died on October 18, 1931, plans to dim the lights of the nation for a full minute as a memorial gesture had to be scrapped. Electric lighting was just too important.

Sound and Light Captured

Although the incandescent lamp was Edison's most pervasive invention, it was not his personal favorite. Two years before he demonstrated his lamp, he designed a device intended to raise some quick cash for his laboratory. Edison drew a quick sketch of a simple machine he wanted built and then turned it over to one of his mechanic-technicians, John Kruesi.

"Build this," Edison had scrawled in the margin of the drawing, and Kruesi dutifully followed his employer's instructions, without any idea of what the device was supposed to do. A grooved metal cylinder was turned by a hand crank; a sheet of tinfoil was stretched over the cylinder; the point of a stylus rested against the tinfoil, and the other end of the stylus was affixed to a flexible diaphragm. Kruesi presented the finished model to Edison, who took it, turned the crank, and spoke into the diaphragm. The stylus, moving with the vibration of his voice, embossed the tinfoil. Then Edison stopped cranking and speaking, reapplied the stylus to the cylinder, and turned the crank. From the diaphragm, the machine recited "Mary Had a Little Lamb." Thomas Edison had invented the phonograph.

After recording sound and producing light, the Wizard of Menlo Park (as an enthralled press had dubbed the inventor) *recorded* light. Edison became interested in the photography of motion after he attended a lecture by Eadweard Muybridge (1830–1904) on his experiments with recording motion on film using multiple cameras. In 1882, a French scientist, E. J. Marey, invented a means of shooting multiple images with a single camera, and Edison patented his own motion picture camera in 1887. Edison then worked with William Kennedy Laurie Dickson to create a practical means of recording the images, using flexible celluloid film created by George Eastman (1854–1932). (Eastman's Kodak box camera would bring photography to the masses in 1888 and make Eastman an extraordinarily wealthy man.) By the 1890s, Dickson had shot many 15-second movies using Eastman's film in Edison's Kinetograph camera.

Bridge and Skyscraper, Kitty Hawk and Detroit

The end of the Civil War brought many monuments—statues, arches, and tombs—but more significant than these were the monuments to American civilization itself. In 1857, a German immigrant named John Augustus Roebling (1806–1869), a master bridge builder who had constructed suspension bridges over the Monongahela River and at Niagara Falls, proposed a spectacular span over the East River to unite Manhattan and Brooklyn, which were, at the time, separate cities. Roebling completed his plans in 1869 but suffered a severe leg injury at the construction site and died of tetanus. His son, Washington Augustus Roebling (1837–1926), took over the epic task. It very nearly killed him as well. He spent too much time in an underwater caisson, supervising construction of the bridge-tower foundations. Roebling developed a permanently crippling, excruciatingly painful case of "the bends," a disorder caused by nitrogen bubbles in the blood. The bridge, finally completed in 1883, was and remains a magnificent combination of timeless architecture and cutting-edge nineteenth-century technology.

If the Roeblings' masterpiece brought to its grandest expression the union of nineteenth-century art and science, the American skyscraper looked forward to the next century. William LeBaron Jenny's Home Insurance Company Building in Chicago (built 1883–1885) is generally considered the first skyscraper, but it was Louis Sullivan (1856–1924), one of the nation's greatest architects, who became the most important pioneering master of the new building form, which depended on a steel cage framework, not masonry walls, for support. With his partner Dankmar Adler, Sullivan based his practice in Chicago, a city he helped to raise, phoenix like, from the catastrophic fire of 1871. Thanks to Sullivan and those who followed him, American cities became vertical, aspiring passionately heavenward, bristling with the spires of new cathedrals founded not on religious faith, but on the wealth and raw energy of the age.

The very name *skyscraper* seemed to proclaim that nothing could contain the spirit of a nation that, like Chicago, had been reborn from the ashes. In 1903, the bicycle mechanic sons of Milton Wright, bishop of the United Brethren in Christ Church in Dayton, Ohio, transported to a beach at Kitty Hawk, North Carolina, a spindly, gossamer machine that resembled an oversized box kite. While his brother Wilbur (1867–1912) observed, Orville Wright (1871–1948) made history's first piloted, powered, sustained, and controlled flight in a heavier-than-air craft on December 17. Orville flew a distance of 120 feet over a span of 12 seconds. Within 2 years, the Wright brothers achieved a flight of 38 minutes over 24 miles and, by 1909, were manufacturing and selling their airplanes.

Of course, in 1909, flight was still out of the reach of most "ordinary" people. But the year before, a farm boy from Dearborn, Michigan, gave the masses wings of a different sort. True, Henry Ford (1863–1947) did not actually lift purchasers of his Model T off the ground, but he did give them unprecedented physical freedom.

Ford did not invent the automobile—a gasoline-fueled road vehicle first appeared in Germany, the handiwork of Gottlieb Daimler in 1885, and commercial production began in France about 1890—but he did make it practical and affordable. In 1908, he designed the simple, sturdy Model T and began to develop assembly line techniques to build it. The price of the car plummeted, and demand increased; with increased demand, Ford further perfected his assembly line, turning out more and more cars at lower and lower prices, which put them within reach of most Americans.

 Vital Statistics

In 1908, Ford manufactured 10,607 cars retailing for $850 each. In 1916, he turned out 730,041 Model T cars at $360 each.

The Model T, a landmark achievement in mass production, transformed the way Americans lived. The car created a mobile society and it created a skyrocketing demand for mass-produced consumer goods of all kinds. The Model T also changed the American landscape, veining it with a network of roads. Where the nation had been sharply divided into city and farm, suburbs now sprouted. Even more than the transcontinental railroad had done in 1869, the automobile unified the United States, connecting city to city, village to village.

Yet for all this, there was a cost well beyond the $360 price tag of a 1916 Model T. It often seemed as if the automobile was an invader rather than a liberator. Worse, American labor lost a certain degree of humanity, compelled now to take its pace from the relentless rhythms of assembly line machinery. The gulf between management and labor, always wide, broadened into a bitter chasm, and if the moneyed classes welcomed the technological revolution, they now had reason to fear a political one.

The Least You Need to Know

◆ The rise of the cattle industry in the West produced a colorful worker who, even in his own time, became an American icon: the cowboy.

◆ The kind of raw energy that animated the "Wild West" seemed to drive the rest of the country as well during the latter half of the nineteenth century.

◆ After the Civil War, big business grew largely unchecked, even at the expense of the public welfare, creating a roller-coaster boom-and-bust economy.

Chapter 24

Octopus and Jungle (1877–1906)

In This Chapter

- Immigration and opposition to immigration
- The Oklahoma land rush
- Development of labor organization to fight oppression
- Corruption and reform

"The history of the world," said the English writer Thomas Carlyle, "is but the biography of great men." For a long time, most historians thought of their craft in this way. They might have told the tale of the last quarter of the nineteenth century exclusively through the lives of Carnegie, Gould, Rockefeller, Ford, and their ilk. However, more recent historians have come to realize that such biographies relate only part of the story. More adequately told, history is also an account of ordinary people, the working men and women whose lives were influenced, even shaped, by the actions of politicians and (to use another phrase from Carlyle) the "captains of industry." While the moneyed elite fought one another for control of more and more capital, the nation's working people were tossed on the brutal seas of an economic tempest. Fortunes were being made and great inventions created, but for plain folk, the waning century presented plenty of hard times.

The Golden Door

America is a nation of immigrants. During the sixteenth century, the majority were Spanish. By the seventeenth century, colonial entrepreneurs actively recruited new settlers, most of whom were English. But by the eighteenth century, waves of German immigrants arrived as well, causing alarm and resentment among the English-speakers, especially those who had been born on these shores. Yet gradually, the German immigrants and those of the Anglo-American mainstream came to coexist peacefully.

> **American Echo**
>
> Give me your tired, your poor,
> Your huddled masses yearning to breathe free,
> The wretched refuse of your teeming shore,
> Send these, the homeless, tempest-tost, to me,
> I lift my lamp beside the golden door!
>
> —Emma Lazarus, from "The New Colossus," verse inscription (composed in 1883) for the base of the Statue of Liberty (unveiled in 1886)

The next great wave of immigration began in 1841, when Ireland suffered a great potato famine, which caused untold hardship and even starvation. Millions left the country, most of them bound for the United States. The influx of Irish-Catholics into what was principally an Anglo-Protestant nation prompted many to believe that "their" American culture had come under attack. Some worried that the Catholics would put allegiance to a foreign pope before allegiance to the government of their adopted nation. Feared and despised, the Irish immigrants were subjected to abuse and prejudice, some of it even backed by local legislation.

Beginning around 1880, the clamoring demands of American industry began to drown out the anti-immigrant chorus. Immigrant labor was cheap labor, after all, and employers looked for unskilled and semiskilled workers to feed newly emerging assembly lines and do the heavy lifting required to build bridges and raise skyscrapers. American employers called not only on the German states and Ireland, but also on southern and eastern Europe, encouraging the immigration of Italians, Greeks, Turks, Russians, and Slavs. For the first time, substantial numbers of Jews came to the United States, adding a new ingredient to the nation's blend of ethnic identities and religious faiths.

While the cities of the East and the Midwest tended to assimilate the new immigrants readily, resistance to immigration remained strong in the rural as well as the urban areas of the West and Southwest. Not that employers in these regions scrupled against hiring foreigners; they just didn't want the workers to enjoy the benefits of citizenship. Asians, prized as hard workers, were nevertheless barred by naturalization laws from attaining U.S. citizenship. In the Southwest, migrant labor from Mexico provided a scandalously cheap source of temporary farm workers—with the accent on the word *temporary*.

By 1882, prejudice against Asians resulted in passage of the first of a series of Chinese Exclusion Acts, which blocked the importation of Chinese laborers. However, authorities winked at the continued influx of Mexican migrants, some of whom came lawfully and others not.

By the second decade of the twentieth century, most Americans were eager to slam shut the golden door that opened onto their land. In 1917, would-be immigrants were re-quired to pass a literacy test, and in 1924, Congress set a strict limit on immigration—154,000 persons annually. Congress also established quotas aimed at reducing immigration from southern and eastern European countries.

How the Other Half Lived

At the end of the nineteenth century, most large American cities were deeply divided places. Established citizens lived in varying degrees of prosperity, decently clothed, fed, and housed, while many of the newer arrivals languished in overcrowded, dilapidated, and ultimately crime-plagued slums. The middle-class reaction to this "other half" of America was to try to ignore it, and they did just that pretty successfully, at least until Jacob August Riis (1849–1914), a New York journalist, published an eye-opening study in text and photographs of his city's slum life. *How the Other Half Lives* (1890), Theodore Roosevelt declared, came as "an enlightenment and an inspiration." The book heralded reform movements not only in New York, but all across the nation.

 Vital Statistics

In 1892, the U.S. Immigration Bureau opened a major central facility for handling the flood of immigrants. Ellis Island, within sight of the Statue of Liberty in New York Harbor, was a place where immigrants could be received, examined for disease, evaluated as fit or unfit for entry, and either admitted to the mainland, quarantined, or deported. During the 62 years of its operation, from 1892 to 1943, Ellis Island processed immigrants at rates as high as a million people a year.

Rush to New Land

If—at least to East Coast dwellers—the United States seemed to be turning into a nation of teeming slums, the dream of wide-open western spaces was by no means dead. At noon on April 22, 1889, government officials fired signal guns, sending hundreds of homesteaders racing across the border of Indian Territory to stake claims. It was the greatest mass settlement of the West since the Homestead Act of 1862, and the event kindled or rekindled the American Dream not only in those who rushed to new lands, but in other Americans who experienced the excitement vicariously.

The kindling of one dream meant that another was extinguished. The government rescinded its agreements to protect and preserve Indian Territory for the Native Americans who had been forcibly relocated to it by the Indian Removal Act of 1830 and subsequent federal actions. The great land rush led to statehood for Indian Territory, which became Oklahoma on November 16, 1907, and tribal lands were drastically reduced in the process.

The Knights of Labor

The Indians, victimized by U.S. land policy, could do little but appeal, mostly in vain, to the white American conscience. The laboring man, victimized by big business operating in the absence of government regulation, began to fight back by organizing unions. The Knights of Labor was founded in 1878 as a national union of skilled, as well as unskilled, workers. The Knights agitated for the universal adoption of the 8-hour day. Targeting the railroads—the "octopus," as the reform-minded turn-of-the-century novelist Frank Norris had collectively labeled them, evoking an image of greedy, sucking, all encompassing tentacles—the union struck several lines in 1877. The strikes brought rail traffic to a halt and won certain concessions from the companies. However, in 1886, after a general strike failed in Chicago and the bloody Haymarket Riot ensued, the Knights of Labor also dissolved.

Strike!

While the courts generally eased restrictions on labor strikes during the nineteenth century, legislators did not act to protect strikers. As a result, violence between employers and unions was frequent. In 1892, workers struck the Carnegie Steel Company plant in Homestead, Pennsylvania, after company manager Henry Clay Frick imposed a wage cut. On June 29, Frick hired some 300 Pinkerton "detectives" (they functioned more as hired thugs and scabs) to run the plant, and on July 6, an armed confrontation occurred, resulting in several deaths. The state militia was called in to protect nonunion laborers, who worked the mills from July 12 to November 20, at which point the strike collapsed.

As a result of the Homestead Strike, the nation's union movement suffered a severe setback, which was compounded 2 years later during the Pullman Strike of 1894. A violent confrontation between railroad workers and the Pullman Palace Car Company of Illinois tied up rail traffic across the United States from May to July. Workers, who lived in the company-owned town of Pullman (today a neighborhood on Chicago's South Side) were protesting wage cuts that had been made without corresponding reductions in company-levied rents and other employee charges. Laborers belonging to the American Railway Union protested and were summarily fired. Railway union head Eugene V. Debs (1855–1926) called a boycott of all Pullman cars, an action to which Pullman lawyers responded by using the newly enacted Sherman anti-trust legislation against the strikers. On July 2, a court injunction was issued to halt the strike. Federal troops were dispatched to enforce the injunction, and a riot broke out, during which several strikers were killed. The strike was crushed by July 10.

AFL

Although the labor movement would not fully recover from these early blows until the 1930s, one enduring union did emerge in 1886. The American Federation of Labor (AFL) was led by a former cigar maker named Samuel Gompers (1850–1924). What set this union apart from the Knights of Labor was that it did not attempt to lump together all trades, skilled and unskilled. Recognizing that working people had certain common interests but also differing needs, the AFL existed as a coordinating group for separate trades. The union, which agitated for an 8-hour day, workmen's compensation, controls on immigrant labor, and protection from "technological unemployment" (losing your job to a machine), exists today as the AFL-CIO.

I Won't Work

Although reasonably successful, the AFL did little to address the needs of unskilled labor. So in 1905, the Industrial Workers of the World (IWW) was formed by the Western Federation of Miners and a number of other labor organizations. Eugene Debs was an early force in this, the most radical of American labor unions, but leadership soon passed to William "Big Bill" Haywood (1869–1928). The "Wobblies," as IWW members were disparagingly called, vowed permanent class warfare against employers and looked forward to nothing less than a revolution, which would replace capitalism with an "industrial democracy." The many opponents of the Wobblies simply swore that IWW stood for "I Won't Work."

Boss Tyranny

Where unions fell short of looking after the needs, wishes, and demands of the masses, American city governments spawned *bosses* who operated *political machines*. The big-city boss was characteristically a demagogue, who presented himself as a common man looking out for the interests of common men. In reality, bosses were corrupt politicians, enriching themselves and their cronies at the expense of their constituents.

Typical of the big-city bosses was William Marcy Tweed (1823–1878) of New York, who worked his way up through the city's political machine (known as Tammany Hall, after the name of a powerful Democratic club). Tweed eventually came to dominate municipal and then state politics. In 1861, Tweed had scarcely a dollar to his name; by 1871, he had amassed a fortune in excess of $2.5 million—all built on influence peddling and kickbacks from the sale of city contracts and franchises. Tweed gathered about himself a band of cronies, called the Tweed Ring, who collectively siphoned off anywhere from $40 million to $200 million in public funds. Tweed was convicted of fraud in 1873, but jumped bond by fleeing to Spain. During his heyday, he had been ruthlessly caricatured by the great political cartoonist Thomas Nast (1840–1902), and in 1876, Tweed was recognized—in Spain—because of a Nast cartoon. As a result, Tweed was arrested, extradited, and returned to New York, where he died after serving 2 years in prison.

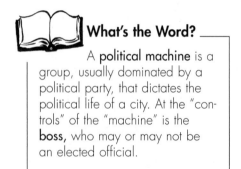

What's the Word?

A **political machine** is a group, usually dominated by a political party, that dictates the political life of a city. At the "controls" of the "machine" is the **boss,** who may or may not be an elected official.

The Age of the Machine soon gave rise to an Age of Reform in response to it. *The Shame of the Cities*, written in 1904 by freelance journalist and passionate reformer Lincoln Steffens, exposed the corruption of St. Louis and showed that it was all too typical of big-city America. Public outrage flared, making way for such crusading politicians as Theodore Roosevelt and Robert M. La Follette.

Chicago Meat

Talk of corruption and reform was all well and good, but to many, the subject seemed rather abstract and remote. It took a novel, *The Jungle*, written in 1906 by a socialist named Upton Sinclair (1878–1968), to bring corruption and reform—quite literally—to the gut level. Sinclair described the plight of one Jurgis Rudkus, a Lithuanian immigrant who worked in a Chicago meat-packing plant. Through the eyes of this downtrodden and exploited worker, Sinclair described in nauseating detail the horrors of modern meat packing. To fatten the bottom line, packers did not hesitate to use decayed meat, tubercular meat, assorted offal, and even rat meat in the manufacture of meat products. Comfortable middle-class Americans may or may not have cared about the exploitation of a blue-collar Lithuanian immigrant, but the idea of big business poisoning *them* and *their* families was downright sickening. "I aimed at the public's heart," Sinclair wrote of his novel, "and by accident I hit it in the stomach." As a result of the indignation stirred by *The Jungle*, Congress enacted the landmark Pure Food and Drug Act a mere 6 months after the novel was published. The federal government now intervened directly in free enterprise and took upon itself the defense of the public welfare.

Muckrakers and Progressivism

Sinclair was one of a group of activists President Theodore Roosevelt, himself a progressive reformer, dubbed *muckrakers*. Sinclair, Lincoln Steffens, Ida Tarbell (author of an epoch-making exposé of the outrageous Standard Oil "trust"), and other writers, caught up in the Progressive movement sweeping the nation, reported on the corruption and exploitation rampant in Gilded Age America. The muckrakers exposed child labor practices, slum life, racial persecution, prostitution, sweatshop labor, and the general sins of big business and machine politics.

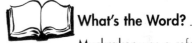

What's the Word?

Muckraker was a reference to *Pilgrim's Progress,* a Christian allegorical novel by the seventeenth-century British writer John Bunyan. One of Bunyan's allegorical characters used a "muckrake" to clean up the (moral) filth around him, even as he remained oblivious of the celestial beauty above.

Government Makes a Stand

The muckrakers succeeded in galvanizing popular opinion and motivating government action. Under President Theodore Roosevelt, antitrust laws were used to break up certain monopolies or, as they were called at the time, "trusts." After a long government assault, Standard Oil, most notorious of the trusts, was broken up into 34 companies in 1911. Under Roosevelt, too, public lands were protected from private exploitation; many historians consider Roosevelt's pioneering environmentalism to be his greatest legacy to the nation. During the Roosevelt era, government also stepped in to establish and enforce standards of purity in food and drugs. The government created safeguards to curb unfair exploitation of workers and restricted child labor.

On a local level, cities embarked on programs to clean up slum districts and to educate immigrants and youth.

Three years after Roosevelt left office, Robert M. La Follette, U.S. Senator from Wisconsin, led a faction of the most reform-minded Republicans to form a third party, the Progressive Party. The new party drafted an enthusiastic Roosevelt as its standard bearer in the 1912 presidential elections. The Progressives sought a middle road between traditional conservatism on the one hand and *populism* on the other, without veering toward socialist radicalism. The Progressives advocated programs of moral uplift, such as Chicago's Hull House, founded in 1889 by social activist Jane Addams.

What's the Word?

Populism is a political philosophy that supports the rights and power of the people versus the privileged, moneyed elite. It was the philosophy of the Populist Party that polled more than a million votes in the presidential election of 1892.

Hull House became a model for providing recreational and educational facilities to slum children, advocating child labor laws, and "American-izing" immigrants. The Progressives also supported clean government, women's suffrage, and prohibition. Although many people, contemporaries and historians alike, have criticized Progressivism as narrow-minded and ultimately reactionary in its support of the middle-class status quo, its spirit of reform changed American government, bringing it more intimately and thoroughly into the everyday lives of everyday Americans.

The Least You Need to Know

- The late nineteenth century was the great age of immigration into the United States—an era followed, early in the next century, by a backlash of immigration restrictions.

- The Oklahoma Land Rush of 1889, the greatest mass settlement of the West since the Homestead Act of 1862, usurped much land specifically set aside as a permanent homeland for Indians displaced by the Indian Removal Act of 1830.

- The greed and corruption rampant after the Civil War triggered a sweeping reform movement, Progressivism, which encompassed politics, social justice, and general moral "uplift."

Part 6

World Power

A "splendid little war" is what Secretary of State John Hay called America's brief armed contest with Spain over the independence of Cuba. Although controversial at home, the Spanish–American War demonstrated to the world that the United States was a power with whom to be reckoned. The war was followed by a period of isolationist retreat, shattered by the United States' entry into World War I. Following the Armistice that ended World War I, the nation was swept by simultaneous waves of a devil-may-care morality and a contrasting mania for sobriety, resulting in an amendment to the Constitution outlawing liquor. Drunk or sober, the country spent money like mad, made unwise investments it couldn't cover, and went broke one dismal Tuesday in 1929. A Great Depression swept the nation and the world, bringing desperation and the rise of dictators to Europe, as well as a new leader, Franklin Delano Roosevelt, to the United States. Here is the story of the century's most frantic and frightening years.

Chapter 25

Over There (1898–1918)

In This Chapter

- ◆ Jingoism, imperialism, and "yellow journalism"
- ◆ The Spanish-American War
- ◆ Woodrow Wilson as a Progressive reformer
- ◆ The United States enters World War I

In his Farewell Address of 1797, George Washington cautioned his fellow Americans to avoid "foreign entanglements," and for a full century thereafter, the nation did just that. Insulated by policy and two oceans from the European and Eastern powers, the United States basked in splendid isolation. The one chink in this isolationist armor was Central and South America. President James Monroe promulgated his Monroe Doctrine in 1823, essentially declaring the entire Western Hemisphere off-limits to European powers with designs on creating new colonies. In the course of the nineteenth century, the United States became the de facto major power of the hemisphere. During the century, too, while other nations amassed far-flung empires throughout the world, the United States expanded exclusively across its own vast continent.

Selling the News

By the end of the century, the nation extended from "sea to shining sea," and a significant number of Americans (some called them "patriots," others "imperialists," and still others *jingoes*) started thinking that it should extend farther. They wanted to see America on an equal footing with the empires of Europe.

What's the Word?

Americans who, in characteristically loud tones, voiced support for a warlike, imperialist foreign policy were called **jingoes** in the 1800s. The word *jingo* apparently came from "by jingo," an expression in the refrain of a bellicose nineteenth-century English music-hall song. "By jingo" also entered into American popular speech as a socially acceptable alternative expletive to "by Jesus."

What's the Word?

Yellow journalism is the sensational, usually nonobjective, even distorted or outright untrue journalistic practices aimed directly at readers' emotions and meant to boost newspaper circulation.

Strange as it may seem, the birth of U.S. imperialism was related to a newspaper cartoon. In 1895, Richard Felton Outcault, a cartoonist for the *New York World*, introduced a single-panel comic that featured as its main character a slum child costumed in a garment that was tinted yellow by a brand-new color printing process. The *World*'s publisher, Joseph Pulitzer (1847–1911), was delighted with "The Yellow Kid of Hogan's Alley," the popularity of which allowed him to close the gap in his circulation race with *The New York Journal*, published by rival news magnate William Randolph Hearst (1863–1951). Not to be outdone, Hearst lured Outcault to the ranks of the *Journal*, whereupon Pulitzer hired George Luks to continue the original comic as simply "The Yellow Kid."

The battle over the comic was but one episode in an ongoing, high-stakes circulation war between Pulitzer and Hearst, both of whom were intent on building mighty publishing empires. The papers continually competed with one another to publish sensational news stories that would attract readers. But it was the yellow ink of the slum kid comics that gave this style of newspaper publishing its name: *yellow journalism*.

"I'll Furnish the War ..."

Sometimes the quest for sensational news led Pulitzer and Hearst to expose social injustice and public fraud. But, noble motives aside, the circulation war kept escalating. Both Hearst and Pulitzer, hoping to bag the "Big Story," dispatched reporters to cover a developing situation in Cuba, a colony of Spain that was a mere 90 miles off the Florida coast. Hearst hired the great painter of life in the American West,

Frederic Remington (1861–1909), and dispatched him to Cuba to sketch dramatic pictures of colonial oppression and the revolutionary response to it. When combat failed to materialize, Remington cabled Hearst: "Everything quiet. There is no trouble. There will be no war. I wish to return." The newspaper tycoon cabled in reply: "Please remain. You furnish the pictures, and I'll furnish the war."

It was true that a full-scale Cuban war of independence was slow to brew. Nevertheless, the island had long been rebellious, and in February 1896, Spain sent General Valeriano Weyler (dubbed "Butcher Weyler" by Hearst) as governor. He created outrage not only in Cuba, but in the United States, when he placed into "re-concentration camps" Cubans identified as sympathizing with or supporting the rebels. Although President William McKinley, like his predecessor, Grover Cleveland, resisted intervening, U.S. popular sentiment, whipped up by atrocity stories published in the papers of Pulitzer and Hearst, moved McKinley to order the battleship *Maine* into Havana Harbor to protect American interests there.

Remember the *Maine!*

The temperature of America's war fever was not raised by popular sentiment alone. U.S. companies had made major investments in the island, especially in sugar plantations—and, not coincidentally, newspaper moguls like Hearst and Pulitzer had investments in such companies. Not only did revolution threaten those companies and their shareholders, but, to put the situation in more positive terms, a pliant puppet "independent" government in Cuba (or better yet, a Cuba annexed to the United States) would be very good for business. On February 9, Hearst scored a journalistic coup by publishing a purloined private letter in which the Spanish minister to the United States personally insulted President McKinley. Having for so long avoided "foreign entanglements," America was now propelled to the brink of war.

On February 15, 1898, the nation held hands and leaped over that brink.

An explosion rocked Havana Harbor, and the USS *Maine* blew up, killing 266 crewmen. The Hearst and Pulitzer papers vied with one another to affix blame on Spain, and cries of "Remember the *Maine* … to hell with Spain!" rang throughout the nation.

President McKinley, still reluctant himself, waited until April to ask Congress to authorize an invasion of Cuba. Congress not only complied, but gave the president something he hadn't asked for: a resolution recognizing Cuban independence from Spain. In response, Spain declared war on the United States on April 24. However, the first action took place in the Spanish-occupied Philippine Islands, not Cuba. U.S.

admiral George Dewey (1837–1917) sailed the Asiatic Squadron from Hong Kong to Manila Bay, where, on May 1, he attacked the Spanish fleet, sinking all 10 ships in the bay. This action was followed by a landing of 11,000 U.S. troops, who, acting in concert with the guerrilla forces of Filipino rebel leader Emilio Aguinaldo, quickly defeated the Spanish army in the islands. In July, Spanish Guam also fell, and the United States gathered up previously unclaimed Wake Island. Most important, Congress passed a resolution annexing Hawaii.

Action on Cuba was equally swift and decisive. On May 29, the U.S. fleet blockaded the Spanish fleet at Santiago Harbor, and in June, 17,000 U.S. troops landed at Daiquiri and assaulted Santiago. The war's make-or-break land battle, at San Juan Hill on July 1, included a magnificent charge by the volunteer Rough Riders, led by Lieutenant Colonel Theodore Roosevelt. (These cavalrymen charged on foot, because the army had failed to ship their horses to them.) In the meantime, Admiral Pasqual Cervera sailed into the harbor of Santiago de Cuba, where he was blockaded by the U.S. fleet. On July 3, after the U.S. victory at San Juan Hill, Cervera decided to run the blockade in order to save his fleet. Within just 4 hours, however, his fleet was almost completely destroyed. On July 17, 24,000 Spanish troops surrendered, and Madrid sued for peace 9 days later. U.S. secretary of state John Hay (1838–1905) summed it all up by dubbing the 10-week conflict a "splendid little war."

Spain withdrew from Cuba and ceded to the United States Puerto Rico and Guam; it sold the Philippines to the United States for $20 million. The United States established a territorial government in Puerto Rico, but temporized on Cuba, first establishing a military government there and then allowing Cuba to draft its own constitution, albeit with certain provisos. These included the right to establish American military bases on the island and to intervene in Cuban affairs "in order to preserve [Cuban] independence."

Theodore Roosevelt, who assumed office after the September 5, 1901, assassination of McKinley and who was subsequently elected to a presidential term in his own right, promulgated the so-called "Roosevelt Corollary" to the Monroe Doctrine. In effect, this policy made the United States policeman of the Western Hemisphere, a step toward establishing the nation as a *world* power.

He Kept Us Out of War

After taking that step, however, Americans had second thoughts. Roosevelt handpicked his old friend William Howard Taft to succeed him as president, and Taft won handily. However, Taft soon proved far more conservative than Roosevelt, although he did continue some of TR's Progressive reforms, including antitrust prosecution and, most significantly, support for the proposed income-tax amendment to the U.S. Constitution. What Taft most assuredly did not pursue was Roosevelt's aggressive foreign policy—and that was clearly fine with most Americans, who wanted nothing more than to return to the comfort of isolationism. Yet Taft lacked the vigor of Roosevelt, and he failed to win reelection in 1912, finishing a poor third to Democrat Woodrow Wilson and TR himself (running as a third-party Progressive—or as he called it, "Bull Moose" candidate).

Democrat Woodrow Wilson (1856–1924), president of Princeton University and, afterward, reform-minded governor of New Jersey, was elected U.S. president on a Progressive platform. During his first term, the income tax was introduced with the Sixteenth Amendment, tariffs were lowered, the Federal Reserve Act (1913) reformed currency and banking laws, and antitrust legislation was strengthened in 1914 by the Federal Trade Commission Act and the Clayton Anti-Trust Act. Labor reform came with the Adamson Act, granting an 8-hour day to interstate railroad workers, and the Child Labor Act, curtailing children's working hours.

But Wilson faced staggering problems in foreign relations. He unsuccessfully attempted to negotiate a Pan-American pact to guarantee the mutual integrity of the Western Hemisphere. Wilson also wrestled with Mexico, embroiled in yet another of its many revolutions. At first, Wilson sought to promote self-government in Mexico by refusing to recognize the military dictatorship of General Victoriano Huerta and instead supporting constitutionalist Venustiano Carranza. But in 1916, Wilson intervened against revolutionary guerrilla leader Pancho Villa after Villa inexplicably raided the border town of Columbus, New Mexico, killing several American citizens. In 1915 and 1916, Wilson also sent troops to rebellion-racked Haiti and Santo Domingo, where he established U.S. protectorates.

Despite these problems and conflicts, the majority of Americans were highly relieved that, under Wilson, the United States remained safely aloof from the cataclysm that had begun in Europe on June 28, 1914. On that pretty day in early summer, the Austro-Hungarian archduke Franz Ferdinand and his wife, the Grand Duchess Sophie, paid a state visit to what was then the remote and obscure Balkan city of Sarajevo, capital of Bosnia, a possession of Austria-Hungary. The couple was gunned down by a young Bosnian nationalist named Gavrilo Princeps, who was backed by a secret Serbian nationalist organization, the Serbian Black Hand. Austria-Hungary chose to respond to the assassination by accusing not the Black Hand but the Serbian government itself of having plotted the deaths of the Archduke and Grand Duchess. A tangled series of threats, ultimatums, and alliances was suddenly set into motion—quite mindlessly, it seemed—as if a switch had been thrown, starting some terrible machine. And between the great gears of that mindless machine, the people of Europe, especially the flower of the continent's young manhood, would be crushed.

Remember This _____

The Sixteenth Amendment to the Constitution was ratified by the required two thirds of the states in February of 1913, and the federal government was henceforth authorized to collect income taxes. Hard to believe today, the income tax was very popular, because (people felt) it forced the rich to pay taxes proportionate to their incomes, taking some of the tax burden off the poor and middle class. Initially, rates were set at one percent of taxable income above $3,000 for individuals and $4,000 for married couples. The highest rate was seven percent, imposed on those with incomes in excess of $500,000. The century's two world wars would temporarily send income tax rates sky high—as high as 77 percent during World War I and 91 percent during World War II. In the middle of the second war, in 1943, Congress enacted an automatic payroll withholding system, thereby greatly increasing taxpayer "compliance" (as the IRS politely terms it) and doubling tax revenues by 1944.

At first, it looked as if the war would be a short one. The German armies made a spectacular drive through France, sweeping all resistance before them. Then, in a moment of strategic uncertainty, the Germans paused, turned, and, about 30 miles outside Paris, dug in along the Marne River. For the next 4 years, Europe was doomed to the fruitless horrors of trench warfare, an unmovable line of trenches stretching from Belgium in the north to Switzerland in the south. To the grinding tattoo of machine-gun fire, the ceaseless pounding of artillery, and the strangled moans of asphyxiation by poison gas, the nations of Europe fought one another to a standstill. France, Britain, Russia, and lesser allies were on one side; Germany, Austria-Hungary, and their lesser allies were on the other.

Lusitania Lost

President Wilson adroitly managed to keep the American nation out of this charnel house. Anxious to preserve the rights of American neutrality, he sternly warned Germany in February 1915 that the United States would hold it strictly accountable for the loss of American lives in the sinking of neutral or passenger ships. Just 4 months later, on May 7, 1915, a German U-boat torpedoed the British passenger liner *Lusitania*, killing 1,200 people, including 128 Americans.

Many in the United States—among them Theodore Roosevelt—clamored for immediate entry into the war. Wilson demurred, but he issued a strong protest to Germany, demanding reparations and the cessation of unrestricted submarine warfare. Although Germany protested that the *Lusitania* carried munitions (a truth that was vigorously denied by the British), the kaiser's diplomats were anxious to avoid having to face yet another enemy. Germany ordered its *U-boats* to give passenger ships ample warning before firing upon them. Wilson's firmness with Germany, which seemed feebly insufficient to Roosevelt and other hawks, seemed overly warlike to Wilson's isolationist Secretary of State William Jennings Bryan, who promptly resigned in protest. But most popular sentiment was on the side of Wilson, who had retained American honor without shedding American blood. He ran successfully for a second term, propelled by the slogan "He kept us out of war."

What's the Word?

American David Bushnell (ca. 1742–1824) invented a submarine that was used during the Revolution in 1776. Then in 1864, the Confederate navy operated the submarine *Hunley* with disastrous results—for the crew of the *Hunley*. By the early twentieth century, all the major European powers built submarines. By far, the best were the German vessels, which were called *Unterseebooten*, or *U-booten* for short, **U-boats**.

Zimmermann Note

Although the Germans had backed down on unrestricted submarine warfare, relations between the United States and Germany deteriorated steadily after the *Lusitania* sinking. In February of 1917, Germany, stalled in the trenches and wanting to tighten its stranglehold on British and French supply by sea, announced the resumption of unrestricted submarine warfare. Subsequently, on February 3, the U.S. Navy's *Housatonic* was torpedoed and sunk without warning. In response, President Wilson severed diplomatic relations with Germany. In the meantime, evidence of German espionage in the United States mounted, and on March 1, the American public learned of the "Zimmermann Note" or "Zimmermann Telegram." It was a coded message, sent on January 19, 1917, from German foreign secretary Alfred Zimmermann to his nation's ambassador to Mexico outlining the terms of a proposed German-Mexican alliance against the United States: In return for an alliance against the United States, Germany would help Mexico get back what it had lost in the U.S.-Mexican War. Public sentiment suddenly shifted toward war, and Woodrow Wilson likewise no longer saw an alternative to entering, on the side of the Allies, what was called the Great War. On

April 2, 1917, he asked Congress for a declaration of war. The declaration was voted up on April 6 and signed the same day.

Safe for Democracy

Wilson told Congress that America must go to war in order "to make the world safe for democracy." With this statement, the nation's role as guardian of the Western Hemisphere expanded to an assertion of the United States as truly a world power. In terms of domestic policy, Woodrow Wilson was the typical Progressive reformer. Now he meant to take the Progressive spirit onto the world stage.

The puny U.S. Army numbered fewer than 200,000 men and officers in 1917; by the end of the war, it would swell to 4 million. In May 1917, Wilson pushed through Congress a Selective Service bill, by authority of which 2.8 million men were drafted (in excess of a million more enlisted voluntarily). About half the army—some two million men—served in the AEF (Allied Expeditionary Forces) led by the very able General John J. Pershing. Naval forces sailed under the command of Admiral William S. Sims.

Pershing arrived in Paris on June 14, 1917, at a low point in the fortunes of the Allies. Every major French offensive had failed, and the demoralized French army was plagued by mutinies. The British had made a major push in Flanders, which ended in a costly stalemate. The Russians, fighting on the Eastern Front, had collapsed and were rushing headlong toward a revolution that would end centuries of czarist rule and introduce communism into the world. This revolution would also result in a "separate peace" between Russia and Germany, freeing up masses of German troops for service on the Western Front. Although the first AEF troops followed Pershing on June 26, it was October 21, 1917, before units were committed to battle and the spring of 1918 before masses of Americans actually made a difference in the fighting.

Patriots and Slackers

Pershing's first battle was not with the Germans, however, but with his French and British allies, who demanded that U.S. forces be placed under their direct control. Pershing fended off this demand, which would have fed American soldiers piecemeal into the slaughter, and he retained direct authority over U.S. troops, which were used, in large cohesive units, to great effect.

There was yet another battle to fight. Although a majority of Americans supported the war effort, a minority objected to spilling blood in a "foreign war." Under journalist George Creel, Wilson built a powerful propaganda machine, which produced hundreds of films, posters, pamphlets, and public presentations to portray the "Great War" as a titanic contest between the forces of good and evil. And wherever propaganda failed, the government used emergency war powers to censor the press and to silence critics of the war. Little was done to protect the rights of U.S. citizens of German ancestry, many of whom were threatened and persecuted. In many places, local laws were passed banning the use of the German language itself. Small midwestern towns that had been settled by Germans and given names like Berlin or Hamburg were suddenly rechristened with names like Liberty or Libertyville. Even sauerkraut became "liberty cabbage." As to America's young manhood, the noblest thing one could do was to enlist. And if waiting to be drafted was considered less than patriotic, protesting or attempting to evade the draft was downright treasonous. Those who were suspected of avoiding service—even legally—were branded as "slackers" and publicly humiliated. The word disappeared after the end of the war, only to resurface during the 1990s to describe the drop-out lifestyle some young people adopted.

 Vital Statistics

A total of 65 million men and women served in the armies and navies of combatant nations during World War I. Of this number, at least 10 million were killed and 20 million wounded. Of the 2 million U.S. troops who fought, 112,432 died, and 230,074 were wounded. An influenza epidemic produced by the filthy living conditions of the war killed even more—some 21.64 million people worldwide—1 percent of the world's population.

Over the Top

Between June 6 and July 1, 1918, the "Yanks" recaptured for the Allies Vaux, Bouresches, and Belleau Wood. The Americans also managed to hold the critically important Allied position at Cantigny against a great German offensive between June 9 and 15. If ever the cliché about a "baptism by fire" was appropriate, it was then. American troops quickly came to know what the soldiers of Europe had experienced for the past 4 years: the results of humanity gone mad.

A Blooding at the Marne

Between July 18 and August 6, 85,000 American troops broke the seemingly endless deadlock of the long war by decisively defeating the German's last major offensive at the Second Battle of the Marne. Here, at last, was a battle that could be deemed a genuine turning point. The victory was followed by a series of Allied offensives—at the Somme, Oise-Aisne, and Ypres-Lys—during August.

St. Mihiel Victory

Although Americans fought in each of the major August offensives, they acted independently—and brilliantly—against the St. Mihiel *salient* during September 12 to 16. This battle initiated a campaign involving a massive number of U.S. troops—some 1.2 million of them—who pounded and then cut German supply lines between the Meuse River and the Argonne Forest. The campaign, which continued until the very day of armistice, November 11, 1918, was highly successful, but terribly costly. American units suffered, on average, a casualty rate of 10 percent.

What's the Word? _____

In a military context, a **salient** is a line of battle, especially a concentrated area of defense.

Not Peace, but Armistice

It became apparent to Germany that American soldiers were not only willing and able to fight (a matter of doubt among optimistic German strategists the year before), but that their numbers were inexhaustible, as was the American capacity for producing the hardware of war. The German government agreed to an armistice—a cessation of hostilities—to be concluded at the eleventh hour of the eleventh day of the eleventh month of 1918.

The Least You Need to Know

- The end of the nineteenth century saw the end of America's long tradition of isolation from world affairs.

- The Spanish-American War (1898) was a symptom of U.S. imperialism in the guise of a struggle against tyranny.

- An zealous idealist, Woodrow Wilson devoted his first presidential term to sweeping political and social reform; this same idealism prompted him to lead the United States into World War I in 1917 "to make the world safe for democracy."

- The United States emerged from World War I, the most terrible war the world had seen up to that time, as the champion of world democracy.

26

Booze, Boom, Bust (1918–1929)

In This Chapter

 ◆ Wilson's "Fourteen Points"

 ◆ Rejection of the League of Nations

 ◆ The "Lost Generation" and the "Roaring Twenties"

 ◆ Women's right to vote and advancement of African Americans

 ◆ Prohibition and the birth of organized crime

 ◆ The crash of the stock market

The United States had entered World War I late, but nevertheless in time for the American Expeditionary Force to suffer a ghastly 10 percent casualty rate—even higher if deaths from the influenza epidemic are included. President Wilson was determined that these losses in a "foreign war" would not be in vain. He had told the American people that the "Great War" was a "war to end all war," and he meant it. On January 8, 1918, almost a year before the Armistice, Wilson announced to Congress "Fourteen Points," which he called "the only possible program" for peace. After a complex web of treaty obligations had escalated an obscure Balkan conflict into a worldwide conflagration, Wilson's dream was that his Fourteen Points would create a single international alliance, making armed conflict among nations impossible. The alliance would be called the League of Nations.

Wilson's Dream

As vigorously as Wilson had worked to mobilize his nation for war, he now struggled to bring about a peace meant to spell the end of war. Wilson personally headed the American delegation to the Paris Peace Conference, which was charged with creating a final treaty. Driven by his intense and idealistic vision of a world league and a world of perpetual harmony, Wilson made the fatal political error of disdaining to develop strong bipartisan support for his peace plans. Correctly fearing that Republican isolationists would be hostile to the League of Nations, he unwisely chose to appoint no prominent Republican to the delegation. Worse, Wilson made peace a partisan issue by appealing to voters to reelect a Democratic Congress in 1918. In fact, the 1918 contest went to the Republicans, who won majorities in both houses. To many, this election seemed a no-confidence vote against Wilson and his crusade for world peace.

In Europe, Wilson was at first greeted with nothing but confidence in his leadership of the treaty-making process. However, it soon became apparent that the other major Allied leaders—Georges Clemenceau of France, David Lloyd George of Great Britain, and Victoria Orlando of Italy—wanted to conclude a settlement that did neither more nor less than impose severely vengeful punishment on Germany with the object of permanently crippling it, rendering it incapable of ever going to war again.

In a climate of mean-spirited vengeance, Wilson nevertheless hammered away at his "Fourteen Points," ultimately seeing them embodied in the Treaty of Versailles, which, however, also imposed on Germany the ruinous terms advocated by the other Allies. Gratified that he had won inclusion of the League of Nations as part of the treaty, Wilson presented the Versailles document to his fellow Americans as the best obtainable compromise. He naively believed that the League of Nations itself would, in the fullness of time, rectify some of the injustices presently imposed upon Germany.

Reds!

Even as Wilson was trying to engineer world harmony, popular American sentiment was already retreating into isolationism. The Russian Revolution of 1917 and the Bolshevik Revolution that followed it toppled the long regime of the czars and then installed a Communist government. Few Americans greeted these events as a victory over autocracy, but regarded them with fear and loathing as an assault on established order. In the years following World War I, a "Red Scare" swept Western Europe and the United States.

Remember This _____

Wilson addressed Congress on January 8, 1918, and promulgated his "Fourteen Points":

I. Open covenants of peace, openly arrived at ...

II. Absolute freedom of navigation upon the seas ...

III. The removal ... of [international] economic barriers ...

IV. Adequate guarantees ... that ... armaments will be reduced ...

V. ... impartial adjustment of all colonial claims ...

VI. The evacuation of all Russian territory ...

VII. Belgium ... must be evacuated and restored ...

VIII. All French territory should be freed and the invaded portions restored ...

IX. A readjustment of the frontiers of Italy should be effected along clearly recognizable lines of nationality.

X. The peoples of Austria-Hungary ... should be accorded the freest opportunity of autonomous development.

XI. Rumania, Serbia, and Montenegro should be evacuated ...

XII. The Turkish portions of the present Ottoman Empire should be assured a secure sovereignty ...

XIII. An independent Polish state should be erected ...

XIV. A general association [league] of nations must be formed ...

On the evening of January 2, 1919, U.S. Attorney General A. Mitchell Palmer launched simultaneous raids on the headquarters of radical organizations in 33 cities, indiscriminately rounding up 6,000 persons, U.S. citizens and noncitizens alike, who were *believed* to be "sympathetic to communism." Palmer and others lumped Communists, radicals, and "free thinkers" together with out-and-out anarchists, who, in the wake of the revolutions in Russia, were indeed committing acts of terrorism in the United States. Anarchists mailed bombs to Palmer, Rockefeller, J. P. Morgan, and more than 30 other wealthy, prominent conservatives. Fortunately, many of the bombs failed to reach their destinations—due, incredibly enough, to having been mailed with insufficient postage!

In a climate of intense fear, outrage, and confusion, Palmer created the General Intelligence Division, headed by a zealous young Justice Department investigator named J. Edgar Hoover. With meticulous enthusiasm, Hoover (in those recomputed days) directed the laborious manual compilation of a massive card index of 150,000 radical leaders, organizations, and publications. As all too often happened in American history, beginning with the Alien and Sedition Acts passed at the end of the eighteenth century, legislators and administrators did not hesitate to take totalitarian measures in the name of defending American liberty.

The Dream Ends

Fear of Communism was not the only thing that chipped away at Wilson's dream. Although the president tried to persuade the American people—and himself—that the Treaty of Versailles was the best compromise possible, it was actually one of the most tragic documents in history. Although Wilson succeeded in persuading France to concede its key demand—that the left bank of the Rhine be severed from Germany and put under French military control—the treaty dictated humiliating, economically devastating terms. Germany was forced to accept full guilt for the war, to cede huge sections of territory, and to disarm almost completely.

The Allies hoped that, by weakening Germany, that nation could never again threaten Europe's peace. However, the punitive terms of Versailles so destabilized Germany that it became ripe for the dark promises of Adolph Hitler, who came into prominence during the 1920s and 1930s. Instead of preventing another war, the Treaty of Versailles *guaranteed* one—a war that would prove even more devastating than the conflict of 1914–1918.

At home, Wilson's lapse of political savvy was taking its toll as staunch conservative Henry Cabot Lodge (1850–1924) led Senate Republican opposition to the U.S. commitment to the League of Nations. Believing the League to be above politics, Wilson would brook virtually no compromise and decided to bring popular pressure on the Senate by taking his case directly to the people. He embarked on a grueling 9,500-mile transcontinental whistle-stop speaking tour. On September 25, 1919, exhausted by war, by the heartbreaking labors of making peace, and by his battle on behalf of the League of Nations, Woodrow Wilson collapsed following a speech in Pueblo,

Colorado. He was rushed back to Washington, but his condition deteriorated and, a week later, he suffered a devastating stroke that left him partially paralyzed. Ill, desperate, frustrated, and embittered, Wilson instructed his followers to accept absolutely no compromise on the League.

American politics has always thrived on compromise; and now, without it, the Senate rejected the Treaty of Versailles, as well as the League of Nations. Woodrow Wilson, his health continuing to decline, could only watch as the "war to end all war" came to look more and more like just another war fought in vain. Warren G. Harding (1865–1923), the Republican who succeeded Wilson in the White House, ran on a pledge of a "return to normalcy." Shortly after taking office, Harding told Congress that "we seek no part in directing the destinies of the world … [the League] is not for us."

A Generation Lost and Found

Woodrow Wilson was not the only embittered individual in postwar America. Four years of European carnage had shown the worst of what humanity was capable. The war broke the spirit of some people; in others, it created a combination of restlessness, desperation, boredom, and thrill-seeking that earned the decade its nickname: the "Roaring Twenties." Some Americans, mostly young intellectuals, found that they could not settle back into routine life at home after the war. A colony of expatriate artists and writers gathered in Paris. Many of these individuals congregated in the apartment of a remarkable medical school dropout named Gertrude Stein—writer, art collector, and cultivator of creative talent. One day, she reportedly remarked to one of these young people, Ernest Hemingway, "You are all a lost generation." That phrase stuck as a description of those individuals cast adrift after the war, their former ideals shattered by battle, yet unable to find new values to replace those they had lost.

Stein, Fitzgerald, Hemingway, and Co.

The United States, land of liberty and opportunity, had much to be proud of. The nation touted its superiority over Europe, whose masses often suffered under conditions of political enslavement and spiritual and physical want. Yet, in matters of art and culture, America had not outgrown its "colonial" status, even by the 1920s. True, the United States did produce a number of remarkable world-class writers during the nineteenth century—including Washington Irving, Edgar Allan Poe, Ralph Waldo Emerson, Henry David Thoreau, Nathaniel Hawthorne, Walt Whitman, Herman Melville, Emily Dickinson, Mark Twain, and others. And America had some extraordinary

American Echo

I remember riding in a taxi one afternoon between very tall buildings under a mauve and rosy sky; I began to bawl because I had everything I wanted and knew I would never be so happy again.

—F. Scott Fitzgerald, "My Lost City" (1932)

visual artists—such as the unparalleled group of landscape painters dubbed the Hudson River School, who emerged under the leadership of Thomas Cole and Frederick Edwin Church before the Civil War. Despite this prominent talent, the United States entered the twentieth century still bowing to the aesthetic culture of Europe, as if Americans could never quite measure up.

During the 1920s, however, a group of American writers made an unmistakable impact on the cultural life of the world. Two of the most important, Ernest Hemingway (1899–1961) and F. Scott Fitzgerald (1896–1940), were frequent guests at Gertrude Stein's salons (informal gatherings of artists and writers), where they discussed how they would write "the great American novel." Francis Scott Key Fitzgerald (named for the ancestor who wrote "The Star-Spangled Banner") burst onto the literary scene in 1920 with *This Side of Paradise*, a novel that ushered in the "Jazz Age" (Fitzgerald's own coinage) with a vivid portrait of Lost Generation youth. Two years later came *The Beautiful and Damned* and, in 1925, *The Great Gatsby*. This story of the enigmatic Jay Gatsby explored the American Dream in poetic, satirical, and ultimately tragic detail. The theme was plumbed again a decade later in *Tender Is the Night* (1934).

Women Get the Vote

The American woman also came of age in the 1920s, emerging from long subjugation to straitlaced Victorian ideals of decorum and femininity. During the war, women had joined the workforce in increasing numbers, and, afterward, became lively participants in the intellectual life of the nation. The most profound step toward the liberation of American women was the ratification of the Nineteenth Amendment to the U.S. Constitution, which gave women the right to vote.

Harlem Lights and Harlem Nights

There was growing liberation, too, for another long-oppressed group: African Americans. Slavery had ended with the Civil War, but African Americans hardly enjoyed the same opportunities and privileges as most other Americans. In the North as well as the South, they were discriminated against in education, employment, housing, and in just about every other phase of life. Segregation was *de facto* in the North—unofficial, but nonetheless real—and *de jute* in the South—actually mandated by law. African Americans had served with distinction during World War I, but always in segregated units. The French did not discriminate, and for some African American soldiers, the overseas experience was an eye-opener. They returned to the States no longer willing to accept second-class citizenship.

Many white Americans did not so much discriminate against African Americans, as they failed to *see* them, as if they were invisible. Excluded from positions of power and influence, African Americans simply did not matter much—as far as mainstream white society was concerned.

The humble peanut helped to change this attitude. In 1921, George Washington Carver, who had been born a Missouri slave in 1864, testified before Congress on behalf of the National Association of Peanut Growers to extol and explain the wonders of what had been a minor crop. Against all odds, Carver had worked his way through college, earning a Master's degree in agriculture in 1896 and accepting a teaching position at Tuskegee Institute. Tuskegee had been founded in Alabama by African American educator Booker T. Washington (1856–1915) as a source of practical vocational education for the black community. At Tuskegee, Carver concentrated on developing new products from crops—including the peanut and the sweet potato—that could replace cotton as the staple of southern farmers. Cotton was a money maker, but it quickly depleted soil, and farmers solely dependent on cotton soon were ruined. Carver transformed peanuts and sweet potatoes into plastic materials, lubricants, dyes, drugs, inks, wood stains, cosmetics, tapioca, molasses, and most famously, peanut butter. His contribution to revitalizing the perpetually beleaguered agricultural economy of the South was significant; but even more, Carver showed both white and black America that an African American could accomplish great things. For the black community, he was a source of pride; for white Americans, he was among the very first culturally *visible* black men.

Indeed, although oppression was still a fact of black life during the 1920s, white intellectuals became intensely interested in African American intellectual and artistic creations. Black artists and writers were drawn to New York City's Harlem neighborhood, where they produced works that commanded widespread attention and admiration. This literary and artistic movement was called the Harlem Renaissance and drew inspiration from the black political leader W. E. B. Du Bois (1868–1963). A sociologist, Du Bois had a Harvard doctorate (he was the first African American Ph.D. in the United States) and founded *The Crisis*, the magazine of the National Association for the Advancement of Colored People (NAACP), an important organization created in 1909 by Du Bois and a mostly white group of social activists. In opposition to Booker T. Washington, who was willing to sacrifice social and political equality for black economic progress,

Du Bois argued that African Americans had to achieve social equality and their full political rights as well as economic self-sufficiency. Moreover, he argued, they could not achieve these goals by merely emulating white people, but had to awaken within themselves black racial pride by discovering their own African cultural heritage.

> **American Echo**
>
> The dark world is going to submit to its present treatment just as long as it must and not one moment longer.
>
> —W. E. B. Du Bois, "Dark water," in *The Souls of Black Folk*, 1920

Some significant American writers associated with the movement Du Bois was instrumental in launching were poet Countee Cullen (1903–1946), novelist Rudolph Fisher (1897–1934), poet-essayist Langston Hughes (1902–1967), folklorist Zora Neale Hurston (1891–1960), poet James Weldon Johnson (1871–1938), and novelist Jean Toomey (1894–1967).

Harlem developed into a gathering place for avant-garde white intellectuals who did what would have been unthinkable just a decade before: they spoke and mingled with African American writers, artists, and thinkers. Yet among whites, Harlem was not known only to intellectuals. The community also became a popular spot for white night-clubbers seeking first-class jazz from great African American musicians like Fletcher Henderson (1898–1952), Louis Armstrong (1900–1971), and the young Duke Ellington (1899–1974).

America Goes Dry

The general liberalization of morals that accompanied America's entry into World War I fueled a reactionary countermovement in the form of a drive toward temperance, which culminated in the Eighteenth Amendment to the Constitution, prohibiting the sale, importation, or consumption of alcoholic beverages anywhere in the United States. The Vested Act, passed after ratification, provided for federal enforcement of Prohibition.

Greeted by some as what President Herbert Hoover called a "noble experiment," Prohibition was for a large number of ordinary Americans an open invitation to violate the law. The 1920s, therefore, became by definition a lawless decade. Otherwise law-abiding citizens made bathtub gin, brewed homemade beer, fermented wine in their cellars, and frequented "blind pigs" and "speakeasies"—covert saloons that served booze in coffee mugs and teacups. Police raids on such establishments were common occurrences, but mostly, officials looked the other way—especially if they were paid to do so.

Corruption hardly stopped with the cop on the street. City and state governments were receptive to payoffs, and indeed, the presidential administration of Warren G. Harding rivaled that of Ulysses S. Grant for corruption and scandal. In this national atmosphere, mobsters was born and thrived. Underlying the violence was the idea of crime as a business, and by the end of the decade, a quasi-corporate entity called the Syndicate would be formed to "organize" crime.

Countdown to Black Tuesday

If morals, mores, and ideas were freewheeling in the 1920s, so was spending. For most—except farmers and unskilled laborers—the decade was prosperous, sometimes wildly so. Americans speculated on stocks in unprecedented numbers, often overextending themselves by purchasing securities "on margin," putting down as little as 10 cents on the dollar in the hope that the stock would rise fast and far enough to cover what amounted to very substantial loans based on miniscule equity.

Joy Ride

The fact was that so much stock had been bought on margin—backed by dimes on dollars—that much of it amounted to little more than paper. Even worse, although production in well-financed factories soared, the buying power of consumers failed to keep pace. Soon, industry was making more than people were buying. As goods piled up and prices fell, industry began laying off workers. People without jobs do not buy goods. As more workers were laid off, the marketplace shrunk smaller and smaller. Companies do not make new hires in a shrinking marketplace. And so the cycle went.

 Vital Statistics

Stocks lost an average of 40 points on Black Tuesday, October 29, 1929. In 1932, the Dow Jones Industrials hit an all-time low of 40.56 points, having fallen 89 percent from a September 1929 high of 386. In 1930, 1,300 banks failed. By 1933, another 3,700 would fail, and one in four workers would be jobless.

Paying the Fare

Despite this cycle, stock prices continued to spiral upward. But the market began to exhibit the warning signs of instability. During the autumn of 1929, stock prices fluctuated wildly; then, on October 24, the stock market was seized by a selling spree. Five days later, on October 29, "Black Tuesday," the bottom fell out and stock prices plummeted. With prices falling, brokers "called" their margin loans, demanding immediate payment in full on stocks that were now worthless. Many investors were wiped out in an instant. President Calvin Coolidge had declared during the booming mid-decade years that "the business of America is business." Herbert Hoover, elected president in 1928, found himself nervously assuring his stunned and fearful fellow Americans that "prosperity was just around the corner." As it so happened, that corner would not be turned for a full decade.

The Least You Need to Know

- The failure of the United States to join the League of Nations doomed that precursor of the United Nations to ultimate failure.

- The Eighteenth Amendment finally gave American women the right to vote.

- The Nineteenth Amendment ended Prohibition and brought on the heyday of organized crime in America.

- The climate of the 1920s, at once wildly creative, liberating, desperate, and reckless, was in large part the result of the aftereffects of World War I.

- The stock market crash of 1929 was the culmination of a cycle of careless, credit-based investments and increased industrial output versus a shrinking market for industrial goods.

Chapter 27

A New Deal and a New War (1930–1941)

In This Chapter

- The Hoover administration during the Great Depression
- FDR's New Deal
- An era of "organized crime"
- The approach and outbreak of World War II

Herbert Clark Hoover was born on August 10, 1874, the son of a West Branch, Iowa, blacksmith. He learned the meaning of hard work practically from the cradle, and at age eight, he also came to know the tragedy of loss. Orphaned, Hoover was sent to live with an uncle in Oregon and enrolled in the mining engineering program at California's Stanford University, graduating in 1895. For some 20 years, Hoover traveled the world, earning a fortune as a mining engineer. The Quaker ideals acquired from his uncle prompted him to aid in relief efforts during World War I, and Hoover earned a reputation as a tireless and effective humanitarian. During the period of U.S. participation in the "Great War," Hoover served as food administrator, charged with promoting agricultural production and food conservation. At the end of the war, President Woodrow Wilson sent

Hoover to Europe to direct the American Relief Administration. Hoover served as U.S. Secretary of Commerce in the cabinets of Warren G. Harding and Calvin Coolidge.

When Coolidge declined to seek a second term (privately observing that an economic disaster was on the way, and he didn't want any part of it), Hoover easily won election as the nation's thirty-first president. He ran on the optimistic platform that, if everyone would just put their heads together, poverty could be eliminated in America. The future looked bright. And who should know this better than a man justly hailed as "the great humanitarian?"

Brother, Can You Spare a Dime?

After the Wall Street crash came, Hoover was slow to react and did nothing more than assure the public that "prosperity was just around the corner." As each month brought worse financial news and lengthened the lines of the jobless, the homeless, and the desperate, Hoover proposed a number of relief programs, but insisted that state and local governments take responsibility for funding them. In principle, this arrangement was prudent. Who better knew the needs of the people than their local governments? In practice, however, the policy was doomed for a very simple reason: like just about everyone else, state and local governments had no money.

Most significantly, Hoover steadfastly refused to make federal aid available directly to individuals. He feared that big-government intervention would compromise individual liberty and integrity. Most of all, reflecting his midwestern, up-by-your-own-boot-straps heritage, Hoover believed federal assistance would sap the gumption and initiative of the individual citizen. Like many others, Hoover believed the depression was nothing more than a brief downturn in the economy, and he thought it far better to tough it out than radically alter the established capitalist system.

In the meantime, shanty towns constructed of boxes and crates sprouted like weeds across the American landscape to house the homeless. "Hoovervilles" they were called, and the great humanitarian's reputation was forever tarnished. Unjustly—but understandably—blame for the Great Depression was laid almost entirely at the doorstep of the White House.

America had had its share of boom and bust before. But the Great Depression of the 1930s was unparalleled in magnitude, scope, and duration. Fifteen to 25 percent of the workforce was jobless in an era without government unemployment insurance and other elements of a social safety net. Families lost their savings, their homes—in fortunately rare instances, some even their lives—to disease, malnutrition, and outright starvation.

The depression was not confined to the United States. It gripped the world, including the citadels of democracy—the Western capitalist nations. Worst of all, the depression showed no signs of abating. As the difficult years went by, want and misery became a way of life.

Tyranny Abroad

Discontent and despair bred revolution. The nations of Europe seethed, especially Germany, which was already economically crippled by the punitive Treaty of Versailles and was now brought utterly to its knees by the depression. First in Italy and then in Germany—and to a lesser extent, elsewhere in Europe—two major ideologies came into violent opposition: *fascism* versus *communism*. To most Americans, both of these *totalitarian* ideologies seemed clearly repugnant to democracy.

What's the Word?

Fascism, a system of government marked by centralization of authority under an absolute dictator, was masterminded in Italy by Benito Mussolini (1883–1945). The name comes from the Latin word *fasces*, meaning "a bundle or rods bound together around an ax," which was the ancient Roman symbol of authority. Communism, as proposed by Karl Marx (1818–1883), was a system of collective ownership of property and the collective administration of power for the common good. In practice, communism was a system of government characterized by state ownership of property and the centralization of authority in a single political party or dictator. Totalitarianism describes any system of government in which the individual is wholly subordinate to the state.

But Democracy was not putting beans on the table. Among American intellectuals and even some radical workers, communism appeared to offer a viable alternative to what seemed a lot like a failed political and economic system. Could the nation be on the precipice of revolution?

The Epoch of FDR

Born to great wealth in Hyde Park, New York, in 1882, Franklin Delano Roosevelt never suffered poverty himself. The product of Groton School, Harvard College, and Columbia University Law School, young Roosevelt became a Wall Street lawyer. He devoted some of his time to free legal work for the poor and by this came to know and sympathize with the plight of the so-called common man. FDR worked his way to prominence in Dutchess County (New York) politics and was appointed assistant secretary of the Navy in the Wilson administration. In 1920, FDR was running mate to James M. Cox, the democratic presidential hopeful who lost to Republican Warren G. Harding.

Then came Roosevelt's darkest—and finest—hour. In the summer of 1921, while resident at his family's summer home on Campobello Island (New Brunswick, Canada), Roosevelt was stricken with polio. Desperately ill, he recovered, but was left paralyzed from the waist down. His mother urged him to retire to Hyde Park. His wife, the remarkable Eleanor Roosevelt—FDR's fifth cousin once removed and the niece of Theodore Roosevelt—persuaded her husband instead to return to public life. With great personal strength and courage, Roosevelt underwent intensive physical therapy, learned to stand using heavy iron leg braces, to walk with the aid of crutches, and even to drive his own car, specially modified with hand-operated accelerator, brake, and clutch. He ran for governor of New York and won, bringing to the state such progressive measures as the development of public power utilities, civil-service reform, and social-welfare programs.

When he decided to run for president, Roosevelt faced opponents who objected that he was neither intellectually nor—as detractors pointed out—physically fit for the White House.

FDR proved his opponents dead wrong. Having overcome the odds in his personal fight against polio, Roosevelt set about proving himself capable of overcoming the even grimmer odds in the national fight to lift America out of the Great Depression. The candidate flew to Chicago and addressed the 1932 Democratic National Convention, pledging to deliver to the American people a "New Deal," a *federally* funded, *federally* administered program of relief and recovery.

When he accepted the 1932 Democratic presidential nomination, Franklin D. Roosevelt declared: "I pledge you, I pledge myself, to a new deal for the American people." Following Roosevelt's inauguration, the phrase "New Deal" caught on in a way that transformed the federal government as well as people's attitudes about the role of government. Within the first 3 months of the new administration—dubbed with Napoleonic grandeur by the press the "Hundred Days"—FDR introduced to Congress his program of relief legislation, which promised to stimulate industrial recovery, assist individual victims of the depression (something Hoover and all previous presidents had refused to do), guarantee minimum living standards, and help avert future crises.

Most of the actual legislation of the Hundred Days was aimed at providing immediate aid and relief. The Federal Deposit Insurance Corporation (FDIC) was established to protect depositors from losing their savings in the event of bank failure. The measure did much to restore confidence in the nation's faltering banking system. The Federal Reserve Board, which regulates the nation's money supply, was strengthened. The Home Owners Loan Corporation was established to help beleaguered home owners avoid foreclosure. A Federal Securities Act reformed the regulation of stock transactions—an effort to avert the kind of wild speculation that helped bring about the crash of 1929.

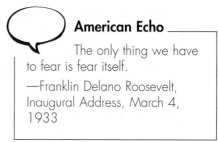

American Echo

The only thing we have to fear is fear itself.

—Franklin Delano Roosevelt, Inaugural Address, March 4, 1933

Next, the Civilian Conservation Corps, the CCC, put thousands of unemployed young men to work on projects in national forests, parks, and public lands; the National Recovery Act (NRA), the most sweeping and controversial of the early New Deal legislation, established the Public Works Administration (PWA) and imposed upon industry a strict code of fair practice. The act set minimum wages and maximum working hours and gave employees the right to collective bargaining.

In sharp contrast to the world's Communist regimes, the Roosevelt administration showed equal concern for the industrial worker and the agricultural worker. Farmers were in a desperate plight during the depression, and in May 1933, FDR called on Congress to create the Agricultural Adjustment Administration, a program of production limits and federal subsidies. Perhaps the single most visible manifestation of the New Deal program of agricultural reform was the establishment of the Tennessee Valley Authority (TVA), which built roads, great dams, and hydroelectric plants in seven of the nation's poorest states.

More programs followed the Hundred Days. In 1935, the Works Progress Administration (WPA) was formed, which put 8.5 million people to work between 1935 and 1943—the year the program ended. WPA workers built public projects out of concrete and steel, and they also created cultural works through the Federal Theater Project, the Federal Writers' Program, and the Federal Art Project. The most enduring of the New Deal programs was Social Security, introduced in 1935, which created old-age pension funds through payroll and wage taxes.

Vital Statistics

Despite the New Deal, 9.5 million people remained unemployed by 1939.

None of the New Deal programs brought full recovery, but they helped restore confidence in the American government and propelled Roosevelt to a landslide second-term victory over Republican Alf Landon in 1936. A "Second New Deal" went into effect, which concentrated on labor reforms.

Street Wars

In the end, it would take the approach of World War II, with its insatiable demand for the industrial materials of strife, to end the Great Depression. But years before the United States entered that war, another, different kind of combat was being waged on the streets of the nation's cities. Prohibition had spawned a gangster culture in the 1920s, which many Americans found colorful, almost romantic. After all, the urban outlaws supplied the public with the good times that government denied them.

Then came St. Valentine's Day, 1929, the day Al Capone decided to eliminate rival Chicago gangland leader "Bugs" Moran. Capone dispatched gunmen, disguised as policemen, who rounded up seven members of the Moran gang, stood them up against the wall of Moran's commercial garage, and brutally executed them with the gangster's weapon of choice, the "Tommy gun"—the Thompson submachine gun, cheaply available in great quantity as U.S. Army surplus in the years following World War I. (Moran himself wasn't present and escaped assassination.) Mobsters had been rubbing one another out for years, but the blatant butchery of the St. Valentine's Day Massacre hit a public nerve. Suddenly, Capone and other gangsters were no longer viewed as Robin Hoods, but as the cold-blooded murderers they had been all along. Yet, as gangsters became more viciously violent, they also became increasingly organized.

In the same year as the St. Valentine's Day Massacre, Capone proposed to the gang leaders of New York and other cities that they meet to *organize* crime throughout the United States. The meeting took place in Atlantic City and included such underworld luminaries as Lucky Luciano, Joe Adonis, Alberto Anastasia, Frank Costello, and Meyer Lansky. The national crime "Syndicate" was born, consolidating—albeit in loose fashion—gambling, prostitution, extortion, and liquor trafficking nationwide. After 1933, when the Eighteenth Amendment was repealed, thereby ending Prohibition, the Syndicate began to enter the trade in narcotics, hoping heroin and the like would replace booze as the public's illicit substances of choice.

The economic conditions of the 1930s brought at least two durable legacies into American life: one, a federal government that takes an active role in the welfare of its citizens (witness the enormous popular resistance that, beginning in 2005, met President George W. Bush's proposals to "reform" Social Security) and, two, organized crime.

Bloodlust

The Great Depression brought the United States close to the brink of revolution, but a deeply ingrained tradition of democratic capitalism, combined with FDR's inspired leadership, which restored and maintained faith in the government, averted a violent breakdown. In Europe, also hard hit by the depression, the people of Italy and Germany hungered not for democracy, but for the strongman dictatorships promised by a political journalist named Benito Mussolini (1883–1945) and a failed artist, sometime house painter, and full-time political agitator named Adolf Hitler (1889–1945). Exhausted humanity had assumed that the horrors of World War I, combined with the peaceful prosperity of the 1920s, guaranteed the permanent rise of international stability and liberal constitutionalism. But Germany, crippled by the harsh conditions of the Versailles treaty, had been excluded from any postwar prosperity. Then the depression drove its desperate people to even deeper desperation. In Germany and Italy, militaristic authoritarianism burst into iron blossom with promises of a return to national glory and national prosperity.

Remember This

The depression-born longing for a bright future was summed up in two great World's Fairs. The Century of Progress Exhibition of 1933 to 1934, held in Chicago, did much to popularize modern architecture. And the New York World's Fair of 1939 to 1940 was built around the theme of "The World of Tomorrow"—even as the nightmare of total war broke once again upon Europe.

Lightning War

In Germany, Hitler and his Nazi Party won a popular following that propelled him to the position of chancellor under the aged and infirm President Paul von Hindenburg in 1933 and into absolute dictatorship after Hindenburg's death in 1934. Hitler took Germany out of the League of Nations in 1933 and, in defiance of the Treaty of Versailles, initiated a massive rearmament program. In 1936, the dictator sent troops into the Rhineland, even though it had been officially "demilitarized" by the Versailles treaty. The League of Nations stood by helplessly, as did the Allies of World War I. Indeed, one of those erstwhile Allies, Italy, openly sided with Nazi Germany. Seeking an easy foreign conquest to solidify popular support, Benito Mussolini, like some monstrous incarnation of a schoolyard bully, sent Italy's modern army into Africa against Ethiopians who were armed, if at all, with weapons from the last century. Ethiopia collapsed by 1936, and although the nation's emperor, Haile Salassie (1892–1975), appealed for international aid to the League of Nations with great dignity and eloquence, that world body proved impotent.

Hard on the heels of the Italian conquest of Ethiopia came the Spanish Civil War (1936–1939), a complex struggle between factions allied with the nation's liberal-leftist republican government, on one side, and the Fascist-sympathizing rightists led primarily by General Francisco Franco (1892–1975) on the other. Hitler and Mussolini eagerly sent military aid to Franco, and Hitler's Luftwaffe (air force) in particular used Spanish towns as practice targets in preparation for the greater conflict looming on the dark horizon. Although Soviet dictator Joseph Stalin (1879–1953) gave military equipment to the Spanish republicans, the United States, Britain, and France—fearing the outbreak of a general war—remained neutral.

Their reluctance was as understandable as it was tragic. After all, in 1914, a tangle of alliances had escalated a local Balkan conflict into a conflagration that engulfed the world. Yet while the former Allies waffled and waited, Germany and Italy forged the Rome-Berlin Axis in 1936. That same year, in Asia, the Empire of Japan concluded the Anti-Comintern Pact (an alliance against communism) with Germany; in 1937, Italy signed on to the pact as well. The following year, 1938, Hitler invaded Austria and annexed it to his Third Reich. The year 1938 also saw Hitler's demand for annexation of the Sudetenland—western Czechoslovakia, where many ethnic Germans lived. France and Britain were bound by treaty to defend the territorial integrity of Czechoslovakia, but they nevertheless yielded the Sudetenland to Germany in an effort to "appease" Hitler. British prime minister Neville Chamberlain told the world that the cession of the Sudetenland (by means of the 1938 Munich Agreement) ensured "peace in our time."

He was wrong. In 1939, Hitler seized the rest of Czechoslovakia, then took a part of Lithuania and prepared to gobble up the so-called Polish Corridor, a narrow strip of land that, by the terms of the Treaty of Versailles, separated East Prussia from the rest of Germany. At this time, Mussolini's Italy annexed Albania. Finally, at four o'clock on the morning of September 1, 1939, Germany invaded—and quickly crushed—Poland, conquering the country in less than a month by means of a rapid, violent, all-out attack, using aircraft, tanks, mobile artillery, and troops. *Blitzkrieg*, the Germans called these tactics: Lightning War. France and Britain could no longer stand by. World War II had begun.

Infamy at Pearl Harbor

While American eyes focused nervously on Europe, Asia was heating to the point of crisis. Despite a 1922 pledge to respect China's territorial integrity, Japan invaded Manchuria in 1931 and transformed it into the puppet state of Manchukuo the following year. The League of Nations protested feebly, prompting nothing more than Japan's withdrawal from that moribund organization in 1933. By 1937, Japan and China were engaged in full-scale war. On September 27, 1940, Japan signed the Tripartite Pact with Italy and Germany, thereby enlarging the Berlin-Rome Axis into the Berlin-Rome-Tokyo Axis.

Although it remained officially neutral, the United States, guided by Roosevelt, edged steadily closer to war. The sale of military supplies to the Allies was authorized, and then, in March 1941, Congress passed the Lend-Lease Act, permitting the shipment of material to nations whose defense was considered vital to U.S. security—Great Britain and, later, China and the USSR. In September 1940, the first peacetime draft law in U.S. history had been passed, authorizing the Selective Service registration of 17 million men. In August and September of 1941, U.S. merchant vessels were armed for self-defense.

The powder was packed in the keg. All it took was a flame for the war to explode upon America.

That came on December 7, 1941. At 7:50 on a quiet Sunday morning, Japanese aircraft struck with stunning surprise at Pearl Harbor, Hawaii, where some 75 major U.S. Navy ships were moored. By 10 A.M., the attack was over.

The next day, President Roosevelt asked Congress for a declaration of war, calling December 7, 1941, a "date which will live in infamy." Suddenly, the Great Depression dissolved in a headlong rush of young men into the armed forces and of others, women as well as men, into the nation's factories. Industries now tooled up—for the second time in the century—to serve as the "arsenal of democracy."

American Echo

A Japanese attack on Pearl Harbor is a strategic impossibility.

—Historian George Fielding Eliot, "The Impossible War with Japan," *American Mercury*, September 1938

The Least You Need to Know

♦ Although unjustly, Herbert Hoover is often blamed for having caused the depression; however, the federal government did not take major steps to bring economic relief until Roosevelt assumed office.

♦ The massive programs of the New Deal probably averted social breakdown and revolution in the United States, but it was the economic demands of World War II that finally ended the Great Depression.

♦ U.S. policy was officially neutral at the outbreak of World War II in Europe, although President Roosevelt negotiated an aid program to England.

♦ The surprise Japanese attack on Pearl Harbor on December 7, 1941, immediately brought the United States into World War II.

Chapter 28

Saving the World (1941–1945)

In This Chapter

- ◆ Early defeats
- ◆ Turning points: victories in North Africa and at Midway
- ◆ The collapse of Germany
- ◆ The use of the atomic bomb against Japan

When America had entered World War I, it rushed to mobilize forces for a *European* war. Now, even as Europe was being overrun by Nazi Germany, Japan had struck directly at United States territory (Hawaii did not become a *state* until August 21, 1959). Preparations for war were even more urgent in 1941 than they had been in 1917, and the blow at Pearl Harbor was just one of many Japanese assaults. Japanese forces attacked Wake Island and Guam (both U.S. possessions), British Malaya, Singapore, the Dutch East Indies, Burma, Thailand, and the Philippines (at the time a U.S. commonwealth territory). The tiny U.S. garrison on Guam was overwhelmed and surrendered. On Wake Island, a small body of Marines and civilian defense contractors heroically repelled the first Japanese attack, but yielded to a second assault by vastly superior forces. Britain's crown colony of Hong Kong collapsed, soon followed by Singapore (another British possession), and then the Dutch East Indies. Burma likewise fell, despite the efforts of Claire L. Chennault (1890–1958), a former U.S. Army Air Corps officer and then air advisor to China's premier Chiang Kai-Shek. Chennault led his American Volunteer Group—the famed "Flying Tigers," a small force of U.S.-made Curtiss P-40 fighter planes piloted by American civilian mercenaries—in cripplingly effective action against the enemy's far superior numbers of aircraft.

For the United States, as for the rest of the formerly "free" world, the opening years of World War II were humiliating, dismal, and terrifying.

"I Shall Return"

After Pearl Harbor, the severest blow in the Pacific came in the Philippines, where General Douglas MacArthur (1880–1964), commanding 55,000 Filipinos and Americans, made a heroic stand on the Bataan Peninsula, but at last, in February 1942, was ordered to evacuate to Australia to assume command of the Allied forces in the southwestern Pacific. Reluctantly, MacArthur left his troops to their fate. "I shall return," he pledged, but it would take until 1944 for the Allies to put him into a position to make good on that promise.

Under Lieutenant General Jonathan M. Wainwright, the Filipino-American forces held out until May 6, 1942, when they surrendered and were subject to unspeakable brutality at the hands of Japanese captors.

Remember This

The Japanese military was guided by the *bushido*, code of the samurai warrior, as ancient as it was harsh. To be killed in battle was an honor, but to be taken prisoner, a disgrace. Accordingly, the Japanese treated their prisoners of war as dishonored men. America learned this fact the hard way when U.S. and Filipino soldiers who surrendered at Corregidor on April 9, 1942, were sent on a forced march to captivity in Bataan. The infamous Bataan Death March resulted in the deaths of 10,000 POWs, victims of abuse, starvation, and illness.

Desperate for a counterstrike against Japan, the Army Air Forces approved a mission led by Lieutenant Colonel James Doolittle (1896–1993). In what very nearly amounted to a suicide mission, he took 16 B-25s aboard the aircraft carrier *Hornet* and launched, on April 18, 1942, a surprise bombing raid against Tokyo and other Japanese targets. Everyone knew that the twin-engine bombers could not carry sufficient fuel to return to any American base. Even if they had had enough fuel capacity to return to the

Hornet, the bombers, not designed for carrier flight, would have been unable to land. The plan was to ditch the planes in China, find safe haven among Chinese resistance fighters, and somehow find a way to return home. Miraculously, most of the bomber crews were, in fact, rescued, and although the damage to Tokyo and other targets was minor, the psychological effect on the Japanese people, as well as the Japanese high command, was profound. The attack shocked the Japanese, who were forced to tie up valuable fighter aircraft in home defense. As for the American home front, morale was given an incalculable boost.

Don't Sit Under the Apple Tree

For all its horrors, World War II is recalled by many Americans as an almost magical time, when the nation united with single-minded purpose in a cause both desperate and absolutely just—a struggle, quite literally, of good against evil. Everyone pitched in to produce the materials of war, and women joined the workforce in unprecedented numbers as the men were inducted into the armed forces. They promised to be faithful to their freedom fighters, awaiting their return from battle. "Don't sit under the apple tree," the popular Andrews Sisters sang, "With anyone else but me ... 'Til I come marching home."

Activity on the homefront also had a far less noble and attractive side. On February 19, 1942, responding to pressure from West Coast politicians, FDR signed Executive Order 9066, requiring all Japanese Americans living within 200 miles of the Pacific shores—citizens and resident aliens alike—to report for relocation in internment camps located in California, Idaho, Utah, Arizona, Wyoming, Colorado, and Arkansas. Military officials feared sabotage, but non-Japanese farmers in the region feared competition even more and were eager to get rid of their Japanese-American farming neighbors.

American Echo

For many Americans, the most stirring voice of the war was that of British prime minister Winston Churchill:

"... I say to the House as I said to Ministers who have joined this government, I have nothing to offer but blood, toil, tears, and sweat. We have before us an ordeal of the most grievous kind. We have before us many, many months of struggle and suffering .... You ask, what is our aim? I can answer in one word. It is victory. Victory at all costs—victory in spite of all terrors—victory, however long and hard the road may be, for without victory there is no survival. ..."

—Address to Parliament, May 13, 1940

The Dark Genius of Erwin Rommel

In 1941, North Africa was held by Field Marshal Erwin Rommel (1891–1944), known as the "Desert Fox," whose Afrika Korps was seemingly invincible. The British and Americans agreed to conduct a North African campaign, defeat the Germans and Italians there, and then attack what Britain's great wartime Prime Minister Winston Churchill called the "soft underbelly of Europe." Forces under British general (later, field marshal) Bernard Law Montgomery and American generals Dwight D. Eisenhower and George S. Patton Jr. decisively defeated the Germans and Italians in North Africa by May of 1943.

Coral Sea and Midway

While the Germans began to lose their grip on Africa, U.S. forces also started to turn the tide in the Pacific. Between May 3 and 9, 1942, at the Battle of the Coral Sea, the Navy sank or disabled more than 25 Japanese ships, blocking Japan's extension to the south and preventing the Japanese from severing supply lines to Australia. However, the Japanese soon resumed the offensive by attacking the island of Midway, some 1,100 miles northwest of Hawaii. Mounting a task force of 200 ships and 600 planes, Japanese naval commanders counted on the element of surprise to achieve a rapid victory. But, unknown to them, American intelligence officers had broken the key Japanese naval codes, and the U.S. Navy, therefore, had advance warning of the approach of the task force.

The battle commenced on June 3, 1942. American aircraft, launched from the *Hornet*, *Yorktown*, and *Enterprise*, sank four Japanese carriers. Reeling from this blow, the Imperial Navy withdrew its fleet, but the Americans gave chase, sinking or disabling two heavy cruisers and three destroyers, as well as shooting 322 planes out of the sky. Although the U.S. Navy took heavy losses—the carrier *Yorktown*, a destroyer, and 147 aircraft—Midway Island remained in American hands, and the Japanese were never able to resume the offensive in the Pacific. The battle is considered the turning point of the Pacific war.

Island Hopping

After suffering defeat at Midway, the Japanese turned their attention to mounting a full-scale assault on Australia. They began by constructing an airstrip on Guadalcanal in the southern Solomon Islands. In response, on August 7, 1942, a U.S. task force

landed Marines at Guadalcanal, where the Japanese resisted for 6 months. Guadalcanal was the beginning of a U.S. strategy of "island hopping": a plan to take or retake
Japanese-held islands, one after the other, but also "hopping" over some, which would
be isolated and cut off from support. In this
way, American progress against the Japanese
could proceed much faster and farther than
the enemy, even in its worst-case scenarios,
had anticipated. Gradually, island by island,
U.S. forces began to close in on the Japanese
homeland itself.

This campaign promised to be a very long and
bloody haul. Guadalcanal, having taken 6 hell-
ish months to conquer, was a full 3,000 miles
from Tokyo.

 Vital Statistics

Japanese soldiers and
sailors characteristically fought to
the death. Of the 5,000 Japanese troops defending Tarawa,
for example, only 17 were taken
prisoner when the island fell on
November 26, 1943.

The next step was to neutralize the major Japanese air and naval base at Rabaul, on the
eastern tip of New Britain Island, just east of New Guinea. Under General MacArthur,
U.S. and Australian troops attacked through the Solomons and New Guinea. When
the Japanese rushed to reinforce their position on the islands of Lae and Salamaua, on
March 3 and 4, 1943, U.S. B-24 Liberators and B-17 Flying Fortresses attacked troop
transports and their naval escorts with devastating results. The Battle of the Bismarck
Sea cost the Japanese 3,500 men; the Allies lost only 5 planes. The defeat was a severe
blow to the Japanese presence in the southwest Pacific. By the end of 1943, Rabaul
had been destroyed, severing some 100,000 Japanese troops from any hope of supply,
support, or reinforcement. This was "island hopping" at its most devastatingly effective.

In the central Pacific, U.S. forces moved against Tarawa and Makin islands. Makin
fell quickly, but Tarawa was defended by veteran Japanese jungle fighters, and the battle, begun on November 20, 1943, was extraordinarily costly to both sides. Although
victorious, the U.S. Marines who fought there called the island "terrible Tarawa."

On Mediterranean Shores

By mid-May 1943, Roosevelt and Churchill agreed to postpone crossing the English
Channel to invade France until the "soft underbelly" of Europe had been penetrated
by means of an invasion of Sicily from North Africa. This way, German forces could
be entrapped in a three-way vise, with British and American armies pressing upward

from the south, and eastward from the coast of France while the Russians pushed the German invaders out of the Soviet Union and shoved them ever westward.

On July 9 and 10, 1943, British and American forces landed in Sicily, and the Italian army crumbled before them. German resistance was a different matter, however, and costly fighting ensued. The invasion of Sicily culminated in the fall of Messina to General Patton's Seventh U.S. Army on August 17, 1943.

By this time, Benito Mussolini had been overthrown by his own Fascist Council (July 25, 1943) and was saved from imprisonment and, ultimately, perhaps, execution only by a daring German commando rescue mission. The Italian government, now under Marshal Pietro Badoglio (1871–1956), made secret peace overtures to the Allies while the Germans dug in on the Italian peninsula and awaited an invasion.

On September 3, 1943, British and U.S. forces left Messina and landed on the toe of the Italian boot. The Fifth U.S. Army, under General Mark W. Clark (1896–1984), landed at Salerno, and within a month southern Italy fell to the Allies. The Germans evacuated the key city of Naples on October 1, but then, under Field Marshal Albert Kesselring, very effectively stiffened their resistance, struggling to hold Rome while exacting a terrible toll on Clark's Fifth Army. After Badoglio's government signed an armistice with the Allies and, on October 13, declared war on Germany, Hitler installed Mussolini as head of a puppet regime in northern Italy.

For the balance of 1943, the Allied and German armies in Italy were deadlocked. On January 22, 1944, 50,000 U.S. troops landed at Anzio, just 33 miles south of Rome, but were pinned down by German forces. Not until June 4, 1944, did Rome fall to the Allies. From this point on, the Germans steadily retreated northward. On April 28, 1945, Mussolini and his mistress, Claretta Petacci, were captured by Italian anti-Fascists, then shot to death and hung by the heels on an iron fence bordering a gas station near a Milanese public square.

D-Day

Although U.S. forces entered Europe through Italy, combat on the main part of the continent was more widespread. The Soviets, who suffered the heaviest casualties of the war and who had been devastated by a surprise German invasion begun on June 22, 1941, were fighting back with a vengeance across their vast homeland. The Battle of Stalingrad (present-day Volgograd), fought from July 17 to November 18, 1942, resulted in the loss of 750,000 Soviet troops, but also 850,000 Nazis. This battle turned the grim tide of the war on the Eastern Front. Although Hitler continued to commit troops to that theater, the German army was doomed there.

In the meantime, British Royal Air Force (RAF) bombers and U.S. Army Air Forces bombers pummeled industrial targets throughout Germany. At sea, the Battle of the Atlantic had raged since early 1942. From January to June of that year, German U-boats sank three million tons of U.S. shipping. However, the development of longer-range aircraft, capable of dropping underwater depth charges, and more advanced radar systems led to effective defenses against U-boats, and by the spring of 1943, the U-boat threat had been greatly reduced.

 Vital Statistics

Approximately 5,000 Allied ships, 11,000 Allied aircraft, and more than 150,000 troops participated in the June 6 D-Day landing.

With pressure applied from the south, from the east, from the air, and at sea, the time was at last right for the major Allied thrust from the west: a full-scale assault on what Hitler liked to call *Festung Europa*—"Fortress Europe." For this offensive, the Allies mounted in Britain the largest and most powerful invasion force in history. Officially dubbed Operation Overlord, the invasion of Normandy became popularly known by the military designation of the day of the landings: D-Day, June 6, 1944.

U.S. General Dwight David Eisenhower, Supreme Allied Commander, the single most powerful Allied military figure in World War II, was in charge of the high-stakes operation, which—astoundingly—caught the Germans off guard. True, the Germans expected an invasion, but not at Normandy. Through an elaborate program of decoys, deceptions, and misinformation, the Allies had led the Germans to believe that the invasion would come not at Normandy, but at the Pas de Calais, geographically the far more likely spot for an invasion. Nevertheless, German resistance was stiff at Normandy and in places nearly impenetrable. Yet the Allies prevailed and, on August 15, 1944, they launched a second invasion of France, this time in the South between Toulon and Cannes. The objective was to trap German forces in France within the jaws of a mighty pincers. On August 25, Paris—beloved capital of France, in German hands since 1940—was liberated by the Allies.

Retaking Europe

From France, the Allies launched an invasion into the German homeland itself. By early September, British forces liberated Brussels, Belgium, and American troops crossed the German frontier at Eupen. On October 21, the First U.S. Army captured Aachen, the first German city to fall to the Allies. It was, however, the Third U.S. Army, led by the war's single finest field commander, General George S. Patton Jr.

(1885–1945), that spearheaded the main breakout from Normandy, across France, and into Germany, in 9 months moving faster and farther and destroying or capturing more of the enemy than any army had in World War II and, perhaps, in the history of warfare itself.

As 1944 came to a close, it was abundantly clear that the Germans had lost the war. At least, that is how any rational leader would have viewed it. But Adolf Hitler was no longer rational—if it can be said that he ever had been. Hitler ordered his soldiers to fight to the last man, and he reinforced his thinning lines with the *Volkssturm*, consisting of underage boys and overage men. Although the Germans continued to retreat, resistance was always fierce. Then, on December 16, 1944, General Gerd von Rundstedt (1875–1953) led a desperate and entirely unexpected counteroffensive, driving a wedge into Allied lines through the Ardennes on the Franco-Belgian frontier. His object was to divide the Allied forces and advance all the way to Antwerp, now functioning as a key port of supply for Allied operations. With German forces distending the Allied line westward, the ensuing combat was called the Battle of the Bulge. In the most desperate battle of the war in western Europe, the First and Third U.S. Armies pushed back the "bulge," which was wholly contained by January 1945. The battle was the last great German offensive, and it had been Germany's last chance to stall the Allies' advance into its homeland.

During February 1945, U.S. forces advanced to the Rhine River and, after clearing the west bank, elements of the 9th Armored Division captured the bridge at Remagen, near Cologne, on March 7. Allied forces crossed this bridge at other points along the Rhine and were then poised to make a run for Berlin. However, General Eisenhower, believing Hitler would make his last stand in the German south, chose instead to head for Leipzig. Moreover, Eisenhower was far more interested in destroying the enemy army than in taking its capital, an operation that, he believed, would cost many American casualties. With U.S. troops just 96 miles west of Berlin, the Supreme Allied Commander sent a message to Soviet dictator Joseph Stalin, telling him that he was leaving Berlin to the Red Army. It was a controversial decision with profound implications for postwar Europe; however, Ike was right about the casualties. The Red Army lost some 300,000 men, killed or wounded, in the Berlin campaign.

While the British and Americans had been closing in from the West, the Soviets executed a massive assault on Germany's Eastern Front. By the end of January, the Red Army had pushed through Poland into Germany itself. In truth, little was left of Berlin. A combination of U.S. and British air power and Soviet artillery had razed the capital of Hitler's vaunted "Thousand-Year Reich." Nevertheless, the ruined capital was fiercely defended, and it was April 16, 1945, before Soviet Marshal Georgy

Zhukov finally moved his troops into the city proper. Many German soldiers and civilians, terrified of the vengeance the Soviets would surely exact, fled westward to surrender to the Americans and the British.

Vital Statistics

Civilian deaths in World War II exceeded 25 million, of whom 6 million were Jews systematically murdered, for the most part in specially constructed death camps, by order of Adolf Hitler.

Indeed, Germans could have found few places of refuge in the spring of 1945, for the entire world was learning of war crimes committed on an unimaginably vast scale. In their drive toward Berlin, the Allies liberated one Nazi concentration camp after another—to which Jews, Gypsies, Slavs, homosexuals, and others deemed "undesirable" by the Reich had been sent for inhuman confinement or outright extermination. Such names as Auschwitz, Buchenwald, Bergen-Belsen, Treblinka, and Dachau seared themselves into history. The Nazis had not been content with conquest; they intended nothing less than genocide in what they called the "Final Solution to the Jewish Question" and the rest of the world, after the war, called "the Holocaust."

Remember This

Franklin Delano Roosevelt, elected to an unprecedented four terms as president of the United States and having seen his nation through the Depression and the blackest days of World War II, succumbed to a cerebral hemorrhage on April 12, 1945. Roosevelt was succeeded by his vice president, Harry S. Truman (1884–1972). Truman attended the last wartime Allied conference at Potsdam, Germany, July 17 to August 2 with Churchill (who was replaced by his successor, Clement Attlee, during the conference) and Stalin.

The conference crystallized plans for the postwar world, confirming the four-zone division of Germany (among the U.S., Britain, France, and the USSR), establishing plans for de-Nazification and demilitarization, and establishing a tribunal to prosecute those guilty of war crimes and atrocities. The group resolved that nothing less than unconditional surrender would end the war against Japan. Truman also revealed at Potsdam that the United States had successfully tested an atomic bomb, which could be used against Japan.

Westbound Soviet and eastbound American troops met at the river Elbe on April 25, 1945. Five days later, Adolf Hitler, holed up in a bunker beneath the shattered streets of Berlin, shot himself while biting down on a glass cyanide ampule in a double suicide with his mistress-turned-bride, Eva Braun. On May 7, 1945, senior representatives of

Germany's armed forces surrendered to the Allies at General Eisenhower's headquarters in Reims. The very next day came a formal unconditional surrender. From the pages of American newspapers, headlines shouted the arrival of V-E (Victory in Europe) Day.

Fat Man and Little Boy

German scientists discovered the possibility of nuclear fission—a process whereby the tremendous energy of the atom might be liberated—in 1938. Fortunately for the world, Hitler's anti-Semitic reign of terror drove many of Germany's best thinkers out of the country, and the nation's efforts to exploit fission in a weapon came to nothing. Three Hungarian—born American physicists—Leo Szilard, Eugene Wigner, and Edward Teller—were all intimately familiar with what a man like Hitler could do. They asked America's single most prestigious physicist, Albert Einstein (himself a fugitive from Nazi persecution), to write a letter to President Roosevelt, warning him of Germany's nuclear weapons research and urging that the United States begin research in the field.

Heeding Einstein's letter, FDR authorized late in 1939 the atomic bomb development program that became known as the Manhattan Project. Under the military management of Brigadier General (later Major General) Leslie R. Groves (1896–1970), who had directed construction of the Pentagon, and the scientific direction of the distinguished and dynamic physicist J. Robert Oppenheimer (1904–1967), the program grew into the greatest and most costly military enterprise in the history of humankind. The Manhattan Project employed the nation's foremost scientific minds and put at their disposal a virtually limitless industrial facility. A prototype bomb—called "the gadget" by the scientists—was completed in the summer of 1945 and was successfully detonated at Alamogordo, New Mexico, on July 16, 1945.

At this time, the Allies were planning the final invasion of Japan, which, based on the bloody experience of "island hopping," was expected to add perhaps a million more deaths to the Allied toll. Hoping to avoid the necessity of invasion, President Truman authorized the use of the terrible new weapon

Vital Statistics

Dropped on Hiroshima, with a population of about 300,000, "Little Boy" killed 78,000 people instantly; 10,000 more were never found; more than 70,000 were injured; and many subsequently died of radiation-related causes. Nagasaki, with a population of 250,000, instantly lost some 40,000 people when "Fat Man" was dropped. Another 40,000 were wounded.

against Japan. On August 6, 1945, a lone B-29 bomber, named *Enola Gay* after pilot Paul Tibbets's mother, dropped "Little Boy" on Hiroshima, obliterating the city in three fifths of a second. Three days later, "Fat Man" was dropped on Nagasaki, destroying about half the city.

On August 10, the day after the attack on Nagasaki, Japan sued for peace on condition that the emperor be allowed to remain as sovereign ruler. On August 11, the Allies replied that they and they alone would determine the future of Emperor Hirohito. At last, on August 14, the emperor personally accepted the Allied terms. A cease-fire was declared on August 15, and on September 2, 1945, General MacArthur presided over the Japanese signing of the formal surrender document on the deck of the U.S. battleship *Missouri*, anchored in Tokyo Bay.

The Least You Need to Know

◆ Never before or since World War II have Americans fought with such unanimity and singleness of purpose.

◆ If ever a war was a contest of good versus evil, such was World War II, and America's role in achieving victory elevated the nation to "superpower" status in the postwar political order.

◆ The United States waged a war on two vast fronts, concentrating first against Germany in Europe and then against Japan in the Pacific.

◆ The war in Europe was ended by massive application of conventional weapons, while that in the Pacific was brought to a terrible close by the dropping of two atomic bombs on the Japanese cities of Hiroshima and Nagasaki.

Part 7

Superpower

World War II was a contest between fascist, Nazi, and Japanese imperialist powers on one side and an alliance of democratic and communist powers on the other. Following the defeat of the fascist-Nazi-imperialist Axis, democracy and communism squared off as the great opposing ideologies of the postwar world. The World War II alliance shattered in a long contest of diplomatic maneuvering and military posturing called the Cold War. This period saw two costly shooting wars as well, one in Korea and one in Vietnam. In the meantime, the homefront after World War II was both a booming and a turbulent place. The economy soared, the civil rights movement went into full swing beginning in the late 1950s, and the Vietnam War proved the catalyst for a general social protest movement during the 1960s. The chapters in this part cover what poet W. H. Auden aptly called "the Age of Anxiety."

Chapter 29

War Served Cold—and Hot (1944–1954)

In This Chapter

- ◆ The United Nations and other postwar peace programs
- ◆ The descent of the "Iron Curtain" and the start of the Cold War
- ◆ The CIA and McCarthyism
- ◆ The Korean War

Rejoicing at the end of World War II was intense, but all too brief. The Soviet Union, portrayed by U.S. politicians and press alike as a valiant ally during the war, once again became an implacable ideological and political enemy. The Eastern European nations occupied by the Red Army became unwilling satellites of the USSR, and the postwar world found itself divided between the Western democracies, led by the United States, and the Eastern Communist "bloc," dominated by the Soviets. It seemed as if the seeds of yet another war—World War III?—had been sown. At least Americans could take comfort in their monopoly on the atomic bomb … but that, too, would soon change.

Winning the Peace

It was clear to America's leaders that the Allies had won World War I, only later to "lose the peace." They were determined not to make the same mistake again.

United Nations

During World War II, the powers aligned against the Axis called themselves the "United Nations." The concept that label conveyed held great promise; after all, had the League of Nations been a more effective body, World War II might have been averted altogether. From August to October 1944, the United States, Great Britain, the USSR, and China met at Dumbarton Oaks, an estate in the Georgetown section of Washington, D.C., to sketch out plans for a new world body. The wartime allies— plus France—would constitute a peacekeeping ("security") council, while the other nations of the world, though represented, would play secondary roles. Later in the year, a formal United Nations Charter was drawn up and adopted by 50 nations at the San Francisco Conference. The charter became effective after a majority of the signatory nations ratified it on October 24, 1945. The United Nations, the most significant world body in history, had become a reality.

Divided Germany

Another element vital to winning the peace was the postwar treatment of Germany. American, British, and French leaders, mindful of how the punitive Treaty of Versailles had created the conditions that brought Hitler to power and plunged the world into the second great war of the century, did not, this time, clamor for revenge. On the other hand, the demands of the Soviet Union, which had suffered the greatest losses in the war, went far beyond mere vengeance. Stalin called for the utter subjugation of Germany. For the present, a compromise was reached among the Allies, by which Germany was carved up into four "zones of occupation," each under the control of a different ally: the United States, Britain, France, and the USSR.

Marshall's Bold Plan

The single boldest step toward winning the peace was proposed on June 5, 1947, by George C. Marshall. The former Army Chief of Staff, now Secretary of State in the cabinet of President Harry S. Truman, described in an address at Harvard University a plan whereby the nations of Europe would draw up a unified scheme for economic reconstruction to be funded by the United States. Although the Soviet Union and its satellite nations were invited to join, in the growing chill of the Cold War, they declined. Sixteen Western European nations formed the Organization for European Economic Cooperation to coordinate the program formally known as the European Recovery Program, but more familiarly called the Marshall Plan.

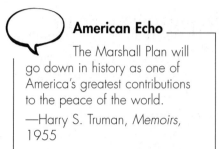

American Echo

The Marshall Plan will go down in history as one of America's greatest contributions to the peace of the world.
—Harry S. Truman, *Memoirs*, 1955

Winston Churchill called the Marshall Plan the "most unsordid" political act in history, but it was, above all, a *political* act. Although Marshall assured the Soviets that the plan was not directed "against any country or doctrine, but against hunger, poverty, desperation, and chaos," it was, in fact, a powerful economic salvo fired against communism. Having witnessed totalitarian regimes rush to fill the void of postwar economic catastrophe, Marshall and other U.S. leaders were eager to restore the war-ravaged economies of the West. Economic well-being, they felt, was the strongest ally of democracy.

The United States poured $13 billion into Europe and established a Displaced Persons Plan, whereby almost 300,000 homeless Europeans (including many Jewish survivors of the Holocaust) were welcomed to the United States.

Curtain of Iron

On March 5, 1946, Winston Churchill addressed little Westminster College in Fulton, Missouri. "From Stettin in the Baltic to Trieste in the Adriatic," he declared, "an iron curtain has descended across the continent." The former prime minister's phrase took root, and the term *Iron Curtain* was used for more than 50 years to describe the economic, social, and military barriers created against the West by the Communist countries of Eastern Europe.

"Containing" Communism

In 1823, President James Monroe issued his famous "Monroe Doctrine," warning European powers that the United States would act to halt any new attempts to colonize the Americas. In 1947, President Harry S. Truman promulgated the "Truman Doctrine," warning the Soviet Union, which supported a threatened Communist takeover of Greece and Turkey, that the United States would act to halt the spread of communism wherever in the world it menaced democracy.

The Truman Doctrine had its basis in a proposal by State Department official George F. Kennan (1904–2005), that the most effective way to combat communism was to *contain* it, confronting the Soviet Union wherever it sought to expand its influence. Thus, the *Cold War* began in earnest, and the conflict prompted rapid passage of the National Security Act of 1947. This sweeping legislation reorganized the War Department into the Department of Defense (under which the Armed Forces were effectively unified), created the U.S. Air Force as an independent military arm, and also established the Central Intelligence Agency, which had as its mission covert intelligence gathering. This meant that the CIA sometimes functioned with neither executive nor legislative knowledge, let alone approval. In the name of fighting communism, the National Security Act had created the closest thing to a secret police (long a mainstay of oppressive Eastern European regimes) this nation ever had.

What's the Word? _____

Coined in a 1947 speech by financier and presidential adviser Bernard Baruch (or by his speechwriter, journalist Herbert Bayard Swope), **Cold War** refers to the postwar strategic and political struggle between the United States (and its Western European allies) and the Soviet Union (and Communist countries). A chronic state of hostility, the Cold War was associated with two major "hot wars" (in Korea and Vietnam) and spawned various "brushfire wars" (small-scale armed conflicts, usually in Third-World nations), but it was not itself a shooting war. The end of the Cold War was heralded in 1989 by the fall of the Berlin Wall.

Berlin Lifeline

Truman's policy of containment prompted the United States and its Western allies to take a strong stand in Germany after the Soviet Union began detaining troop trains bound for West Berlin in March of 1948. (Although Berlin was deep inside the Soviet sector of occupied Germany, the city, too, was divided into zones of Allied occupation.) In response, on June 7, the Western allies announced their intention to create the separate, permanent capitalist state of West Germany. Two weeks later, the Soviet Union blockaded West Berlin.

Would the West back down? Would this be the start of World War III?

President Truman did not take armed action against the Soviets. Instead, he ordered an airlift, a spectacular chain of round-the-clock supply flights into West Berlin—277,569 flights over 321 days, carrying 1,325,499.7 tons of food and other supplies. The airlift was a political and logistical triumph, which caused the Soviet Union to lift the blockade. The success of the airlift was also a vindication of the policy of containment, and in April 1949, it led to the creation of the North Atlantic Treaty Organization—NATO—a key defensive alliance of the Western nations against the Communist East.

Witch-Hunts

While national leaders and the military were scrambling to "contain" communism abroad, certain Americans looked homeward. Joseph R. McCarthy (1908–1957) was a thoroughly mediocre senator from Wisconsin whose popularity was flagging. McCarthy made a provocative speech to the Women's Republican Club of Wheeling, West Virginia, on February 9, 1950. He held up a piece of paper, which he said was a list of 205 known Communists in the State Department.

The audience was electrified. The speech was reported nationally, and the nation likewise was stunned. McCarthy suddenly became famous and, over the next 4 years, spearheaded a legislative crusade to root out Communists in government and other positions of power. No one, of course, had actually seen the list of names McCarthy held up, and only a few people were disturbed when the number of communists was repeatedly, almost randomly, revised, finally getting pegged at 57.

American Echo

The crux of the North Atlantic Treaty, which created NATO, is Article 5: "The parties agree that an armed attack against one or more of them in Europe or North America shall be considered an attack against them all."

Crusade is a word with which McCarthy and his followers would have been comfortable. Others, however, called what happened a *witch-hunt*. McCarthy pointed fingers and leveled charges. Due process of law, the rules of evidence, and the presumption of innocence mattered not at all to "Tail Gunner Joe" McCarthy. He gained chairmanship of the powerful Senate Subcommittee on Governmental Operations and, from this post, launched investigations of the Voice of America broadcasting service and the U.S. Army Signal Corps. That McCarthy pointed a finger was quite enough to ruin a reputation and destroy a career—even if no actual evidence of subversion or disloyalty was presented. Those called to testify before the committee were asked to "name names"—expose other individuals with Communist affiliations. If the witnesses refused, they were found to be in contempt of Congress and subject to imprisonment. If a witness exercised his constitutional right not to testify against himself, McCarthy (and much of the public, it seemed) presumed him guilty.

McCarthy was aided in his witch-hunt by an oily, ruthless, and thoroughly unprincipled young lawyer named Roy Cohn (1927–1986), who was instrumental in one of the most highly publicized phases of the witch-hunt, an investigation of Communist influence in the Hollywood film industry. A parade of executives, producers, directors, and movie stars appeared before the Senate committee. Some witnesses "named names." Some refused. Those who failed to "cooperate" with the committee and those who stood accused were *blacklisted*, which meant that no studio would hire them.

The McCarthy witch-hunts were certainly not born of fantasy. Many influential Americans did have ties to Communist organizations, although most of these associations came and went with the 1930s, when intellectuals and liberals flocked to socialist and Communist groups in order to oppose fascism, which was then menacing the world. The Cold War also spawned a veritable legion of spies, including those who communicated U.S. atomic secrets to the Soviets, thereby enabling the USSR to develop an atomic bomb in 1949 and a hydrogen bomb in 1954. (The atomic bomb operates on the principle of nuclear fission—the splitting of the nuclei of uranium or plutonium atoms—which suddenly releases an incredible amount of explosive energy. The hydrogen bomb is a fusion rather than fission device, joining the nuclei of hydrogen atoms together in an uncontrolled nuclear reaction. The hydrogen bomb releases about 1,000 times more energy than an atomic bomb.)

McCarthy, however, made no effort to separate fact from fantasy, and even after the Republican Party captured the White House in 1952, he continued his strident attacks. In 1954, McCarthy accused Secretary of the Army Robert T. Stevens and others of deliberately hampering the investigation of communist infiltration of the U.S. military. This accusation was sufficient to provoke President Eisenhower—a career army man—to encourage Congress to form a committee to investigate McCarthy's attempts to coerce army brass into granting preferential treatment for a former McCarthy aide, Private G. David Schine.

From April to June 1954, the "Army-McCarthy Hearings" were broadcast on an infant medium called television. Joseph McCarthy was exposed as the reckless, self-serving demagogue that he was. Censured by action of the Senate later that year, he was overtaken by the alcoholism that had always dogged him. McCarthy died in 1957, at the age of 49.

Remember This _____

On June 19, 1953, Julius Rosenberg (born 1918) and his wife, Ethel Greenglass Rosenberg (born 1915), became the first United States civilians in history to be executed for espionage. Their trial and their punishment were sources of great bitterness and controversy during the Cold War.

Julius Rosenberg, a member of the American Communist Party, had been employed as an engineer by the U.S. Army Signal Corps during World War II. He and Ethel were accused of supplying Soviet agents with atomic bomb secrets during 1944 and 1945. Their chief accuser was Ethel's brother, David Greenglass, who had worked on the "A-bomb" project at Los Alamos, New Mexico, and had fed the Rosenbergs secret information. Because Greenglass turned state's witness, he received a 15-year sentence, whereas, under the Espionage Act of 1917, the Rosenbergs were sentenced to death on April 5, 1951. The sentence provoked protests worldwide—including accusations of anti-Semitism—but President Eisenhower, convinced of the couple's guilt, refused to commute the sentences.

Soviet documents released in the 1990s after the collapse of the USSR suggest that Julius Rosenberg was, in fact, guilty of espionage, but that his wife was innocent. Experts continue to debate the actual value to the Soviets of the material Julius Rosenberg obtained for them.

"Police Action" in Korea

The Cold War was not just a contest of rattling sabers and strong language. As Eastern Europe had fallen behind an Iron Curtain, so China, the world's most populous nation, became a Communist nation in 1949. China was long the subject of a struggle between Communist forces (led primarily by Mao Zedong) and capitalist-nationalist forces (whose strongest leader was U.S. World War II ally Chiang Kai-shek). Elsewhere in Asia, Communist factions were positioning themselves to take power. After World War II, Korea was divided along the 38th parallel between a Soviet occupation zone in the north and a U.S. zone in the south. In November of 1947, the United Nations resolved to create a unified independent Korea, but the Communists barred free elections in the north. Only in the U.S. southern zone were elections held, and on August 15, 1948, the Republic of Korea was born. In North Korea, the Communists created the Democratic People's Republic of Korea in September 1948.

What's the Word? _____

Congress never declared war against North Korea or China. Officially, the conflict was called a **police action**—a localized war without a declaration of war.

Invasion, Counterstrike, Invasion

On June 25, 1950, Communist-backed forces from the north invaded South Korea. The United States secured a United Nations sanction against the invasion and contributed the lion's share of troops to repel it. World War II hero of the Pacific Douglas MacArthur was put in command of the UN forces.

The North Korean troops—trained by the Soviets and the Chinese—quickly pushed the South Koreans back toward the southern tip of the Korean peninsula. MacArthur struggled to hold the critical southern port of Pusan to buy time until reinforcements arrived. He then executed a controversial and extremely risky landing at Inchon, on the west coast of Korea, *behind* North Korean lines. The landing was a stunning success—surely MacArthur's single greatest military feat—and by October 1, 1950, the North Koreans had been forced out of South Korea in a long, disorderly retreat. UN forces were now arrayed along the 38th parallel.

Within the Truman administration, debate raged over whether to cross the 38th parallel and invade North Korea. To do so might trigger World War III. To do less might mean the loss of Korea to the Communist camp. President Truman compromised, authorizing the crossing, but taking steps to avoid provoking the Chinese and the Soviets directly. No UN troops would enter Manchuria or the USSR, and only South Koreans would operate near international borders. On October 7, the UN General Assembly called for the unification of Korea and authorized MacArthur to invade. On October 19, the North Korean capital of Pyongnang fell, and the North Korean armies were pushed far north, to the Yalu River, the nation's border with Manchuria.

The war seemed to be over, but then, between October 14 and November 1, some 180,000 Communist "volunteers" crossed the Yalu from China. MacArthur launched an offensive on November 24, only to be beaten back by massive Chinese resistance, which forced UN troops back across the 38th parallel. The South Korean capital of Seoul fell to the Communists in January 1951.

Meatgrinder

Halting their retreat south of Seoul, U.S. and other allied troops began probing northward once again in an offensive that front-line soldiers dubbed the "meatgrinder." By March of 1951, UN forces had returned to the 38th parallel and established a strong defensive position.

Old Soldiers ...

In light of the Chinese intervention, General MacArthur demanded permission to retaliate against the Chinese by bombing Manchuria. President Truman and the United Nations—fearing that direct aggression against China would trigger nuclear war with the Soviets—turned MacArthur down. The confrontation was controversial, and many Americans vociferously sided with the general against the president. Contrary to the accepted military practice of refraining from publicly differing with the civilian administration, MacArthur freely blamed his military setbacks in Korea on Truman's policies. Finally, on March 25, 1951, just after Truman had completed preparation of a cease-fire plan, MacArthur broadcast an unauthorized and provocative ultimatum to the enemy commander. MacArthur also sent a letter to Republican House minority leader Joe Martin, criticizing Truman's war policy. Martin read the letter into the *Congressional Record*. In response to this final act of insubordination, Truman relieved MacArthur of command in Korea on April 11, 1951.

Thrust, Counterthrust, and Stalemate

The highly capable General Matthew B. Ridgway assumed command of United Nations and U.S. forces after the dismissal of MacArthur, and Lieutenant General James A. Van Fleet led the Eighth U.S. Army northward. But on April 22, nearly half a million Chinese troops drove the Eighth Army to within five miles of Seoul. On May 10, the Chinese launched a second offensive, concentrating on the eastern portion of the UN line; however, Van Fleet counterattacked in the west, north of Seoul, taking the Communists entirely by surprise. In full retreat, the Communists suffered their heaviest casualties and withdrew into North Korea. By the beginning of summer 1951, the war was stalemated at the 38th parallel. For the next 2 years, both sides pounded one another fruitlessly.

Vital Statistics

Just how many Chinese and North Korean troops were killed in the Korean War is unknown, but estimates range between 1.5 and 2 million, in addition to at least a million civilians. The UN command lost 88,000, of whom 23,300 were American. Many more were wounded. South Korean civilian casualties probably equaled those of North Korea.

Talking Peace and Talking Some More

Armistice negotiations began at the behest of the Soviets in June of 1951 and dragged on for 2 years. It took until July 26, 1951, even to agree on an agenda for the conference.

The participants decided that an armistice would require agreement on a demarcation line and demilitarized zone, impartial supervision of the truce, and arrangements for return of prisoners of war. The toughest single issue involved the disposition of POWs. UN negotiators wanted prisoners to decide for themselves whether they would return home; the Communists, fearful—as Communist governments always are—of mass defection, held out for mandatory repatriation. In an effort to break the negotiation deadlock, General Mark Clark, who had succeeded Ridgway, stepped up bombing raids on North Korea. At last, during April 1953, the POW issue was resolved; a compromise permitted freed prisoners to choose sides, but under the supervision of a neutral commission.

The Unhappiest Ally

After this long and frustrating process, the only individual who remained thoroughly displeased was Syngman Rhee (1875–1965), president of South Korea. Rhee vowed to accept nothing less than unification of Korea (under himself) and wholly voluntary repatriation as absolute conditions for cease-fire. So, he threw a monkey wrench into the proceedings by suddenly ordering the release of 25,000 North Korean prisoners who wanted to live in the South. To regain Rhee's cooperation, the United States promised him a mutual security pact and long-term economic aid. Nevertheless, the armistice signed on July 27, 1953, did not include South Korea. Still, the cease-fire held, and the shooting war was over.

The Korean War did succeed in containing communism—confining it to North Korea—but in all other respects, this costly conflict was inconclusive, except that it provided a precedent for intervention in another Asian war, beginning in the next decade, in a place called Vietnam.

The Least You Need to Know

- ◆ Jubilation at the end of World War II was short lived, as the Western capitalist nations and the Eastern European and Asian Communist nations squared off for a Cold War.

- ◆ The Marshall Plan was a humanitarian, as well as political triumph for the forces of democracy.

- ◆ A policy of "containing" communism and a fear of touching off a nuclear World War III dominated American foreign policy in the postwar years.

- ◆ The Korean War demonstrated the horrible dilemma of fighting worldwide communism: defeat an enemy without touching off a new—atomic—world war.

From the Back of the Bus to the Great Society (1947–1968)

In This Chapter

- ◆ The African American struggle for civil rights

- ◆ The start of the "Space Race"

- ◆ The Bay of Pigs and Cuban Missile Crisis

- ◆ Idealism and social reform in the Kennedy and Johnson years

- ◆ Assassinations

With the ruins of Europe, ravaged by World War II, still smoldering, much of the planet's population was hungry, politically oppressed, or both as the first half of the twentieth century came to an end. But Americans, having triumphed over evil incarnate in the form of Nazi and Japanese totalitarianism, basked in the blessings of liberty and had much to be proud of. True, the post-war world was scary, with nuclear incineration just a push of a button away, but the 1950s would find America a rather complacent place—prosperous and spawning a web of verdant (if rather bland) suburbs interconnected by new highways built under the Interstate Highway Act of 1956.

Postwar suburbia was an expression of the long-held American Dream: a house of one's own, a little plot of land, a clean and decent place to live. But if suburban lawns were green, the suburbs themselves were white. As usual, the overwhelming majority of African Americans had been excluded from the dream.

Executive Order 9981

On July 26, 1948, President Harry S. Truman (1884–1972) issued Executive Order 9981, which mandated "equality of treatment and opportunity to all persons in the Armed Services without regard to race." African Americans had regularly served in the armed forces since the Civil War, but always in separate—racially segregated—units, though usually under white officers. Truman's order did not use the word *integration*, but when he was asked pointblank if that is what the order meant, the president replied with his characteristic directness: "Yes."

The Dream Deferred

Truman's executive order did not instantly integrate the armed forces, but it gave the process a much-needed shove, so that by the time of the next war—in Korea, beginning in 1950 (see Chapter 29)—whites and black fought side by side in integrated units.

Nor, of course, did Truman's order transform American society as a whole, let alone transform it overnight. Racial prejudice was deeply ingrained in American life, and in some places, particularly the South, prejudice was even mandated by law. In most Southern states, the "Jim Crow" legislation that had been passed during the bitter years following Reconstruction remained on the books in one form or another. In its 1896 decision in the case of *Plessy* v. *Ferguson*, the U.S. Supreme Court upheld the segregation of public services and facilities, such as schools, provided that such services and facilities were "separate but equal." In the South there was no question that services and facilities were separate. But they were hardly equal. Indeed, African Americans were invariably treated as an underclass. In somewhat subtler form, this was true in the North as well, where segregation was typically *de facto* (a fact) rather than de jure (a legally sanctioned policy).

 What's the Word?

Ghetto is an Italian word that was originally applied to the Jewish quarter in Venice during the Middle Ages. Over the years, the word has been applied to any urban neighborhood—usually run-down and crime-plagued—in which minority groups are compelled, by social pressure and economics, to live.

During and following both world wars, African Americans migrated in large numbers from the rural South to the industrial cities of the North. Northern industry welcomed their cheap labor, but many whites, fearing they would lose their jobs to the newcomers, met them with hostility. Up North, blacks typically found themselves restricted to menial labor and compelled to live in slum districts that became known as *ghettos*.

Looked at objectively, the entire American nation was both separate *and* unequal.

Rosa Parks Boards a Bus

On December 1, 1955, Montgomery, Alabama, was a typical Southern city, its social fabric shot through with the threads of major injustice and trivial humiliation carefully (if no longer quite consciously) interwoven to keep African Americans "in their place." Rosa Parks (1913–2005) boarded a city bus to return home from her job as a department store seamstress-tailor. Like any other commuter, she was tired after a hard day's work. She settled into the first available seat.

 Remember This

The year before Rosa Parks's bus ride, the U.S. Supreme Court effectively declared segregation illegal when, on May 17, 1954, it handed down a decision in the case of *Brown v. Board of Education of Topeka, Kansas*. The decision was the culmination of a long series of lawsuits first brought against segregated school districts by the National Association for the Advancement of Colored People (NAACP) in the 1930s. Repeatedly, the Supreme Court ruled consistently with its 1896 decision in *Plessy* v. *Ferguson* that found "separate but equal" accommodations for black people constitutional as long as all *tangible* aspects of the accommodations were, indeed, equal. But in 1954, Thurgood Marshall (1908–1993) and other NAACP lawyers demonstrated that segregated school systems were inherently unequal because of *intangible* social factors. The high court agreed. Desegregation of the nation's schools became the law of the land. In some places, the process of integration proceeded without incident; in others, it was accompanied by violent resistance that required the intervention of federal marshals and even federal troops. (In 1967, President Lyndon B. Johnson appointed Thurgood Marshall to the Supreme Court; he was the first African American to serve.)

In most parts of the world, this mundane action would have gone entirely unnoticed. But in Montgomery, in 1955, where one sat could be a criminal matter. Parks had taken a place in the front-most row occupied by blacks. When a white passenger boarded, the driver told her and the other blacks in the row to stand—for the law required black passengers to yield their seats to whites, and it further prohibited whites and blacks from occupying the same row of seats. The others in the row obediently rose. Parks refused. For that, she was arrested and jailed. Active in the emerging civil rights movement and secretary in the local branch of the NAACP, Rosa Parks was well aware that her action was provocative. In fact, she was hoping that it would provoke precisely the response it did.

The arrest launched a boycott. If the town's African Americans could not ride wherever they wished in a city bus, they would not ride at all.

The year-long boycott not only desegregated Montgomery buses, but focused the attention of the entire nation on the great issues of equality and civil rights.

A Preacher from Atlanta

The Reverend Martin Luther King Jr., pastor of the Dexter Avenue Baptist Church in Montgomery, emerged during the Montgomery boycott as moral and spiritual leader of the developing Civil Rights Movement. Born on January 15, 1929, in Atlanta, Georgia, King was educated at Morehouse College, Crozer Theological Seminary, and Boston University. Along with the Reverend Ralph David Abernathy and Montgomery NAACP head Edward Nixon, King entered the national spotlight during the boycott. He used his sudden prominence to infuse the national Civil Rights Movement with what he had learned from the example of India's great leader, Mahatma Gandhi, who taught the Hindu-inspired principle of *satyagrapha*—"holding to the truth" by nonviolent civil disobedience.

After Montgomery, King lectured nationally and became president of the Southern Christian Leadership Conference (SCLC). He conducted major voter registration drives, demonstrations, marches, and campaigns. In August 1963, King organized a massive March on Washington, where he delivered one of the great speeches in American history, "I Have a Dream."

American Echo

... I have a dream that one day on the red hills of Georgia sons of former slaves and the sons of former slave-owners will be able to sit down together at the table of brotherhood .... I have a dream that one day down in Alabama, with its vicious racists, with its governor having his lips dripping with the words of interposition and nullification, one day right there in Alabama little black boys and black girls will be able to join hands with little white boys and white girls as sisters and brothers.

—Martin Luther King Jr., speech of August 28, 1963

In 1964, King was recognized with the Nobel Peace Prize, then went on to conduct desegregation efforts in St. Augustine, Florida. King organized a voter-registration drive in Selma, Alabama, leading a march from Selma to Montgomery in March 1965.

At Selma, on the Edmund Pettis Bridge, King and the other marchers were met by a phalanx of club-wielding state troopers. King responded by asking the marchers to kneel in prayer, and then he turned back with them. Some—especially younger black civil rights activists—saw this as a gesture of defeat, and, in this moment, some fell away from commitment to nonviolence. From 1965 on, the civil rights movement developed an increasingly strident and outraged militant wing, willing, in the words of one of their leaders, Malcolm X, to claim racial justice "by any means necessary."

As for King, after 1965, he expanded the Civil Rights Movement into the North and began to attack not just legal and social injustice, but economic inequality, seeking to unite the poor of all races and ethnicities.

It was while King was planning a multiracial "poor people's march" on Washington in 1968, aimed at securing federal funding for a $12 billion "Economic Bill of Rights," that he flew to Memphis, Tennessee, to support striking sanitation workers. In that city, on April 4, Martin Luther King Jr., fell to a sniper's bullet.

James Earl Ray, a small-time career criminal, was apprehended in London and accused of King's assassination. He confessed, pleaded guilty, and was sentenced to life imprisonment. Almost immediately after his incarceration, however, he recanted his confession and his plea, claiming that he had been "set up" by a shadowy figure he knew only as Raul and that the King assassination was really the result of a conspiracy involving the FBI and other agencies of the federal government, perhaps as well as the Mafia. Ray's appeals for a new trial (really, a first trial, since, because he pleaded guilty, his case hadn't been tried) were turned down, despite support from civil rights leaders and the King family, which found Ray's story credible. Ray died of liver disease, in prison, on April 23, 1998. The case was never reopened.

Or Does It Explode?

The assassination of Dr. King, compelling apostle of nonviolent social change, sparked urban riots across a number of the nation's black ghettos. These riots were not the first of the decade, however. Despite the nonviolent message of Dr. King, racial unrest had often turned violent. NAACP leader Medgar Evers was assassinated in Jackson, Mississippi, in 1963; Birmingham, Alabama, was the site of the bombing of a black church, in which four girls were killed (the last of the bombers evading justice until May 22, 2002, when 71-year-old Ku Klux Klansman Bobby Frank Cherry was convicted of murder); and three civil rights activists—including two whites—were killed in Mississippi while working to register black voters. (The trial of one of the accused murders, a KKK leader named Edgar Ray Killen, resulted in a hung jury. He was not retried until 2005, when, at age 80, he was found guilty, on June 21, of three counts of manslaughter.) On August 11, 1965, a 6-day riot ripped apart the Watts section of Los Angeles after a police patrolman attempted to arrest a black man for drunken driving. Riots broke out the following summer in New York and Chicago, and in 1967 in Newark, New Jersey, and Detroit. Following the King assassination in 1968, more than 100 cities erupted into violence.

The racial violence of the 1960s was dramatic evidence of the pent-up frustration and outrage long simmering within black America, but not until the emergence of Malcolm X in the early 1960s was African American militancy given truly compelling and eloquent direction. Malcolm X had been born Malcolm Little in Omaha, Nebraska, in 1925. He turned bitter and rebellious after his father, an activist preacher, was murdered by white racists in 1931, presumably for advocating black nationalism.

Malcolm Little moved to Harlem, where he embarked on a criminal career and, convicted of burglary, was imprisoned from 1946 to 1952. While in prison, he became a follower of Elijah Muhammad (1897–1975), leader of the Lost-Found Nation of Islam, popularly called the Black Muslims. Rejecting his surname as a "slave name," Malcolm Little became Malcolm X and, upon his release from prison, served as a leading spokesman for the Black Muslim movement.

What Malcolm X said electrified many in the black community, giving young black men in particular a sense of pride, purpose, and potential, even as his rhetoric intimidated and outraged many white people, who saw Malcolm X as just another of several very angry young activists. These included such figures as Stokely Carmichael, who called for "total revolution" and "Black Power"; H. Rap Brown, leader of the Student National Coordinating Committee (SNCC), who exhorted angry blacks to "burn this town down" in a 1967 speech in Cambridge, Maryland; and Huey Newton, leader of the militant Black Panther Party.

American Echo

The great African American poet Langston Hughes (1902–1967) asked in a poem called "Harlem" …

"What happens to a dream deferred? Does it dry up like a raisin in the sun? … *Or does it explode?*"

Yet Malcolm X evolved ideas that were not only quite different from those of Martin Luther King, but also from the others identified as militants. Initially advocating the separation of blacks and whites, whom he condemned as a race of "devils," Malcolm X became increasingly committed to Islam and, during a *hajj*, or pilgrimage to Mecca in 1964, he worshiped with whites as well as blacks. Breaking with the Black Muslims, he founded the Organization of Afro-American Unity in June 1964 and advocated a kind of socialist solution to the corruption of American society that had led to racial hatred and the subjugation of black people. His original message of racial separation was now transformed into a religiously inspired quest for racial equality.

The evolution of Malcolm X was cut short on February 21, 1965, when he was gunned down by three Black Muslims during a speech at Harlem's Audubon Auditorium. His *Autobiography* (dictated to Alex Haley, who would later gain fame as the author of *Roots*, a sweeping novel of black history told as the history of a family), published just after his assassination, became an extraordinarily influential document in expanding and redefining the Civil Rights Movement.

The journey of black America, like the life of Malcolm X, remained incomplete during the 1960s and remains incomplete to this day. The fact is that most African Americans live less affluently, amid more crime, and with less opportunity than most white Americans. Yet the range of black leaders of the 1950s and 1960s, from Rosa Parks, to Martin Luther King Jr., to Malcolm X, brought hope and social visibility to black America.

> **American Echo**
>
> If you are born in America with a black skin, you're born in prison.
>
> —Malcolm X, interview, 1963

Sputnik and the New Frontier

Despite growing racial disharmony, the United States was a fairly self-satisfied place in the 1950s. Then, on October 4, 1957, the world learned that the Soviet Union had successfully launched a 184-pound satellite into Earth orbit. Called *Sputnik I*, its simple radio transmitter emitted nothing more than electronic beeps, but each of these electronic emissions sent a shockwave through the American nation. Suddenly, the USSR, our adversary in the postwar world, the embodiment of godless communism, had demonstrated to the world its technological superiority. The launching of *Sputnik* began a "Space Race," in which the United States came in dead second during all the early laps. The Soviets put a man, "cosmonaut" Yuri Gagarin, into orbit 4 years after

Sputnik and almost a month before American "astronaut" Alan B. Shepard was launched on a 15-minute suborbital flight on May 5, 1961.

Sputnik shook Americans out of their complacency. The 1960 presidential race, between Eisenhower's vice president, Richard M. Nixon, and a dashing, youthful senator from Massachusetts, John F. Kennedy, almost ended in a tie. But the nation rejected the proffered security of Eisenhower's man and instead voted into office a candidate who embodied a new energy, vigor, and challenge.

JFK

At 43, John F. Kennedy was the youngest elected president in American history. (Theodore Roosevelt was slightly younger when he assumed office in 1901 after the assassination of William McKinley.) Kennedy's administration established the Peace Corps (an organization of young volunteers assigned to work in developing nations), created the Alliance for Progress (which strengthened relations with Latin America), and set a national goal of landing an American on the moon before the end of the 1960s. Despite these accomplishments, Kennedy is best remembered for the *magic* (there is no better word) he and his beautiful wife, Jacqueline, brought to the White House and the national leadership.

"The Torch Has Been Passed ..."

Intelligent (his books included the Pulitzer Prize–winning *Profiles in Courage*), handsome, idealistic, athletic, irreverently witty, and a war hero, Kennedy declared in his inaugural address that the "torch has been passed to a new generation"—of which *he* was clearly the embodiment.

From the Bay of Pigs to the Edge of Armageddon

Although he was adored by many, Kennedy never succeeded in winning the support of Congress. He and his brother, Attorney General Robert F. Kennedy (1925–1968), sought (sometimes less than enthusiastically) to further civil rights, but were repeatedly thwarted by Congress. Kennedy tried to create programs to fund broad social and educational initiatives, only to see them diluted by Congress.

Early in Kennedy's administration, the nation suffered the tragic humiliation of a bungled attempt to invade Cuba, which had been under the communist rule of Fidel Castro

(b. 1926) since 1959. In March of 1960, President Eisenhower had approved a CIA plan to train anti-Castro Cuban exiles for an invasion to overthrow the Cuban leader. When he assumed office, Kennedy allowed the preparations to proceed, and some 1,500 exiles landed on April 17, 1961, at Bay of Pigs on the island's southwestern coast.

The result was an unmitigated military disaster. Not only had the attack's secrecy been breached, but Kennedy, fearing Soviet reprisal, decided at the eleventh hour not to authorize promised U.S. air support. Worse, the CIA had badly misread the political climate of revolutionary Cuba. In a spectacular failure of intelligence, the CIA assured Kennedy that the invasion would touch off a general popular uprising against Castro. Nothing of the kind happened, and by April 19, the invasion was crushed and 1,200 survivors were captured. (They were released in December 1962, in exchange for $53 million worth of U.S. medicines and provisions.)

Soviet Premier Nikita Khrushchev saw the failure of the Bay of Pigs as a sign of the new administration's weakness. Khrushchev quickly rushed in to exploit this flaw by covertly sending nuclear-armed missiles to Cuba along with the technical and military personnel to install and operate them. An American U-2 spy plane photographed the missile bases under construction, and on October 22, 1962, President Kennedy addressed the nation in an urgent television broadcast, announcing a naval blockade (officially called a "quarantine") of the island. Kennedy demanded that the Soviets withdraw the missiles, and by October 24, the blockade was in place.

The idea of hostile nuclear warheads parked a mere 90 miles from the United States was terrifying, but so was the prospect of a naval battle off the coast of Cuba, which might ignite a thermonuclear World War III. For the next 4 days, Americans braced themselves for Armageddon.

However, on October 28, Khrushchev backed down, offering to remove the missiles under UN supervision. For his part, President Kennedy pledged never again to attempt to invade Cuba, and he also secretly promised to remove U.S. ICBMs from Turkish bases near the Soviet border. On October 29, the blockade was lifted, and JFK had scored a signal victory in Cold War *brinkmanship*.

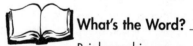 **What's the Word?**

Brinkmanship was a word coined during the Cold War. It signified winning an advantage in international politics by demonstrating a willingness to push a dangerous situation to the very brink of nuclear war.

Motorcade in Dallas

On November 22, 1963, President Kennedy visited Texas to bolster his popularity as he geared up for the reelection campaign. *Air Force One* touched down at Dallas's Love Field that morning, and the president was gratified by the unexpectedly warm reception the Texans accorded him. A man who enjoyed contact with voters, Kennedy declined to ride beneath the bullet-proof bubble top normally affixed to the armored presidential limousine. As the motorcade passed by the Texas School Book Depository, a warehouse, three shots rang out, the second of which ripped into the president's head, fatally wounding him. Texas governor John Connally, riding in the front seat of the car, was also grievously wounded, but recovered.

American Echo

A piece of each of us died at that moment.

—Mike Mansfield, U.S. Senator from Montana, shortly after the Kennedy assassination

The accused assassin, captured later in the day (although not before murdering Dallas police officer J. D. Tippett), was Lee Harvey Oswald, a misfit who had lived for a period in the Soviet Union, having renounced his U.S. citizenship. As he was being transferred from the city to the county jail, Oswald himself was assassinated on November 24 by Dallas nightclub owner and small-time mobster Jack Ruby.

LBJ

John Fitzgerald Kennedy was pronounced dead at Dallas's Parkland Hospital at 1 P.M. local time. Lyndon Baines Johnson (1908–1973), the popular Texas senator tapped by Kennedy as vice president to improve his standing in the South and West, took the oath of office inside *Air Force One* at 2:39 P.M. One of Johnson's first acts was to appoint a commission, headed by Supreme Court Chief Justice Earl Warren, to investigate the assassination. Despite the Warren Commission's finding that Oswald had acted alone, rumors and theories of elaborate conspiracies—some involving the CIA, FBI, Mafia, and Cuba's Castro—proliferated. In 1976, a congressional investigation reached conclusions that gave these added weight, and speculation persists to this day. Whether JFK was the victim of a conspiracy or not, Americans continue to find it difficult to believe that a life such as his could be ended by a nondescript loner like Lee Harvey Oswald.

War on Poverty

Americans had much to admire, as well as much to criticize, about the "thousand days" of the Kennedy administration, but the youthful president's sudden, terrible martyrdom cast an aura of enchantment and heroism over Kennedy and his programs. President Johnson was able to refashion the JFK social programs that had foundered in Congress and, in the name of the slain president, he effectively oversaw their passage into law. When Johnson ran for president in his own right in 1964, he called upon America to build a "Great Society," one that "rests on abundance and liberty for all."

The phrase *Great Society* became, like FDR's New Deal, the label for an ambitious, idealistic package of legislation, including Medicare, which helped finance medical care for Americans over 65; Medicaid, which provided healthcare for the poor of all ages; elementary, secondary, and higher education acts to enhance education and provide financial aid to college students; and legislation relating to what Johnson called a "War on Poverty."

Civil Rights Act of 1964

Of all the creations of the Great Society, none has had more lasting and profound impact than the Civil Rights Act of 1964. The act banned segregation and discrimination in public accommodations such as restaurants, theaters, and hotels, and it barred employers from discriminatory hiring practices based on race.

The Civil Rights Act of 1964 was followed the next year by a Voting Rights Act of 1965, which tore down the last vestiges of local legislation intended to prevent or discourage African Americans from voting. By the end of the Johnson years, equality in America was certainly not a fact of life, but at least it was no longer a condition of law—anywhere in the United States.

The Least You Need to Know

◆ The modern Civil Rights Movement began with the integration of the armed forces in 1947 and developed through a nonviolent program of civil disobedience led by Dr. Martin Luther King Jr., and others.

◆ The record of the Kennedy administration is ambiguous, but the young president became and remains a potent symbol of the great potential of American democracy.

♦ Although John F. Kennedy attempted to create an ambitious program of civil rights and social legislation, it was the administration of Lyndon Baines Johnson that secured passage of legislation creating the "Great Society."

♦ The landmark Civil Rights Act of 1964 extended civil rights protection into the nongovernmental sector by banning segregation and discrimination in public accommodations such as restaurants, theaters, and hotels, and barring employers from discriminatory hiring practices based on race.

Chapter 31

Nam (1946–1975)

In This Chapter

- ◆ The background of the Vietnam War
- ◆ Escalation and deception
- ◆ Protest on the home front
- ◆ U.S. withdrawal and Communist victory

In 1964, the beacon of the Great Society shone brightly. Motivated by the memory of JFK and energized by the moral passion of Lyndon Johnson, the program of social reform, even more ambitious than FDR's New Deal had been, seemed unstoppable.

Then, on August 2, 1964, the American destroyer *Maddox*, conducting electronic espionage in international waters, was reported as having been attacked by North Vietnamese torpedo boats. Undamaged, *Maddox* was joined by a second destroyer, the *C. Turner Joy*. On August 4, both ships reported coming under fire. In 1971, *The Pentagon Papers*, a top secret history of the Vietnam conflict leaked to *The New York Times* (Chapter 32), revealed that the ships had been in North Vietnamese territorial waters and not (as originally reported) in international waters and that the second attack had not, in fact, occurred. In 1964, however, LBJ was looking for a provocation to expand the war in Vietnam in order to push it to a conclusion, and the "Tonkin Gulf Incident" provided just that provocation.

Based on the second attack—that is, the nonexistent attack—President Johnson ordered retaliatory air strikes against North Vietnam, and, at his request, on August 7, the U.S. Senate passed the Tonkin Gulf Resolution, giving LBJ almost unlimited authority to escalate American involvement in what turned out to be a heartbreakingly long war destined to wreck the Great Society, nearly tear the United States apart, spawn an idealistic, albeit drug-oriented, youth counterculture, and cost the lives of more than 58,000 young Americans.

History

World War II left much of the world, including Southeast Asia, dangerously unstable. During the nineteenth century, France had colonized Laos, Cambodia, and Vietnam, and when France collapsed under German invasion in 1940, the Japanese allowed French colonial officials puppet authority in Southeast Asia until the Allied liberation of France in 1945. Japan then seized full control, purging the French police agencies that had kept various nationalist groups in check. In Vietnam, Ho Chi Minh (1890–1969) led the most powerful of these independence-seeking groups, the Viet Minh.

When the war in Europe ended, Allied forces were free to turn their attention to Vietnam (and the rest of Southeast Asia). Nationalist Chinese troops (under Chiang Kai-shek) occupied northern Vietnam. The British secured southern Vietnam for reentry of the French, who, when they returned, ruthlessly suppressed supporters of Ho Chi Minh. A state of low-level guerrilla warfare developed, which escalated sharply when Chiang Kai-shek, hoping to checkmate communist ambitions in the region, withdrew from northern Vietnam and turned that region over to French control.

The March to Dien Bien Phu

Like Chiang Kai-shek, U.S. leaders feared communist incursions in Southeast Asia and began to supply the French with funding, military equipment, and—on August 3, 1950—the first contingent of U.S. military "advisors." By 1953, the United States was funding 80 percent of the cost of France's war effort.

France assigned General Henri Eugene Navarre to strike a decisive blow against the Communists on the strategically located plain of Dien Bien Phu, near Laos. President Eisenhower stepped up military aid, but despite Navarre's massing of troops, Dien Bien Phu fell to the forces of Ho Chi Minh on May 7, 1954. This disaster was followed by a string of Viet Minh victories, and, in a July peace conference, the French and the Viet Minh concluded a cease-fire and agreed to divide Vietnam along the 17th parallel.

Domino Theory

During the thick of the Dien Bien Phu campaign, on April 7, 1954, President Eisenhower presented reporters with his rationale for aiding France—a foreign colonial power—in its fight against Communism in Vietnam—a remote country. "You have a row of dominoes set up," he explained, "you knock over the first one, and what will happen to the last one is the certainty it will go over very quickly." This offhanded and clumsily expressed metaphor was immediately christened the Domino Theory, and it became the basis for an escalating U.S. involvement in Vietnam.

American "Advisors"

As a condition of the armistice agreement concluded in Geneva, Switzerland, between Ho Chi Minh and France, the divided Vietnam was to hold elections within 2 years with the object of reunification. South Vietnam's President Ngo Dinh Diem assumed that Ho Chi Minh would win a popular election; therefore, he simply declined to abide by the Geneva accords, refusing to hold the promised elections. The United States, more concerned with blocking Communism than with practicing democracy in Vietnam, backed Diem's position. Under John F. Kennedy, who succeeded Eisenhower in 1961, the number of military "advisors" sent to Vietnam steadily rose.

Flaming Monks and the Fall of a "Friend"

The Kennedy administration's desire to stop the toppling dominoes caused U.S. officials to turn a blind eye toward the essential unpopularity and universal corruption of the Diem regime. Diem's cronies were put into high civil and military positions, and although a small number of urban South Vietnamese prospered under Diem, the rural majority fared poorly. Moreover, the Catholic Diem became tyrannical in his support of the nation's Catholic minority while openly abusing the Buddhist majority. The world was soon horrified by a series of extreme protest demonstrations: buddhist monks doused themselves in gasoline and set themselves ablaze in the streets of Saigon.

By mid-1963, the Kennedy administration determined that the Diem regime was no longer viable. President Kennedy secretly allowed the CIA to plot the murder of Diem in a U.S.-backed military coup that overthrew him on November 1, 1963. Diem's death unleashed a series of coups that made South Vietnam even more unstable over the next 2 years and encouraged the Communists to escalate the war.

Rolling Thunder

After the death of Kennedy, Lyndon B. Johnson moved vigorously to oppose North Vietnamese insurgents, authorizing the CIA to oversee diversionary raids on the northern coast while the Navy conducted electronic espionage in the Gulf of Tonkin. The new president also named General William Westmoreland to head the Military Assistance Command, Vietnam (MACV) and increased the number of military "advisors" to 23,000, far more than were actually needed merely to "advise." Nevertheless, faced with a succession of weak Saigon governments, President Johnson continued to weigh the odds. The Domino Theory was persuasive, but the conflict began to look increasingly hopeless. In February 1965, LBJ sent his personal advisor, McGeorge Bundy, on a fact-finding mission to Saigon.

On February 7, Viet Cong units attacked U.S. advisory forces and the headquarters of the U.S. Army 52nd Aviation Battalion, near Pleiku, killing 9 Americans and wounding 108. U.S. forces retaliated against an enemy barracks near Dong Hoi, provoking a Viet Cong counterstrike on February 10 against a U.S. barracks at Qui Nhon. The next day, U.S. forces struck back with a long program of air strikes deep into the North. Code named Rolling Thunder, the operation formally began on March 2, 1965, and marked the start of a course of escalation as 50,000 new ground troops were sent to Vietnam, ostensibly to protect U.S. air bases. They were the first U.S. soldiers openly identified as combat troops rather than "advisors."

"Escalation" and "Vietnamization"

Johnson's strategy was to continue a gradual escalation, bombing military targets in a war of attrition intended to wear down the North Vietnamese without, however, provoking overt intervention from China or the USSR. This scheme proved to be a no-win strategy that served only to prolong the war. In an aggressive military campaign, success is measured by objectives attained—cities captured and military targets eliminated—but in a war of attrition, the only measure of success is the body count. To be sure, American forces produced a massive body count among the enemy, but, just as Buddhist monks were willing to set themselves aflame, this enemy was prepared to die.

 Vital Statistics

In 1965, 75,000 Americans were fighting in Vietnam. In 1966, the number jumped to 375,000, and to half a million by 1968.

Motivated by nationalistic passion, the North Vietnamese did more than send combat troops to infiltrate the South. Special political cadres won widespread grassroots support from the rural populace of the South. With this support, the Viet Cong enjoyed great mobility throughout the country, often fighting from a complex network of tunnels that were all but invisible. True, the growing numbers of U.S. troops were successful in clearing enemy territory. Yet U.S. numbers could never be great enough to *hold* and *occupy* that territory, and, once cleared, battle zones were soon overrun again.

President Johnson and his advisors began to recognize that the war would not be won by U.S. intervention, and military efforts were increasingly directed toward *Vietnamization*—giving the ARVN (Army of the Republic of Vietnam) the tools and training to take over more and more of the fighting, so that U.S. troops could ultimately disengage as the South Vietnamese forces occupied the cleared territory.

Hearts and Minds

In the early stages of the war, President Kennedy had spoken of the need to win the "hearts and minds" of the Vietnamese people. And even as America's technologically advanced weaponry destroyed the country, the hearts and minds of the people remained elusive targets.

The fact is that American war policy had not only failed to win the hearts and minds of the Vietnamese, but it was rapidly losing influence over the hearts and minds of citizens of the United States. President Johnson increasingly relied on the Selective Service System—the draft—to supply troops, although most combat soldiers were, in fact, volunteer enlistees. Relatively well-off young people could often avoid conscription through student deferments (college enrollment skyrocketed during the war) and by other means, including, at the most extreme, fleeing to sanctuary in Canada or other countries. The options of minority youth seemed more limited—a fact that stirred resentment and unrest, especially in the African American community.

But antiwar sentiment was hardly confined to black America. What rapidly evolved into a full-blown antiwar movement began with leftist college students and peace activists. And as more

 Vital Statistics

Popular perceptions aside, two thirds of U.S. soldiers who served in Vietnam were voluntary enlistees; most draftees served Stateside duty or assignments in other noncombat regions. Eighty-six percent of the U.S. troops who were killed in Vietnam were white, 12.5 percent were black, and 1.2 percent were members of other races—percentages that accurately reflected the racial makeup of the general civilian population.

Americans came home maimed or in body bags, the movement spread into the mainstream, including a series of marches on Washington starting in 1965 and continuing through 1968 and again in 1971.

Antiwar protest widened what was popularly called the generation gap, pitting young people against "anyone over 30." The antiwar movement became associated with a general counterculture movement, which featured young people in long hair (for both sexes) and wearing what to their elders seemed bizarre gypsy-hobo outfits. Such youngsters called themselves "hippies" and ostentatiously indulged in "recreational" drugs (such as marijuana and the hallucinogenic LSD) and "recreational" sex. Government officials assumed that the entire peace movement was backed by Communists and used the FBI as well as the CIA (illegally, because this agency was forbidden by law to conduct domestic espionage or counterespionage) to infiltrate antiwar organizations.

Remember This _____

The most visible and violent "confrontation" of the 1960s took place from August 26 to August 29, 1968, in Chicago, during the Democratic National Convention. Earlier, on March 31, 1968, President Johnson had announced to a stunned nation that he would not run for reelection. However, probably the most electable antiwar candidate, Robert F. Kennedy, was assassinated on June 6, following his victory in the California primary. Hubert H. Humphrey then became the most likely candidate—and, unlike RFK, he did not oppose the war. Some 10,000 individuals massed in Grant and Lincoln parks along Chicago's lakefront to protest the war, to protest the nomination of Humphrey ("Dump the Hump!" they chanted), and to vent rage against Chicago mayor and Democratic "boss" Richard J. Daley, whom they scorned as a reactionary, racist, fascist, and, as the demonstrators saw him, all-around "pig."

The Light at the End of the Tunnel

By the end of 1967, it was clear that the Vietnam War was gruesomely deadlocked. President Johnson repeatedly went before the nation, assuring television viewers that there was "light at the end of the tunnel," but the increasing numbers of U.S. casualties created something the media and media-savvy politicians dubbed a "credibility gap" between what the administration claimed and what the public believed.

Tet Offensive

In this period of growing doubt, the North Vietnamese staged a series of massive offensives, first along the southern border, with attacks against the U.S. base at Khe Sanh, then against South Vietnamese provincial capitals and principal cities beginning on January 30, 1968, a traditional Vietnamese lunar holiday called Tet. The offensive, which included an assault on the U.S. Embassy in Saigon, was costly to U.S. and ARVN forces, but far more costly to the Viet Cong. Militarily, the United States and its ally prevailed; nevertheless, the 3-week campaign came across as a devastating psychological victory for the Communists, convincing many Americans, including politicians and policy makers, that the war was unwinnable.

With American casualties now topping 1,000 a month, it was hard to believe official (and quite accurate) military pronouncements that Tet was by no means a defeat. Tet hardened public opposition to the war and sharply divided legislators, with *hawks* (war supporters) on one side and *doves* (peace advocates) on the other.

A President Opts Out

On March 31, President Johnson made two surprise television announcements. He declared that he would restrict bombing above the 20th parallel—that is, refrain from bombing the North Vietnamese homeland—thereby opening the door to a negotiated settlement of the war, and he announced that he would not seek another term as president. Johnson recognized that his advocacy of the war and his close identification with it were tearing the nation apart.

Cease-fire negotiations began in May, only to stall over Hanoi's demands for a complete bombing halt and NLF (National Liberation Front) representation at the peace table. Johnson resisted, but in November agreed to these terms. Despite the boost this move gave the sagging presidential campaign of Democrat Hubert Humphrey, Richard M. Nixon (whom many had counted out of politics after he lost the race for California governor in 1962) emerged victorious in the presidential contest.

Nixon's War

Richard Milhous Nixon (1913–1994) was a man who believed in winning at any cost. To ensure victory in the 1968 election, he made repeated—although very vague—promises that he had a plan to end the war. Yet, after he was elected, Nixon did not hesitate to *expand* the war into neighboring Laos and Cambodia, nations whose neutrality the United States had guaranteed by treaties signed years earlier. Nixon had evolved a grand strategy with his foreign policy advisor, Henry Kissinger (b. 1923). The strategy called for détente—improving relations with the Soviets (mainly through trade and an arms-limitation agreement)—in order to disengage Moscow from Hanoi, and for normalizing relations with China. After the USSR and China had cut the North Vietnamese loose, Nixon and Kissinger reasoned, the United States could negotiate "peace with honor" in Vietnam.

The strategy didn't work. The Soviets announced their recognition of the Provisional Revolutionary Government (PRG) formed by the NLF in June 1969, and the peace talks stalled.

Remember This

On March 16, 1968, a U.S. infantry company commanded by Lieutenant William L. Calley marched into the South Vietnamese hamlet of My Lai, supposedly a Viet Cong sanctuary and stronghold. The company massacred 347 unarmed civilians, including women, old men, and children, some of whom were herded into ditches to be shot. The grisly scenes were recorded by Army photographers.

The "My Lai Incident" was not made public until 1969, and then only through the efforts of Vietnam veteran Ronald Ridenhour, who threatened to go to the media with what he had heard about the massacre if the U.S. Army failed to initiate an inquiry itself. That proceeding resulted in the court martial of several soldiers, of whom only Calley was convicted on March 29, 1971.

For many Americans, My Lai symbolized the essential brutality of the Vietnam War, a conflict in which the defenders of democracy were seen as slaughterers of innocent women and children. As to Calley, some people saw him as likewise a victim, thrust into a war in which everyone was a potential enemy.

Sentenced to life imprisonment, Calley was released in September of 1974 when a federal court overturned the conviction. He always maintained that he was only following orders and that he was being scapegoated to cover up official policy concerning the rules of engagement in Vietnam.

Paris, Cambodia, and Laos

As negotiators spun their wheels in Paris, the Nixon administration sought to accelerate the Vietnamization process by turning more and more of the responsibility for the war over to ARVN forces, which, however, continued to perform poorly. Despite the discouraging results, U.S. casualties did drop, and President Nixon was able to commence and then accelerate the withdrawal of U.S. ground troops.

In an attempt to force the North to negotiate favorable peace terms, Nixon ordered an invasion of Vietnam's neighbor Cambodia in order to attack communist supply and staging areas there. This incursion, made without even consulting Congress, triggered angry protests at home, including a campus takeover by students at Kent State University in Ohio on May 4, 1970. The event resulted in the killing of four unarmed students and the wounding of nine more when inexperienced National Guardsmen, called in to "restore order" to the campus, fired on them. Subsequently, 100,000 demonstrators marched on Washington, and Congress registered its own protest by rescinding the Tonkin Gulf Resolution. Nixon withdrew troops from Cambodia, but stepped up bombing raids, and when communist infiltration continued unabated, the United States supplied air support for an ARVN invasion of Laos in February 1971.

By the end of 1971, withdrawals had reduced ground-troop strength to 175,000 in Vietnam, somewhat calming protests at home but destroying front-line morale, as remaining troops saw themselves as expendable pawns in a lost cause. Drug and alcohol abuse assumed epidemic proportions among soldiers, who were often openly rebellious; some transformed search-and-destroy missions into "search-and-avoid" operations, the object of which was to get home safely—sometimes even if this entailed *fragging* one's company commander.

> **What's the Word?**
>
> Officers who ordered their men into dangerous situations risked **fragging**—that is, assassination by their own troops—often by fragmentation grenade.

Death for Easter

In March 1972, the communists launched a new invasion, initially routing ARVN troops until President Nixon retaliated by redoubling air attacks, mining Haiphong harbor, and establishing a naval blockade of the North. Following the communist "Easter Offensive," Henry Kissinger and North Vietnamese representative Le Duc Tho finally formulated a peace agreement. The terms called for the withdrawal of U.S. troops, the return of all POWs, and the laying of a foundation for political settlement through establishment of a special council of reconciliation. South Vietnamese president Nguyen Van Thieu rejected the peace terms because they permitted Viet Cong forces to remain in place in the South.

Bombs for Christmas

The fact that Nixon's negotiator, Henry Kissinger, had been able to announce that "peace is at hand" ensured the president's re-election in 1972. Once in office, however, Nixon supported Thieu, repudiating the peace terms Kissinger had negotiated. Nixon then ordered massive B-52 bombing raids north of the 20th parallel, which forced the North Vietnamese back to the negotiating table.

The agreement reached after the bombing was not materially different from what Kissinger had originally negotiated. This time, President Thieu and his renewed objections were ignored.

Peace with Honor

On January 31, 1973, the United States and North Vietnam signed the Paris Peace Accords, which brought U.S. withdrawal and the return of the POWs, some of whom had been languishing in North Vietnamese prisons for nearly a decade. A four-party Joint Military Commission and an International Commission of Control and Supervision supervised the cease-fire. However, the Nixon administration continued to send massive amounts of aid to the Thieu government, and both the North and South freely violated the cease-fire accords. To pressure the North into abiding by them, the United States resumed bombing Cambodia and menaced North Vietnam with reconnaissance over-flights.

But a war-weary Congress had turned against the president, whose administration (as you will see in the next chapter) was now wallowing and disintegrating in the Watergate Scandal. In November 1973, Congress passed the War Powers Act, which required the president to inform Congress within 48 hours of deployment of U.S. military forces abroad; the act also mandated the forces' withdrawal within 60 days if Congress did not approve. In 1974, U.S. aid to South Vietnam was reduced from $2.56 billion to $907 million, and to $700 million in 1975.

What hopes Thieu held for continued support from the Nixon administration were dashed when the American president, facing certain impeachment, resigned in August 1974. Beginning in early 1975, the dispirited South suffered one military defeat after another. After Congress rejected President Gerald Ford's request for $300 million in supplemental aid to South Vietnam, Nguyen Van Thieu unceremoniously resigned his office. He left the leadership of his nation to Tran Van Huong, who promptly resigned, turning over power to General Duong Van Minh. Minh's single official act was to make an unconditional surrender to the North on April 30, 1975. A dramatic, frenzied evacuation of Americans remaining in Vietnam followed. At a cost of more than $150 billion and 58,000 Americans killed, the Vietnam War had ended in defeat for South Vietnam and (as many saw it) for the United States as well.

The Least You Need to Know

- ◆ U.S. involvement in the Vietnam War was an extreme result of the Cold War policy of the "containment" of communism.

- ◆ The Vietnam War was the most unpopular and divisive war in American history, wrecking the grand social programs of Lyndon Johnson and badly undermining popular faith in the federal government and the nation's leaders.

- ◆ Taking over the war from LBJ, President Richard Nixon attempted to do more with fewer U.S. troops, simultaneously expanding the war while withdrawing from it.

- ◆ President Nixon sought "peace with honor" in Vietnam, but the war ended in the total defeat of ostensibly democratic South Vietnam after the United States completed its total disengagement from the country in 1975.

Part 8

Identity Crisis

By the late 1960s, a deep division opened up between a rebellious under-30 generation and their elders, with youngsters developing a colorful separate culture compounded of "psychedelic" art and music, as well as (on a more dangerous note) mind-altering, mind-expanding, and mind-numbing drugs. The nation reached a great technological and human pinnacle in the successful lunar mission of *Apollo 11*, and the Cold War began to thaw. Yet Americans were stunned by the revelation of democracy's failings in *The Pentagon Papers* and by the Watergate scandal that forced President Nixon to resign from office in 1974.

The women's liberation movement was finally taken seriously. But if men were now compelled to readjust their attitudes and egos, so was the entire nation, as it found itself held hostage to the oil sheiks of the Middle East, the industrial giants of Japan, a sluggish economy at home, and the religious fanaticism of the Ayatollah Khomeini in Iran. This part recalls a most unquiet period in American history.

32

Of Love, the Moon, and Dirty Tricks (1968–1974)

In This Chapter

- ◆ The counterculture movement
- ◆ The landing of *Apollo 11* on the moon
- ◆ Nixon's foreign-policy breakthroughs
- ◆ Crisis of national trust: Pentagon Papers and Watergate

Who were the victims of the Vietnam War? Two, perhaps three million Indochinese died, and 58,000 American lives were lost. Many thousands more were wounded, some disabled for life. U.S. Vietnam veterans were not welcomed home with parades, but were looked on with guilt and suspicion. By some Americans, veterans were seen as "baby killers;" by others, they were regarded as damaged goods—young men who may have escaped physical wounds, but who bore psychological scars that made adjustment to civilian life difficult, if not impossible. (This, as it turns out, was a popular perception not supported by fact. Vietnam veterans did not suffer from psychological illness or adjustment problems at any higher rate than the general population.) The fact is that all of America was a victim of the war, which had created a rift—or to use a term from the era, a credibility gap—between citizens and government. Vietnam killed people, and it killed trust.

Turn On, Tune In, Drop Out

Since the early twentieth century, illegal drug abuse had been associated with the fringes of society, with desperate and disturbed individuals, and to some extent, with urban African Americans. By the 1950s, addiction to such narcotics as heroin was becoming a major and highly visible problem in many American cities and was linked to the increasing incidence of violent street crime. Yet drug use was still far from a mainstream affliction.

This all changed by the mid-1960s. A new generation of middle-class youth, characterized by relative affluence and the advantages of education, became passionately dedicated to forms of music and other types of popular art that expressed a turning away from much that had been accepted as the American Dream: material prosperity, a successful career, a happy marriage, a house set amid a green lawn and surrounded by a white picket fence. Youngsters craved the experience of new music (a development of the rock 'n' roll that had started in the 1950s) and new clothing—colorful, wild, casual, sometimes evoking the bygone world of British Edwardian extravagance and sometimes suggesting the realm of that ultimate thorn in the side of the American Dream, the hobo. As they looked with distrust on their elders ("anyone over 30"), 1960s youth indulged in so-called recreational drugs.

With thermonuclear war an ever-present danger, with an ongoing war escalating in Vietnam—a meatgrinder into which American youth were regularly tossed—and with social justice still an elusive goal in America, there was much to protest and reject in mainstream society. Marijuana was one form of protest, alternative, and escape (all rolled up into a cigarette called a *roach* or *joint*). Sex (which many youths in the 1960s saw as a synonym for love) was another. Yet another alternative was religion—not the "outworn" faiths of the Judeo-Christian West, but the apparently less materialistic beliefs of the East. The decade spawned a series of spiritual leaders, or *gurus*, including the Maharishi Mahesh Yogi (b. 1911?), who introduced a generation to Transcendental Meditation. "The Maharishi" gained renown as spiritual counselor to a bevy of celebrities, including The Beatles.

A guru of a different kind exhorted his followers to "expand" their minds with a hallucinogenic drug

What's the Word?

D-lysergic acid diethylamide, also known as **LSD, LSD-25,** and **acid,** is a hallucinogenic drug discovered in 1943 by Swiss chemist Albert Hofmann. LSD produces powerful sensory distortions, with visual (and sometimes auditory) hallucinations. In the 1960s, such LSD experiences were called **acid trips** and were thought to be mind- or consciousness-expanding.

called *LSD*, which (it was claimed) offered users a universe of "psychedelic" experience. "My advice to people today is as follows," proclaimed Harvard psychologist and LSD advocate Timothy Leary (1920–1996) in 1966: "If you take the game of life seriously, if you take your nervous system seriously, if you take your sense organs seriously, if you take the energy process seriously, you must turn on, tune in, and drop out."

By taking drugs—"turning on"—one would "tune in" to what was really worthwhile in life and, as a consequence, be prompted to "drop out" of a life lived in the hollow mainstream. The phrase became the banner slogan of a generation: turn on, tune in, drop out.

Peace and Love

Americans who had, to one degree or another, turned on, tuned in, and dropped out characteristically called themselves *hippies* (derived from *hip*, slang for being attuned to the latest social trends). The movement placed emphasis on kindness, on affection, on looking out for one's fellow being, on caring for the natural environment, on social justice, on freedom of expression, on tolerance, on fostering creativity, on general peaceful coexistence, and on other life-affirming values.

The *Eagle* Has Landed

As much as the counterculture wanted to believe it, the Establishment did not fail in all it put its hand to. Beginning with the launch of *Sputnik I* in 1957, the United States had consistently come in second to the Soviet Union in the Space Race. In 1961, President Kennedy made a speech in which he set a national goal of putting a man on the moon before the end of the decade. At the time, few Americans thought this goal was realistic, but on July 20, 1969, at 4:17 P.M. (Eastern Daylight Time), the people of a world shaken by a multitude of fears, gnawed by myriad acts of injustice, and racked by a terrible war in Southeast Asia, watched live television pictures of two American astronauts setting foot on the lunar surface, a quarter-million miles from Earth.

"That's one small step for [a] man," Neil Armstrong declared as he hopped down off the ladder of the lunar excursion module (LEM) *Eagle*, "and one giant leap for mankind." The

American Echo

Houston, Tranquility Base here. The *Eagle* has landed.

—Neil A. Armstrong, radio message from *Apollo 11*, July 20, 1969 successful mission of *Apollo 11* was a national—and human—triumph in a time of bit-terness, pain, doubt, and rejection of long-cherished values.

Pentagon Papers

Unfortunately, the government that put men on the moon was about to reveal that it was also capable of moral lapses as deep as its lunar aspirations were lofty. During June of 1971, *The New York Times* published a series of articles on a secret govern-ment study popularly called *The Pentagon Papers*. The 47-volume document, compiled between 1967 and 1969 by Defense Department analysts, meticulously revealed how the federal government had systematically deceived the American people with regard to its policies and practices in Southeast Asia. Among many other things, the study showed how the CIA had conspired to overthrow and assassinate South Vietnam president Diem, and it revealed that the Tonkin Gulf Resolution was actually drafted months in advance of the purported attacks on the destroyers *Maddox* and *C. Turner Joy*, the events that supposedly prompted the resolution. (At least one of the claimed attacks was either an error or an outright fabrication.)

In 1971, Daniel Ellsberg, an MIT professor and government consultant who had originally contributed to the study but who had subsequently become disgusted and disillusioned with the Vietnam War, leaked *The Pentagon Papers* to *The Times*.

The revelations of *The Pentagon Papers* marked a low point of popular faith in the American government and the continued prosecution of the Vietnam War. The effect of these documents was profoundly depressing precisely because Americans had long taken for granted that theirs was a free, open, honest, and noble government—as Abraham Lincoln had put it, "the last best hope of the world."

SALT, China, and the Middle East

Last best hope. President Nixon, who had risen to power in Congress through his un-compromising, at times virulent stance against Communism, now worked with his advi-sor Henry Kissinger to engineer détente with the Soviets and with the communist Chinese. His most immediate motivation was to cut them loose from North Vietnam, but the ramifications of the Nixon–Kissinger diplomacy extended far beyond the Viet-nam War. The consummate "cold warrior," Richard M. Nixon initiated the long thaw that ultimately led to the end of the Cold War and the beginning of a safer world.

In 1968, the United Nations sponsored the Nuclear Non-Proliferation Treaty, which sought to limit the spread of nuclear weapons by persuading nations without nuclear arsenals to renounce acquiring them in return for a pledge from the nuclear powers that they would reduce the size of their arsenals. The following year, the United States began negotiations with the Soviet Union to limit strategic (that is, nuclear-armed) forces. These Strategic Arms Limitation Talks (SALT) produced a pair of important arms-control agreements in 1972. Then, from 1972 to 1979, the talks of SALT II were conducted, extending provisions formulated in 1972. Although the U.S. Senate never ratified SALT II (President Jimmy Carter asked that ratification be suspended after the Soviets invaded Afghanistan in 1980), the two nations generally abided by its arms-limitation and arms-reduction provisions.

Perhaps even more remarkable was President Nixon's February 1972 journey to China, where he was received in Beijing by Chairman Mao Zedong, the very incarnation of the Communism Nixon had spent his life opposing. In a single stroke of diplomacy, Nixon reversed the long-standing U.S. policy of refusing to recognize China's communist government, and by January 1979 (under President Jimmy Carter), full diplomatic relations were established between the nations.

The third of Nixon's major triumphs in diplomacy came in the war-torn Middle East. Following the Arab-Israel War of 1973, Nixon's emissary Henry Kissinger presided over negotiations that led to a cease-fire, troop disengagement, and ultimately, the foundations of a more lasting peace in the region.

CREEP

Intelligent and boldly creative on the international front, Richard Nixon never won total trust and confidence at home. A vigorous, merciless political campaigner, Nixon had a reputation for stopping at nothing to crush his opponent. "Tricky Dick," he was called, and never affectionately.

As the 1972 elections approached, there was little doubt that Nixon would be re-elected. Henry Kissinger had announced that peace in Vietnam was "at hand," international relations were dramatically improving, and Americans were generally loath to (in Lincoln's homely phrase) change horses in midstream. Yet, oddly, none of this optimism was sufficient for the President. He directed his re-election organization, the Committee to Re-elect the President—known (incredibly enough) by the acronym CREEP—to stack the deck even more strongly in his favor. The committee engaged in a campaign of espionage against the Democratic Party and a program of what CREEP called "dirty tricks" aimed at smearing Democratic challengers.

Plumbers at Work

On June 17, 1972, during the presidential campaign, five burglars were arrested in the headquarters of the Democratic National Committee at the Watergate office building in Washington, D.C. This was hardly front-page news, except that these burglars were really "Plumbers." That's what White House insiders called the men, because their original mission had been to plug any leaks (security breaches) that developed or might develop in the aftermath of the publication of *The Pentagon Papers*. The Plumbers' original role was expanded so that they served the Nixon administration as a kind of palace guard, assigned to do jobs that lay not only beyond the chief executive's constitutional mandate, but outside the law. One such job involved planting electronic bugs (listening devices) at the headquarters of the political opposition.

The five Plumbers included three anti-Castro Cuban refugees, all veterans of the ill-fated Bay of Pigs invasion, and James McCord Jr., former CIA agent and now "security" officer for CREEP. McCord reported directly to CREEP's head, Nixon's campaign manager, former U.S. Attorney General John Mitchell. In a slapstick security *faux pas*, one of the burglars carried in his pocket an address book with the name of E. Howard Hunt. A former CIA agent (he'd been in charge of the Bay of Pigs operation) and writer of pulpy spy novels, Hunt was assistant to Charles Colson, special counsel to President Nixon. Hunt's address? "The White House."

What President Nixon later tried to dismiss as a "third-rate burglary" pointed to conspiracy at the very highest levels of government, which began to unravel due to the investigative journalism of two young and very persistent *Washington Post* reporters, Bob Woodward and Carl Bernstein. Guided in part by a super-secret government source they dubbed "Deep Throat"—revealed in 2005 as Mark Felt, the deputy director of the FBI—Woodward and Bernstein wrote a series of articles pealing back the layers of a vast and vastly illegal covert White House operation.

In September 1972, the burglars and two co-plotters—Hunt and former FBI agent G. Gordon Liddy, CREEP's general counsel—were indicted on charges of burglary, conspiracy, and wiretapping. After their convictions, Nixon's aides, one after the other, began to talk.

All the President's Men

Despite the arrests and early revelations, President Nixon, running against George McGovern, an obscure senator from South Dakota, won re-election. However, soon after Nixon began his second term, the Watergate conspiracy rapidly unraveled. As each of the "president's men" gave testimony to federal authorities, the conspiracy tightened around Nixon's inner circle. In February 1973, the Senate created an investigative committee headed by North Carolina Senator Sam Ervin Jr. Like the Army-McCarthy Hearings two decades earlier, the Watergate Hearings riveted Americans to their television sets. After each key disclosure, the president announced the resignation of an important aide, including John Ehrlichman and H. R. Haldeman, his closest advisors. Nixon's counsel, John W. Dean III, was dismissed. Patiently, persistently, and with the cunning of a country lawyer educated at Harvard, the drawling Ervin elicited testimony revealing crimes far beyond Watergate:

- Mitchell controlled secret monies used to finance a campaign of forged letters and false news items intended to damage the Democratic party.

- Major U.S. corporations had made illegal campaign contributions amounting to millions.

- Hunt and Liddy had in 1971 burglarized the office of Daniel Ellsberg's psychiatrist in order to discredit *The Pentagon Papers* whistle-blower.

- A plan existed to physically assault Ellsberg.

- Nixon had promised the Watergate burglars clemency and even bribes in return for silence.

> **American Echo**
>
> People have got to know whether or not their President is a crook. Well, I'm not a crook.
>
> —Richard M. Nixon, press conference, November 11, 1973

- L. Patrick Gray, Nixon's nominee to replace the recently deceased J. Edgar Hoover as head of the FBI, turned over FBI records on Watergate to White House counsel John Dean.

- Two Nixon cabinet members, Mitchell and Maurice Stans, took bribes from shady "financier" John Vesco.

- Illegal wiretap tapes were in the White House safe of Nixon advisor John Ehrlichman.

- Nixon directed the CIA to instruct the FBI not to investigate Watergate.

- Nixon used $10 million in government funds to improve his personal homes.

- During 1969 and 1970, the United States had secretly bombed Cambodia without the knowledge (let alone consent) of Congress.

In the midst of all this turmoil, Vice President Spiro T. Agnew was indicted for federal income tax fraud and for bribes taken when he had served as Maryland governor. He resigned as vice president in October of 1973 and was replaced by Congressman Gerald Ford of Michigan. Finally, it was revealed that President Nixon had covertly taped White House conversations; the tapes were subpoenaed, but the president claimed "executive privilege" and withheld them. Nixon ordered Elliot L. Richardson (who had replaced John Mitchell as attorney general when Mitchell resigned that post to head up CREEP) to fire special Watergate prosecutor Archibald Cox. On October 20, 1973, Richardson refused and resigned in protest; his deputy, William Ruckelshaus, likewise refused and was duly fired. The duty to discharge Cox fell to Nixon's solicitor general, Robert H. Bork, who apparently had no scruples about complying. This so-called "Saturday night massacre" served only to suggest that Nixon had more to hide. Much more.

At length, the president released transcripts of some of the White House tapes (containing a highly suspicious 18½-minutes of gaps), and on July 27 through 30, the House Judiciary Committee recommended that Nixon be impeached on three charges: obstruction of justice, abuse of presidential powers, and attempting to impede the impeachment process by defying committee subpoenas. Nixon released the remaining tapes on August 5, 1974. They constituted what the press called "the smoking gun," irrefutably revealing that the President had taken steps to block the FBI's inquiry into the Watergate burglary. On August 9, 1974, Richard Milhous Nixon became the first president in U.S. history to resign from office.

The Least You Need to Know

- As World War I had produced a lost generation in America, so Vietnam spawned a youth counterculture movement, founded on idealism, rock music, sexual freedom, and "recreational" drugs.

- Through a deviousness that was characteristic of his style, President Nixon simultaneously withdrew U.S. troops from Vietnam, even as he (sometimes illegally) intensified the war by ordering massive air strikes.

- Perhaps the most disturbingly complex leader the United States has ever had, Richard Nixon was both a ruthless "cold warrior" and the president who opened the door to sane relations with the Soviets and the Chinese.

- The turbulent Nixon years saw men land on the moon and the Cold War begin to thaw, but the era ended in the gravest national crisis since the Civil War.

Chapter 33

Women Rise, the Nation Drifts, Reagan Rallies (1963–1980)

In This Chapter

- ◆ Feminism and the fate of the ERA
- ◆ An energy crisis triggered by OPEC
- ◆ A plague of economic and social woes
- ◆ The Iran hostage crisis
- ◆ The election of 1980

The 1960s marked a period of self-examination in the United States, an era of sometimes liberating reflection and sometimes debilitating self-doubt. During the decade, women joined African Americans and other minorities in calling for equal rights and equal opportunity. In the course of the following decade, all Americans were forced to rethink attitudes and assumptions about limitless economic growth, unrestrained spending, and the natural environment as the vulnerability of the nation's sources of energy was dramatically exposed. Then, in 1980, after 20 years of often painful introspection, Americans elected a president whose resumé included two terms as California's governor, part of a lifetime as a B-movie actor, and nearly a decade hosting

General Electric Theater on TV. His message to the nation was to be proud and feel good—a message Ronald Wilson Reagan's (1911–2004) beleaguered fellow Americans were more than ready to embrace.

A Woman's Place

The sweet land of liberty was largely a man's world until 1920, when the Nineteenth Amendment gave women the constitutional right to vote. Yet that giant stride changed American society surprisingly little. Pundits of the period speculated that women would introduce an enduring liberal note to American politics, yet the first presidential election in which women had a voice brought Warren G. Harding (1865–1923) into office, product of the GOP's conservative "old boy" consensus. No, it would take a *second* world war to bring even temporary substantial change to gender roles and sexual identity in the United States.

From Rosie the Riveter to *The Feminine Mystique*

The national war effort spurred into action by the December 7, 1941, surprise attack on Pearl Harbor required maximum military force and all-out industrial production. But if the men were off fighting the war, who would "man" the factories? Women answered the call in massive numbers, invading traditionally male workplaces. Posters exhorting workers to give their all for war production often depicted a woman in denim overalls and bandanna, expertly wielding a rivet gun or flexing her muscular bicep. She was Rosie the Riveter, radical new symbol of American womanhood during World War II.

For most American women, the war was their first experience of life in a workplace other than the home. Yet when the war ended, most women quit their jobs, married the returning soldiers, and settled into lives as homemakers.

Throughout the 1950s, few women questioned their role among home and family. Then, in 1963, writer Betty Friedan sent a questionnaire to graduates of Smith College, her alma mater. She asked probing questions about the women's satisfaction in life, and the answers she received were sufficiently eye opening to prompt her to write a book, *The Feminine Mystique*. Its thesis was that American women were no longer universally content to be wives and mothers. They were, in fact, often the unhappy victims of a myth—the "feminine mystique"—that the female of the species could gain satisfaction only through marriage and childbearing. *The Feminine Mystique*, an instant best-seller, struck a chord that caused many women to re-examine their lives and the roles in which society had cast them.

The Power of the Pill

In May 1960, just a few years before Friedan's book appeared, the U.S. Food and Drug Administration (FDA) approved Enovid, the world's first effective oral contraceptive, the birth control pill. "The Pill" was destined not only to bring radical change to the nation's sexual mores—contributing to the so-called "sexual revolution" of the 1960s—but also to liberate women, allowing them to choose to delay having children (or not to have them at all) and use the time to establish a career.

NOW and *Ms.*

In 1966, three years after publishing *The Feminine Mystique*, Friedan helped found the National Organization for Women (NOW) and served as NOW's first president. An organized feminist movement—popularly called Women's Liberation or (sometimes derisively) "women's lib"—crystallized around NOW. The organization advocated equality for women generally in society and more specifically in the workplace, liberalized abortion laws, and passage of the Equal Rights Amendment (ERA), a proposed constitutional amendment declaring that "equality of rights under the law shall not be denied or abridged by the United States nor by any State on account of sex." ERA had been drafted years earlier by radical feminist Alice Paul (1885–1977), founder of the National Woman's Party, and introduced in Congress in 1923, where it was essentially ignored until NOW revived it in 1970.

By the end of the 1960s, the Women's Liberation Movement was in full swing. In 1972, journalist and feminist Gloria Steinem started *Ms.* magazine, which became a popular, entertaining, and immensely profitable vehicle for the feminist message. Its masthead title came from the new form of female address that had been gaining ground since the 1960s: Both "Miss" and "Mrs." linked a woman's identity to her marital status, as if she had no legitimacy of social standing apart from her relationship to a man, but *Ms.* was the equal counterpart of *Mr.* in that it defined a self without reference to a spouse.

NOW met with opposition not only from conservative men, but also from many women, some of whom claimed that the feminist movement ran contrary to the natural (or, more usually, God-given) order; other women feared the movement would defeminize women and lead to the disintegration of the family. By the 1970s, NOW was also under attack from more radical feminists, such as Shulamith Firestone, Kate Millet, and Ti-Grace Atkinson, for being too conservative. Nevertheless, NOW and the entire range of feminist activism have had an impact on American life. Today 99 out of 100 women work for pay at some time in their lives, and, as of 2004, 59 percent of the American workforce is female. Today, about half of all professional and corporate executive positions are held by women. As of 2005, women hold four of thirteen positions in the Cabinet of George W. Bush. A record 77 women were serving in Congress in 2004, 63 in the House and 14 in the Senate. As of 2005, two women were serving as associate justices of the U.S. Supreme Court and more than 20 percent of federal judges were women. However, as of 2004, women were still being paid at a lower average rate than men. The U.S. Bureau of Labor Statistics reported men's median earnings as $713 per week, whereas women made $573. Overall, American women are paid 77 cents for each dollar paid to men.

 Remember This _____

In 1973, the Supreme Court ruled in the case of *Roe* v. *Wade*, which had its origin in a suit brought by a woman against the state of Texas for having denied her the right to an abortion. In a seven-to-one vote, the high court determined that women have a constitutional right to abortion during the first 3 months of pregnancy.

Abortion is the most controversial right women have asserted, and the *Roe* v. *Wade* decision gave rise to a so-called Right to Life antiabortion movement. Usually motivated by religious conviction, Right to Life advocates have campaigned for a constitutional amendment banning abortion (except in cases of rape, incest, or threat to the mother's life). In recent years, some opposition to abortion has been fanatical, leading to the bombing of abortion clinics and the intimidation, even the murder, of medical personnel.

ERA Collapse

Thanks to NOW, the Equal Rights Amendment (ERA) was passed by the House of Representatives in 1971 and by the Senate in 1972. The amendment was then sent to the states for ratification, and when the necessary three-fourths majority of states failed to ratify it by the original March 1979 deadline, a new deadline of June 30, 1982, was fixed. Yet, by this date, ratification was still three states short of the 38 needed. Reintroduced in Congress on July 14, 1982, ERA failed to gain approval and was dead as of November 15, 1983, although it has been repeatedly reintroduced.

Oil

Citizens of the United States, men and women, have always cherished their liberty, and after 1908, when Henry Ford introduced his Model T, they have increasingly identified a part of that liberty with the mobility provided by the automobile. With just 6 percent of the world's population, the United States consumes little more than a third of the world's energy—much of it in the form of petroleum. Through the 1960s, this posed few problems. Gasoline was abundant and cheap. Indeed, at the start of the decade, U.S. and European oil producers slashed their prices, a move that prompted key oil nations of the Middle East—Iran, Iraq, Kuwait, and Saudi Arabia, plus Venezuela in South America—to band together as the Organization of Petroleum Exporting Countries (OPEC) on September 14, 1960, to stabilize prices. (More nations joined later.) In 1970, OPEC first began to press for oil price hikes, and on October 17, 1973, OPEC temporarily embargoed oil exports to punish nations that had supported Israel in its recent war with Egypt. Chief among the embargo's targets was the United States.

The effects of the OPEC embargo were stunning. Not only did prices shoot up from 38.5 cents per gallon in 1973 to 55.1 cents by June of 1974, gasoline shortages were severe in some areas. Americans found themselves idled in gas lines stretching from the pumps and snaking around the block.

 Vital Statistics

Because OPEC nations still hold 77 percent of the world's proven oil reserves, the organization will continue to remain an important force in the world's economy.

Cruising full speed ahead since the end of World War II, Americans were forced to come to grips with an energy crisis, cutting back on travel and on electricity use. The public endured an unpopular, but energy- and life-saving 55-mile-an-hour national speed limit, in addition to well-meaning, if condescending, lectures from President Jimmy Carter, who characteristically sported a cardigan sweater on TV appearances because he had turned down the White House thermostat as an energy-conserving gesture. In a modest way, Americans learned to do without, and oil consumption was reduced by more than seven percent—enough to prompt some OPEC price rollbacks by the early 1980s. By this time, too, OPEC's grip on key oil producers had slipped as various member producers refused to limit production.

The Japanese Miracle

The energy crisis came on top of an economic crisis, characterized by a combination of inflation and recession christened *stagflation* ("stagnant growth" coupled with "inflation"). The crisis had begun during the Nixon-Ford years and continued into the Carter presidency. By the mid-1970s, the heady consumerism of the 1960s was on the wane, and the dollar bought less and less. To use a phrase popular during the period, the economy was "in the toilet."

And so, it seemed, was the American spirit. Accustomed to being preeminent manufacturer to the world, American industry was losing ground to other nations, especially Japan. All but crushed by World War II, Japan had staged an incredible recovery, becoming a world-class economic dynamo. By the 1970s, Japanese automobiles in particular were making deep inroads into the U.S. automotive market. Not only were the Japanese vehicles less expensive than American makes, they were more fuel-efficient (which meant fewer dollars spent on increasing gasoline costs), and they were generally more reliable. In 1981, American auto production would hit a 20-year low of 6.2 million passenger vehicles.

Scary Cities, Crumbling Bridges

Driving through an American city, circa 1975, in one of those Japanese imports could be a pretty distressing experience as well. The post–World War II building boom had developed suburban America, and throughout the 1950s, many middle-class families left the old cities for the new suburbs. The pace of this exodus accelerated following the racial violence that plagued many urban centers during the 1960s. Social commentators began to speak of *white flight*—although, in fact, the abandonment of inner city for suburb was as much a matter of economics as it was of race; middle-class African Americans departed just as quickly as their white neighbors. The result was cities that rotted at their cores.

But deteriorating cities weren't the only symptoms of a crisis in the national economy and spirit. The American infrastructure was in need of general repair. The very roads that had carried the middle class out of the inner city were typically eaten away with potholes, and a growing proportion of the nation's bridges were failing inspection, too old and too neglected to bear the traffic for which they had been designed.

China Syndrome

The single most terrifying event that suddenly and dramatically forced Americans to question their faith in U.S. technology, big business, and government regulation occurred on March 28, 1979. A nuclear reactor at the Three Mile Island electric generating plant, near the Pennsylvania capital of Harrisburg, lost coolant water, thereby allowing an uncontrolled nuclear chain reaction, which generated tremendous heat and initiated a partial meltdown of the reactor's intensely radioactive core.

Nuclear energy had long been a subject of controversy in the United States. During the late 1950s and early 1960s, the peaceful use of the atom was seen as the key to supplying cheap and virtually limitless energy to the nation. But by the 1970s, environmentalists and others were questioning the safety of atomic power, which was also proving far more expensive than had been originally projected. By the end of the decade, a beleaguered nuclear power industry was on the defensive. In a remarkable coincidence, just before the Three Mile Island accident, a popular movie dramatized the consequences (and attempted corporate cover-up) of a nuclear power plant accident. The movie was called *The China Syndrome*, an allusion to the theory that a full-scale meltdown of a reactor's core would burn so intensely that the material would, in effect, sear its way deep into the earth—clear down to China, experts grimly joked.

> **American Echo**
>
> A normal aberration.
>
> —Metropolitan Edison Company vice president Jack Herbein's description of the Three Mile Island incident, quoted in *Time* magazine, April 9, 1979

The movie was very much on people's minds when a shaken Pennsylvania governor Richard Thornburgh appeared on television to warn residents to remain indoors and to advise pregnant women to evacuate the area entirely. The partial meltdown had already released a quantity of radioactive steam and gases into the atmosphere. There were also fears that a giant bubble of hydrogen, which had accumulated within the reactor containment building, might ignite and explode, catastrophically releasing even more radiation that could render a large portion of Pennsylvania more or less permanently uninhabitable.

Subsequent inquiries showed that plant officials improperly delayed notifying public authorities of the accident, and, during the incident, industry experts issued contradictory assessments of the seriousness of the emergency; however, despite human lapses, automatic backup safety features built into the plant did successfully prevent a major disaster (such as what would occur on April 26, 1986 at Chernobyl in the Soviet Ukraine, where a meltdown killed 31 persons almost immediately and untold additional numbers over the years). Nevertheless, Three Mile Island seemed to many people just one more in a long string of terrible failures of American technology, know-how, and corporate accountability.

The Fanatics

The year 1979 brought a shock of a different kind to national pride. A revolution in Iran, led by the *Ayatollah* Ruhollah Khomeini (1900–1989), toppled longtime U.S. ally Muhammad Reza Shah Pahlavi, the Shah of Iran, who fled into exile in January of

What's the Word?

An **ayatollah** is a religious leader among the *Shiite* Muslims, whose religious zeal and orthodoxy are often compared to those of Christian fundamentalists.

1979. In October, desperately ill with cancer, the Shah was granted permission to come to the United States for medical treatment. In response to this gesture, on November 4, 1979, 500 Iranians stormed the U.S. Embassy in Tehran and took 90 hostages, including 65 U.S. nationals. Non-Americans and 13 American women and black hostages were released on November 19–20, leaving 52 in captivity. Their captors demanded the return of the Shah.

Although President Carter refused to yield to this demand, the Shah, hoping to end the crisis, voluntarily left the United States in early December. Still, the hostages remained in captivity. President Carter authorized an elite army Delta Force unit to attempt a rescue on April 24, 1980. A combination of hasty planning and mechanical and human errors resulted in aborting the mission, and although its failure did not result in harm to the hostages, it came as yet another humiliating defeat for a battered superpower.

Not until November 1980 did the Iranian parliament propose definitive conditions for the liberation of the hostages, including a U.S. pledge not to interfere in Iranian affairs, the release of Iranian assets frozen in the United States by President Carter, the lifting of all U.S. sanctions against Iran, and the return of the Shah's property to Iran. An agreement was signed early in January 1981, but the Ayatollah Khomeini deliberately delayed the release of the hostages until January 20, the day Jimmy Carter left office and Ronald Reagan was inaugurated. Although the new president, in an act of moving grace, sent Carter as his special envoy to greet the returning hostages at a U.S. base in West Germany, many Americans saw the Iran hostage crisis as the crowning failure of the Carter administration, and the release was widely regarded as a kind of miracle performed by the incoming president.

The Great Communicator

Depressed and downcast, a majority of the American people looked to smiling, unflappable Ronald Reagan for even more miracles. Certainly, his own life had much magic to it. Born above a grocery store in the central Illinois town of Tampico in 1911, Reagan worked his way through college, became a sportscaster and then an actor—less than a spectacular talent, perhaps, but with 53 films and many TV appearances to his credit, he was never out of work. A Democrat during his on-screen years, Reagan left acting to enter Republican politics with a strong stop-communism and end-big-government message. In 1966 he handily defeated incumbent Democrat Pat Brown for the governor's office in California and served two terms, during which he made a national reputation as a tax cutter. Delivering a feel-good message to the nation and promising large tax cuts, a vast reduction in the size of government ("getting government off our backs," he called it), and a return to American pride and greatness, Reagan defeated the incumbent Carter by a wide margin in 1980: 42,797,153 to 34,434,100. Even those who bitterly opposed what they saw as his shallow conservatism admitted that Reagan deserved the title of *The Great Communicator*.

The Least You Need to Know

- ◆ The 1960s and 1970s saw Americans re-examining themselves and struggling to redefine their nation in an effort to renew the American Dream.

- ◆ The United States economy suffered a severe recession, which also dragged down American morale.

- ◆ The unshakable American faith in technology was severely shaken by a faltering auto industry, decaying infrastructure, and a near nuclear meltdown at the Three Mile Island reactor in Pennsylvania.

- ◆ Ronald Reagan took his sweeping victory over Jimmy Carter in 1980 as a mandate for a rebirth of patriotism and a revolution in economics.

Part 9

A New World Order?

An economically and spiritually beleaguered America was highly receptive to the tax-cutting promises and patriotic feel-good message of Ronald Reagan. Although the 1990s saw the end of the Cold War in the breakup of the Soviet Union, which left the United States as the world's only superpower, the decade was also marked by profound dissatisfaction with domestic "politics as usual" and by a sinister undercurrent of political rage that exploded into incidents of "homegrown" terrorism. As you see in this concluding part, sensational criminal cases—the videotaped police beating of Rodney King and the televised murder trial of O. J. Simpson—revealed the persistence of deep national divisions along racial lines.

At the turn of a new century, the American democracy passed through the crucible of scandal, a tortured presidential election, and an attack by ruthless terrorists, followed by a highly divisive war with no clear end in sight.

Chapter 34

A New Economy, a Plague, a Fallen Wall, and a Desert in Flames (1980–1991)

In This Chapter

- ◆ The rise and fall of Reaganomics
- ◆ The AIDS crisis
- ◆ Victory in the Cold War and the Persian Gulf
- ◆ The Iran-Contra scandal

The presidency of James Monroe (1817–1825) ushered in an "era of good feelings," a time of perceived (if somewhat less than actual) national well-being. Much the same happened during the two terms of Ronald Reagan, the most popular president since Ike Eisenhower. Where President Carter took a stern moral tone with the nation, admonishing his fellow Americans to conserve energy, save money, and generally do with a little less of everything, President Reagan congratulated his countrymen on the very fact of being Americans and assured them that all was well—or *would* be well, just as soon as he got "big government off our backs."

For a time, business boomed during the Reagan years, although the boom was mostly the result of mega-mergers and large-scale acquisitions and the shifting back and forth of assets, rather than any tangible strides in production. True, too, the Reagan administration saw the beginning of the end of the Cold War and the disintegration of the Soviet Union, which the president called an "evil empire." Yet, during the Reagan years, the national debt also rose from a staggering $1 trillion to a stupefying $4 trillion. And the period was convulsed by a terrible epidemic of a new, fatal, and costly disease, AIDS, which the administration met largely with indifference and denial.

The Trickle-Down Solution

Following his inauguration, President Reagan lost no time in launching an economic program formulated by his conservative economic advisors. The program was quarterbacked by Office of Management and Budget (OMB) director David Stockman (b. 1946), whose ascetic, even pinched, appearance seemed to signal his ruthlessness as a slasher of taxes and domestic social welfare spending. The new administration marched under the banner of supply side economics, a belief that the economy thrives by stimulating the production of goods and services (the supply side) because (according to advocates of the theory) supply *creates* demand.

The Reagan revolution turned on three major policies: a reduction in government regulation of commerce and industry; aggressive budget cutting; and aggressive tax cutting—albeit not for middle- and lower-income individuals, but for the wealthy and for businesses. Reducing the tax burden on the rich, Reagan and his circle claimed, would free up more money for investment, the benefits of which would ultimately "trickle down" to the less affluent in the form of more and better jobs.

If *trickle down* was a hard concept for many to swallow, Reagan's insistence that a *reduction* in tax rates would actually *increase* government revenues seemed downright bizarre to some. When Ronald Reagan and the man who would be his vice president, George H. Bush, were battling one another in the Republican primaries, Bush had branded the notion "voodoo economics," but conservative economist Arthur Laffer (b. 1940) theorized that tax cuts would stimulate increased investment and savings, thereby ultimately increasing taxable income and generating more revenue for the government's coffers. President Reagan made frequent reference to the "Laffer Curve," which illustrated this process.

Plausible or not, a majority of the American people were prepared to take the leap with their new president. In 1981, a bold program was hurried through a sometimes bewildered Congress, including a major tax cut, a staggering $43 billion reduction in the budget for domestic programs, and broad cutbacks in environmental and business regulation. The "Great Communicator" brushed aside all resistance. When catastrophe struck on March 30, 1981, in the form of would-be assassin John Hinckley Jr., the 70-year-old president's calm and heroic response to his having been shot in the lung drew even more support for his programs.

 Remember This _____

President Reagan had been in office only 2 months when he exited the Washington Hilton Hotel on March 30, 1981, after delivering a speech. Six shots rang out, fired from a .22-caliber revolver loaded with explosive "Devastator" bullets. Secret Service agent Timothy J. McCarthy and Washington police officer James Delahanty were hit, as was White House press secretary James S. Brady, who suffered a severe head wound.

The president was bundled into his limousine, where it became apparent that he, too, had been injured. Only in the hospital emergency room was it discovered that his injury was a gunshot wound in the chest. Fortunately, the explosive bullet, lodged in his lung, had failed to detonate and was removed in a 2-hour emergency operation. "I hope you're all Republicans," the president quipped to his surgeons just before the anesthetic was administered.

The shooter, 25-year-old John Warnock Hinckley Jr., was the drifter son of a wealthy Denver oil engineer. Hinckley was obsessed with screen actress Jodie Foster, who had made a sensation as a teenage prostitute in *Taxi Driver*, a 1976 film dealing in part with political assassination. Hinckley apparently decided to kill the president to impress Foster.

A jury found Hinckley not guilty by reason of insanity, and he was confined to a psychiatric hospital. All of his victims fully recovered, except for Brady, who was left partially paralyzed. Brady became a passionate advocate of federal regulation of handguns—a policy President Reagan continued to oppose.

Greed Is Good

A relatively small number of people made a lot of money as a result of what was dubbed Reaganomics. Most of the new wealth was generated not by the stimulated production that the supply side theory promised, but by a frenzied crescendo of corporate acquisitions and mergers. The stock market buzzed and churned in a way that (for some) disturbingly recalled the late 1920s. Companies were bought and either merged for efficiency (with resulting loss of jobs) or broken up, their component parts and assets sold at a profit to stockholders (with resulting loss of jobs). Unemployment generated by the high-level financial manipulations of the 1980s was hard on the man and woman on the street, but the movement of masses of wealth benefited those who could afford to invest in the right companies at the right time. The average American may have been raised to believe that businesses existed to make products and provide employment, but the manipulators of wealth insisted that companies existed exclusively to enrich investors, and if that meant destroying a company, breaking it up, so be it. In the words of Gordon Gecko, a fictional tycoon played by Michael Douglas in the popular movie *Wall Street*, directed by Oliver Stone in 1987, "Greed is good."

 **American Life**

The words put into Gordon Gecko's mouth were paraphrased from a real-life Wall Street manipulator, Ivan Boesky, who told the graduating class of the School of Business Administration at the University of California, Berkeley, on May 18, 1986: "Greed is all right, by the way ... I think greed is healthy. You can be greedy and still feel good about yourself."

Early confidence in Reaganomics faltered when the recession of the Nixon-Ford-Carter years deepened further, and public-opinion polls began to suggest that many people believed the tax cuts had benefited only the rich. Inflation did roll back, though interest rates remained high, as did unemployment. However, by 1983, acquisitions and mergers made the stock market a very active place, and prices began to rise sharply. This change, combined with relatively low inflation and (at last) rising production, as well as slowly decreasing unemployment, happily portended recovery.

What hopeful observers tended to ignore was the prodigiously growing national debt—this under a president whose economic theory called for a *balanced* budget!—and the often corrupt sources of the profits being turned on Wall Street. Beginning in 1985, Wall Street was rocked by a series of massive insider trading scandals. Trader Dennis B. Levine pleaded guilty to making $12.6 million by trading on nonpublic information, and Ivan Boesky admitted buying huge blocks of stock as a result of receiving inside information.

To finance the buyout of companies, traders turned to junk bonds, high-risk investments (usually issued by a company without an established earnings history or burdened by poor credit) acquired cheaply and paying a high rate of interest. Such transactions, called leveraged buyouts (the takeover of a company financed by borrowed funds, the debt to be serviced by the income anticipated to flow from the merged company) were pioneered in the 1970s by the Wall Street firm of Kohlberg Kravis and Roberts (KKR) and brought to a point of frenzy by Michael R. Milken. Often, junk bonds were purchased with very little expectation that the issuing company would ever actually repay the loan, but in the short run, interest payments were so high that the underlying "junkiness" of the bond hardly seemed to matter.

 Vital Statistics

On "Black Monday," October 19, 1987, $870 billion in equity simply evaporated as the market dropped from a Dow of 2,246.73 to 1,738.41 points.

Black Monday

The junk being bought and sold hit the fan on October 19, 1987, when the Dow Jones Industrial Average (key measure of stock market performance) plunged 508 points—a far steeper fall than that of the 1929 crash, which brought on the Great Depression. Much as Herbert Hoover had assured the American public that "prosperity was just around the corner," President Reagan dismissed the crash as "some people grabbing profits." Fortunately, the market gradually recovered, but the high-flying era of Reaganomics had careened to a gut-wrenching end.

"Gay Plague" and a Blind Eye

Although many Americans stared with envy, admiration, or disgust at the Wall Street roller coaster, they turned a blind eye to the growing legion of homeless people who haunted the nation's large cities and even many of its smaller towns. Certainly, the Reagan administration, having drastically cut back federal welfare funding, did little for America's poorest. The administration likewise turned away from a terrifying plague that developed initially among homosexual men, but was soon also diagnosed in heterosexual men, in women, and in children.

What's the Word?

AIDS—Acquired Immune Deficiency Syndrome—is caused by infection with the Human Immunodeficiency Virus (HIV), which attacks immune system cells, ultimately producing severe suppression of the body's ability to resist other infections. The disease is transmitted sexually, through the blood (for example, through transfusion with infected whole blood or plasma), and during birth, from infected mothers to their children.

Throughout the 1980s, grass-roots *AIDS* organizations—including, most notably, Gay Men's Health Crisis (GMHC) and AIDS Coalition to Unleash Power (ACT UP)—mobilized. The organizations accused the government of failing to respond to an epidemic perceived to affect socially marginal groups—homosexuals and intravenous drug abusers (who contract the disease by sharing hypodermic needles tainted with infected blood). President Reagan failed even to make public mention of the disease until April 1987, fully 6 years after health officials had determined that the epidemic was underway. Only through the efforts of AIDS activists was federal funding increased—from $5.6 million in 1982 to more than $2 billion a decade later.

"Mr. Gorbachev, Tear Down This Wall!"

If the Reagan administration did not engage AIDS vigorously, it did not hesitate to take on the Soviet Union, assuming an aggressive stance against what the president called an "evil empire." Defense spending was dramatically stepped up, dwarfing domestic budget cuts in welfare and other programs.

The president also acted aggressively to meet perceived military threats throughout the world, sending U.S. Marines in the summer of 1982 to Lebanon as a peacekeeping force. On October 23, 1983, 241 marines were killed in their sleep, and another 70 wounded, when a truck laden with 25,000 pounds of TNT was driven into the marines' Beirut headquarters building by an Islamic suicide bomber. Just 2 days after this disaster, the president ordered an invasion of the Caribbean island nation of Grenada. Cuban troops had been sent to the tiny country (population 110,100) at the behest of its anti-American dictatorship, and the president expressed his absolute determination to protect the approximately 1,100 U.S. citizens there, mostly students at a medical school. The president also saw the liberation of the country as a collective national "feel-good" compensation for the death of the marines in Beirut.

Ronald Reagan's saber-rattling was gratifying to some Americans and alarming to others, who were distressed by the deadlock of U.S.-Soviet arms-control talks as a fresh deployment of American nuclear missiles began in Europe during November of 1983.

A War Without Bullets

During 1983, President Reagan announced the most spectacular, ambitious, elaborate, and expensive military project in world history. It was called the Strategic Defense Initiative (SDI), but the popular press dubbed the system *Star Wars*, after the popular George Lucas science-fiction movie of 1977. Using an orbiting weapons system, the idea was to create a shield against intercontinental ballistic missile attack by destroying incoming ICBMs before they could begin their descent. The weaponry was so far beyond even the foreseeable cutting edge as to be fanciful. Critics pointed out that Star Wars was not only a violation of the 1972 SALT I (Strategic Arms Limitation Talks) Treaty ("On the Limitation of Anti-Ballistic Missiles") concluded between the United States and the Soviet Union, but also a brazen temptation to wage thermonuclear war because it promised to make such a war survivable. Others suggested that the system could never be made to work, and still others protested that the staggering cost of the program—$100 to $200 billion—would permanently cripple the nation.

Yet presidents Reagan and George H. W. Bush pursued Star Wars to the tune of $30 billion, even though the program produced few demonstrable results. Finally, in 1993, anonymous SDI researchers revealed that at least one major space test had been "rigged" to yield successful results. Caspar Weinberger, who had served as President Reagan's secretary of defense, at first denied these charges, but subsequently claimed that the test in question—and perhaps the entire Star Wars program—had been something on the order of an elaborate decoy. The program (Weinberger said) had been designed primarily to dupe the Soviet Union into spending a huge proportion of its resources on a Star Wars program of its own—a program that U.S. scientists already knew was unworkable. (Weinberger's assessment notwithstanding, Star Wars survived in reduced form, under the Ballistic Missile Defense Organization, as the National Missile Defense [NMD]. In 2001, President George W. Bush called for accelerated development of the NMD system and withdrew from the ABM treaty to permit the system's development and deployment. Bush ordered the deployment of a modest missile defense system by 2004, but flawed tests have repeatedly delayed deployment.)

An Ideology Crumbles

Whether one views Star Wars and the rest of the gargantuan Reagan defense budget as a vast misjudgment, which quadrupled the national debt from one to four trillion dollars, or as a very costly but very effective strategy to win the Cold War, the fact is that the Cold War *did* end, and President Reagan is widely credited with this victory. The government of the Soviet Union was first liberalized and then fell apart, the nation's economy in tatters and the people clamoring for democratic capitalist reforms. Even though Mikhail Gorbachev (b. 1931), General Secretary of the Soviet Communist Party (1985–1991) and president of the USSR (1988–1991), introduced unheard of liberal reforms—under the banners of *perestroika* (social restructuring) and *glasnost* (openness)—President Reagan prodded him to go even further. In 1987, standing near the Berlin Wall—brick, stone, and razor-wire symbol of a half-century of Communist oppression—the president made a stirring speech calling out to the

What's the Word?

Americans learned two important Russian words during the 1980s. **Perestroika** (literally, "restructuring") was how Gorbachev described his program of liberal political and economic reforms. **Glasnost** ("openness") described how the traditionally secretive and closed USSR would now approach its own people and the rest of the world.

Soviet leader: "Mr. Gorbachev, open this gate! Mr. Gorbachev, tear down this wall!" Two years later, ordinary Berliners, in the West and in the East, began chipping away at the wall, tearing it down piece by piece, as a liberalized Soviet Union merely looked on.

Although Communist hardliners staged a revolt against Gorbachev in 1991, progressive army officers refused to follow KGB (Soviet secret police) directives, and the coup failed. Gorbachev then disbanded the Communist Party and stepped down as leader of the Soviet Union. Boris Yeltsin (b. 1931), reformist president of the Russian Republic, assumed leadership not of the Union of Soviet Socialist Republics, which ceased to exist, but of a commonwealth of former Soviet states.

Ollie, Iran, and the Contras

In November 1986, President Reagan confirmed reports that the United States had secretly sold arms to Iran, an implacable enemy since the hostage crisis of the Carter years. The president at first denied rumors and media leaks that the purpose of the sale had been to obtain the release of U.S. hostages held by terrorists in perpetually war-torn Lebanon, but he later admitted to the existence of an arms-for-hostages swap. Then, the plot thickened—shockingly—when Attorney General Edwin Meese learned that a portion of the arms profits had been diverted to finance so-called Contra rebels fighting against the leftist Sandinista government of Nicaragua. As part of the ongoing U.S. Cold War policy of containing communism, the Reagan administration supported a right-wing rebellion in Nicaragua, but Congress, not wanting to become mired in a Central American version of the Vietnam War, specifically prohibited material aid to the Contras. The secret diversion of the secret arms profits was blatantly unconstitutional.

A congressional investigation gradually revealed that, in 1985, a cabal of Israelis had approached National Security Advisor Robert MacFarlane with a scheme in which Iran would use its influence to free the U.S. hostages held in Lebanon in exchange for arms. Secretary of State George Schultz and Secretary of Defense Caspar Weinberger objected to the plan, but (MacFarlane testified to Congress) President Reagan agreed to it. In a bizarre twist, U.S. Marine Lieutenant Colonel Oliver (Ollie)

North then modified the scheme in order to funnel profits from the arms sales to the Contras. The reasoning was this: the illegal arms sales produced illegal profits, which could be hidden from Congress by illegally funneling them to the Contras. It would be as if the money—and the whole twisted scheme—had never existed.

As was the case with Watergate during the 1970s, investigation and testimony implicated officials on successively lofty rungs of the White House ladder—through national security advisors John Poindexter and MacFarlane, through CIA Director William J. Casey (who died in May 1987), and through Defense Secretary Caspar Weinberger. Few people believed that President Reagan had been ignorant of the scheme, but even if he had been the unwitting dupe of zealots in his administration, the implications were bad enough, painting a picture of a passive chief executive blindly delegating authority to his staff.

In the end, Ollie North was convicted on 3 of 12 criminal counts against him, but the convictions were subsequently set aside on appeal; Poindexter was convicted on 5 counts of deceiving Congress, but his convictions were also set aside; CIA administrator Clair E. George was indicted for perjury, but his trial ended in mistrial; and Caspar Weinberger was indicted on 5 counts of lying to Congress. All of those charged were ultimately pardoned by President Reagan's successor, George H. W. Bush. Although the 1994 report of special prosecutor Lawrence E. Walsh harshly criticized both Reagan and George H. W. Bush, neither was charged with criminal wrongdoing.

Measuring the Reagan Years

President Reagan's second term, marred by the Iran-Contra affair, a bumbling performance at the 1986 summit with Mikhail Gorbachev, and the 1987 stock market crash, nevertheless saw the "Teflon president" emerge personally unscathed. For a few years following the end of his second term, a number of academic historians issued scathing assessments of the Reagan years, some ranking him as one of the worst of American presidents. However, the public assessment of Reagan seemed, if anything, to improve with age. Before his death in 2004 at the age of 93, public buildings, roads, and even Washington's in-town National Airport had been named in honor of Ronald Reagan. After his death, there was talk of putting his likeness on coins, perhaps ousting FDR on the dime or JFK on the half-dollar. Many more years will have to pass before consensus can be reached on the Reagan presidency, but it seems undeniable that no president since Franklin Roosevelt put his personal stamp on the character of the nation more deeply than Ronald Wilson Reagan.

Desert Shield and Desert Storm

Vice President George H. W. Bush sailed to easy victory in the presidential race of 1988. Where the "Great Communicator" Reagan had been charismatic, however, Bush was widely perceived as aloof, even somewhat testy, and, with the economy faltering (the principal issue was high unemployment), his popularity rapidly slipped in the polls. Bush seemed doomed to a one-term presidency.

 Vital Statistics

Combined U.S. and coalition forces in the Gulf War amounted to 530,000 troops as opposed to 545,000 Iraqis. U.S. and coalition losses were 149 killed, 238 wounded, 81 missing, and 13 taken prisoner (they were subsequently released). Iraqi losses have been estimated in excess of 80,000 men killed or wounded, with overwhelming loss of materiel.

Then, on August 2, 1990, Iraqi president Saddam Hussein, a dictator whose florid mustache recalled Joseph Stalin and whose ruthlessly irrational actions summoned to mind Adolf Hitler, ordered an invasion of the small, oil-rich Arab state of Kuwait. It was the beginning of a tense and dramatic crisis, but it was also President Bush's finest hour. His administration brilliantly used the United Nations to sanction action against Iraq, and with masterful diplomacy, the president assembled an unprecedented coalition of 31 nations to oppose the invasion. Particularly delicate was the process of acquiring the support of the Arab countries while keeping Israel, which was even subject to attack by Iraqi Scud missiles, out of the fray. As to the U.S. commitment, it was the largest since Vietnam: more than a half-million troops, 1,800 aircraft, and some 100 ships.

In early August of 1990, King Fahd of Saudi Arabia invited American troops into his country to protect the kingdom against possible Iraqi aggression. Called Operation Desert Shield, this was a massive, orderly buildup of U.S. forces. In January of 1991, the U.S. Congress voted to support military operations against Iraq in accordance with a UN Security Council resolution, which set a deadline of January 15, 1991, for the withdrawal of Iraqi forces from Kuwait. When Saddam Hussein failed to heed the deadline, Operation Desert Shield became Operation Desert Storm, a massively coordinated lightning campaign against Iraq from the air, the sea, and on land. After continuous air attack beginning January 17, the ground war was launched at 8:00 P.M. on February 23 and lasted exactly 100 hours before Iraqi resistance collapsed and Kuwait was liberated.

Bush, who consistently earned high marks from the American public for his conduct of foreign relations, now enjoyed overwhelming popular approval in the wake of the successful outcome of the Persian Gulf War. Moreover, military success in the Gulf seemed to exorcise the demons of failure born in the Vietnam War, and with the liberalization and ultimate collapse of the Soviet Union, Americans felt that their nation was in the vanguard of what President Bush called a "new world order." Not only had the long ideological struggle between communism and democracy ended in a victory for democracy, but a bully from the Third World, Saddam Hussein, had been defeated—and he was defeated with the cooperation of many nations and to the applause of most of the world.

The Least You Need to Know

◆ President Reagan started a conservative revolution in America, introducing supply-side economics and undoing much of the welfare state that had begun with FDR.

◆ President Reagan's second term was marked by economic decline and the Iran-Contra scandal, neither of which seemed greatly to damage Reagan's unassailable popularity.

◆ The Reagan-Bush years saw victory in the 50-year Cold War (as well as victory in the brief but dangerous Persian Gulf War), but at the cost of quadrupling an already staggering national debt and sidelining such domestic issues as welfare and the AIDS crisis.

◆ President George H. W. Bush, his popularity declining in a listless American economy, realized his finest hour as commander in chief during massive military operations against Iraq's Saddam Hussein.

Chapter 35

E Pluribus Unum (1991–1999)

In This Chapter

- ◆ The end of the Reagan–Bush years
- ◆ The New Right and the ascendancy of the Libertarians
- ◆ Domestic terrorism: militias and fanatics
- ◆ A new role in world peace

In 1980 and again in 1984, the American electorate voted Ronald Reagan into office with gusto. In 1988, Americans had relatively little enthusiasm for either Democrat Michael Dukakis, governor of Massachusetts, or Republican George H. W. Bush, vice president of the United States. Nor was there much enthusiasm in 1992, when the incumbent Bush was opposed by the youthful governor of Arkansas, Bill Clinton. However, during the Bush administration, the American Dream seemed somehow to have slipped further away. True, from an American perspective, the world certainly seemed a safer place than it had been at any time since the end of World War II. Yet the electorate felt that President Bush habitually neglected domestic issues and focused almost exclusively on international relations. Candidate Bill Clinton's acerbic campaign manager, James Carville, put it directly, advising Governor Clinton to write himself a reminder lest he forget the issue on which the election would be won or lost: "It's the economy, stupid."

The Economy, Stupid

The economy. It was not that America teetered on the edge of another depression in 1992, but a general sense existed among the middle class that this generation was not "doing as well as" previous generations. Sons were not living as well as fathers, daughters not as well as mothers. So Bill Clinton, promising a return to the domestic agenda, entered the White House by a comfortable margin.

Vital Statistics

Even though third-party candidate H. Ross Perot dropped out of the race for a time (stunning his many supporters), he won 19,237,247 votes, an astounding 19 percent of the popular vote total.

But if voters had rejected Bush, a sizable minority of them had also turned away from Clinton. For the first time since Theodore Roosevelt ran as a Bull Moose (Progressive) candidate in 1912, a third-party contender made a significant impact at the polls. Presenting himself as a candidate dissatisfied with both the Republicans and the Democrats, billionaire Texas businessman H. Ross Perot (b. 1930) told Americans that they were the "owners" of the nation and that it was about time they derived real benefit from what they owned.

The New Right

The Perot candidacy was not the only evidence of widespread discontent with politics as usual. Beginning in the 1970s, a conservative movement gained increasing strength. Its values rested upon the family as traditionally constituted (father, mother, kids), a strong sense of law and order, reliance on organized (Christian) religion, a belief in the work ethic (and a corresponding disdain for the welfare state), a passion for "decency" (even to the point of censorship), and a desire for minimal government.

Right to Life

Many who have identified themselves with the "New Right" hold passionately to a belief that abortion, even in the first trimester of pregnancy (when the fetus cannot survive outside the womb), is tantamount to murder. The so-called Right to Life movement has spawned a fanatic fringe, whose members have bombed abortion clinics and have intimidated, assaulted, and even murdered physicians who perform abortions. However, the mainstream of the movement has relied on legal means to effect social change, with the ultimate object of obtaining a constitutional amendment barring abortion. The Right to Life movement became so powerful a political lobby that the Republican Party adopted a stance against abortion as part of its 1992 platform.

Christian Right

The First Amendment to the Constitution specifies that "Congress shall make no law respecting an establishment of religion." Church and state are explicitly separated in the United States; but the government nevertheless freely invokes the name of God in most of its enterprises. Our currency bears the motto *In God We Trust* and both houses of Congress employ full-time chaplains. When, on June 26, 2002, a federal appeals court of the Ninth District ruled unconstitutional the phrase "one nation, under God" in the Pledge of Allegiance most of us grew up reciting at the start of each school day, the public as well as lawmakers protested vigorously—members of Congress describing the decision with such adjectives as "nuts," "outrageous," and "stupid." President George W. Bush called the decision "ridiculous."

 **What's the Word?**

In God We Trust is plain enough English. The Great Seal of the United States, reproduced on the dollar bill, also includes two phrases of Latin: *Annuit coeptis* ("He has favored our undertakings") and *Novus ordo seclorum* ("A new order of the ages").

Although many Americans shake their heads over their perception that religious worship has somehow gone out of fashion in America, and some "faith-based" political lobbyists speak of an emerging "anti-Christian" element in American government, most opinion polls agree that approximately 96 percent of the population actively profess belief in God and (as of 2001) 76.7 percent of Americans call themselves Christian.

In recent years, one of the most significant political manifestations of the Christian Right has been the powerful lobbying group called the Christian Coalition of America, which was spun off of the unsuccessful 1988 presidential campaign of religious broadcaster Pat Robertson (b. 1930). Based in Washington, D.C., the coalition boasts a membership of nearly 2 million members belonging to 1,500 local chapters in all 50 U.S. states and has claimed responsibility for the Republican sweep of Congress during the midterm elections of 1994. In 1995, the organization spent more than a million dollars mobilizing its "born-again" evangelicals behind the conservative "Contract with America" promulgated by Republican Newt Gingrich when he was

Speaker of the House. Although some people welcomed what they saw as a return of morality to American political life, others viewed the Christian Right as narrow, coercive, and intolerant.

The Age of Rage

In turn, the Christian Right has viewed liberal America as too tolerant of lifestyles and beliefs that they regard as alien or offensive to their religious principles and a threat to the moral fiber of the nation.

This was hardly a new dialogue in the 1990s. Right and left have been taffy-pulling national life since well before the Revolution. Indeed, Americans might be too accustomed to thinking in terms of right versus left; for another body of American belief appears to want little to do with either side. In its mildest form, this group has expressed itself in a third political party, the Libertarians, founded in 1971. Libertarians oppose laws that limit personal behavior (including laws against prostitution, gambling, sexual preference), advocate a free-market economy without government regulation or assistance, and support an isolationist foreign policy (including U.S. withdrawal from the United Nations).

But those who really listened during the 1990s did not hear a Libertarian dialogue. The dominant voice was rage. Most of the time, it was part of the background: angry slogans on bumper stickers, endless staccato of sound bites from the television tube, a jagged litany that issued from talk-radio, and the remarkable volume of violence that was played out across movie screens. And sometimes the rage exploded, front and center.

Waco and Oklahoma City

April 19, 1993, saw the fiery culmination of a long standoff between members of a fundamentalist religious cult called the Branch Davidians and federal law officers. Followers of David Koresh (his real name was Vernon Howell) holed up in a fortified compound outside of Waco, Texas, had been holding off agents of the U.S. Treasury Department's Alcohol, Tobacco, and Firearms Unit (ATF) who were investigating reports of a stockpile of illegal arms, as well as allegations of child abuse in the compound. When ATF officers initially moved on the compound on February 28, the cultists opened fire, killing four agents. Koresh was wounded in the exchange, and at least two of his followers were killed. The FBI was called in, and, for the next 51 days, the FBI and ATF laid siege to the Branch Davidians, until April 19, when agents commenced an assault with tear gas volleys. The Branch Davidians responded (according

to law-enforcement officials) by setting fire to
their own compound, a blaze that killed more
than 80 cultists, including 24 children.
Millions witnessed both the February 28 shoot-
out and the April 19 inferno on television.

In August 1999, the FBI reversed its 6-year-old
position that it had never used munitions capable of starting a fire and admitted that it had
used "a very limited number" of incendiary tear
gas cartridges during the final day of the Branch
Davidian siege. U.S. Senator John Danforth
was appointed to chair an independent inquiry
into how the FBI handled the Branch Davidian siege and, in May 2000, issued a report
concluding that the FBI did not start the fire or shoot at members of the Branch
Davidian cult during the fire, that the government did not improperly use the military, and that it did not engage in a cover-up. Officially laid to rest by the Danforth
report, the Waco siege continues among some in the public to raise questions of a
federal conspiracy.

 Vital Statistics

In the 1980 presidential
election, Libertarian candidate
Ed Clark polled 920,859 votes,
but candidate David Bergland
received only 227,949 votes
in 1984. Ron Paul garnered
409,412 votes in 1988, and
Andre Marrou received 281,508
votes in 1992.

Millions also saw the bloody aftermath of the bombing of the Alfred P. Murrah
Federal Office Building in Oklahoma City on April 19, 1995, which killed 168 persons, including children at play in the building's daycare center. Timothy McVeigh
and Terry Nichols, two disaffected U.S. Army veterans, were indicted and tried in
connection with the bombing. In June 1997, Timothy McVeigh was found guilty on
11 counts of murder and sentenced to death. He was executed at the Federal
Penitentiary in Terre Haute, Indiana, on June 11, 2001—the first federal execution
since 1963. Nichols, found guilty by a federal jury on December 23, 1997, of eight
counts of involuntary manslaughter and conspiring with McVeigh, was sentenced to
life imprisonment. Subsequently, the state of Oklahoma charged him with capital
murder. Convicted on August 9, 2004, of 161 counts of first-degree murder, he was
given additional life sentences.

McVeigh and Nichols were loosely associated with what was widely called in the
1990s the "militia movement," a phrase that described militant groups organized in
several states after the Waco raid and a 1992 government assault on extreme conservative and white supremacist Randy Weaver and his family in Ruby Ridge, Idaho.

The incidents at Waco and Ruby Ridge, together with passage of federal gun-control
legislation, inspired the formation of these armed cadres, groups opposed not only to

what they deemed excessive government control of everyday life, but also to what they saw as a United Nations plot to take over the United States in a drive toward "One World Government." Yet even self-proclaimed militia activists generally disavowed the Oklahoma City bombing, and few Americans could accept that attacking a federal office building—which contained no military installations, no CIA secret headquarters, but only such mundane offices as the local Social Security unit—was in any meaningful sense a blow against government tyranny.

At Heaven's Gate

After Waco and Oklahoma City, Americans were becoming both more aware of and simultaneously desensitized to extreme political and social "statements." Then came the discovery, on March 26, 1997, of 39 bodies in a mansion-cum-commune perched atop a hill in the upscale community of Del Mar, California. They were suicides, apparently having died as a result of swallowing sedative pills with vodka, and then suffocating themselves by putting plastic bags over their heads.

They were all members of a cult calling itself Heaven's Gate and led by one Marshall Applewhite. Since the 1970s, Applewhite had described himself as a Space Age "shepherd," destined to lead his "flock" to a higher level of existence. To underscore this identity, he called himself "Bo" and his wife, Bonnie Nettles (who had succumbed to cancer in 1985), "Peep." The suicide of Applewhite and his flock was a first step toward a promised rendezvous with extraterrestrial beings whose coming was heralded by the appearance of the Hale-Bopp comet, which loomed in the skies during several months of 1997.

Bizarre? Yes. But even stranger was the way in which all of this had been offered up all along as public knowledge. The Heaven's Gate cultists had maintained themselves in their Del Mar compound, in part, through income raised by an increasingly profitable cottage industry: designing Internet web pages for a variety of clients. One of the pages they created was for themselves. It offered prophecy, including the scenario involving the comet and the coming deliverance at the hands—if hands they were to be—of extraterrestrial beings.

To be sure, Heaven's Gate is a very strange and sad story, but what could the deaths of 39 tragically deluded persons mean to American history?

Perhaps little or nothing at all—were it not for the Internet. For Heaven's Gate is not the story of a religious fanatic hawking his revelations on a street corner, but of a self-proclaimed prophet using Internet technology to publish his "word" to the world.

Through most of history, such potent technology was available only to a select few. In the past, "to publish" meant that you had persuaded a number of powerful people, representing major corporations, of the value of what you had to say. Producing books or films or radio or television broadcasts was, after all, complicated and expensive. But the development of the Internet and the World Wide Web during the closing decade of the twentieth century put within reach of anyone the ability to publish or broadcast just about anything.

American Echo

… there is a true Kingdom of "God"—a truly Evolutionary Kingdom Level Above Human, above all mammalian or any other reproductive species. It is a many-membered Kingdom that exists in the literal Heavens, with its own unique biological "containers" or bodies, and modes of travel—spacecrafts or "UFOs" …. This Kingdom Level created the physical world, as we know it, as a "holographic classroom," and the human-mammalian kingdom as a stepping stone. That hologram is about to be "rebooted"—canceled and restarted—for its usefulness and serviceability as a classroom has come to an end.

—From a poster announcing a Heaven's Gate membership recruitment meeting

The potential benefit this represents is, of course, extraordinary, perhaps immeasurable. But could the potential liability likewise be without measure? Probably not. Or, rather, it will be measured by the strength of our democracy's ability to weigh and evaluate the onrush of information. The suicide of 39 human beings is a tragedy. Yet we may take some comfort in the fact that, while the message of Heaven's Gate was broadcast to millions, the deaths were confined to a house on a hill in Del Mar. Even in 1997, the advance of technology had not replaced the faculty of judgment.

And It Was *Still* the Economy …

Not that most Americans spent many hours pondering Heaven's Gate. At the time, many were giving much more thought to where they should invest their surplus cash.

Bill Clinton had run his first presidential campaign largely on issues of the sluggish economy. In 1996, when he stood for reelection, the economy, lackluster during the second term of Ronald Reagan and even duller during the only term of George H. W. Bush, had at last taken fire, and Wall Street was now aflame. In contrast to the stock market boom during the early Reagan years, however, the new wealth was not generated exclusively by acquisitions and mergers. Even more significantly, it was spreading well beyond a few high rollers.

"Ordinary people" were investing—and doing quite well at it. Even those who didn't play the market enjoyed the benefits of the lowest rates of unemployment in decades. There was no need to talk about the "trickle down" of wealth that Ronald Reagan had promised. For large numbers of people, the money came, if not in a torrent, at least on tap. And, finally, as if the nation were being strung along the plot line of some economic fairy tale, the high stock prices, the high rate of employment, the high salaries were *not* accompanied by the "necessary evil" of high inflation. Economists were baffled, but the person on the street was delighted. And Bill Clinton sailed into a second term, handily defeating the caustic and much older Robert Dole, Republican senator from Kansas, who was in the unenviable position of having to argue with success.

We Fight for Peace

President Clinton had been reelected on the strength of his domestic performance at a time when most of the public gave little thought to the international scene. However, the president was soon faced with a series of international crises, which were especially difficult to deal with because in each the direct interest of the United States was not clear.

Shortly before Clinton had taken office at the start of his first term, American soldiers arrived in Somalia, on the east coast of Africa, pursuant to a pledge of military and humanitarian aid that had been made by President George H. W. Bush. The government of that nation had crumbled, and the people, dying from famine and civil war, were at the mercy of competing warlords. The name of the UN mission in which U.S. troops participated suggested its humanitarian purpose: Operation Restore Hope. American soldiers were to function as peacekeepers and, above all, to protect relief supplies from being stolen by the warring factions.

But President Clinton soon discovered the futility of being a cop in a place without law. Pressed by the Democratic left to maintain the humanitarian mission and by the Republican right to avoid further entanglement in an obscure civil war, the president authorized an action he hoped would bring decisive and rapid results. Among all the warlords, the most powerful and intractable was Mohamed Farah Aideed, gangster leader of a large "militia" force. At 3:40 P.M. on October 3, 1993, an elite cadre of

U.S. Army Delta Force commandos swooped down on Somalia's capital, Mogadishu, in Black Hawk helicopters, disembarked, then swept through the Olympic Hotel in search of Aideed and his principal lieutenants. Aideed was not present, but the operation netted a number of his lieutenants. After 15 minutes, the commandos and their prisoners made for the Black Hawks.

That is when the unit came under heavy attack from Aideed's militia in a gruesome street battle that lasted for 15 bloody hours. In the end, 18 American soldiers were killed, and American television screens beamed an image of the body of one soldier being dragged triumphantly through the streets of Mogadishu by militiamen.

The grim image stuck painfully in the American imagination. No more raids were ordered in Mogadishu, and, on March 31, 1994, all U.S. forces were withdrawn from Somalia by order of President Clinton. Operation Restore Hope came to an end.

Waking from the Bosnian Nightmare

It was nearly impossible for Americans and other Westerners to comprehend what was happening in Africa, where war combined modern weapons, including AK-47 assault rifles and RPGs—rocket-propelled grenades—in conflicts motivated by ancient tribal hatreds and rivalries. U.S. foreign policy and military strategy had long been formulated to fight Communism, a discrete ideology held by one-party nations led by absolute dictators. One thing was clear: the "new world order" George H. W. Bush had spoken of following the collapse of Communism had a very dark side, with cons including a morass of clan and tribal agendas having nothing to do with clear-cut ideology or legally constituted nations.

If this situation was difficult to understand in an African context, Americans found it even harder to grasp in a European setting. But that is precisely what the Clinton administration had to deal with in the region that had been until recently Yugoslavia.

Yugoslavia was a twentieth-century invention, cobbled together from the fragments of the old Austro-Hungarian Empire, which had been broken up by the Treaty of Versailles after World War I. Political and ethnic fragments do not make a nation, however, and until World War II, Yugoslavia was a collection of strongly nationalistic, ethnically diverse, and largely irreconcilable factions. What brought them together into something resembling genuine nationhood was their mutual opposition, under the powerful leadership of Josep Broz—known as Tito—to German Nazi and Italian fascist invasion.

Following World War II, Tito continued to hold Yugoslavia together until his death in 1980. After that, the Croatians and Slovenes, the largest nationalist groups in the country, developed opposing separatist movements. In January of 1990, the Communist Party voted to relinquish its constitutional monopoly on power in Yugoslavia—a move that came too late to satisfy the Slovenes and Croatians, who, later that year, declared their independence from Yugoslavia and proposed a new, decentralized union.

Slobodan Milosevic, Communist leader of Serbia, another of the Yugoslav republics, opposed the new plan of union. Urged on by Milosevic, the Serbian minority in Croatia rebelled against the Croatian government, and Milosevic sent the Serbian-led Yugoslav army into Croatia to support the Croatian Serbs. Almost instantly, this civil war ceased to be a political struggle and appeared as what it really was—the reemergence of violent ancient ethnic allegiances. Twentieth-century Europe was experiencing primitive tribal warfare among the Serbs, the Croats, and the Moslems of what had been Yugoslavia.

In January of 1992, the United Nations imposed a truce on all factions in the region, but it proved short-lived when Bosnia seceded from Yugoslavia in March of 1992. The Serb population of Bosnia rebelled, and the breakaway republic was reduced to bloody anarchy. Its capital city, Sarajevo, scene of the 1914 assassination that had triggered World War I, re-emerged as a symbol of modern warfare—warfare employing modern weapons to fight age-old ethnic feuds.

Beginning in August of 1995, the Clinton administration helped to bring about a peace settlement among the warring factions in Bosnia. On November 21, 1995, after protracted negotiations, the "Dayton Accord," a comprehensive peace agreement, was initialed at Wright-Patterson Air Force Base near Dayton, Ohio. The agreement was formally signed in Paris the following month, and President Clinton joined the ranks of such chief executives as Theodore Roosevelt and Jimmy Carter in having brokered peace in an apparently intractable foreign conflict.

Kosovo "Crisis"

Bosnia was not the only hot spot in what commentators clumsily referred to as "the former Yugoslavia." In the breakup of that nation, a place called Kosovo was accorded the ambiguous status of an "autonomous province" within Serbia. This arrangement was bound to create trouble; for ethnic Albanians—mostly Moslems—made up 90 percent of Kosovo's population, with Serbs accounting for the other 10 percent. The Albanian majority protested Serbia's taking control of the Kosovar administration, and, in 1992, Kosovo voted to secede from Serbia as well as from Yugoslavia, with the intention of merging with Moslem Albania. Slobodan Milosevic at first responded by tightening his control on Kosovo. When this failed, he waged all-out war against the Albanian majority there.

The problem was that, despite Kosovo's overwhelming Albanian majority, the Serbs considered the province the ancient and hallowed source of Serbian culture. To complicate matters further, Kosovo was caught between the violent passion of Serbia and the political opposition of other European powers, which feared that Kosovar independence would trigger a wider war in the Balkans, one that might engulf the whole of Europe, as had happened in 1914.

At this juncture, President Clinton brought the prestige of the United States to bear in proposing a solution: wider autonomy for Kosovo, but autonomy well short of independence. The ethnic Albanians accepted the compromise plan, but Slobodan Milosevic rejected it. Beginning in February 1998, Milosevic launched an offensive against the Kosovo Liberation Army (KLA), resulting in the deaths of at least 2,000 people and the forced exodus of some 300,000 more. In response to the offensive, NATO, with the United States leading, launched massive airstrikes against Serbian forces.

The United States, NATO, and the United Nations attempted to broker peace, but talks in Rambouillet, France, dissolved early in March 1999. On March 24, again spearheaded by the United States, NATO launched air strikes on Serbian Yugoslavia. After weeks of unremitting attacks, on June 10, 1999, the Milosevic government agreed to a military withdrawal from Kosovo. Since then, there has been something very close to peace in Kosovo (despite terrorist bombings of a U.N. headquarters, a government building, and a newspaper early in July 2005), which may be counted a victory of American diplomacy.

The Least You Need to Know

- The 1990s were characterized by discontent, political extremism, and rage that threatened democracy, but also by a renewed passion to gather and share information and ideas, the very elements that keep democracy strong.

- During this period, the Christian conservatism or the Christian right emerged as an increasingly powerful force in American politics.

- Despite continued political and racial divisions in America, unprecedented economic prosperity buoyed the nation's confidence during much of the 1990s.

- The United States closed the century by intervening in civil wars in Africa and Eastern Europe.

36

Democracy at the Turn of the Millennium (1991–2005)

In This Chapter

- Three American trials: Rodney King, O. J. Simpson, Bill Clinton
- Dot.com boom and dot.com bubble
- Instant gratification via the Internet
- The disputed election of 2000

Chapter 24 began with Thomas Carlyle's observation that the "history of the world is but the biography of great men." As many saw it, however, the history of our nation in the closing years of the twentieth century and the opening of the twenty-first more often encompassed the lives of high-profile figures who fell far short of greatness.

American Trials

Few Americans welcome a summons to jury duty, but millions glued themselves, voluntarily and for weeks at a time, to press and television coverage of the three highest-profile trials of the 1990s.

"Can't We All Just Get Along?"

On March 3, 1991, Rodney King, an African American, was arrested for reckless driving and speeding (in excess of 100 miles per hour) through a Los Angeles residential neighborhood. By chance, a witness carrying a video camera videotaped the arrest, which included a brutal beating by four nightstick-wielding Los Angeles police officers, who inflicted 56 baton blows and six kicks, resulting in 11 skull fractures, brain injury, and kidney damage. The tape was broadcast nationally, sending shockwaves of outrage from coast to coast. Courtroom testimony revealed that King had refused police orders to exit his car and violently resisted arrest, throwing more than one officer on his back. Twice, the police attempted to subdue him with 50,000-volt tasers. When this failed, the beating began. It was believed that King was under the influence of pain-numbing street drugs, including the animal tranquilizer PCP.

An all-white jury in the upscale California community of Simi Valley acquitted the officers on April 30, 1992, their verdict touching off three days of rioting, arson, and looting in Los Angeles, especially in the city's predominantly black South-Central neighborhood. Some 50 square miles of Los Angeles were engulfed, and lesser disturbances erupted in Atlanta, Pittsburgh, San Francisco, and Seattle. The L.A. riot resulted in 54 deaths, 2,383 reported injuries, the arrest of 13,212 persons, and property damage of at least $700 million dollars. Even President George H. W. Bush, who rarely commented on such domestic matters, remarked that the verdict "has left us all with a deep sense of personal frustration and anguish."

On April 17, 1993, in a separate trial on federal civil rights charges, two of the officers were convicted; however, the first verdict and the riots that followed—the worst urban disorder in the United States since the Civil War–era New York "Draft Riots" of July 13 to 16, 1863—were heartbreaking, suggesting that we as a nation had not come very far in learning to live harmoniously and productively together. Yet the sad episode was also a demonstration of how technology could serve the ends of democracy. For despite the first jury's verdict, the beating, videotaped and broadcast, united most of the nation not in rage, but in outrage. As those brutal images flickered across television screens everywhere, unquestioning belief in law and order dissolved. Middle-class white people were forced to ask themselves, *Is this what it means to be black in America?* At the very least, those millions who saw the beating had to ponder: *This is exactly what American democracy was created to prevent.*

> ### American Echo
>
> People, I just want to say, you know, can we all get along? Can we get along? Can we stop making it, making it horrible for the older people and the kids?
>
> —Rodney King, spoken during the Los Angeles riots, May 2, 1992

The Juice Is Loose

Television brought another racially charged legal battle into the nation's living rooms when O. J. Simpson, an African American football star turned sports broadcaster and all-around celebrity, was tried for the brutal murder of his ex-wife, Nicole Brown Simpson, and her friend Ronald Goldman. For almost a year, the televised "Trial of the Century" mesmerized a significant portion of the population. On October 3, 1995, after having been sequestered for 266 days and then in deliberation for less than four hours, the Los Angeles jury found Simpson not guilty. Although television had once again united the nation in focus on a single event, the televised verdict revealed a deep national division along racial lines. In a Gallup Poll conducted during October 19 through 22, 1995, 36 percent of whites thought the verdict was correct and 53 percent believed it wrong, whereas 73 percent of blacks thought it right and only 16 percent wrong; 11 percent of whites had no opinion, whereas only 5 percent of blacks were undecided. Clearly, despite what Simpson's prosecutors called a "mountain of evidence" against him, a majority of African Americans believed he had been the innocent victim of racist police officers determined to frame him for the murder of his white ex-wife and her white friend.

Remember This

After the Simpson verdict was announced, the catch-phrase "The Juice is loose!" was heard on the streets—a reference to O. J. Simpson's nickname from his football years, "The Juice." Yet after the initial jubilation faded, many in the African American community were disturbed by those who would hold Simpson up as a black role model, let alone a hero. Simpson had never earned a reputation as an African American activist or as a social activist of any kind. Supported through his trial by many in the African American community, he seemed detached from it and even oblivious to it.

Many white Americans were deeply disturbed by the verdict, and they took some satisfaction in the outcome of a 1997 civil trial of a wrongful death suit brought by the families of Nicole Brown Simpson and Ron Goldman. Simpson, found liable, was ordered to pay $33,500,000 in damages. Because California law protects pensions from being used to satisfy judgments, Simpson was able to continue living affluently on his NFL pension. In 2000, after another court battle, he won custody of his children, and he moved with them to Miami, Florida, where state law bars a person's residence from being seized for debt.

High Crimes and Misdemeanors?

In 1935, Richard Bruno Hauptmann, a German American carpenter, was tried for and convicted for kidnapping and murdering the infant son of Charles and Anne Morrow Lindbergh. At the time, it was called the "Trial of the Century," and it held that unofficial title until the O. J. Simpson trial 60 years later. The Simpson matter would not long retain the dubious distinction of "Trial of the Century," however.

On September 11, 1998, the Republican-controlled U.S. Congress published on the Internet the full text of a report written under the direction of Kenneth Starr, an "independent counsel" appointed to investigate allegations of possibly impeachable offenses committed by President Bill Clinton. Millions of Americans were free to read laboriously detailed accounts of the president's sexual liaison with a 21-year-old White House intern, Monica Lewinsky.

The so-called Starr Report was the culmination of a 4-year, $40 million-dollar investigation into a number of questionable aspects of Clinton's conduct. It had begun as an inquiry into the involvement of the President and First Lady in a shady real-estate undertaking known as Whitewater (a name that coincidentally echoed "Watergate," the culminating scandal of the Nixon presidency) and other possible financial improprieties. When Starr failed to find evidence of wrongdoing in these areas, he focused instead on the president's sexual behavior.

Bill Clinton was no stranger to sexual scandal. In 1992, Gennifer Flowers, an aspiring rock 'n' roll singer and, later, a Little Rock, Arkansas, TV news reporter, announced that she had had a 12-year sexual affair with Clinton, had become pregnant by him in 1977 (she aborted the baby), and had smoked marijuana and used cocaine with him. The affair, according to Flowers, did not end until 1989.

Candidate Clinton coolly and earnestly denied the accusations, and his wife, Hilary Rodham Clinton, voiced absolute faith in her husband. Defying pollsters and pundits, the Clinton candidacy not only survived the scandal, but the Arkansas governor went on to spoil George H. W. Bush's bid for a second term.

> **American Echo**
>
> I did not have sexual relations with that woman—Miss Lewinsky.
> —President Bill Clinton, televised address to the nation

The Starr Report appeared when the president was midway through his second term. The lurid details of the report notwithstanding, Starr and the others involved in the investigation insisted that sex was not the issue in question. The issue, they claimed, was that the president had violated his oath of office by lying about the affair in a sworn deposition he had given in a sexual harassment civil lawsuit brought against him by a former Arkansas state employee, Paula Jones. It was alleged that the president had also lied about the affair to a grand jury.

Based on the Starr Report, the House of Representatives voted, along strict party lines, to *impeach* President Clinton, and, for the first time since Andrew Johnson was impeached in 1868, the United States Senate was the scene of an impeachment trial.

Although Republicans held a simple majority of Senate seats, removal of a president from office requires more: a two-thirds Senate vote. Because no one believed that such a vote was even remotely possible, the months of Congressional proceedings that followed made for engrossing television but also struck many Americans as a time-wasting exercise in partisan vindictiveness. Although most people deplored President Clinton's unbecoming personal behavior, they also overwhelmingly approved of his performance as a chief executive presiding over a booming economy. In any case, as most saw it, the charges against the president, even if true, did not "rise to the level" of impeachment, and in the very midst of the impeachment proceedings, public-opinion polls gave Clinton his highest approval ratings ever.

What's the Word?

To **impeach** is to charge an office holder with offenses that, if proven, warrant removal from office. Impeachment is not synonymous with such removal.

Heedless of popular sentiment, the Republican-controlled Senate pressed on with what members solemnly called their "constitutional duty." Nevertheless, on February 12, 1999, to no one's surprise, the Senate acquitted the president, bringing the latest "Trial of the Century" to an end.

Of Wall Street Riches and the Great American Smokeout

In 1925, President Calvin Coolidge declared in a speech to the American Society of Newspaper Editors that "the chief business of the American people is business." This famous pronouncement would seem a cruel mockery 4 years later, after the October 1929 stock market crash that precipitated the Great Depression, but in 1925, in the midst of a booming economy, it rang with truth. Some 70 years later, it seemed even truer.

Paper Money

Americans who had come of age in the economically troubled 1970s and the economically volatile 1980s could hardly believe the bounty of the 1990s. With each passing year, the optimism became a little less cautious. The Dow Jones Industrial Average, traditional benchmark of economic performance, shattered one record after another, ultimately topping the 10,000 mark and even venturing well into 11,000 territory. The new information-technology industries, centered on computers, digital communications, and the Internet, spawned major new companies seemingly every day, creating what was touted as the "dot.com economy," because so many of the new firms did business exclusively on the Internet and therefore had corporate names ending with the digital-style *.com* suffix.

Far from approaching these startups with healthy skepticism, investors rushed to fund each new venture, sending Internet and other computer-related stocks soaring, in turn propelling the equity markets to ever greater heights. More and more people made more and more money—at least on paper.

Sitting on fat stock portfolios, a good many investors felt rich, and they spent as rich people spend, thereby driving the economy to even greater heights. Productivity was up. Employment was way up.

Dot.Com

Even near its height, the boom had its price. In Atlanta, on July 29, 1999, a disgruntled investor walked into a brokerage in an upscale office complex and shot 9 persons to death, wounding 12 more. The killer, Mark Barton, was one of a new breed of investors known as "day traders." *Day trader* was just one of a torrent of strange-sounding phrases Americans were learning in the 1990s. Traditionally, investors have bought stocks on a long-term basis. The idea had always been to choose a promising firm, buy its stock, hold it—perhaps for years, as the company developed—and then sell the stock at a profit. In contrast, a *day trade* is a stock trade that is opened and closed on the same day.

What's the Word?

A **day trade** is a stock trade opened and closed on the same day.

In fact, many day traders open and close a trade not within hours, but within minutes—sometimes even seconds. The explosive growth of technology and Internet companies, whose perceived value changes minute by minute, made for sharp, sudden rises and falls in the stock market. In the late 1990s, high-tech stocks had the potential to rise or fall by 5 to 10 percent in a day, so buying 1,000 shares of a major computer chip maker at 63 7/8 on August 5, 1999, and selling them at 68 5/8 at the end of the day would yield $4,750, a 7.6 percent return in a single day. Of course, if the numbers happened to go the other way—68 5/8 in the morning and 63 7/8 that afternoon—the *loss* is that same $4,750.

Some saw the day-trading phenomenon as a cutting-edge way to wealth, an example of a technological dream-come-true wrought by our digital age. Others saw it as a nightmare of greed, a forsaking of such traditional values as patience, commitment, prudence, and loyalty. Reportedly, Mark Barton, the Atlanta gunman, had recently lost a six-figure sum in day trading.

American Echo

I hope this doesn't ruin your trading day.

—Mark Barton, July 29, 1999, just before he opened fire on traders and others at an Atlanta brokerage firm

But if the technology enabling day trading was new and its morality at least questionable, the roots of day trading ran deep in American history as well as in human nature. Columbus sailed to the New World in the hope of finding a shortcut to the riches of the East. In 1849, hundreds of thousands of working men left their desks or dropped their tools and lit out for the gold fields of California.

The explosion of digital technology during the last decade of the twentieth century did not refashion human nature or remodel the American Dream, but it did enable instant access to information that had once been the privileged domain of a relatively few professionals. And, perhaps of even greater consequence, it provided a means of acting on much of that information—instantly, perhaps impulsively.

"The business of America," Calvin Coolidge said in 1925, "is business." Whatever else the history of this nation is, it is the story of one American selling something to another. In the past, this involved the buyer coming to the seller's place of business or the seller traveling to the buyer. In 1872, Chicago merchant Montgomery Ward began sending copies of his 280-page dry goods catalog to thousands of farmers across the Midwest, and the mail-order business was born. During the last half-decade of the twentieth century, both the brick-and-mortar store and the paper catalog lost ground to buying and selling electronically over the Internet. Increasingly rare was the firm that had *not* raised a dot.com banner on the World Wide Web. One could now get up in the morning and, before consuming a cup of coffee, buy a book or an automobile. Whether that purchase was the result of long, careful thought, a weighing of need against the capacity of one's personal finances, or a spur-of-the moment impulse hardly mattered to the computer. For better and for worse, the gratification of desire had become instant.

Dot Bomb

Online investors weren't the only people looking for a fast buck on the Internet. Investors avidly sought dot.com start-ups to sink their money into, and Internet entrepreneurs were more than willing to oblige. The problem was that in their haste to set up new companies, entrepreneurs as well as investors often overlooked such fundamentals as a sound business plan, reasonable market studies, and a realistic assessment of operating costs. People invested not in fully formed companies, but in mere ideas and concepts, many of which failed in the realization.

Greedy to get in on the ground floor of an IPO (initial public offering), investors bid up dot.com stocks wildly. Then, as the bubbles started to burst one by one—costs soared, markets proved ephemeral, profits were nil—they let the stocks fall just as precipitously. Between September 1999 and October 2000, for example, more than 117 dot.coms imploded.

Pillars of the Community

The failure of so many dot.coms—"dot bombs" they were dubbed—and the disappointing performance even of most of those that survived precipitated a slump in the stock market as a whole. The Dow, which had ascended into the stratosphere of the 11,000-point range before the end of the 1990s, receded into the four figures.

The business community was shaken and depressed, and ordinary folk, who had invested in the stock market as never before, joined that community in its misery.

The finger-pointing was fast and furious. During the first disappointing year of the new century, older investors scolded their younger colleagues for having failed to consider "the fundamentals." What nobody realized as 1999 gave way to 2000 and even as 2000 became 2001 was just how "fundamental" some business problems really were.

Big Tobacco in a Public Burning

No American business is older than tobacco. The weed was America's first money-making export, and the tobacco industry got its start in the sixteenth century, some two centuries before there even was a United States. Over the years, it grew into one the nation's largest and most powerful business interests. Yet, in contrast to most big businesses, it was regarded as benign, even beloved—an industry that made products providing comfort and satisfaction.

Then, gradually, America's romance with cigarettes turned sour, as the link between cigarettes and such plagues as cancer and heart disease became increasingly apparent. On January 11, 1964, the U.S. Surgeon General issued a report that found cigarette smoking to contribute "substantially to mortality from certain specific diseases and the overall death rate." In 1970, the Federal Communications Commission banned cigarette ads from television. In 1979, the Surgeon General issued a stronger report on cigarettes and health, and in 1984, the American Cancer Society and other organizations sponsored the first annual Great American Smokeout, in which some five million smokers swore off the habit.

 Vital Statistics

In 1954, when cigarette smoking was at its height, 45 percent of the adult American population smoked at least one pack a day: 60 percent of the male population and 30 percent of the female.

But the revolution got under way in earnest on June 13, 1988, when a federal jury in New Jersey awarded $400,000 in damages to Antonio Cipollone. He had sued the Liggett Group for the wrongful death of his wife, who had succumbed to cancer after smoking heavily for 40 years. Of more than 300 similar suits filed since 1954, it was the first in which a tobacco company lost. Most important, the Cipollone trial revealed a 1972 confidential report prepared by the Philip Morris Research Center of Richmond, Virginia, titled "Motives and Incentives in Cigarette Smoking." "The cigarette should be conceived not as a product but as a package," the report said. "The product is nicotine. … Think of the cigarette as a dispenser for a dose unit of nicotine. … Think of a puff of smoke as the vehicle of nicotine. … Smoke is beyond question the most optimized vehicle of nicotine and the cigarette the most optimized dispenser of smoke." Judge Lee H. Sarokin, presiding over the Cipollone trial, concluded that the evidence had revealed a conspiracy by three tobacco companies that is "vast in its scope, devious in its purpose, and devastating in its results."

Although the award to Cipollone was later overturned on a technicality, the trial unleashed a series of suits from individuals and a torrent of legislation from various levels of government. In 1994, the CEOs of the nation's seven major tobacco companies testified under oath before Congress that they did not believe nicotine to be an addictive drug. Following this, a scientist who had worked for Philip Morris presented evidence that his former employer had carried out and then suppressed animal studies proving nicotine to be addictive. Later in the year, Mississippi became the first state to sue tobacco companies to recoup the costs of health care to treat diseases caused by smoking. In 1998, after many other states followed Mississippi's example, the major tobacco companies entered into talks with the federal government, hoping to arrive at a definitive settlement, which would bring an end to further liability in exchange for a huge payment. By the end of the year, however, negotiations had broken down.

Cooked Books

The spectacle of seven CEOs lying to Congress and the American people was a shock, even to the cynical and savvy. As it turned out, however, big tobacco had no monopoly on bad business ethics.

The "Gilded Age" of the post–Civil War years reveled in unregulated capitalism, the excesses of which promoted the reforms introduced by the "trust-busting" Theodore Roosevelt and other Progressives as the nineteenth century gave way to the twentieth. And so it went for much of the century, with business under the watchful eye of government regulators, until the election of pro-business governments under presidents Ronald Reagan and George H. W. Bush, who promoted the "deregulation" of business across the board. It all seemed to work remarkably well. As a Democrat, President Clinton might have been expected to try to reintroduce more government regulation, but he had no wish to interfere with an economic recovery that was becoming an economic boom.

Many firms flourished in the climate of deregulation. One, a company called Enron, emerged during the 1990s as the veritable poster boy of deregulation.

The company began in 1985 as nothing more than an oil pipeline enterprise in Houston. During the heady years of Reaganomics, which lifted the lid on American energy policy, and in the long economic expansion under Bill Clinton, Enron morphed from running pipes to trading electricity and other energy-related commodities. It became a new kind of business: an energy broker.

By the start of the twenty-first century, Enron had gone even beyond that role. A broker brings buyers and sellers together. Enron, as the *Washington Post* pointed out, "entered the contract with the seller and signed a contract with the buyer, making money on the difference between the selling price and the buying price." Moreover, by processing—camouflaging, really—transactions through incredibly complex bookkeeping and a maze of partnerships and subsidiaries, Enron became the only party privy to all sides of its baroquely complex contracts. This allowed the company to post losses as apparent profits by passing expenses off to one of its many "partners." Moreover, the greatly loosened federal laws under which the firm operated actually permitted it to show *projected* profits as *realized* profits, without distinguishing between the two.

No wonder that, from the outside, Enron looked like one terrific company—a no-brainer investment if there ever was one. On the basis of fictitious profits, its all-too-real stock soared. In August 2001, Sherron Watkins, an Enron vice president, warned Kenneth L. Lay, the company's founder and chairman, that the company was liable to "implode in a wave of accounting scandals." Within another month or two, even Enron had run out of places to hide the losses. On October 16, the company sent a shockwave through the financial markets by posting a devastating $638 million loss for the third quarter. That same day, Wall Street reduced the value of stockholders' equity by $1.2 billion. On November 8, company officials admitted having overstated earnings for the past 4 years—by some $586 million. Worse—if anything could be worse—Enron also owned up to liabilities of some $3 billion in obligations to various partnerships.

After Enron's lenders downgraded the company's debt to junk-bond status in November, a much hoped-for merger with chief rival Dynegy, representing a life-giving $23 billion infusion of funds, was unceremoniously withdrawn.

The value of Enron stock plummeted to pennies, and the company began proceedings to consummate the biggest bankruptcy in American corporate history, whereupon Congress opened a round of investigations and hearings, politicians rushing to the rostrum to express their outrage, rarely if ever alluding to the fact that, during the 2000 elections, Enron had spent $2.4 million in individual, PAC, and soft-money contributions to federal candidates and parties.

There was more to come. Amid a slipping stock market and the shriveling of retirement funds nationwide, the talk of political reform and "new" government regulation grew in volume, even as other major firms—communications giants Global Crossing and WorldCom among them—came under investigation for "accounting irregularities."

The New Ethics?

The new century saw top Enron, WorldCom, and other executives facing indictment, trial, and, in many cases, conviction for various shades of fraud and other financial malfeasance. Even Martha Stewart, creator and CEO of a multimedia empire devoted to her personal guidance in the areas of cooking, gardening, etiquette, arts and crafts, and general lifestyle, was laid low by corporate scandal.

On June 4, 2003, a federal grand jury indicted Stewart and her former broker, Peter Bacanovic, on nine criminal counts growing out of charges of insider trading. The government alleged that Stewart had sold stock in a drug firm after she obtained illegal insider information that an anticipated Food and Drug Administration approval for one of the company's emerging wonder drugs was about to be withheld. In the end, Stewart was not indicted for insider trading, but for her attempts to cover up activities associated with it. On March 5, 2004, Stewart was found guilty of conspiracy, obstruction of justice, and two counts of making false statements, and she was subsequently sentenced to 5 months in prison, 5 months of home confinement, 2 years probation, and a fine.

Many took a guilty pleasure in the spectacle of America's "domestic diva" spending time in the slammer. Others believed she had been unfairly singled out as a celebrity scapegoat, a sacrifice on the altar of public outrage—outrage more properly directed against the corporate criminals at Enron, WorldCom, and elsewhere.

Some feared that Stewart's fate was a symptom of what might well become a destructive public, political, and regulatory backlash against the deregulated excesses of corporate culture.

The relationship between American business and American government looked to be on the verge of a new Progressivism, with government ending the hands-off policy born in the Reagan era. However, as of 2005, despite a welter of congressional hearings and some high-profile verdicts (including a 25-year prison sentence handed to WorldCom CEO Bernard Ebbers for fraud), no great reform movement seemed likely. What did begin to emerge was an increased level of sophistication among investors, who now routinely insisted on proof of sound ethics as well as a sound balance sheet before they put their money into a firm. Gone, it seemed, were the days in which CEOs could eat their fill at the corporate trough. Investors now demanded that top-level bosses *earn* their top-level salaries by producing top-level returns on investment. Reform came less from the government than from investors making themselves heard in the marketplace.

Too Close to Call

If the ethical failings of American business were especially troubling because capitalism and democracy go hand in hand, even more urgently distressing was a convulsion at democracy's very core: the institution and process of electing national leaders. In 2000, the entire procedure fell under a shadow.

Democrat Al Gore, Bill Clinton's vice president, ran against Republican George W. Bush, son of Clinton's predecessor, George H. W. Bush. The two ran campaigns that failed to generate much enthusiasm and that resulted in a neck-and-neck election too close to call. The first complete tally gave Gore 50,996,116 votes against 50,456,169 for Bush. However, it is the Electoral College, not the popular vote, that puts a candidate into the White House, and it is on this point that democracy seemed to falter.

In Florida, governed by candidate Bush's younger brother, Jeb, the popular vote was almost a dead heat. Initial counts gave Bush a razor-thin lead of 1,784 votes over Gore, which would deliver to Bush the state's 25 electoral votes and, with them, the presidency. Florida law, however, prescribed an automatic recount when results were this close. After the recount on November 9, the Bush lead was narrowed to 327 votes.

The notion that a choice made by 327 Floridians would determine who would become the most powerful political leader on the planet was stupefying to contemplate. But this was just the beginning.

Unsatisfied with an automatic recount, Democrats demanded a recount by hand in four counties where they had reason to believe significant numbers of Gore votes had not been counted. The basis of this assumption was Florida's reliance on an antiquated punch-card ballot, on which voters indicated their choices by pushing a stylus through a card. If a voter failed to push the stylus all the way through, the resulting hole might be blocked by a tiny rectangular fragment of cardboard—called a "chad"—which prevented the tabulating machine from registering the vote. It was not unusual in Florida elections for a number of ballots to be spoiled in this way. Fortunately, most elections are sufficiently decisive to render the rejected ballots insignificant. But not this one.

Acting in accordance with Florida law, which required election officials to evaluate disputed ballots in a way that attempts to "determine the intention" of the voter, Democrats called for each ballot to be inspected for "hanging chad." Where such was found, the vote was to be counted. Some called as well for election officials also to examine ballots for so-called "pregnant chad," chad that had not been punched out on *any* of its four sides, but merely bulged—evidence that *some* stylus pressure had been applied.

Now it seemed that the future of the nation and, perhaps, the world depended not just on 327 Floridians, but on a few tiny fragments of scrap cardboard, each smaller than a piece of confetti.

As if that weren't sufficiently surreal, Democrats also pointed to another flaw in the election process. In Palm Beach County, the list of candidates for local office was so long that election officials designed a ballot that opened into *two* facing pages, referred to as a "butterfly ballot." The design created confusion because the punch hole for Bush was directly to the right of his name, whereas those for right-wing extremist Patrick J. Buchanan and Democratic candidate Al Gore were placed differently. No sooner had the polls closed than officials were flooded with calls, mostly from elderly Jewish voters, who protested that they had mistakenly punched the hole for Buchanan—widely regarded as an anti-Semite—when they had intended to vote for Gore.

On November 11, the Bush camp filed suit to stop the ongoing manual recounts, even as Katherine Harris, Florida's secretary of state, declared that she was prepared to certify Bush as winner on the legal deadline for certification, November 14. Democracy in action? Harris, the state's top election official, was not only a Republican, but had served as a Bush delegate to the Republican National Convention and was one of eight co-chairs of the Bush campaign in Florida.

Over the next several days, recounts stopped and started and stopped again in several Florida counties, and the Democrats and Republicans battled in court. On November 16, the Florida Supreme Court, the majority of whose judges had been appointed during Democratic administrations, ruled that the manual recounts were legal, thereby prompting Palm Beach County to resume a manual recount it had suspended. However, on November 17, Judge Terry P. Lewis of the Leon County Circuit Court ruled that Harris could certify the election without the inclusion of the hand recounts. The Florida Supreme Court responded by enjoining such certification and set November 26 as the deadline for completion of all the counts. The Bush legal team appealed the Florida Supreme Court decision to the U.S. Supreme Court, which, on December 12, by a five-to-four vote, overturned the Florida Supreme Court and barred all further manual recounts. Defeated in the courts and the Electoral College, though not by the popular vote, Al Gore conceded the election to George W. Bush on December 13. Bush had carried Florida, it was decided, by 537 votes.

> **American Echo**
>
> [W]e may never know with complete certainty the identity of the winner of this year's Presidential election, [but] the identity of the loser is perfectly clear. It is the Nation's confidence in the judge as an impartial guardian of the rule of law.
>
> —Associate Justice Stephen Breyer, December 12, 2000, in his dissent from the majority decision ending the Florida recount of the 2000 election

Later unofficial recounts sponsored by the *Miami Herald*, *USA Today*, and others came to ambiguous conclusions. Some suggested that, even if a full manual recount had been completed in the counties where Democrats demanded recounts, Bush would have prevailed. Others, however, concluded that if manual recounts had been conducted throughout Florida, Gore would have won, although only by 393 votes.

However one looked at it, the first election of the new century stood as a disturbing testament to voter apathy and to the arbitrary nature of some aspects of democracy.

The Least You Need to Know

- Around Rodney King, O. J. Simpson, and Bill Clinton revolved three of the most important trials of the closing decade of the twentieth century.

- As the century ended, the Internet emerged as a great force in our economy, our culture, and our lives.

- Political and corporate ethics was a hot-button issue during this period, which saw the impeachment of Bill Clinton and the trials of high-profile corporate moguls.

- George W. Bush defeated Democratic candidate Al Gore in a disputed election, which was ultimately arbitrated by the Supreme Court. The nation emerged from the 2000 presidential contest deeply divided.

37

Terror and Freedom (2001–)

In This Chapter

◆ Terrorists attack the United States

◆ War in Afghanistan and Iraq

◆ The Bush re-election and a divided America

◆ Faith-based politics

◆ The nation, the world, and democracy

Were Florida's voting machines flawed? Absolutely. Was the U.S. Supreme Court flawed? Perhaps. Was democracy itself flawed? As it turned out, not fatally. Like it or not, the people and the candidates willingly accepted the rule of law, and George W. Bush entered the White House on the day appointed by that law and without violence.

9/11

Nine months after the resolution of the disputed election, at 8:45 (EDT) on the morning of September 11, 2001, a Boeing 767 passenger jetliner (later identified as American Airlines Flight 11 out of Boston) crashed into the north tower of the World Trade Center in lower Manhattan. The usual morning TV shows were interrupted by live coverage of the disaster, cameras focused on the thick black smoke that billowed from the wound torn in the gleaming silver skin of the 110-story skyscraper.

Stunned

Television news pictures of the burning World Trade Center began to be broadcast just 3 minutes after the impact. Accounts, including more than one from the president himself, vary regarding when Mr. Bush was informed of what appeared to be a terrible accident. That morning, the president was in a motorcade heading to the Emma E. Booker Elementary School in Sarasota, Florida, for a "photo op" to promote his new "No Child Left Behind" education bill. He later claimed that he first saw an airplane hitting the World Trade Center on television while he was waiting to enter the classroom. In this regard, however, his recollection was clearly faulty, because there was no broadcast of what turned out to be only the first of two impacts, and the second did not occur until the president was in the classroom.

Did President Bush know about the first impact and simply fail to respond, assuming it was just a terrible accident? Or was he uninformed of it? Presumably, his aides, especially national security advisor Condoleeza Rice—who would later be criticized for failing to heed a "Presidential Daily Briefing" that warned of an impending terrorist attack—were aware of what millions of Americans were now watching on television. Or perhaps, in a modern technologically driven democracy, information routinely reaches the masses *before* it reaches the powerful. In any case, U.S. Navy Captain Deborah Loewer, director of the White House Situation Room, was traveling in the motorcade when she received a message from an assistant back in Washington about the first crash. She informed the president as soon as he got out of his limousine and before he entered the school.

While the president prepared to listen to a class of second graders read, cameras rolled in lower Manhattan, and the nation bore witness as, at 9:03, a second 767, United Airlines Flight 175, hit the World Trade Center's south tower.

In Sarasota, members of the Secret Service saw the second impact on television in another room, but, apparently, neither said nor did anything. The president's

American Echo

Clandestine, foreign government, and media reports indicate bin Laden since 1997 has wanted to conduct terrorist attacks in the U.S. Bin Laden implied in U.S. television interviews in 1997 and 1998 that his followers would follow the example of [1993] World Trade Center bomber Ramzi Yousef and "bring the fighting to America."

—from a Presidential Daily Briefing (PDB) dated August 6, 2001, entitled "Bin Laden Determined to Strike in U.S."

chief of staff, Andrew Card, was also in a nearby room when he heard the news. He waited until there was a pause in the reading drill to walk into the classroom and whisper in Bush's ear. Reports vary as to whether this moment came at 9:05 or 9:07. Whatever the precise time, the president said nothing, asked no questions, and gave no orders. Instead, with the United States under attack, the commander-in-chief picked up *The Pet Goat* and followed along as the children read aloud: "The - Pet - Goat. A - girl - got - a - pet - goat. But - the - goat - did - some - things - that - made - the - girl's - dad - mad."

Back at the White House, Secret Service agents were evacuating Vice President Dick Cheney. In the Sarasota classroom, according to a *Washington Times* reporter, presidential press secretary Ari Fleischer, standing at the back of the room, held up a pad of paper on which he had written in block letters, "DON'T SAY ANYTHING YET."

But the president did talk—to the children—praising them as "great readers. Very impressive! Thank you all so much for showing me your reading skills. I bet they practice, too. Don't you? Reading more than they watch TV? Anybody do that? Read more than you watch TV?" Hands went up. "Oh, that's great! Very good. Very important to practice! Thanks for having me. Very impressed." Not quite through, he advised the children to stay in school and be good citizens, and when one child asked him a question, he politely paused to give a quick response.

Accounts vary as to when the president finally left the classroom. Some say 9:12 A.M.; some as late as 9:16. It was 9:30 before President Bush appeared on television to announce that the nation had suffered "an apparent terrorist attack."

More Attacks

The attack was by no means over. At 9:43, American Airlines Flight 77, a Boeing 757, plowed into the Pentagon, headquarters of the U.S. military. Two minutes later, the entire White House staff was evacuated. Back in New York, at 10:05, the south tower of the World Trade Center collapsed, appearing to telescope into itself, swallowing up 110 stories of steel, concrete, and humanity. Five minutes after this, United Airlines Flight 93, another 757, cratered the earth of rural Somerset County, Pennsylvania, not far from Pittsburgh. At 10:28, the north tower of the World Trade Center collapsed. It looked as if a volcano had suddenly erupted in Lower Manhattan.

In the meantime, President Bush did not rush back to Washington, but instead flew from Florida to what was described as a "secure location" within Barksdale Air Force Base, Louisiana. At 1:04 P.M., he appeared on television to pledge that "the United States will hunt down and punish those responsible for these cowardly acts."

It was 7 P.M. before he returned to the White House, by which time the 47-story Building 7 of the World Trade Center had collapsed.

The Terrorists

Before the day was over, the media reported that the airplane downed in Pennsylvania had been headed for the White House or the United States Capitol, and it was quickly learned that all four planes had been hijacked by terrorists willing to sacrifice themselves in order to take the lives of untold thousands by using the giant jets, loaded with thousands of pounds of jet fuel, as guided missiles.

Days after the attacks, the nation learned that cell phone calls made by crew members and passengers on the doomed planes described how the terrorists had commandeered the aircraft using weapons no more sophisticated than box cutters. The first three planes hit their targets, but by the time the fourth plane had been seized, passengers who surreptitiously phoned loved ones were told of the attack on the World Trade Center. Apparently understanding that this hijacking was part of a larger attack against the nation, a group of Flight 93 passengers resolved to try to regain control of the plane. They apparently stormed the cockpit and rushed the hijackers. In the struggle, the plane crashed—but it did so in rural Pennsylvania, and not into the White House or the Capitol.

> **American Echo**
>
> Let's roll.
>
> —Todd Beamer, passenger, Flight 93, signaling the start of an attempt to overcome the terrorist hijackers (heard via cell phone transmission)

Also before the end of the day, CNN correspondent David Ensor reported that U.S. officials believed that Osama bin Laden, a Saudi multimillionaire sponsor of terrorism living under the protection of the radical Islamic Taliban government in Afghanistan, was behind the attacks. He led al-Qaeda (Arabic for "The Base"), an Islamic guerrilla organization of perhaps 10,000 men (at the time) dedicated to fighting a *jihad*—a holy war—against Israel, the West, and the United States.

A Rush to War

In 2004, a blue-ribbon panel christened "The 9/11 Commission"—"9/11" having become the awful shorthand for the attacks of September 11, 2001—issued its nearly 600-page report on the events of that terrible day and all that led up to it. Chillingly, the commission concluded that federal officials at every level had been unprepared "in every respect" to stop the suicide hijackings. The commission cited failures to gather intelligence, failures to process intelligence, failures to act on intelligence, failures to communicate and coordinate among the agencies charged with national security, and a general failure to respond with appropriate urgency to what, in hindsight, seemed to have been the clear and present dangers of terrorism.

First War of the Twenty-First Century

In the hours and days following the attacks, officials did move quickly to identify the perpetrators. They were 19 Middle Eastern terrorists, who had (for the most part) entered the United States illegally but quite easily and who had, for months before the attacks, lived in American motels and apartment complexes, paid cash to train in small American flight schools, hardened their bodies in American gyms, and banked at American banks. They had been prepared by and were financed by al-Qaeda, whose chief, Osama bin Laden, was well known to the American intelligence community as having masterminded bombings of two U.S. embassies in 1998 and an October 12, 2000, attack on the U.S. destroyer *Cole* while it was in port at Yemen. It was also well known that Osama bin Laden and al-Qaeda enjoyed the protection and support of the fundamentalist Islamic government of Afghanistan, known as the Taliban.

On September 12, President Bush remarked, "We have just seen the first war of the twenty-first century." Eight days later, in an address to a special joint session of Congress on September 20, he issued a warning, announcing that the United States would attack the Taliban in Afghanistan unless it surrendered "all the leaders of al-Qaeda who hide in your land." The Taliban replied with defiance, and the United States unleashed an air war followed by a limited ground war, which quickly toppled the Taliban. Osama bin Laden, however, was neither captured nor heard from again, except on three videotaped messages of uncertain date. Some believed he had fled Afghanistan and found refuge in another country; others believed he had been killed during the general assault on the Taliban.

The Toll of Terror

While the war was being fought in Afghanistan, crews completed months of hazardous and heartbreaking clean-up operations at the World Trade Center. The death toll there was fixed at 2,893—added to 189 killed at the Pentagon, including the 64 passengers and crew of Flight 77.

Vital Statistics

While the Taliban government in Iraq quickly collapsed and was replaced by a provisional regime friendly to the United States, fighting (as of July 2005) was ongoing. As of spring 2005, more than 8,500 Afghan troops had been killed and some 26,000 wounded. As of May 2005, 211 U.S. troops had been killed and 633 wounded.

In the Pennsylvania crash, everyone on the plane, 44 persons, had died. Among those killed at the World Trade Center were 23 New York City police officers, 37 Port Authority police officers, and 343 New York City firefighters. They had begun September 11, 2001, as ordinary people. Before the morning was over, they were the heroic defenders of a democracy under attack.

With the fall of the Taliban, a new, democratic government was installed in Afghanistan, although the war continued at a low, albeit deadly, level.

Next Target: Iraq

Throughout the summer of 2002, there was much debate about where the "war on terrorism" should be taken next. The administration fixed its sights on Iraq, but other government, political, and military leaders questioned the wisdom, justice, and feasibility of invading that country, which, after all, had not been implicated (as the Afghani Taliban had) in the 9/11 attacks.

In the meantime, elsewhere in the Middle East, Israelis and Palestinians killed one another with a rhythm of nauseating regularity. And, at home, health and law enforcement officials were investigating a wave of human anthrax infections that had been disseminated by weapons-grade spores sent through the mail beginning just weeks after the events of September 11. Whether the attacks were the work of al-Qaeda, domestic terrorists, or simply some unbalanced individual was not determined. (As of July 2005, the source of the attacks remained unknown.)

Remember This

On October 4, U.S. health officials reported that a Florida man had contracted anthrax—the first case in the United States since 1975. At first authorities played down any link between the infection and terrorism, but anthrax was well known as a bioterrorist weapon. More cases followed, most of which were traced to letters sent to prominent media figures (including NBC news broadcaster Tom Brokaw) and government officials (including Senate majority leader Tom Daschle). By the end of November, scores of people had been exposed to anthrax, several became ill, and six victims died.

A year after the terrorist attacks on America, on September 12, 2002, President Bush addressed the United Nations General Assembly, declaring that Iraq presented a threat to the United States and other nations and that the Iraqi regime of Saddam Hussein was a direct threat to the authority of the United Nations itself. Next, on October 11, the president secured congressional resolutions authorizing the use of military force against Iraq. On November 8, the United Nations approved U.S.-sponsored Resolution 1441, pressuring Iraq to comply with its disarmament obligations by proving that it had divested itself of all weapons of mass destruction.

Pursuant to the resolution, UN inspectors were sent to Iraq. Although the inspectors found nothing of significance, the Iraqis had submitted a provocatively evasive disclosure report, and the Bush administration, citing its own intelligence reports, persisted in asserting that Iraq possessed the "WMDs" (weapons of mass destruction). On February 5, 2003, U.S. Secretary of State Colin Powell (b. 1937) took the administration's case to the UN Security Council.

Despite Powell's presentation, most of the international community withheld support for a war against Iraq and some, most notably France and Germany, actively opposed it. Only Great Britain offered substantial military support.

Operation Iraqi Freedom

While both international and domestic debate over the prospective war was under way, President Bush suddenly shifted his definition of what constituted an appropriate cause for war. No longer were the putative WMDs the sole issue. On March 16, 2003, the president issued an ultimatum to Saddam Hussein, demanding that he and his immediate cohorts (including his sons, Uday [1964–2003] and Qusay [1966–2003]) permanently leave Iraq within 48 hours. When this deadline passed, on March 19, President Bush authorized a "decapitation" attack on the Iraqi leadership, an aerial bombardment of a bunker in Baghdad believed to shelter Saddam. This attack, from which Saddam emerged uninjured, was the commencement of the undeclared war called Operation Iraqi Freedom.

The evening of the 19th was the beginning of surgically targeted air strikes, using satellite-guided Tomahawk Cruise Missiles fired from American warships in the Red Sea and Persian Gulf and bombardment by guided "smart weapons" launched from aircraft to destroy government and military installations.

On March 20, the ground phase of the war commenced, as U.S. Army troops and Marines captured strategically vital oil fields. The invasion of Iraq progressed with lightning speed and resulted in very few U.S. or British casualties. Anticipated Iraqi use of chemical and biological weapons did not occur, and on April 2, U.S. forces began the taking of Karbala, 50 miles from Baghdad. This signified the opening of the "Battle of Baghdad."

After Karbala fell, U.S. Special Forces troops seized the Thar Thar presidential palace, just northwest of Baghdad, on April 3. Simultaneously, an attack was launched against Baghdad's Saddam International Airport. That same day, the holy city of Najaf fell to the U.S. 101st Airborne Division. On April 4, American forces secured Saddam International Airport, renaming it Baghdad International Airport. From this base of operations, the occupation of Baghdad proper began.

The Fall of Baghdad

On the April 6, U.S. and British troops began the encirclement of the Iraqi capital, and on the 7th, U.S. forces advanced into the city itself. On this same day, an air strike was made against a building in a residential neighborhood of Baghdad said to harbor Saddam Hussein. Once again, however, the dictator apparently evaded death. By this time, too, after a long struggle, the British finally took control of the important port city of Basra.

On April 9, international television broadcasted images of massive statues of Saddam Hussein being pulled down in Baghdad and other cities, apparently by jubilant Iraqis. In some places, U.S. and British soldiers were clearly welcomed as liberators. In other places, they found themselves the targets of gunfire, booby traps, and explosive devices. By the 10th, however, President Bush confidently announced that the regime of Saddam Hussein was indeed being removed from power, and on April 14, 2003, the Pentagon announced that the "major combat phase" of Operation Iraqi Freedom appeared to have ended.

"Mission Accomplished"

On April 20, the U.S. Marines left Baghdad, turning it over to U.S. Army occupying forces. Lt. Gen. Jay Garner (Ret.) (b. 1938) arrived in the capital to lead U.S. reconstruction efforts in Iraq and arrange for an interim civil authority in Baghdad. However, these efforts got off to a slow and unsteady start, and, on May 11, 2003, Garner was replaced by a new civilian administrator, diplomat L. Paul Bremer (b. 1941).

On May 2, 2003, President Bush landed on the deck of the aircraft carrier *Abraham Lincoln* in an S-3 Viking aircraft. Emerging from the jet, attired in a flight suit, the smiling president stood before a banner emblazoned with the phrase "MISSION ACCOMPLISHED" and affirmed that major combat had indeed been concluded in Iraq.

As of May 2, 139 U.S. military personnel had been killed and 553 wounded in combat, and Saddam Hussein and his sons were still at large. The latter two, Uday and Qusay Hussein, would be killed in a July 22 raid. Saddam Hussein was discovered on December 14, 2003, hiding in a hole on a farm near Adwar, 10 miles from Saddam Hussein's hometown of Tikrit.

Yet even after the capture of Saddam, the fighting continued as so-called "insurgents," apparently pro-Saddam loyalists and "foreign fighters" (mostly Saudi nationals), attacked with ambushes, "IEDs" (improvised explosive devices—roadside bombs), and suicide bombings. As of July 10, 2005, 1,752 U.S. military personnel had been killed in Iraq and another 13,190 wounded. Notably, 1,615 of the deaths occurred after the day President Bush declared the end of the war's "major combat" phase.

Charles A. Duelfer, who was a weapons expert the Bush administration chose to complete the U.S. investigation of Iraq's weapons programs, concluded in October 2004 that Iraq's ability to produce nuclear weapons had "progressively decayed" since 1991 and that there was no evidence of "concerted efforts to restart the program."

Red State, Blue State

No war since Vietnam was more unpopular or divisive than "Operation Iraqi Freedom," and, quite possibly, no president was more routinely ridiculed by political satirists and television comics than George W. Bush, who struggled with the English language even as he seemed to wrestle with thought process itself. Given these strikes against him, many political pundits believed that he would be defeated in his re-election bid. After all, he had gained office by virtue of a few hundred disputed votes in Florida, a state governed by his brother.

The Christian Right

Those pundits misread the mood of the nation. President Bush, a self-proclaimed, born-again Christian, had the support of a socio-political bloc that had been growing since the Reagan years: the Christian conservatives or the Christian right. By the end of the millennium, this group exerted a powerful grip on the Republican agenda, which included such issues as funding for "faith-based" social services and charities (despite the constitutional separation of church and state), federal funding (through tax credits) for educating children in parochial schools, support of a constitutional amendment banning abortion, and support for a constitutional amendment banning same-sex (gay and lesbian) marriage. Moreover, although many Americans supported the Iraq war as an opportunity to introduce democracy to an important and dangerous part of the world, a significant number of Christian conservatives also saw it as a battle between the forces of Christianity and those of Islam, and they believed it imperative that Christianity emerge triumphant.

 Vital Statistics

As of September 2005, only the state of Massachusetts recognized same-sex marriages, while Vermont, Maine, Hawaii, California, New Jersey, Connecticut, and the District of Columbia offered same-sex partners benefits similar to those of legally married couples. Eighteen other states had constitutional provisions that explicitly limit marriage to one man and one woman, and 25 states had statutes containing similar definitions of the institution. During 2004, 13 states amended their constitutions to define marriage as being only between one man and one woman.

President Bush was opposed by John Kerry, liberal senator from Massachusetts, who failed to excite much interest in voters. The result was a close but solid second-term victory for President Bush, who captured 51 percent of the popular vote.

One Nation, Divisible

Those who watched the election returns on television saw a new map of the United States emerging, one consisting of predominantly Republican-voting states (colored red by TV broadcasters) and predominantly Democratic-voting states (colored blue). The political and ideological divisions between the "red states" and "blue states" were almost as absolute, if not nearly so violent, as those between the Confederacy and the Union during the Civil War. The red states encompassed the entire South, most of the Midwest, and the western "heartland"; however, within this vast area, many large cities remained democratic enclaves—lone blue islands in a sea of red. The blue states included the Northeast, much of the upper Midwest (that is, Michigan, Illinois, and Minnesota), and the West Coast. Red states were not only Republican, but politically, culturally, and spiritually conservative, whereas blue states tend toward liberalism in all of these areas. Racially, red voters were overwhelmingly white, whereas blue voters were a more diverse group.

![American Life logo] **American Life**

The life and death of Terri Schiavo dramatically illustrates the growing role of religious faith, especially fundamentalist Christianity, in American government. Terri Schiavo was born Theresa Marie Schindler on December 3, 1963, and grew up near Philadelphia. She married Michael Schiavo in 1984, and moved to St. Petersburg, Florida, in April 1986. Those who knew Terri Schiavo suspected that she had an eating disorder, and in 1989, Schiavo's weight dropped dramatically and she stopped menstruating—typical signs of anorexia.

On the morning of February 25, 1990, Schiavo experienced cardiac arrest and lapsed into a coma, which evolved into an irreversible "persistent vegetative state," in which she remained for the last 15 years of her life, sustained by nourishment delivered through a surgically implanted feeding tube.

By 1993, Michael Schiavo and the Schindler family began a legal dispute over whether or not to remove the feeding tube. Michael Schiavo sought to remove the tube; Terri Schiavo's parents and other relatives sought to keep it in place. During 2003, the dispute escalated through the appeals courts, and the Schindlers received financial and moral support from Christian conservative groups, which professed an absolute belief in the sanctity of life, even in the case of a person effectively brain dead. Also in 2003, Florida governor Jeb Bush, brother of President George W. Bush, intervened against Michael Schiavo. Nevertheless, state and federal courts repeatedly upheld Michael Schiavo's right, as his wife's guardian, to remove the tube. At this juncture, the majority-Republican U.S. Congress, shortly after 12:30 A.M. on March 21, 2005, passed a "private bill" granting Schiavo's parents the right to continue suing for the maintenance of the feeding tube and to order its reinsertion while the suit was pending. President Bush, professing his commitment to a "culture of life," signed the bill at 1:11 A.M.; however, a federal district court refused to order the tube reinserted; the U.S. Supreme Court refused to hear the parents' appeal; and, amid much controversy and rancor, Schiavo slipped away at 9:05 A.M., March 31, 2005.

America in the World

The criticism frequently leveled against George W. Bush's father, George H. W. Bush, was that his interest in international relations eclipsed his interest in the nation's domestic affairs. When his son ran for his first term in 2000, precisely the opposite criticism was advanced. It was said he knew and cared little about the world beyond Texas. Indeed, candidate Bush frequently voiced his opposition to intervention in the affairs of other countries, what he called "nation building," and it seemed to many that, were he elected, the United States would retreat into the kind of isolationism favored by Republicans at the beginning of the twentieth century.

In fact, after 9/11, George W. Bush embarked on the most aggressive possible course of nation building: a war to effect regime change in Iraq, a war aimed at bringing democracy to that country and, ultimately, by irresistible example, to the entire Middle East region.

Not since Woodrow Wilson, who brought the United States into World War I in order (he said) "to make the world safe for democracy," had an American president committed the nation to war on so ambitious and explicit an ideological basis. True, Presidents Truman, Eisenhower, Kennedy, Johnson, and Nixon had committed American troops to fight for the "containment" of communism, but the Bush agenda was more aggressively positive. His purpose was not to *contain* tyranny or terror so much as it was to "spread freedom."

The problem was that much of the rest of the world did not credit Bush for his idealism, but instead condemned him as an international bully, forcing the "American way" upon a region and a people who did not necessarily want to receive it. Moreover, President Bush had opted out of major international conventions and treaties, including the Kyoto Protocol addressing global warming, the Rome Statute establishing the International Criminal Court, and an important Protocol to the United Nations' Convention against Torture and Other Cruel Inhuman or Degrading Treatment or Punishment. All of this, coupled with graphic evidence presented in 2004 that U.S. military personnel abused and tortured prisoners of war and other detainees in Baghdad's Abu Ghraib prison, tended to isolate the United States in the world community to a degree unprecedented since World War II.

Mortgage on the Future

Beginning with Ronald Reagan, Republicans have painted themselves as the party of fiscal responsibility in contrast to the "tax and spend" Democrats. It has proved to be a compelling self-image, although often at odds with reality. During the Reagan administration, the national debt rose from one trillion dollars to four, whereas, during the two terms of Bill Clinton, the United States not only balanced the federal budget, but accumulated a surplus.

Debt and More Debt

President George W. Bush aggressively championed bold tax cuts, arguing (as President Reagan had) that the cuts would stimulate the economy and, therefore, ultimately increase rather than reduce federal revenues. He maintained the cuts even after the

Iraq war got under way. As of 2005, operations in Iraq were consuming $4 to $5 billion per month. Although the Bush administration's budget request for 2005 proposed deep reductions or funding freezes in domestic programs, including the elimination of grants for firefighters' assistance, low-income schools, family literacy, and rural housing and economic development, the federal deficit reached $400 billion in 2005 and the national debt climbed to about $8 trillion.

Fixing Social Security

For most Americans, the deficit and national debt figures are just too astronomical to be comprehensible. Although personal income decreased slightly during the Bush presidency and unemployment rose, the economy, on a personal level, remained strong, at least as it directly and immediately affected most Americans. Productivity was high, and inflation low, although skyrocketing oil and gas prices in 2005 threatened this.

If most Americans were little bothered by the growing burden of the federal deficit and the national debt, they were very concerned about the administration's proposal to "fix social security." President Bush argued that, left alone, the Social Security program would soon be bankrupt. He advocated cuts in benefits and giving workers the choice of putting at least some portion of their Social Security tax payments into private investment accounts (a proposal that warmed hearts on Wall Street).

But most Americans resisted "fixing" a program they did not believe broken, and, as of July 2005, the future direction of Social Security was very much an open question.

Freedom on the March—or on the Run?

Referring to events in the Middle East, President Bush several times invoked the phrase "freedom is on the march." There could be no denying that many in Iraq, as in the United States, were willing selflessly to struggle and sacrifice for a better life and a better world. It was also clear that at least some leaders in the Islamic world wanted closer ties with the United States (as was the case with Pakistan's President Pervez Musharraf) or were willing to liberalize their regimes (as with Libya's formerly saber-rattling Mohmmar Qadaffi). But fear of terror all too readily breeds fear and intolerance of dissent and variety of opinion, the key constituents of freedom itself.

In "post-9/11 America," the Patriot Act, passed by Congress in 2001 and renewed thereafter, gave law enforcement agencies unprecedented powers of surveillance, search, seizure, and arrest. Those of the right wing painted as unpatriotic any who questioned the legislation, and those who did question it tended to accuse supporters of the act of trampling American liberties. The dialogue between right and left grew increasingly intemperate and intolerant, obscuring the very real and dangerous dilemma facing democracy: an open and free society is also open and free to those who would destroy it, yet closing an open society to protect it likewise destroys it.

We have seen all this before, and worse. During the Civil War, Abraham Lincoln, a presidential apostle of freedom if there ever was one, suspended *habeas corpus*, an act for which many condemned him as a tyrant. During World War I, Woodrow Wilson, fighting to make the world safe for democracy, approved some of the most repressive anti-protest and "loyalty" legislation the country has ever had. As for incivility in government, Aaron Burr killed Alexander Hamilton in duel on July 11, 1804, and, on May 22, 1856, Representative Preston S. Brooks of South Carolina viciously beat Massachusetts senator Charles Sumner senseless with a cane.

We have seen all this before, and yet democracy has surely survived, emerging from each spasm, each struggle, all the stronger for having been so sorely tested.

When he committed the United States to what he knew would be a long, lonely, often disheartening course in the Cold War, Harry S. Truman had faith that, whatever the temporary tribulations, democracy would ultimately trump communism. Democracy, after all, is a human ideology, whereas communism is brutishly mechanical and can be maintained only by force. That which is more congenial to humanity tends to survive and thrive, while that which works contrary to humanity tends to wither and die.

In fighting oppression of any kind, the great thing is not to become oppressive oneself. In the post-World War II contest against communism, America drifted left then veered sharply right, but it never allowed itself to become totalitarian on either extreme. And so it will be with the contest between democracy and terror—provided that, in defense of democracy, we take care not to become terrorists ourselves.

The Least You Need to Know

- The terrorist attacks on the United States (September 11, 2001) motivated the United States to topple the terrorist-supporting Taliban government of Afghanistan and to wage war against Saddam Hussein's Iraq.

- Despite the unpopularity of the war in Iraq, which had devolved into a long and bloody American occupation, President George W. Bush was re-elected to a second term, supported in large measure by a Christian conservative movement, which favored his "faith-based" politics.

◆ Acting aggressively to disseminate democracy to the Middle East, the Bush administration drew both praise and criticism at home and alienated many of the world's other leaders.

◆ During 2004 and 2005, Americans debated President George W. Bush's plan to reform and partially privatize Social Security, which had remained largely unchanged since the system was introduced during the FDR administration.

Index

S

X-Y-Z